Who Runs

Police?

Secrets of a Top Cop

Attention Authors

'We Convert Fighters into Writers.' That's the motto of Manas Publications since more than four decades. Our message to the world is that India can win the battle not only by the bullet but also by the pen. There is no dearth of intellectuals in our country, but their knowledge is confined to them only. No sincere effort has been made by any other publisher to channelise their knowledge in national interest. That is why the talent of a large number of intellectuals remains latent. An author transforms his knowledge into a manuscript, and it is our job to spread his/her knowledge by converting it into a beautiful book. For over four decades, Manas has been motivating the intellectuals by publishing their manuscripts and would like to publish your manuscript too. So if you or your colleagues have any manuscript ready for publication or are working on it, kindly contact us with detailed synopsis and list of contents. We will transform your work into a valuable publication. If you wish, we can also suggest you the suitable subjects for writing the books related to your area of expertise. Manas is known for its publishing quality and commitments. We take utmost care in production and give wide publicity to the book as well as its author through our national and international distribution network.

Who Runs Police?

Secrets of a Top Cop

Hans Raj Swan, IPS

(Former Director General of Police, Haryana)

Manas Publications

(We Convert Fighters into Writers)

New Delhi-110002 (INDIA)

MANAS PUBLICATIONS
(We Convert Fighters into Writers)
(Publishers, Library Suppliers, Importers & Exporters)
4402/5-A, Ansari Road (Opp. HDFC Bank)
Darya Ganj, New Delhi-110 002 (India)
Off. (23260783, 23265523, Fax: 011-23272766
E-mail: manaspublications@vsnl.com
manaspublications@gmail.com

ISBN 978-81-7049-430-0
₹ 695/-

Designed at
Manas Publications

Printed in India at
HS Offset Press, Delhi
and published by Mrs Suman Lata for
Manas Publications, 4402/5-A, Ansari Road
(Opp. HDFC Bank),
Darya Ganj, New Delhi-110 002 (INDIA)

Contents

Annexures

Opinions

HYMN IN GLORY TO OMNIPOTENT LORD

1. AISEE LAAL!
TUJH BINU KAUNU KAREY.
GAREEB NIWAAJU GUSAAEEAA MERAA
MAATHAI CHHATAR DHARAI-RAHAO.

2. JAA KEE CHHOTI JAGAT KAU LAAGAI
TAA PAR TUHEE DHARAI.
NEECHAH OOCH KARAI MERAA GOBINDU
KAAHOO TAY NA DARAI.

3. NAAMDEV KABEER TILOCHAN SADHNAA SAIN TARAI.
KAHI RAVIDAASU SUNHU RAY SANTAHU
HARI JEEO TAY SABHAI SARAI.

(GURU GRANTH SAHIB, Page 1106)

"O Divine Beloved
Who else can create such a wonderful creation save Thou.
The Omnipresent Supreme Cherisher of the humble,
Thou blesseth them with the honour of enlightenment.
Those whose touch considered defiling the people,
Thou alone shower the grace of Thy benevolence on them.
Salvaging the humble from the abyss of humility,
O my Supreme Sovereign Lord, Thou exalt them to the apex of glory.
The humble Namdev, Kabeer, Trilochan, Sadhna and Sain were, thus, salvaged.
Sayeth Ravidaas, listen O the Truth seekers, Lord alone is the Prop of all."

Paying homage and tribute to my parents in their heavenly abode,

I dedicate this Book to my beloved wife-

Nasib Kaur and her "Naseeb".

Foreword

With joyous feelings, I associate myself with this book, an autobiography written by Hans Raj Swan IPS, former Director General of Police, Haryana State. The book is a monumental work containing graphic details from his childhood to, not only the time when the author hung up his police uniform in July 1988, but still further to his retreat in public life for the last 23 years. A 'Karmayogi' from a scheduled caste who has an energetically straight bearing that belies his age of 81 years explains philosophically "The human life is a wondrous momentary play that can be blissfully enjoyed by playing spontaneously as it comes. The panacea for perennial human sorrows, miseries and sufferings lies in being with love and living that comes, as everything happens in a moment in this momentary world." He further says that accepting life as the bounty of the bounteous nature, he has loved, lived and relished the way it has come, moment by moment to him, taking head on when it came as a challenge and realizing into reality when it came as a dream.

Born to parents from humble background under the roof of their thatched dwelling, without even one rusty spoon around, much less, the proverbial silver spoon in the mouth, the author went to a non-descript school in his equally non-descript remote village at the age of 7 years. Later he shifted to a school in a nearby village and established his mettle as an outstanding student. While in the 5th primary class, he as class head boy suffered uncalled for corporal punishment at the hands of an uncouth, crude, rude and intemperate teacher who unabashedly abused him calling names to his low caste origin. Sensitivities of his tender mind made him to drop out of school. To be of some assistance to his poor parents, he took to grazing and tending the family cattle for two years. Though out of school, yet the spark in him to get educated never lost its glow. Coming under the spell of some noble teachers, he rejoined school and was moulded into, not only an outstanding student, but also was imbibed deeply into his consciousness, the beauty of nature and *Japuji Sahib*, devotional hymns sung by Baba Nanak. Soon after passing his Matriculation examination with distinction, he was married at the very young age. It is to the credit and vision of his hard working parents that despite their meager resources the author was still sent to Khalsa College Mahilpur to pursue his FSc and graduation.

Yearning for social justice to fellow downtrodden people, was deeply ingrained in author's conscience. While as a college student, the author challenged and cudgeled the vicious conduct of SHO Police Station Mahilpur, who had sexually abused a newly wed scheduled caste girl, after calling her to the Police Station, based on some ill-conceived pretext and detaining her wrongfully for days. The author mobilized fellow college students in a big way and launched virulent agitation against the immoral and debased police officer, demanding his immediate arrest. Though the rogue police officer escaped due punishment for his grave crime because of his high links, yet his ignominious shunting out of the district to an insignificant post was a standing warning to his alike to behave in a manner befitting to their official position. The rogue police officer before demitting charge, recorded a vicious note in the police station record to wreak vengeance against the author that he had leftist tendencies and was prone to indulge in disruptive activities.

Following the saying "Shoot to the moon, you may land at the stars", the author went to Delhi, got a government job in the Central Civil Secretariat and continued pursuing post graduation studies by attending evening classes in Punjab University Camp College, Delhi. Here the vendetta game of erstwhile Station House Officer of Police Station Mahilpur overtook all the plans of the author. He was unceremoniously discharged from Government job, based on adverse police report. Once on the road, his indomitable spirit to fight against blatant in justice, got extra-energized and in a dare devilry action the author, breaching security rules, gate crashed into the residence of Deputy Union Home Minister to seek justice. The author suffered severe thrashing at the hands of the police personnel posted at the residence of Deputy Home Minister. His cries attracted the attention of the Minister. The woeful tale of the author made the Minister to take up the matter with Punjab Government for re-verification of his antecedents. He got his job back and those police officials responsible for making tainted report against the author were punished. Shortly thereafter, the author got a Central Secretariat Grade-IV job on his own merit. It was at this stage that the erstwhile cattle grazer, now a father of two kids and still pursuing his post graduation studies, started dreaming for All India Civil Services. Lo! he turned his dreams into reality in the very first attempt in 1956 and was selected in the Indian Police Service – a unique achievement.

After getting into the Indian Police Service, the author once again faced abominable brahminical mindset of caste prejudice at the hands of CPTC Commandant (G K Handoo). Undeterred the author continued achieving higher goals.

I must confess that reading this book has reaffirmed my faith in the motto "Nothing is impossible". The author, born and raised in extremely adverse environment, a school drop out, having been a victim of the venom of caste system, through his sheer grit, determination and steely resolve, rose to the highest pedestal in the Indian Police Service. In addition, he achieved the distinction of being the first schedule caste IPS officer of the country to achieve the position of State DGP and holding twin decorations of the Police Medal for Meritorious Service 1977 and President's Police Medal for Distinguished Service 1987.

Enforcing rule of law, refusing to bend backwards and calling spade a spade without bothering about the rewards, such as plum postings, is author's special trait, which is rare in these times. The author belongs to the rare breed of officers who are on the brink of extinction. It is often said "Those who do not bend will break". Is it really true? The right answer lies in this extremely gripping and exceptionally rendered life saga of the author. It is an appropriate lesson for those who believe that compromise in life is the order of the day. I must say that the generation of the day needs to be patient in their approach to life and career. The world around us is changing very rapidly and so are our aspirations and dreams. All this is leading the youth to adopt any possible means to achieve their so-called targets. Righteousness, morality and honesty have taken a back seat. The book is a great motivator for all to understand that results achieved through principled stands taken in life, are far sweeter than those achieved through compromises.

Sixty-four years after Independence, the future of India needs to introspect whether we should still continue to live in a narrow and fragmented society or should we rise over and above the same and give all dues to those having been discriminated socially for ages. The journey of the author is nothing short of "Agnipath". This book will serve as motivational reading to all sections of society, including budding and serving officers in the three pillars of criminal justice system. To others this book provides a valuable insight into the historical facts and social practices as they existed in early post Independent India, such as the customs, familial bonds, practice of untouchability, lack of means of transport/communication/education, working style of the then administration including judiciary, politics and politicians of the times.

On a personal front, the chapter on his getting college education from SGGS Khalsa College, Mahilpur, district Hoshiarpur, Punjab has made me nostalgic as I too belong to Mahilpur town of Hoshiarpur district. It is true that this college boasts of producing many stalwarts in different spheres of administration and armed forces. But, considering the handicaps of the author I would rate him as the tallest among the brood.

In conclusion, having dispensed justice throughout my life, I can only say that the author has done justice to his existence. Justice has, certainly been delivered.

Justice Ajit Singh Bains

Former Judge, Punjab and Haryana High Court,
Chairman, Punjab Human Rights Organization,
Chandigarh

Preface

R C Majumdar, the doyen of Indian historians lamented, "One of the greatest defects of Indian culture which defies rational explanation, is the aversion of Indians to writing history". The IPS officers have generally shunned from penning down their life stories. Writing autobiography for any senior police officer is undoubtedly, a very sensitive task. With the vigilant media, eagle eyes of the Social and Human Rights activists always on the prowl, awakened intelligentsia fully conscious of their Fundamental Rights and every act of senior police officers coming under the lens of watchful judicial scrutiny, the private and the official life of every police officer becomes a matter of wide interest. Unprincipled politicians, whose number unfortunately continues swelling, often nurture deep prejudices and spread all sorts of canard against the senior police officers, who do not fall in line. In the fast changing world of technology and electronics, the people at large feel utterly disgusted with extra slow moving wheels of justice delivery system, rampant corruption and failure of grievances redressal machinery. They very often take law in their own hands for instant justice. In the process, every accusing finger is pointed at the police. In these circumstances, it would be in the larger interest of the police force to educate the public in a proper perspective about the ground realities if the senior police officers narrate objectively, their own experiences – sweet and sour.

If we recall the history of the Indian Police, we find that its present hierarchical structure evolved in 1861 in the shadow of the Mutiny of 1857. The Police Commission of 1860, while making its recommendations, *inter alia* observed that organized police by them, would be "politically more useful" to the British regime in India. police system, therefore, continued operating ruthlessly throughout the country as an instrument for retaining the government in power. The British reviewed the working of the Indian police system through Indian Police Commission of 1902-03. The said Commission found the police far from efficient, defective in training and organization, corrupt and oppressive in public perception, causing serious injury to the psyche of the people and discredit to the Government. The Commission emphasized the necessity for radical reforms. However, observations/recommendations of Police Commission notwithstanding, the character of Indian police remained the same, until we won the Independence on 15th August 1947.

Unfortunately, no radical change in the system of police functioning took place after the Independence of India. Newspapers and Periodicals continued often carrying reports of incidents of police excesses, criticizing police behaviour and depicting the Indian police as undemocratic and uncivilized brute force. The public at large continued passively tolerating the Police system unworthy of the governance as envisioned in the Constitution of India. Thanks to the infamous Emergency of 1975-76, the brazen manner in which the police force were used by the authorities that were, to subvert lawful procedures and serve purely political ends, the general public in the country and political figures of every stature experienced the real heat of the wretched and putrefied police system obtaining in the country.

The top leaders of Janata Party– a loose conglomeration of top leaders of all non-Congress political parties, who had formed a newfound fraternity while languishing in jails for 19 months constituted their government at the Centre on 23rd March 1977 with Morarji Desai as the Prime Minister and Charan Singh as the Home Minister. This Government constituted a National Police Commission (NPC) on 15th November 1977 under the Chairmanship of Dharmvira, former ICS and a former Governor. The Commission made an in-depth study about the entire gamut of police system obtaining in the country and submitted seven reports to the Central Government, from February 1979 to May 1981, containing recommendations for wide range reforms in the policing system, so as to meet the aspirations of the general public as well as police personnel of various ranks. Unfortunately, these reports continued eating dust in the dingy record room. Prakash Singh IPS, former DGP Uttar Pradesh and subsequently of Boarder Security Force (BSF) filed a Public Interest Litigation (PIL) Petition in the Supreme Court of India in nineties, pleading for the implementation of the recommendations of the said NPC. The Supreme Court's Judgment of 2006 marks a defining moment in the history of Indian police. It endorsed the view of National Police Commission (1978-81) that Indian police has become the handmaiden of the ruling party, alienated from the people and has become professionally incompetent. The Supreme Court issued seven points directive to the centre and the states to implement the recommendations.

Though the Apex Court gave fixed period to the states for compliance of various points, yet political masters continued to scuttle meaningful reforms. Many top police officers of gone-by days and the Human Rights activists have been forcefully projecting through the media, the need of the hour to transform the Police into an effective instrument of social defence and social change. Unfortunately, many state governments are dragging their feet and trying to stall police reforms under various pretexts. Some states have made a few cosmetic changes far from being systematic police reforms. The full gamut of police reforms endlessly debated and refined for over thirty years since the submission of comprehensive reports by Dharmvira Commission needs to be enforced. It is unfortunate that even after the Union Home Minister's plaintive cry in Parliament that "malafide transfers have reduced the police to football" nothing seems to have happened to end the charade.

The idea to write this book germinated in my mind when I relinquished charge as Superintendent of Police district Rohtak on 30th July 1969. My transfer from Rohtak had matured after I pressed for it persistently with the Chief Minister. I decided then that I would record everything whatever I experience until the age of 80 and write my autobiography. In this book, I have attempted to place before the worthy readers, two distinct aspects of my life. In the first four chapters, I have described, in minute details, how with humble rural background from a downtrodden community, I struggled hard to overcome various difficulties and hurdles in acquiring education, both during pre and post Independence era and then successfully competed in the All India/Central Civil Services Examination, conducted by the UPSC in 1956. In the next sixteen chapters, I have described the character, attitude, behaviour and quality of the police personnel of various ranks and relationship between bureaucrats, police and politicians – intrigues, revenge, sealing the ladder. I have also described the conduct and approach of various politicians including the top political executives holding the reins of the state's administration from time to time and the approach, patterns, postulations, converses and unifications of various political forces as I could discern throughout my police career.

"Nostalgia is like a grammar lesson; you find the present tense, but the past is perfect," said Owens Lae Pomeroy. A journey through the memory lane can be fun to some but painful to others. Majority among the intelligentsia remember their lives not in years, months or days but in moments – freeze frames – as if time had stood still to enable them to commit to memory every detail. Significant happenings are stored not in fast forward but in slow motion mode. During various stages of my life, I had to tread an undulating path strewn with thorns, making it a saga of challenges and fulfillment. I dropped out from fifth primary class, when the class teacher made disparaging remarks about my caste. I became the family cattle grazer for two years. I was unceremoniously discharged from Government service on adverse police report. Police thrashed me on my surreptitiously sneaking into the residence of Union Deputy Home Minister to seek justice. I was rebuked badly, during basic training as IPS probationer by GK Handoo, Commandant Incharge Central Police Training College Mount Abu, for no reasons. I had to suffer wickedness and revengeful conduct of Range DIG. A false story was concocted by state vigilance agency, linking me with an imaginary murder case. These events are so vivid in my memory that the passage of time has not been able to fade out their intensity. Some of these events are really very painful and vile in nature but in the end proving to be fulfilling as William Shakespeare said "Sweet are uses of adversity which like the toad, ugly and venomous, wears yet a precious jewel in his head".

Many moments of fulfillment came in my life with the success stories. I successfully competed for Civil Services Competitive Examination 1956, held by the UPSC, in the first attempt. I successfully steered through storms and straits during my posting as Superintendent of Police, district Rohtak and was adjudged as a model police officer. Investigating the murder case of village Jasrana, Police Station Gohana district Rohtak was a challenging episode. In this case, five innocent persons were falsely named in the FIR to wreak vengeance. SHO and the Dy SP endorsed the story of FIR. However, after holding on the spot investigation I found the alleged five accused as falsely implicated. Unfortunately, the trial Court of District and Session Judge rejected my investigation and believing the FIR story as true, convicted them to life imprisonment. However, the High Court accepting, in toto, the investigation conducted by me found these accused persons as innocent and acquitted them. I got Police Medal for Meritorious Service in 1977 and further got President's Police Medal for Distinguished Service in 1987. In June 1987 I was recalled to head the police department as the State DGP, thus the invisible glass ceiling for a scheduled caste IPS officer was broken. The most important and significant day in my police career was 20th June 1988 when I refused to go off the lawful path and in upholding the rule of law, I preferred to hang my police uniform, five weeks ahead of my date of superannuation from the service. Kaleidoscopic view of all these events, though to some would seem to be amusingly incredible, has been inspiring for me to live long.

I have throughout been conscious of the fact that writing recent political history of the state as described in chapter eight onwards of the book was a highly sensitive affair. It has been my humble endeavour to present to the readers a comprehensive account to understand the police dilemma. "With malice towards none; with charity to all; with firmness in the right as God gives us to see the right, let us strive on to finish the work we are in," said Abraham Lincoln. In true spirit of this quote, I have described, with respect to all and malice to none, every event in its true perspective and have offered detailed information on contemporary political history of Haryana State since its inception believing that it would be useful to the generation next to mine. Some of the players of the game of politics and also the governance of the country, relevant for the period of my term of over three decades in the IPS, as outlined in this book, are no longer alive. May their souls be in peace! All my narrations are in historical perspective and I repeat, are without any ill-will or disregard to anybody as human being, alive or dead.

Acknowledgments and Thanks

My sincere thanks and heart-felt acknowledgments are due to my kind friends who assisted and guided me with their very valuable advice enabling this monumental work to see the light of the day in this form. Sh Baljit Rai IPS, DGP (Retd.) and Dr J D Dhingra, M.A. (English) M.A. (History) and Ph.D. (English), who both have authored books on diverse subjects, helped in completing this book with their precious advice. Sh TD Jogpal, IAS, Former Financial Commissioner and Secretary to Haryana Government, later Haryana State Election Commissioner, examined the draft and made very useful suggestions. Sh KC Sulekh, former Taxation Officer, a prolific writer with scholarly bent of mind and ex-editor of an erstwhile famous magazine "Ujala"; who has authored numerous books and articles on a variety of subjects was very helpful by going through word to word to suggest and correct the matter. Col Prithvi Raj Kumar, a former Chief Postmaster General, a learned person with sound knowledge of Hindi, Sanskrit and English literature and evincing keen interest in subjects like social and moral sciences with philanthropic mission, has also made very useful suggestions in finalizing the format of the book.

Most important has been the role played by Sh Nagendra Tiwary from Bihar. He extended his willing and helping hand for typing about four hundred pages of this work with unstinted and untiring hard work put in meticulously and intelligently. No words of thanks would ever be good enough for the labour and sincerity of purpose, displayed by Sh Tiwary. May God bless him!

My thanks are also due to Sh. Jaibir Ranga, a prominent social activist of Panchkula, who enthusiastically extended his helping hand in carrying out corrections in the manuscript of this book.

Hans Raj Swan

Chapter – 1

Ancestors – Their Origin and Dispersion, Present Village and Kins

Origin and Dispersion

I have not been able tc lay hands on any authentic documents regarding the origin of my ancestors. However, I have mentioned hereinafter various circumstantial factors, which have come around to my firm belief about their origin.

Evolutionary historical facts are in evidence that the growth process of immigration and emigration has been in vogue among the humans ever since man raised boundaries between various regions and countries. However, within various regions and countries, reshuffling of population has been a continuous phenomenon and in that, different factors at different times have led the inhabitants of different places leaving their homes and hearths and moving out to places, in their quest for better surroundings and opportunities, more convenient and favourable environments. For many historical reasons, a view point comes around that my ancestors, many centuries ago, had their abodes in the Sohaan Valley of erstwhile Una Tehsil of district Hoshiarpur, presently a full fledged district of Himachal Pradesh State and were from Chauhan Rajput lineage.

My ancestors, after leaving Sohaan valley settled in village Khan Khaana, district Jalandhar. However, with the passage of time, as the family expanded, during a span of few generations, their offspring started diverging out to other places within the doab of Beas and Sutlej rivers. Some had gone still too far off places. Presently their main concentrations are in villages Sakrulli, Barot Randhawa, Doogri, Deowal all in district Hoshiarpur; villages Khan Khanna, Lodipur and Khamano in district Nawanshahar; villages Pandori Nijjran, Adampur, Alawalpur, Phillaur in district Jalandhar; various suburbs which have sprung up on the out–skirts of Ludhiana city, village Balliwal in district Ludhiana; village Sirhi in district Hisar (Haryana). Many amongst them are Non-Resident Indians having settled in UK, Germany, Canada, USA, Italy, Greece etc. At the time of initial migration from Sohaan Valley they were economically poor; at their new sojourns they had to take all sorts of odd jobs to make both ends meet.

With the passage of time, Sohaan river of Una's Sohaan Valley came to be known as Swan River. Taming of Swan River "The Sorrow of Una" has ushered in a green revolution changing the economic landscape of the area as never before. The immigrants to the plains, identify themselves with Chauhan or Swan gotra. But they do not inter-marry their boys and girls. Here it should be worthwhile to mention that prohibition of marriage within sagotra, the same gotra, or two gotras, which are akin or believed to have originated from a common ancestry is a social custom prevalent among Hindus under the Hindu system of laws. It has no backing from the Hindu Marriage Act. In addition, there has not been any scientific evidence to prove that biologically marriage within same gotra could be harmful for the health of the offspring produced from such alliance.

German scholar Max Mueller had defined gotra as descending from eight sages and then branching out to innumerable families. PV Kane author of the "History of Dharmashashtra" had said, "The mass of material on *gotra* and *parvara* in *sutra*, the Puranas and Digest is so vast and full of contradictions that it is almost an impossible task to put it to order and coherence". Judicial scrutiny of marriage within the same gotra has not been found invalid. The people from Chauhan and Swan gotras profess that their great grand ancestor who, after migrating from Una's Swan River Valley, had settled and died at village Khan Khaana. Therefore, they assemble in thousands in the month of May, every year, at village Khan Khaana to pay homage to departed soul of their ancestor. A shrine has come up at a place near that village where the first ancestor from among the settlers at village Khan Khaana was laid at rest. That is a place of cynosure for the clan pilgrims. Their claim of coming from Chauhan Rajput clan lineage remains buried, in the debris of historical ruins and they generally came to be known as a depressed class. During the census of 1931 AD, they were listed as Ad-dharmi.

Village Before and After Independence

Having left village Khan Khaana, my ancestors, perhaps only two real brothers had settled down at village Sakrulli, tehsil Garhshankar of district Hoshiarpur, sometimes during the early decades of 17th century. A non-descriptive village Sakrulli then had a small population, but its land holding was of 9976 kanals–large territorial area by all standards. Situated at about 8 km from the Shivalik foothills in its western plain, its vast area was covered under mango grooves, followed next by big chunk of land, which was sandy, barren and not cultivable.

Out of total land holding of 9967 kanals, nearly one third was under plough. No irrigation facilities were available. Sub-soil water being very deep even persian wheels were not feasible and tube wells were not known. Thus, the agriculture depended entirely on the rains. The entire agriculture process was labour intensive, right from the ploughing of field for sowing to harvesting crops. Tractors had not yet come up. Pesticides and insecticides had not been discovered then for agricultural purposes. Ploughing, hoeing and weeding were manual processes. Therefore, there was much interdependence between land owning and landless classes; *jajmani* system was in vogue between the land owning and landless families. This suited well both the sides.

There was no gurdwara or Hindu temple or mosque in the village. Neither was there any school even of primary level. Irregular footpaths and bullock-cart passages with the neighbouring villages linked the village. The nearest semblance of a metalled road was far away. An anglo-vernacular Khalsa middle school was at village Paldi some 3km away. A government middle school and a Khalsa high school with English subject were at Mahilpur. There were quite a few persons both young and middle aged who used to indulge in notorious activities such as sexually exploiting the women from the poor families in the village. Because of my persuasive efforts, the village-panchayat members were generally elected unanimously giving representation to all communities in proportion to their population. After Independence the village got a link-metalled road. Gurmail Singh a resident of this village remained Cabinet Minister holding important portfolios. His efforts gave the village two other link roads and the village government middle school upgraded to high school level. The villagers expected of him to make some spectacular contribution in the development of the village. On that count, they have been feeling disappointed and unhappy.

Kins

When plague struck north India during the years 1899-1904 complete evacuation of villages and towns became the order of the day. My great grandfather and his colaterals set-up their improvised thatched dwellings in the mango grove some 1500 yards away from the village. Other residents likewise settled in thatched dwellings in the open fields away from the village. As the epidemic of plague receded, the people started reverting to the village, but the group of my ancestors as stated above, continued in their improvised thatched dwellings which acquired the name of *kullian mohalla* of main village. After Indepedence, this basti has turned into a cluster of *pacca* houses with brick lined streets. A bhawan for common use for multifarious socio-religious activities has come up. Almost every household has a T.V, a refrigerator, water supply connection and sanitation facilities.

Great Grandfather

Saddhoo Ram had four sons; Sunder Das, my grand father, Rikhi Ram, Hira Lal and Issar Das. Rikhi Ram did not marry and continued to live in the joint family of Hira Lal and died at the age of 70. A grand son of Hira Lal is Phania Ram, who retired as an officer from the Telephone Department and has settled down at Hoshiarpur. Hira Lal was a good-looking person with adventurous disposition. He migrated to USA soon after the First World War. He became alcoholic and fell to the charm of white skinned women and died in the foreign land – when, how and where, have remained a mystery. Issar Das, the youngest son of my great grandfather was a tall, well-built and handsome person. His physical assets proved rather a cause of weakness for worldly pleasures. Dalip Chand, the youngest of his three sons, had inherited physical assets of his father. He appeared to be very promising. After graduation, Dalip

Chand joined the Indian Army as a sepoy. There, he rose to the rank of Subedar and was unfortunately, incapacitated in a road accident while on duty in Assam. His two sons and a daughter got good education and are well settled in government jobs on senior positions.

Grandfather Sunder Das

He was a very affable person, gifted with the art of living in harmony with whom-so-ever he came into contact. My grand mother, Atri Devi was a fair complexioned sweet natured person. She never raised her voice in *saas-bahu* skirmishes. The couple got four sons and two daughters.

My uncle Munshi Ram elder to my father had married Pooro, elder sister of my mother. They got three sons and a daughter. The elder son, Anant Ram got seven sons and two daughters. Three of them are NRIs, one each in USA, UK and Germany; the eldest - Davinder Kumar is well settled in the village with his own miscellaneous business. The second in line Jinderpal Jangi is German NRI. He did his graduation and used to hum folk songs and turned out to be a folk singer of some reckoning. With a guitar, as his pet musical instrument, he set out on a global trotting unmindful of his destination. "If music be the food of love; play on! Music was invented to confirm human loveliness". Plato said, "At the touch of love, every one becomes a poet". "The truest expression of people is in dance and music". "The job of the artist is always to deepen the mystery". Crossing all borders, with his guitar and an enchanting voice, helping him all the way, he landed in Germany and settled down there. His girlfriend, Mahinder Kaur already in London with her NRI parents, joined him at Germany in nuptial bond. After spending some twenty years in Germany, the couple shifted to Chandigarh.

Alla Ram, younger to Anant Ram, now at 86, still gives out a youthful look. His two sons and a grandson with their families settled in Italy. His one grandson is a police officer in Haryana. Chanan Ram, the third son of my uncle had migrated with his family to USA His son and three daughters, all married, are too settled in America.

The two families of my father and uncle remained in an admirable harmony like an extended family and we, three sons of each of them, had mutual love, affection and respect, as if we were real brothers. This was mainly because of healthy influence of the two sisters – my mother and *masiji*. This bond has continued even to their present fourth generation.

Parents

My father, Garib Das was the second son of my grandfather Sunder Das. A *keshadhari*, bearded and a non-baptized Sikh, he was a hardworking person, always cherishing high goals. Though having no formal schooling, he had acquired good workable knowledge in Panjabi language. He had developed interest in Panjabi folklores like *Heer-Ranjha, Sohni-Mehiwal, Mirza-Sahiban, Sassi-Punnu, Keema-Malki* and *Dulla Bhatti*. These folk songs he had committed to his memory and had become a popular folk singer among rural folks. Being in haste to achieve something substantial, he switched over from one profession to another and ultimately settled down to farming and trading in milch buffaloes. There used to be 10 to 12 heads of cattle, at a time to take care of. The habits of my father, for example keeping himself busy like a honey-bee, both mentally and physically and wasting no time on frivolities, instilled in me importance of hard work and respecting every minute of life, for some positive, productive and meaningful objectives. He remained elected member of the village panchayat for many years, and village numbardar, as nominated by the government, for about 25 years until his death on 18th September 1984 at the age of 90.

My mother Gulab Devi was a tall, very fair complexioned, blue eyed, very good-looking woman. She had inherited these physical assets from her father Shobha Ram, my maternal grand father who was 6 feet 2 inches tall with sharp features and impressive personality. Right from her middle age days until 1977 when she expired at the age of 79. She remained a respected woman for her worldly wisdom, liberal habits of helping the women folk, taking side firmly with the aggrieved party in any minor or major dispute. Whatever, I have been in my life, from childhood to the apex stage of my achievements, I owe all to her wisdom, affection, guidance and the meaningful stories, she used to narrate to me from Ramayana, Mahabharata and lives of Guru Nanak Dev, Guru Teg Bahadur and Guru Gobind Singh. It was she, who taught me the meaning of Omnipresence and Omnipotence of God and how a low-caste born Ravidas reached the high pedestal of glory and was called a Guru, worthy of worship, even by the high caste Rajput princess, Mirabai. She used to sing melodiously these stories during small hours of the morning while grinding grains or churning milk overnight turned into curd for preparing white butter and "*lassi*", both famous Panjabi delicacies.

The hard work put in by my parents and their helpful attitude towards the needy and aggrieved persons endeared them to everyone. They started their married life from a thatched dwelling and landless status. Having a reasonably good *pucca* house, owning 10 acres of agriculture land, about 100 Marlas of residential area and ensuring that I though, married at the age of 19 years, continued my studies up to graduation, with their own hard-earned money, speaks volumes of their wisdom and hard working nature. May God bless their souls with eternal peace!

Family of My Parents

My parents got three daughters one after the other, followed by three sons. I was the youngest, born on 4th August 1930. The women folks in the rural area used to administer a very small dose of opium to the infant children to keep them asleep for longer hours during the daytime so that they did not distract their mothers from attending to their household affairs. This intoxicant had adverse effect on the mental growth of the infants. Since I had the privilege of having three elder sisters, grown up enough to attend on me, I was saved from that savage act of having that intoxicant. It is perhaps, because of this fact that from the very childhood, my mental alertness was much higher than that of the other children around.

My eldest brother, Khushi Ram was in the farming profession. His two sons Hem Raj and Ram Bhaj are in the police department. My second elder brother Maluk Chand had four sons, Sewak Raj, Surinder Kumar, Jiwan Lal and Dilbag Rai. The first three of them were in the police department. Sewak Raj the eldest being alcoholic, remained in trouble. Surinder Kumar was martyred at the hands of terrorists in 1988 while on his duty in police department.

Chapter – 2

Childhood and Schooling

Childhood

Born on 4th August 1930, as the youngest sixth child of my parents under a thatch without even one spoon in the entire dwelling, let alone the proverbial silver spoon in the mouth, in a remote village and in equally obscure surroundings. We all eight members of the family had a sizeable thatched hut as our home shared with two buffaloes, having calves, surrounded all around by a cluster of thatched huts of other mohalla dwellers. I became six years old playing with fellow children. Kullian mohalla dwellers had dug out from an adjoining vacant plot, a lot of earth for raising mud walls for their thatched huts over the years and this shallow place, in due course of time, became a good pond to store rainwater for the cattle to quench their thirst and cool themselves from the heat during summer months. Like other mohalla children, I learnt swimming in this pond while tending the cattle. For immunization against child diseases, I had been administered vaccination against Small Pox. No other immunization treatment was given to me against polio and other diseases, which generally afflict the children. Perhaps, it was not then common among the village folk and perhaps the government, at that time, did not practice it.

Admission to School

I was admitted to the 1st standard in the village Lower Primary class in April 1937. My father, who took me to the school for admission, could not tell the teacher the exact date of my birth, saying merely that I was born during the rainy season some six years back. The teacher put in my date of birth as 15.7.1930, by his own calculations. Pandit ji was a very good teacher; single handedly he used to manage both 1st and 2nd lower primary classes, studiously and efficiently. Village panchayat tried its best to get the school upgraded up to 4th class with recognition by the District Board. Their efforts failed and instead Primary school up to 4th class was granted for the adjoining village Langeri some 2 km from my village. The school at my village was, therefore, closed. The students were left with no alternative, except to go to the Primary School at village Langeri, whereto approach was rather difficult. Sant Attar Singh Khalsa Anglo Vernacular Middle School at village Paldi was some 3km from my village. With the best building in the entire area, this was a duly recognized school by the Government and known for being excellently managed by the Managing Committee. Being Khalsa School, all the students from 1st standard to 8th standard used to adorn turban, as their headgear. No other part of the clothings was in any prescribed form. The school would start the teaching session with recitation of a hymn from *GUR-BANI* (Guru Granth Sahib). I had then passed class II and was to seek admission in class III. My parents put me in Khalsa School, at village Paldi in April 1939. Maulvi Umarbux was the teacher–in-charge for the primary classes. He was a very kind hearted, affectionate in dealing with the students and reputed for producing very good results. In the mid-session of class III, Maulvi Umarbux finding me very good in arithmetic and recitation of Urdu poems, appointed me as monitor of the class. This made me not only more self confident, it ignited some sort of spark and excitement within me to excel all others in the class. Results were, indeed, very encouraging for me. In the 4th class, I was made to compete for District Board Merit Scholarship, with students of 4th classes in all other schools of the district. The result was a windfall; I was selected and awarded scholarship to be availed from 5th to 8th class. With this achievement, I was elated. My parents and other elders in the mohalla were boisterous in celebrating the happy occasion. In the 5th standard, English subject was also added. Due to my performance in the 4th class, I was nominated as monitor of the 5th class just from the start of the session.

Dropped Out

In May 1941, an extremely bad patch in my otherwise very smooth and admirable schooling career, overtook and the destiny led me on to a disastrous and path. On a hot mid day of May, 1941 Hazura Singh, the English teacher had not arrived to take the class for 20 minutes or so. The students, all in the age group of 10 to 12 years, feeling free had started playing, gossiping and shouting. As monitor I tried my best to control them but they would only lower their pitch for a while. When the teacher entered the classroom, I was a little late in calling the class to stand up. The teacher perhaps was under some tension. He started abusing me in obscene and unprintable language for my mother, sisters and the caste. In his rage, he gave me very hard slaps and stopped only when I started crying hoarse. The whole class had sunk into the silence of the grave, as if highly terrorized. When I did not stop crying, the teacher perhaps atoning for his uncalled for aggression, tried to console me. Tears are God's gift to us; our holy water. They heal as they flow. In the meanwhile, the episode came to the notice of the senior teacher, then acting as Headmaster. He called Hazura Singh and perhaps reprimanded him.

The acting Headmaster called me to his room and consoled me with all affection, which made me to cry again; perhaps it was an emotional outburst. The acting Headmaster affectionately advised me not to disclose the incident to my parents. Corporal punishment was order of the day during those times.

But I, having been adjudged the best student and scholarship holder had rightly or wrongly, assumed some sort of self importance and my sensitivity to corporal punishment, which I had never experienced, was somewhat excessive. Although slapping by the teacher hurt me a lot yet I perhaps could still tolerate and forget it, but the highly indecent unprintable language the teacher had used for my mother, sisters and caste was something so horrible that it caused a deep scar on my psyche. This incident was the first ever, but very severe assault on my self-respect by the scourge of untouchability.

I returned home crestfallen and deeply depressed. I threw away my bag of schoolbooks, lying flat on the cot, sinking my face into an improvised pillow, I cried and cried saying that I would not go to school any more. My mother and elder sisters, trying to console me, were impatiently enquiring as to what had happened. I refused to divulge anything and insisted for a promise from my mother not to force me for going to school. She did promise but became very tense. For many days, my mother did not make any mention about my schooling and was more worried because I had lost my appetite as the incident had continued haunting me with its painful memory. With her melodious songs about Devaki, Yashodhara and Mata Gujari, she finally extracted the secret of my depressed state of mind. After listening to my woeful story she advised me not to tell anything to my father about the obscene language which the teacher had used for my sisters and mother. After a month or so Pandit Sant Ram of our village who was also a teacher in the school at Paldi came to our residence to inquire about the reasons for my long absence from our school. It was then that my father came to know that it was some serious misconduct on the part of Hazura Singh. Pandit ji tried to persuade my mother to prevail upon me for starting going to the school. However, I continued getting frightened, even on the mention of any more schooling for me. Hazura Singh looked to me a demon incarnate, "Respect for the teachers cannot be ordered; it must be earned."- S. Radhakrishanan. My parents, as ill luck would have it, gave up and there was no more talk about my schooling.

A Cattle Grazer

The family had about a dozen heads of cattle. By that time, my parents had managed to have a big thatch for the cattle, separate from the family's thatched dwelling. I being just about 11 years old not grown up enough to assist the family except that I could take out the cattle for grazing in the vast tract of land in the village, which was not cultivable. Other boys almost of my age were doing the same job for their families. There used to be a herd of about 50 to 60 heads of cattle for a group of 5 to 6 boys. Except me, the other boys had never gone to any school. Time flew fast. I started feeling uncomfortable in the company of other rustic fellow cattle grazers. Young boys of neighbouring village Chandsu used to pass that way while going to the school. I would greet them and try to cultivate friendship with them. My inner conscience started urging me to take out my books. I became keen to learn English lessons from those boys. In the words of Brian Lithrell "Shoot for the moon. Even if you miss, you will land among the stars". The cattle grazing fields were full of various types of shrubs, amidst this wild growth of *Mala* shrubs, bearing a small variety of *Ber* (sannon fruit) was very common. I would collect Ber in good quantity and would present these to the school-going boys. In exchange, I would learn from them a lesson from my English book. This became my daily routine. In about a year's time I learnt all the lessons in my English book reading, writing and understanding the meanings. I also started getting lessons in arithmetic of 5th standard and that too I soon learnt fairly well. My "boy-teachers" would enjoy more in imparting to me lessons in English and Arithmetic than any keenness for getting *Ber* from me. In the words of Winston Churchill "Success is not final, failure is not fatal; it is the courage to continue that counts"**.** Though sparking urge started surging up in my inner conscience, yet the fear psychosis, by the assault of Hazura Singh, which had been inflicted on my mind, would prevent me from asking my parents for sending me again to the school.

Rejoining the School

My routine went on and on until destiny smiled on me. It was mid-April, 1943 when harvesting of wheat crops was in full swing. I was as usual, doing my routine job as a cattle grazer. I saw a well dressed Sardar Ji, possibly in his early fifties, accompanied by an equally well dressed boy, almost of my age, walking with a bicycle, on a nearby sandy footpath. I having an English book in one hand together with my daily collection of *Ber* and a long stick in the other hand approached them. Putting all the articles on the ground, I greeted them with folded hands with the salutation "Sat Sri Akal Sir". Sardar Ji very affectionately responded saying "Sat Sri Akal Beta". He enquired where I was studying. On my telling him, I was not studying in any school he curiously inquired what sort of book I was carrying. On my telling him that it was an English book and that I knew its reading, writing etc, he asked me to show the same to him. Having seen the book he asked me to read out to him from a particular page of the book. He was surprised and then the obvious followed. He became all the more affectionate towards me after listening to my story how I had left the school; he started goading me to rejoin the school. On my saying that my parents would not perhaps agree, he told me that it would be for him to persuade my parents to spare me for rejoining the school. Before departing, he disclosed that he was the new Headmaster of the school. After patting my back and saying "Sat Sri Akal", he moved on towards his destination.

Next day on Monday evening Pandit Sant Ram of our village, a teacher in Khalsa Middle School Paldi, met my parents at our residence and told them the story of my happy chance meeting with the Headmaster of the school on the previous day. My parents asked me whether I would happily rejoin the school at Paldi. I excitedly replied in the affirmative. Next day being Tuesday was considered inauspicious by my mother and she decided to send me to the school on the next day that is Wednesday. My father took me to the school and met the Headmaster accompanied by Pandit Sant Ram. Thus, I once again became a regular student of the 5th Class. For the summer-vacation, the school teachers assigned homework to the students. I was the only student who fully accomplished the homework neatly and correctly. Therefore, I was appointed, as monitor of the class when the session restarted on the expiry of the summer vacation. I was though very excited for my rebirth as a student and becoming again the monitor of the class, yet whenever I would meet my previous class fellows of 5th class then studying in 7th class, I would feel sad and somewhat melancholic. Some of the boys would tease calling me sarcastically a permanent monitor of the 5th class. This however did not dishearten me, as I was then, not grown up enough to realize that I had wasted two very precious years of my life. Then the circumstances around me at both school and home were extra enjoyable and encouraging for me. I could not fully realize the deeper implications of these two wasted years.

My illiterate mother had imparted, deep into my psyche, the urge for learning by narrating enchantingly interesting stories of great men and women who had acquired enviable position in the history because of their high learning. Then the sweet, affectionate and inspiring way of teaching during the primary classes used to attract the children to the school. The urge so created in my psyche had continued prompting me to take to my books even while having been pushed into the most rustic job of a cattle grazer. Anganwadi System has failed because the teachers are themselves ill-educated, ill-mannered and are only mercenaries. The present days teaching staff, at primary and middle school levels, are not trained enough to understand the psyche of the children.

Bajaj Couple–My Foster Parents

I had been a topper in my 5th, 6th and 7th classes. When I was in the 8th class Sardar Sawan Singh Bajaj in his late twenties from Rawalpindi, West Punjab joined as Headmaster of our school. During 1946, communal riots had started in Rawalpindi area and many of his near and dear had come over to East Punjab and Delhi. Bajaj Sahib, then newly married was accommodated in a good house in village Paldi. A tall, fair complexioned, stoutly built, very religious person, he used to dress up impeccably, in three-piece suite and was an impressive personality. He taught English subject to the 8th Class. Soon he became very fond of me and gave me lot of affection. It was after the students of 8th class were given a test to translate some hymns like *Mool-Manter, five first hymns* and *shaloka* of *Holy Japuji Sahib* composed by Guru Nanak Dev and considered to be the very basic and foundational beauty of *Guru Granth Sahib*. Translation done by me was adjudged the best in the class, both by the Headmaster and Giani Sohan Singh, the Moral Science teacher in the school. I got a book, written in Urdu by Khan Bahadur Khuwaja Dil Mohammad, Sub-Registrar, Lahore University and Retired Principal, Islamia College Lahore, as the first prize. This famous book carries translation of *Japuji Sahib* and *Sukhmani Sahib*, in simple Urdu Poetry. This book continues to be my most valued treasure until today. Whenever I feel mentally disturbed, I take solace in reciting hymns and assimilating the translations in the said book. It is my privilege that all the hymns in *Japuji Sahib* are committed to my memory. During those days Urdu was the medium of instructions, English was the second language. The quality of students used to be adjudged from their proficiency and eloquence in English language and Arithmetic. I was considered far ahead of my class fellows in these two subjects in the class.

As per the system followed in the Khalsa School, all the classes, with their respective teachers, would collect together in the school compound for morning assembly to sing hymns from *Bani* followed by prayers, before the classes began. I, flanked by two other students would sing the hymn and the entire assembly of school would repeat, in chorus, melodiously. It used to be a great occasion for every participant including Maulvi Umarbax to enjoy gleefully the *Bani.* This would be followed by a prayer by Giani Sohan Singh. He would conclude the prayer with the words, "Oh Great Lord Bless this little boy Hans Raj with such Bounties as wisdom, hard work and capability that in the Anglo Vernacular Middle School final examination he may come ahead of all students of 8th class in all the schools in the area". *Hey Sachhey Patshah Kaka Hansraj De Sirr Te Hath Rakhna, Iss Nu Annee Buddee Tey Sakht, Mehnat Karan Dee Shakti Tey Hoshiari Bakhshna Ke Eh Bachha Sare Ilakke De Sakoolan De Athmeen De Imtehaan Wichhon Avval Avae.* With joy, gratitude and excitement I would often have goose bums on my body and my eyes would become moist with emotions. This all would have very inspiring effect on my psyche resulting in a renewed determination to come up to the expectation of my kind and noble teachers. Mark Twain very rightly said, "Really great people make you feel that you too can become great."

Bajaj Sahib would take me along to his house very often where his wife, a young highly educated person would treat me very affectionately and give me toffees and biscuit packets every time. Once, on a visit to their house, this graceful and kindhearted person told me that she wanted to see the place where I lived with my parents and also wanted to meet my mother. The school peon Ratan Lal was married in our village. He had already seen our house. He brought a message from Madam Bajaj that she would come to our house on a Sunday afternoon. My mother and all brothers and sisters were highly excited in waiting for the arrival of our VIP. Madam Bajaj, accompanied by school peon, came to our house carrying with her a box of sweets. She talked to my mother about her household matters and went around the house, which by then had come up as brick walled house with wooden logs and rafters ceiling. However, total accommodation was too inadequate to spare a proper separate study room for me. Madam Bajaj proposed to my mother that Hans Raj could stay with them at their house at village Paldi for two months, the remaining period to start final examinations. To the excitement of every one of us in the family, it was a very big offer and a unique favour. My mother had already prepared some 'Pakoras' which she offered to Madam Bajaj with a glass of milk. She enjoyed the 'Pakoras' but declined to take milk.

Next day with all my books and scanty bedding, my eldest brother left me at the house of Madam Bajaj. Bajaj Sahib was in the house. He told Madam Bajaj that her initiative for a social cause was laudable. At this new place, my regular daily routine was very interesting. Madam Bajaj would wake me up at 4 am; I would wash my face with fresh cold water; she would bring a glass full of sweetened milk with two small "matthis". Having consumed that, I would sit up for my study and she would sit on the opposite side of the bed-knitting sweater for about 20 minutes. Finding me fully absorbed in my studies, she would leave to attend to her own household chores saying affectionately to me "Kakkaji continue carefully with your study, if there is any problem, call me". Bajaj Sahib would generally getup at about 5.00 am, take his bath and set on to recite *Japuji Sahib.* He would then come to me enquiring whether I was comfortable and wanted any help from him in my studies. Often I would take his help in English Grammar and Arithmetic. At 6.30 am, I would close up as per daily routine set up by Madam Bajaj, leave for my house in the adjoining village Sakruli hopping joyfully, relieving myself on the way in the open fields. Reaching home, I would hug my mother and tell her my sweet experience of the previous night. Having taken bath at the common well of the mohalla, amidst the mohalla folks assembled there for collecting water in their earthen pots, my mother would feed me with freshly prepared butter mixed with raw sugar "shakkar" spread on a chapatti with a glass of Lassi. Before I start my hopping back to the Bajaj's place, my mother would give me about 100 ml of milk and two big *Laddoos* prepared from *chapatti-shakkar-ghee*, all meshed, for my meals during the recess hours of the school. After collecting my books etc., from the house of Madam Bajaj, I would reach school well before time to take part in morning school recitation of hymns and prayer. After school hours, I would deposit my books etc. at the house of Madam Bajaj and joyfully hop back to my own home. After taking evening meals well before sunset, I would again hop back to the Bajaj's place. I would sit down for my studies at about 7.00 pm, as per the timetable set by Madam Bajaj. At 10.00 pm, she would give me a cup of sweetened milk and bid me to sleep. This happy routine continued for about two months.

The love, affection and kindness showered on me by the kindhearted Bajaj couple and their spiritual way of life and uniquely humane approach left very deep imprints on my life. All this rekindled a new kind of spark within me. During these days, Bajaj Sahib got an offer of Headmaster's job in a High School at Delhi. This was his elevation and then Delhi was the place where his many kith and kin had settled after migrating from Rawalpindi. It was, therefore, an occasion for celebration for the Bajaj couple. However, the very thought of missing them made me gloomy and somewhat restless. The sense of loss of their kind and affectionate patronage left a kind of void in my life. The entire school staff was present to bid farewell to them and I could not control my tears when Madam Bajaj hugged me saying, "Kakka Hans, do continue putting hard work in your studies; remember you have to excel others in the final examinations. I did not get the opportunity to meet them again in my life. Reaching home, I hugged my mother with tearful eyes telling her how badly I was missing them. "Relationships are like a book. It takes a few seconds to burn, but it takes years to write. So write it carefully and never let it burn." When someone you love becomes a memory, the memory becomes a treasure. For some moments in life, there are no words. "As in the sky flies the white clothed crane, keeping its mind behind; In its hearts continually remembering its young ones; So the true guru (teacher) keeps the disciple absorbed in the love of God; And also keeps him in his heart." *–Adi Granth*

Sardar Gurbax Singh Giani

The new Headmaster, Sardar Gurbux Singh Giani was a baptized Sikh. His earlier station was Baba Bakala, a renowned Sikh historical place. He was of a saintly disposition and was very often heard reciting *Japuji Sahib*. He soon learnt about my performance as a student. Since final examination of Anglo Vernacular Middle Class was to be conducted by the Lahore Education Board in February 1946, the Headmaster arranged accommodation in one side of the school hall for 10 students who were considered the best lot in the 8th class. Giani Banta Singh Saini, an Arithmetic and Urdu teacher was, made in-charge of the group. He was also a baptized Sikh and a strict disciplinarian. He would wake us up at 4.00 am and would give intense coaching in Arithmetic, Urdu and Persian until 6.30 am. After that, the boys would disperse. My routine from that time onwards was the same as set by Madam Bajaj. The Headmaster was staying in village Paldi, late in the evening he used to come to the school everyday and give coaching to us in English subject for about one hour. This system of intensive study arranged for our group of 10 boys was though much better than what it used to be at Madam Bajaj's house for me, yet the element of love and affection with which I was blessed by the Bajaj couple was missing and that had become only a sweet memory. By the middle of February 1947, we all students were fully prepared and highly excited waiting for the Final examination to start within a few days.

Still another Assault of the Scourge of Untouchability

Khalsa High School Mahilpur was the centre for final examinations for our school pupils also. We all the students of 8th class about 30 in number, with our bag and baggage were taken to Mahilpur with Giani Banta Singh Saini, as the teacher-in-charge. We were lodged in 30 ft by 10 ft room with a wide verandah, built on a barren piece of land about 500 meters away from the school building. This building, owned by Zaildar of Mahilpur, was completely out of use. About 100 mtrs away was a well. Rattan Lal, the school peon, accompanied our party to cook food for us. Gianiji would leave us at 10.00 pm, go for night's stay to his village Havelli, about 1500 mtrs away, and come in the morning by about 7.00 am. I being a monitor would wake up all my class fellows at 4.00 am and we would set to our studies until 6.30 am. On a Sunday morning at 6.00 am, Giani ji arrived. We used to go to the well with Ratan Lal, the school peon for taking bath. He would pull out water from the well in a bucket with the help of a sturdy long rope. On Sunday, Gianiji was also present at the well site. He commanded all the students to take bath one by one and my turn, as per Gianiji's command, came in the last. It was a cold mid-February morning. Ratan Lal pulled out a bucketful of water from the well and poured it on my head. By my quick movement of hands over my head, the water splashed all around as it happens usually. The splashing water must have fallen in tiny drops on the other boys also. Gianiji, with frightening anger shouted at me saying, "you low caste fool, you have polluted everybody". Hearing this all my upper and lower limbs froze wherever they were. All my class fellows also got stunned. For me, the entire surroundings appeared to have sunk in silence of the grave. Giani ji perhaps felt ashamed of his utterances. He did not speak for at least two minutes and then in a low-pitched voice commanded me to put on my clothes lest I would catch cold. We, all the boys, in a gloomy mood, I particularly highly depressed, came back to our lodging place. Ratan Lal was a Jhiwar by caste which too was reckoned to be a low caste but touchable. I had experienced during the last four years, the love and affection from the Bajaj couple. Bajajs were Sikh from a high caste. The current Headmaster, Giani Gurbux Singh also gave me kind and loving treatment. On the top was, *Ardas* recited by Giani Sohan Singh, the Moral Science teacher in the daily morning assembly of the school praying for special blessings to me. However, the "black" Sunday morning's dirty blare of Giani Banta Singh so much confused me that the agony and pain suffered by me mentally, ventilated only when I wept and cried loudly. Giani Banta Singh did try to console me using affectionate words but it did not have much healing effect. I refused to take meals and loudly declared that I will not sit in the examination next day and requested Giani Banta Singh to permit me to go home. I was once again finding myself at the cross roads, realizing that perhaps destiny would again push me back on the path to become a cattle grazer. In retrospection, I realized that it was my sense of over-sensitivity perhaps. In fact, realization started overtaking me that it would take a long time to become the person I wanted to be! Finding that all his efforts had failed to pacify me, Giani Banta Singh sent Ratan Lal to the school at Paldi to ask the Headmaster to come down to Mahilpur. Ratan Lal had narrated the entire episode to the Headmaster. On reaching our lodging place, he first came to me and hugged me very affectionately saying, "Dear son, teacher is like a Guru; good boys do not mind their tough talk". Then he started admonishing Giani Banta Singh in a raised voice telling him that his conduct was not worthy of a baptized Sikh and he should be ashamed of himself. I felt highly relieved and immediately agreed to sit in the examination, which was to start next morning. However, my excitement for a high position in the examination remained somewhat suppressed. All through the examination days, Giani Banta Singh made every effort to keep me in cheerful mood and finally the examination was over on a happy note.

Examination results were out in April 1947. My performance though turned out to be excellent yet I lagged behind the topper boy of Khalsa High School Mahilpur by a few marks. The boy of our school who was the second highest scorer was behind me by 65 marks. SGPC Punjab had given a promise to Giani Gurbux Singh, the Headmaster of our school to bear all expenses on my studies up to Graduation if I could score the highest marks in the district. The topper happened to be a student of Khalsa High School, Mahilpur. Mine was the second position. The Headmaster took up the matter with the SGPC, recommending me for the free ship of studies, at par with the topper student in view of my coming from a depressed class. The SGPC did agree to the Headmaster's proposal but on the condition that I should become a baptized Sikh. Being a student of a Khalsa School right from class III, I had developed already deep reverence for the *Gur Bani*. The Holy *Japuji Sahib* was committed to my memory and I had known the meaning of most of the hymns contained in *Japuji Sahib*. Therefore, I was prepared to become a baptized Sikh. However, my parents and maternal uncles thought that I was of too tender an age to observe all the daily rituals meant for a baptized Sikh. They were also of the view that my studies might also suffer. The SGPC's offer was, therefore declined. Giani Gurbux Singh, the Headmaster who had bestowed upon me almost father-like love was disappointed. However, when I met him at the school at village Paldi, to seek his blessings, he emotionally advised me to pay closer attention to my studies for getting excellent results in the Matriculation Examination, but should also continue reciting *Japuji Sahib* with equal commitment and should also try to recite *Sukhmani Sahib* and understand the meanings of the hymns.

For my Matriculation, I got admission in Khalsa High School, Mahilpur. I was a welcome entrant in the 9th class. Bawa Gurdit Singh Bedi, the Headmaster of the school, called me to his office and gave me a back handed compliment for excellent performance in the 8th Class. The teaching staff included Sardar Randhir Singh, an English teacher, Sardar Amar Singh Sodhi, the Math's teacher and Sardar Bakhtawar Singh Bains, a Science teacher, who were very experienced and known for their excellence. I was amongst the outstanding students. My performance in the Matriculation Final Examination remained excellent. In the Math papers, which included Arithmetic, Algebra and Geometry, my score was 188 marks out of the 200 marks. This happened to be the highest score, even better than the topper student's score. My parents, other relations and elders in the village were very happy and congratulated me profusely. Since, most of the village-folks were illiterate or semi literate, they were extra curious and appreciative about me, a "low caste" boy achieving that "wonder". "Success is the sum of small efforts repeated day in and day out", said R. Collier.

I got further inspired and motivated. I started dreaming myself to be an Engineer after doing my FSc and Graduation with A and B Course from SGGS, Khalsa College Mahilpur. It is unfulfilled dreams that keep you alive. Dreams are illustrations from the book your soul is writing about you. A British philosopher John Stuart Mills said, "The problem is not with the dreams, but with making that dream any obsession; not with ambition, but with making that dream the be-all and end-all of your existence."

Chapter – 3

College Days and Struggle for being Self-Sufficient

My Alma Mater, SGGS Khalsa College Mahilpur

Temple of learning is nevertheless important than the temple of worship. Shri Guru Gobind Singh Khalsa College Mahilpur, district Hoshiarpur (Punjab), a Post Graduate, Multi Faculty, and Co-educational College is now a premier institution of the rural area. It was established in 1946, by Sant Baba Hari Singh Ji, Kaharpuri, the Founder President of Sikh Educational Council with a missionary zeal of providing higher education to the boys and girls, in general, and particularly belonging to the rural, backward and Kandi areas, who were not able to go to other cities for higher education. It is the oldest educational institute of higher learning in rural and pre-partitioned India and one of the oldest amongst premier institutions of higher education in North of India.

It is a matter of great honour for this institution that its football team (Men) won the Punjab University, A-Division Football Championship for the last 20 years regularly and the newly inducted Fencing Team of men and women swept the Inter-college Championship 2009-10 and won 29 medals including four Gold Medals. In the field of NCC this college Cadet Rohit Kumar led the Punjab, Haryana, Himachal Pradesh and UT Chandigarh Directorate in the Republic Day parade, 2006 in New Delhi.

The college has a well-stocked library to serve as a backbone to all academic activities up to Post Graduate level classes with a volume of more than 35 thousand books and a well furnished/equipped Computer Lab. To begin with, the college had upto Graduate level classes but as per the need, from 1991 it started Post Graduate level Degree in the subjects of Punjabi. Further, it was the first, ever in the state of Punjab, to introduce Computer Science as an elective subject in BA /BSc level classes from 1993 when the Computer was just knocking at the door of education. After successful experience, the college management added Post Graduate degree in the subject of History. From Academic Session 2005-06, MSc Chemistry, MCom MA Economics were added to the faculties to which there has been an overwhelming response from the students coming not only from different parts of Punjab state but also from the neighboring states. Encouraged by this, the management added more Post Graduate faculties like MSc Physics, MA Political Science, BSc Medical, 4 years Degree Course in Physical Education and Bachelor of Education classes from the session 2006-07. MSc Instrumentation and MSc Industrial Chemistry have, also been introduced after getting affiliation from Punjab University Chandigarh. This college has thus become the only one in Punjab, offering such valuable professional degrees. These courses will further provide more avenues and opportunities to the students to ensure their placement in the society at the time when cutthroat competition is taking place at the global level. The college has made rapid strides in constructions, introducing the new professional and career oriented innovative courses and up gradation of infrastructure too.

When I joined this college in 1949, I got concession in college fee and monthly scholarship of Rs. 20/- under the Punjab Government Scheme for SC students. I also got another monthly stipend of Rs. 20/- in view of my meritorious performance in the Matriculation Examination and thereafter being student of Faculty of Science (FSc). These amounts were of great value during those days.

Social Activities

"True happiness comes from a sense of brotherhood and sisterhood. We need to cultivate a universal responsibility for one another and the planet we share" said the Holy Dalai Lama. During the second year of FSc session (1950-51), I had the privilege of closely studying the life story of Baba Sahib Dr BR Ambedkar. His various facets of life inspired me a lot. The urge and inspiration to study this fascinating and extremely enlightening literature emanated within me from the Articles, Editorials, and Poems published in Urdu Magazine *Ujala* by its Editor Shri K C Sulekh. The plethora of amazing knowledge gained by me about Dr. B R Ambedkar and his philosophy raised many a strange question in my mind about the real character of ancestors of the Hindu Priestly Class in whose profession and practice there happened to be a very wide chasm.

Babu Gurbux Singh, a renowned Communist Leader of Mahilpur was known for his high integrity and selfless service to the aggrieved persons against injustice and tyranny committed by the rulers. He had greatly influenced the psyche of the students of our college. His son Jasdeep Singh, my class fellow and close friend was very proficient in English language. Later he did his MA in English and migrated to UK, married an English woman and taught in a university there for many years. His elder brother Justice Ajit Singh Bains having retired as Punjab and Haryana High Court Judge has been an active Human Rights protagonist.

There used to be one active Students' Union – its members were larger in number and generally included those who had long break after Matriculation to join for college education. Socialistic Ideology smote them with pronounced leanings towards Marxism. Initially I too, was somewhat attracted towards them. There was another fringe union of the students with RSS background pursuing communal activities. The students of these two unions would often clash in small skirmishes. My mind however was, more focused on what Dr BR Ambedkar had been doing for the downtrodden people and his virulent campaign against the scourge of untouchability. Soon I organized a separate union of the students coming from schedule castes who were already brimming with a lot of enthusiasm. They elected me as President of this union. We were a group of ten to fifteen students. This group would cycle down to five to ten villages, on every Sunday to interact with young and elderly village scheduled caste people urging them to understand the value of education for their children, to abstain from consuming alcohol, smoking and child marriage, telling them also the fascinating success stories from the life of Dr BR Ambedkar. Our campaign proved very successful. The village folks everywhere would welcome us profusely with milk and "pakoras". Whenever there were any complaints of excess committed by the police on any depressed class person, our union would immediately jump into fray agitating for the just cause of the victims.

During 1952, Baba Sahib Dr B R Ambedkar had toured Punjab. His one well-attended public meeting was held at Jalandhar. Seth Kishan Das a rich scheduled caste leather merchant of Jalandhar was one of the pioneers for arranging Baba Sahib's public meetings. Sh. K C Sulekh, with his brigade of committed workers, was in the forefront for organizing the public meeting at Jalandhar. I as President of the scheduled caste students union of Khalsa College Mahilpur led a group of 20 fellow students to Jalandhar for assisting the management to act as "guards" in the public meeting ground. We had arranged special uniforms for our group; each one of us carried a long stick when deployed at various strategic points. I was deployed immediately behind the podium where Baba Sahib was seated. I felt highly elated to be so close to the giant intellectual, the saviour of the downtrodden masses. This was the first ever opportunity for me to be so close to Baba Sahib.

High Handedness of SHO Mahilpur

Sub Inspector, Raghbir Singh, SHO of Police Station Mahilpur, a tall hefty Sikh fellow from Amritsar district, once committed a very immoral act. He was mischievously informed by a tout, perhaps village chowkidar who used to visit Police Station once a week to report latest births and deaths for recording, as per the system then prevailing, that in his village a very beautiful girl had come as a bride of an Ad-dharmi (scheduled caste) boy who came from a poor family. The SHO summoned the couple to the police station through village numbardar, a notorious tout of the police, concocting a story of couple's involvement in abusing and threatening the Chowkidar. The SHO illegally detained them in the Police Station telling the boy in the evening to go home and that his wife would be sent home after some verification. The SHO left for some unknown place taking along with him the helpless newly wedded girl. The Scheduled Caste College Students Union led by me learnt about this horrible episode after four days of the incident and took up the matter seriously. The Union of Socialists/Marxist students lent us supporting hand. Together, we launched a virulent agitation against the SHO.

District Superintendent of Police Hoshiarpur assured us that he would take necessary action against the SHO and would ensure restoration of the girl to her husband. The SHO, an arrogant Jat Sikh, felt doubly insulted when challenged fearlessly by a low caste college students. Therefore, to avenge his foul feelings of injured ego, the SHO, started frightening me by sending threatening messages of dire consequences, through the village numbardar Charan Singh, who was his tout. This however, did not deter me from pursuing the matter through our Union. The SHO restored the girl to her husband after about a month's time. SP Hoshiarpur, in fact wanted to register a criminal case against the SHO but let him off with some disciplinary action, surely under pressure from a fellow SP rank Police Officer, the husband of the sister of SHO's wife. However, the SHO was immediately transferred from PS Mahilpur. Before leaving Mahilpur, he had made a dirty entry about me in the PS record that I was of extreme radical views and had pronounced leftist leanings. Rogues like the said Sub Inspector have been infesting the Police Department, resulting in serious trust deficit between the police and the public.

The new SHO of PS Mahilpur met our college Principal Sardar Harbhajan Singh Bains and asked him to strongly caution me and other prominent members of our Students Union to desist from "undesirable" activities. All my above-mentioned activities had in fact, distracted me from my studies. The Principal had with him record of my performances in the House Examination of FSc 2nd year wherein I had fared badly in Physics and Math's papers. He called me to his office and snubbed me severely, raising his voice angrily that I was treading the path leading to ruining of my career. He also warned me that if my professors of Physics and Math felt unsatisfied with my improved attention to studies, I would not be allowed to sit in my final Examination of FSc to be conducted by the Punjab University. That was enough to un-nerve me. I totally withdrew from the union activities and started devoting myself to studies. However, the self-inflicted damage to my studies had indeed, been already done by then. In the final FSc University Examination of 1951, I had flunked in one of the two Math's papers, delisting me thus from the list of meritorious students.

Graduation

After passing FSc in 1951, I wanted to do BSc, but this faculty was not then available in the college at Mahilpur. It was not possible for me, for economic reasons, to seek admission in any other college at Hoshiarpur. I therefore, opted for A and B course with the idea to go in for Engineering profession. Prof. of Maths did not agree because of my poor performance in Maths in FSc final examination. There was thus, no option left for me but to go for Humanities and I chose Political Science and History-English medium; English as an independent subject was compulsory. Thus, I did my Graduation in 1953.

Let me not skip over my special tribute to Prof Sadhu Saroop Singh who had done his Masters, both in Political Science and Economics. He taught us Political Science. He was a shinning star among the entire teaching faculty. Impeccably adoring a white neatly tied turban and dressed in a spotless white

'Kurta-Pyjama' and a matching Jacket, he presented a serene look of a philosopher. A repository and purveyor of knowledge, he would dedicatedly transmit to the students, from his rich stock of knowledge, the best he could give out. I had developed a special interest to learn the deeper meanings in the realm of Political Science, thanks to his unique style of teaching.

My village had neither any metalled link road nor domestic or agriculture power connection till then. Throughout my college days, I stayed in the college hostel only twice; once for only two months before the FSc final examination and second time again only for two months before the BA final examination. My elder brothers had started taking care of their own families and lived separately independent of my parents after I had joined the college in 1949. It was therefore necessary for me to help my father in his farming operations during holidays and vacations. During my school days, it was kerosene oil crude lighting tool *(diva)* as my lighting aide for studying during night hours. When I joined the college, the kerosene *diva* had graduated to a kerosene lamp, a little better lighting aide.

Post Graduation and Struggle for being Self-Sufficient

Shri Nanak Chand Rattu and his brother Bhagat Ram Rattu from our village were in Government jobs in Delhi during the forties, after doing their matriculation. They told me that after surviving the partition massacre, Punjabi settlers in West Punjab had come in droves to Delhi leaving behind their homes, immovable assets and business, built over generations. Their massive influx had changed the fabric of Delhi population giving it a Punjabi character from the earlier mix of Rajputs, Baniyas and Muslims who had come to Delhi earlier to serve successive rulers and had stayed back. The refugees were labouring hard in the process of restarting their lives from the scratch. Their success stories were highly inspiring. I was told that Government had set up a college called Camp College at Delhi, affiliated to Punjab University, for holding evening classes upto Post-Graduation. They offered me a welcome assistance of providing accommodation if I would like to shift to Delhi to join the said college for Post-Graduation and doing a Government job during daytime. This was, indeed, a very welcome opportunity for a person like me who being married, had also a daughter in December 1951. The secret of success in life is for a man to grab the opportunity when it comes. Earning while learning for Post-Graduation degree simultaneously was a dream appeared to be looking a reality. I jumped on the idea and shifted to Delhi and got a clerk's job in the Ministry of Commerce and Industries, on 7th November 1953. Further, I got admission in the Punjab University Camp College, Delhi for Post-Graduation degree in Political Science in 1954. On 8th July 1954, I got with the assistance of Delhi Employment Exchange, a Government job, as Upper Division Clerk in the Intelligence Bureau, Ministry of Home Affairs. My wife with our child, joined me at Delhi soon after. Rattu brothers had arranged one room accommodation for us at a nominal rent. My day's routine would commence at 5.00 am for two hours study up to 7.00 am, playing with my child for a while, bathing, taking breakfast and getting ready to leave for the office by 9.00 am by my bicycle, carrying with me a brief Tiffin for my lunch. Reaching office well before 10.00 am, after covering a distance of 10 kilometers on my bicycle, I would dutifully attend to my office work up to 5.00 pm. I would rush to the college to attend my classes starting from 5.30 pm. I would reach my residence by 9.30 pm, would play with my child and finish my dinner by 10 pm and then sit down for studies. By 11.00 pm generally I would retire to bed for quiet night hours' rest and sleep up to 5.00 am, stealing, often, in between, some very enjoyable time to share some moments with my wife. *Youth! Thy yearning for such highly pleasurable moments ever remains a high priority!* Our life was thus rolling on very smoothly and happily. I often used to fantasize what goals would be within my reach after completing my Post-Graduation.

Unceremonious Discharge from Service

Superintendent-in-charge of our branch was the only other Graduate in the branch. He was very happy with my performance in the Office and would often ask me to leave office by 4.30 pm to enable me to reach college comfortably to attend my class. The vicissitude in human life means very bumpy path; adversity and prosperity following the Nature's cycle like dark nights and bright days. Nobody would be an exception to this cycle of Nature. My wife and I were in for an acute shock. It was a pleasant morning of 3rd March, 1955 that I reached my office at 10.00 am and was just settling down to attend to my day's office work when two burly persons came to me announcing commandingly to hand over to them my Identity Card, disclosing that I stood discharged from the service with one month's pay in lieu of notice. Everybody in the office including the Branch Incharge was stunned hearing all this. As for mc the shock overtook me overwhelmingly and I suffered dark flashes to the point of almost my breaking down. The Branch Incharge called those persons to his seat and whisperingly asked them perhaps, the background of such a drastic action. They expressed their ignorance. The Branch Incharge then accompanied them outside and returned after fifteen minutes. He advised me to wind up and hand over all the important papers concerning my seat to him. He also whispered in my ear that in the police verification, my district police made an adverse report. Finally, I left the office room with a heavy heart. Outside the office room were standing the same two persons. They escorted me until we were outside the office building. There they were somewhat polite and told me not to loiter about near office building ever, as that might prove to be very harmful to me. This unfortunate episode had raised a sort of tempest in my mind with no way for navigating.

Completely bewildered, confused and under depression, I reached my residence around 5.30 pm. My wife started making searching queries, if I was all right health wise. I decided not to disclose anything to her and pretending to be somewhat indisposed, told her that I was feeling tired and had missed the classes in the college. I would get up in the morning at about 6.00 am, play with my child for some more time than usual and take my time to take bath and finish my breakfast by 9.30 am and then leave with my Tiffin, pretending to be going to the office. I would spend the day roaming about in the parks meeting friends employed in various other offices during their lunch breaks, to take their advice for my next course of action. Some would advise me to complete my Post-Graduation and then try for a teacher's job back in Punjab. Some would jeer at me saying that I used to boast about reaching the Everest. Some would simply avoid me. I was unable to devote my pointed attention to my studies. About a month passed, I was finding no way to come out of this predicament. My wife was getting worried rightly suspecting that I was in some serious trouble. Still I did not share with her the cause for my worries. One day, concocting a lie, I told her that our parents wanted that she should go to Punjab and stay with them for some time. I was also getting tighter financially after losing my job. Therefore, she along with the child, was sent to our village in the company of a family going to Punjab from Delhi.

"When joy takes leave, friends betray, fortune frowns and springs depart, when you are left to your dismay, alone to face with shattered heart, the tempest on the shore, you feel lost as never before. When things are no more the same, try once more and play the game. Wipe the tear and stop the cry, sky is the limit if you try". History sings of the glory of men and women who have fought with the adverse forces to excel. Despite two physical disabilities, the great Helen Keiler (1880-1968), blind and deaf American Author and an educationist wrote several books and accomplished great tasks only through strong determination. The message from the adversities is loud: Strong will-power can move mountains. So, work with full dedication, devotion, confidence, patience, strong determination and above all faith in God to reach the pinnacle of success. Moments also came when I tried to do all that was not humanly possible. In sheer helplessness, I gave up the entire search. The day search was stopped, the day I was not expecting something to happen, it started happening. A new energy arose in me from nowhere. We turn to God for help when our foundations are shaking only to learn that it is God, who is shaking them, Said C.West. Socrates said, "Remember that there is nothing stable in human affairs, therefore, avoid undue elation in prosperity and undue depression in adversity".

I had been advised by a friend to meet Shankar Das, who was working as PA to B N Dattar then the Deputy Home Minister in the Union Government. I met Shankar Dass at his residence and placed before him my predicament. He was very sympathetic. He advised me to get my name registered in the Delhi Employment Exchange afresh, without disclosing anything about my previous job and that in the meantime he would seriously think over as to how I could be helped to get out of the existing problem. He asked me to meet him again after one week. On my next meeting, Shankar Dass disclosed to me that he had learnt that the Police of my area in Punjab had reported that I had Leftist leaning during my college days at Mahilpur and was prone to indulge in disruptive activities. He advised me to somehow try to meet the Deputy Home Minister at his residence and the rest he would take care of. He also told me that for him arranging my interview with the Minister would not be the right thing. Next day I got my name registered at the Delhi Employment Exchange.

I got an offer of appointment as a clerk in the Ministry of Law. I joined that post on 5th May 1955. After getting no objection certificate from Ministry of Law, I again got my name registered in the Delhi Employment Exchange for a higher post. I did not get mental peace after joining the post of clerk, always apprehending that Police Verification Report on reference by the Ministry of Law might be the repeat of the earlier report. In the meanwhile I got a letter from my wife who was back in the village informing me that numberdar Charan Singh had sarcastically told our dadaji a day before "*Haan bhaai Sunderdas kya Hans Raj pension te aa riha aa*" (is Hans Raj retiring on pension?). She also had mentioned that our parents were highly worried. Expressing her deep anxiety, she asked me to inform her about my welfare. She felt perplexed with dirty remarks by Charan Singh. In my reply letter to her I had so written as to give the impression as if I had not received her letter and falsely mentioned details how, as usual, I remained very busy with my routine programme of attending the office and evening classes in the college, studying during early morning and late night hours. I also mentioned with moist eyes under the stress of emotions how I was sadly missing her and our lovely child. I had to tell her all these lies so that she and our parents did not get over-worried.

Gate Crashing into the residence of Deputy Home Minister

Days passed by but I could not manage to meet the Minister. Then I just thought of a dare devilry method and planned gatecrashing into the residence of the Minister. I used to recall in silence the sweet and inspiring high valued sayings of great men blessed with high valued wisdom. Swami Vivekanand had said, "If you have faith in the three hundred and thirty millions of your mythological gods and in all the gods which others have introduced into your mind and still you have no faith in yourselves, there is no salvation for you. Have faith in yourselves and stand upon that faith and be strong." Sun Tzu said, "Know yourself and you will win all battles." To execute my plan I tried to befriend the security personnel posted at the main gate of the Minister's residence. I would go there very often carrying a book in my hand posing as a student of MA classes. The constables were impressed with my simple looks coming from a remote village in Punjab for studying Post Graduation. Once around 10.30 am, I reached the Minister's bunglow and started conversing with the constable on duty at the gate. I requested him to arrange my meeting with the Minister as I wanted to seek his help in getting some day time job. He said that was not possible for him. During this conversation, I found that he was quite relaxed and his attention diverted towards a vehicle passing on the road and I rushed on the driveway towards kothi's front varandah. The left side of the varandah ended with a room wherein Shankar Das and the rest of the PA staff of the Minister had their office. The constable at the gate whose trust I had betrayed raised an alarm *pakrho pakrho pakrho* (haul him up quickly). Soon I was caught hold by another unarmed constable. He started thrashing me and I started crying very loudly saying repeatedly "I wanted to meet the Minister Sahib". My cries attracted the attention of the Hon'able Minister who was sitting in the drawing room of which the outdoor opened into the varandah. In the meanwhile, the PA staff of the Minister including Shankar Das had come out of their office room inquiring loudly "what is happening? Who is he?" I was crying loudly repeating that I wanted to meet the Minister Sahib. The Minister came out into the varandah and said "Don't beat him, bring him here." My thrashing was stopped and I was released from the tight grip of the constable and taken upto the varandah where Minister was standing. I was awfully sobbing. I touched the feet of the Minister with all humility. He sat down on a cane chair and bid me to calm down and sit down. I squatted on the floor. The Minister told me to get up and sit on the chair.

There were about a dozen cane chairs in the varandah. I sat down on a chair, which was a little away from the Minister's chair. He bid me to pull up my chair nearer to him. He called for drinking water and told me to take water and relax. Then he asked me why I dared violate the security rules by gate crashing. I narrated my whole story to him, from early childhood, schooling and college days, my marital status; my being a father of a child and my being still a student of first year of the two years MA degree course and about my summary discharge from the office of Intelligence Bureau. He summoned Shankar Das and asked him to obtain an application from me. He also warned me not to violate the law ever again, but to pursue my study devotedly and meet him after one month with prior permission through his staff. With deep gratitude to this godly figure, very humane, I paid my heart felt respect to the Minister by touching his feet. The immense patience, cool headedness and the concern writ large on his entirely relaxed face amply manifested his highly admirable qualities of a kindhearted man leaving a very deep imprint on my mind for emulation in my future life. "Nearly all men can stand adversity. But if you want to test a man's character, give him power." "Reputation is what world thinks a man is, character is what he really is." I went with Shankar Das to his office room and wrote the application as guided by him. Shankar Das was somewhat curt; unhappily telling me that it could have been highly embarrassing for him if I had just made even an oblique reference of him while talking to the Minister that I knew Shankar Das earlier. Saying sorry to him and expressing my gratitude to him, I felt both relieved and excited as well. As I was getting out of the main gate, I apologized to the guards for causing embarrassment to them.

Appointment as Assistant in ICAR, Ministry of Agriculture

A few days after getting my name registered with the Delhi Employment Exchange for higher post, I got a letter from the Delhi Employment Exchange asking me to report to the Administrative Officer, Indian Council of Agriculture Research (ICAR) with all my certificates for interview for the post of Assistant/ UDC. There were 135 candidates including 7 coming from scheduled castes. There was a written test. The question paper for one-hour duration carried 50 marks for 25 questions. While collecting the answer books from the candidates, it was announced that the result would be displayed on the notice board at the Reception by 3.30 pm. List of 15 candidates securing twenty five marks and above was displayed at the notice board at 3.30 pm, asking these candidates to report to the Administrative Officer with their certificates immediately. I found my name at serial number three with 32 marks. The toppers were N K Aggarwal and G S Gulabani, both with 33 marks each. After checking our certificates, it was announced that, the selected candidates would get their appointment letters within a week. We all were free by 5.00 pm.

I went straight to the residence of Shankar Das to tell him about this good development. He happily told me that being 2nd in the merit list I would surely get the post of an Assistant, the highest non-gazetted post in the Secretariat and that for a Clerk it would take at least 15 to 20 years to reach that stage. He also happily disclosed that the Minister was deeply touched by listening to my story and after looking into the police report regarding verification of my antecedents, he had sent a letter to Punjab Chief Minister for "Fresh Verification", on urgent basis, through a senior honest police officer and that reply was expected anytime. By the time I reached my residence, my excitement had somewhat receded and I had gone into pensive mood with fear lurking in my mind that even fresh inquiry into my antecedents might confirm the earlier Report. I thought of seeking help from Principal Harbhajan Singh Bains of SGGS Khalsa College Mahilpur where from I had graduated. The Principal was also an MLA from Mahilpur Constituency elected during the first General Election held in 1952. Instead of writing to him, I wrote a detailed letter to Prof. Sujjan Singh who used to be the incharge of our Tutorial Group. He showed my letter to the Principal and he, in turn, spoke to Superintendent of Police Hoshiarpur. Prof. Sujjan Singh was very kind to inform me through a letter about this development.

In the meanwhile, I had received an appointment letter for the post of Assistant in the ICAR. Almost at the same time a message from Shankar Das had come to me through a special messenger, that Minister wanted me to meet him at his residence next day at 11.00 am. With all these happy developments coming up one after the other, my elation knew no bounds. At the Minister's house, breaking the news of the receipt of a Clean Report about my antecedents from Punjab Government, the Minister told me to report to AD (Adm) IB for rejoining duty as he had already spoken to Director IB in this regard. My eyes became moist with tears of happiness and with deep sense of gratitude, I again paid my heartfelt respect to him and I then showed to him my appointment letter as Assistant in the ICAR. He patted me on the back and said twice "Very good". He then called Shankar Das and inquired from him what course I should adopt. Shankar Das told that I should first rejoin my previous post and thereafter request the department to relieve me for joining the new assignment. The Minister smilingly told me to go and do accordingly. When I was paying my gratitude and respect to the Minister while leaving his room, he again exhorted me not to try ever to violate the law. I went to the room of Shankar Das where he disclosed to me that the Chief Minister of Punjab, while sending police verification report to the Minister had mentioned in his letter that he had given orders to take action against the policemen responsible for sending a wrong report earlier. While getting out of Minister's bungalow, I apologized to the policemen for my improper conduct earlier in gatecrashing into the Bungalow. I did not go to the office of Intelligence Bureau; instead, next day, I submitted my application to my earlier employer, Branch Superintendent in the Ministry of Law for relieving me for joining as an Assistant in the ICAR. I was relieved by evening the same day. Next day I reported at the ICAR and joined duty as an Assistant on 10th August, 1955. I had now a feeling of a victorious General in the battle-field. Reaching my residence, I wrote a long letter to my wife with all the details including the trauma I had to suffer but with very happy ending. Normal pleasant life routine started rolling on as usual. Many people even those whom I had not even known would congratulate me for getting an Assistant's post directly. In the meanwhile, my studies for Post-Graduation had been badly disrupted and I was very short of my attendance in the college. Prof. of Political Science was very unhappy with me.

Central Secretariat Service Grade IV

In July 1955, UPSC had held a competitive examination to make direct recruitment of SCs/STs to fill up 100 permanent posts of Assistant – Central Secretariat Service Grade-IV in the Government of India Offices. I appeared in the said Examination. The pattern of the said Examination comprised two papers, one each of two subjects of Graduation standard. I opted for Political Science and History subjects; other compulsory papers were of Arithmetic of Matriculation standard, English Essay, General Knowledge and General English, all of Graduation Standard. About 750 candidates had finally appeared in the Examination. In all 105 candidates were declared successful. With God's grace, I stood 8th in the merit list. My seniors and colleagues in the ICAR and many friends celebrated the occasion with great fervour. I joined on 1st February 1956 Central Secretariat Service Grade-IV as a Probationary Assistant in the Ministry of Transport, Department of Tourism, in the North Block of Civil Secretariat.

Dreaming for All India/Central Civil Services

I had the highest non-gazetted post as a permanent Assistant. That could have taken me up to Director's post in the Civil Secretariat, in normal course by the time of retirement. In the words of Disraeli, "There is no education like adversity". I had experienced a lot of adversity. My inner conscience was sparklingly ignited by the beautiful words of a godly man that "Embers of honest ambitions when fanned by a stormy determination can transform the crudest of dreams into beautiful reality". This all had ignited in me, a new spark of energy and unshakable self-confidence. I started dreaming for All India Services/Central Civil Services Competitive Examination conducted every year by the UPSC. Swami Vivekanand had said, "Take up one idea. Make that one idea your life - think of it, dream of it, and live on that idea. Let the brain, muscles, nerves, and every part of your body be full of that idea, and just leave every other idea alone. This is the way to success". A time comes in your life, when you finally get it, but in the midst of all your fears and insanity, you stop dead in your tracks. Somewhere the voice inside your head cries out enough, enough fighting, crying, blaming, and struggling to hold on then, like a child, quieting down after a tantrum, you blink back your tears and begin to look at the world through new eyes. This is your awakening. Energized with all this inspiration around, I firmly decided to turn my dream into a reality. Forgetting everything else, I challenized all energies in one direction–achieving success in All India Services/Central Civil Services Examinations to be held in October-November 1956. My wife, who had earlier gone to the village, after I had lost my job in the Intelligence Bureau, got another daughter in September 1955. I got Assistant's job in the ICAR and afterwards permanent Assistant's job in the Civil Secretariat of the Union government, much before the arrival of the second child. Having no financial worries, my wife with two children joined me at Delhi in December 1955.

Meeting the Greatest Icon of Social Justice, Dr. B R Ambedkar

As described earlier, I had seen Baba Sahib for the first time, from a very close angle when I was standing as a security guard behind the podium where he was seated during public meeting held at Jalandhar in 1952. It is, well said "The most powerful weapon on earth is human soul on fire, fire to transform the society and bring renaissance in the social sphere." Since I had decided to compete for the Civil Services Examination, with this object in my mind I thought of, meeting Dr B R Amedkar for taking his blessings. Nanak Chand Rattu used to attend to the secretarial work of Baba Sahib, at his residence 26, Alipur Road, Delhi, after office hours and on Sundays too. As arranged by him I got an opportunity to have an audience with Baba Sahib on a Sunday afternoon in March 1956. I greeted him with deep respect. An overbearing impressive personality, in his usual roaring voice, he bid me to sit down in the chair lying opposite his big office table. His table and the wall behind his elegant chair were laden with books. "What are you doing and what has brought you here?" He said. I was little perplexed, from where and how to start. Composing my nerves I started narrating briefly what had happened to me during college days and my struggle for being self sufficient while studying for Post-Graduation. I ended saying that I was preparing for Civil Services Examination and had come to seek his blessings. He had listened to me very attentively and had suddenly raised his eyebrows on hearing that I was preparing for Civil Services Examination. He said, "Why not, why not; Community needs fighters like you, but this competition is very tough and you would have to put in very hard work. Good luck, come on, I would show you my library". He got up from his chair with some difficulty and took support of a walking stick lying by the side of his chair. I was wondering whether there could be any Library over and above the fully laden walls of his office- room and his table. He led me to other three big rooms and his bathrooms. Everywhere there was amazing number of variety of books like the riots of different coloured flowers in the blooming winter spring day. Full 35 minutes had gone as if so quickly while going around his sprawling library and listening to his explaining various subjects covered by various renowned authors. At the end, he said, "Okay young man, Good luck to you" and with deep reverence, I paid him my heartfelt respect before departing from him with moist eyes, the tears of joy and gratefulness to him, for granting me the warmth of his august company for forty minutes. He appeared to me much bigger a person than portrayed by Dhananjay Keer in his book "Dr Ambedkar-Life and Mission", a biography written and published by him in May 1954.

All India Services/Central Civil Services Examination 1956

With all the inspiration I got, including my sweet and happy audience with Baba Sahib Dr. B R Ambedkar, I started preparing for the Civil Services Examination very earnestly. "Time is equal to life, therefore, waste your time and waste your life, or master your time and master your life" –Alan Lakein. I had to attend office from 10.00 am to 5.00 pm, MA classes from 5.30 pm until 9.00 pm; there was no time for getting any coaching for the Civil Services Examination. I, being still on probation in my Assistant's job, it was impossible for me to ask for any leave. Apart from Sundays, there was no extra time available for preparing for the competition except some time stolen from early morning hours and late night hours. Gazetted holidays provided the most welcome break. "Know the true value of time, snatch, seize, and enjoy every moment of it. No idleness, no laziness, no procrastination: never put off till tomorrow what you can do today"- said Chesterfield. As the Examination dates were approaching, I decided to skip my MA classes along with the Final MA Examination, which was held in May 1956. I put my heart and soul in preparing for the competition even at the cost of occasional snubs from my immediate boss in the Tourism Department for ignoring the office work in my "madness for pursuing the studies for Civil Services Competition". UPSC Examination Papers, eight in number, spanned over the months of October and November. After the examination was over, tension vanished. In fact it was total relaxation. There was a wait for about four months for the declaration of the result. Except for leisurely preparing for MA final Examination, which was held in May 1957, there was no pressure of attending classes in the College. The wise words of Avesta Videvdad 4.1 "If one does not perform duty to one whom the duty is due, one becomes a thief of duty," inspired me to do my best to come up to the expectations of my bosses- Branch Superintendent, Under Secretary and Deputy Secretary. Mr. Kadapa the Under Secretary from the South, when in happy mood, would often give me a few toffees, which he was very fond of chewing in the office and would inquisitively ask me often, what sort of competition papers were set by the UPSC and how I had fared. I would happily boast of my sure success. Soon I became a favourite with all my three bosses. During the UPSC Examination days, we had been blessed on 25 November 1956 with our third child; it was a male, our elder son Raj Kamal. His birth after two daughters particularly during Examination days, was considered by my parents and all kith and kin, as an auspicious omen for heralding, happy and prosperous future, for our family.

Civil Services Examination result was out in April 1957. By the kindness and grace of the Almighty, I had come out with flying colours on my own merit and became eligible both for Civil Services Group A and Indian Police Service. The inspiring words of Swami Vivekanand were ringing in my ears "We are responsible for what we are, and whatever we wish ourselves to be, we have the power to make ourselves. You cannot believe in God until you believe in yourselves." I was to join the IPS on 26th October 1957 at Central Police Training College, Mount Abu, for a year's Basic Training. A new phase in my life was thus in the offing with the profound kindness of the Supreme Benevolent and Almighty Lord of this Universe. The prayers, the blessings, the moral and financial support of my respected parents enabled me to cross all hurdles. The love, cooperation and amiability of my wife ever remained a pillar of strength for me during the enormous vicissitudes in my life and this cemented further our nuptial bond after my joining the IPS. For my co-villagers my becoming the first Graduate in the village was a big achievement. However, my getting into the IPS was a unique success story for the rural folks all around my native area. People continued flocking for many days to our place in the village to congratulate my parents; celebrations were in abundance. I was all the time wondering what I could give back to these simple folks for their boisterous celebrations and show of happiness over my success story!

Keeping Good Company Pays

The intellectuals are based with association of slanderers but remain stable in the association of equals and one becomes superior with the association of those who are superior to him. One reaps the kind of fruits according to the kind of company one keeps. Therefore, one should always be careful in selecting the company one has to keep. This used to be often repeated advice of my revered mother right from my childhood even up to the time I became a senior officer in the IPS. To illustrate and drill her point deep into my psyche, she used to narrate various interesting stories and anecdotes. One of her pet story often narrated to me was about the friendship between a crow and a swan. One day the crow took the swan to its nest and made him to sit on a dry and wilted tree. The place was stinking of rotten flesh and bones that were scattered all around. The swan said, "Dear friend! I cannot stay in such a dirt-filled place even for a moment. If you have any clean place please take me there." The crow then took him to the secret grove of the king and made him sit on the tree of which new tender and tiny leaves had started sprouting with the onset of spring season. The crow too sat by the side of his friend, the swan. As the swan looked down, he saw the king sitting under the tree with his bald head exposed to the sun. A swan is a kind bird by nature and out of compassion, it spread out its wings to provide shade to the king who started feeling some relief from the sun. A crow is however, uncaring by nature; it dropped its excreta on the king's head. The king's security man shot an arrow upwards, which brought the swan down while the crow flew off quickly. The dying swan said, "Oh king I am not the crow that dropped the excreta. I am the swan that lives in pure water but due to the company of the mean crow, my life has been ruined." May Providence keep us away from the company of the wicked! Throughout my life, I have remembered the sage advice of my mother and have remained very choosy and selective to cultivate close friendship with the people around. For this reason, I have often been misunderstood as not very sociable person.

We were a group of a dozen close-knit friends aspiring to go high in our career. With me were Bhagat Ram Mehmi, Bhagat Ram Assi, Om Prakash Bali, Darshan Ram Nafari, BR Azad, Pyare Lal, Mela Ram, Mangat Ram, Joginder Singh, Amar Singh Chalia, Hari Ram and Kidar Nath. I was the only lucky one to succeed in the Civil Services Examination held by the UPSC in 1956. Bhagat Ram Mehmi ended as Under Secretary to Gvernment of India,

Ministry of Finance. Bhagat Ram Assi had once qualified much later in written papers for the Civil Services but ultimately could not come up in the merit list. Om Prakash Bali, in due course of time, migrated together with his family, to USA and is a rich NRI doing commendable social service. Darshan Ram Nafari succeeded in getting into UT Civil Service through UPSC's Civil Services Examination. BR Azad had qualified along with me in the written papers but did not come up in the merit list after personality test. He ended up with a senior position in Punjab PCS cadre. Pyare Lal had also joined Punjab PCS cadre but ended with premature retirement while holding the post of a Judicial Magistrate. Mela Ram and Mangat Ram had later succeeded in the Civil Services Examination and joined IRS and Indian Railway Service respectively. Joginder Singh made it to the IAS in 1958 through the Special Recruitment conducted by the UPSC in 1957. Amar Singh Chalia and Hari Ram both joined PCS (Judicial) and retired as District and Sessions Judges. Kidar Nath was a staunch Gandhian by habit. He joined Punjab State Welfare Department and followed a puritan philosophy throughout.

Chapter – 4

Marital Bond and Family

Engagement and Marriage

Marriages are settled in heaven and celebrated on earth, is a common saying. It was early September, 1939 when I was a student of 4th class that Maulvi Umarbux, our class teacher asked me to retie my turban, whispering to me that some persons had come with a proposal for my engagement. He took me along to the verandah outside the classroom. Two persons, already present there, accosted me. One of them was very tall about 6 feet 2 inches of hefty built looking to be in his thirties. He asked me my name, age and details about my parents and my fellow siblings in the family. His tone was affectionate. I was excited and blushingly answered all his queries. He then gave me a back handed compliment saying "Good Boy". I remained with those two persons for about 10 minutes. After saying "thank you Maulvi Sahib", they left. Later, when I narrated this incident to my mother, she told me that they had come to our residence also and were enquiring whether any milch Buffalo was available for sale. Giani Atma Ram, husband of my father's sister, came to our place and disclosed that the overwhelmingly smart looking person was Harnam by name, the youngest brother of the girl's father, proposed for engagement with me. After school hours, many of my class fellows used to tease me that I was to be engaged with a baby girl.

Towards the end of September 1939, about 10 persons, including Harnam, came to our place as prearranged and performed my engagement ceremony. Giani Atma Ram, being the middleman, was proudly telling my mother and other assembled women folk "the girl named Nasib Kaur is an Angrezi doll". She was then about 6 years of age.

During mid 1947, sporadic communal riots had started. I was then about 17 years old and had passed the Anglo Vernacular 8th class creditably and had sought admission in the 9th class in Khalsa High School, Mahilpur. My fiancée's village named Burj was in Jallandhar district. It had predominantly Muslim population with only about two dozen non-Muslim families, including 2 or 3 families each of Sikhs and Brahmins; the rest were the depressed class families. The Sikh/Hindu youths belonging to the adjoining villages had started attacking village Burj frequently, at odd hours to molest and loot the Muslim families. There used to be a lot of panic in the village and the Muslims, collectively, used to give the attackers a determined fight. Nobody seemed to be safe. My fiancée was then about 13 years. Our parents through Giani Atma Ram decided that our marriage should be solemnized immediately so that the girl could shift to our village, a much safer place. On 12th July 1947, our marriage was solemnized. When the marriage party of only a few persons was returning to our village with the bride, the communally frenzied people had set many Muslim villages ablaze because of the mutual bitterness.

The follow-up formal marriage rituals were performed by my parents at our village. Though, my fiancée and I had become husband and wife after all formal marriage ceremonies had been performed, yet consummation of the wedlock was not allowed perhaps because of prior mutual understanding between my mother, mother-in-law and Bhuaji, in view of our tender age. We both used to play various games with my sisters, bhabhis and their kids.

Soon after the marriage, my in-law's village had become a target for the hooligans. The whole lot of people from the non-Muslim families evacuated the village and took refuge in the neighboring Sikh/Hindu dominated villages leaving behind Harnam, the uncle of my wife and two sturdy built young Sikh boys, for a sort of keeping a watch on the locked houses, with two elderly women to cook their meals. Many Muslims were killed particularly the younger ones. Their valuables were looted, young girls were molested and some were kidnapped by the communally frenzied Sikh/Hindu raiders.

The hooligans would invariably take Harnam with them to lead them to prominent Muslim houses. Harnam often narrated, with emotionally charged feelings, various embarrassing and painful scene witnessed by him. The most cruel and gory scenes of helpless and hapless persons, from infants to old, among whom he had grown and maintained friendly relations for years, being mercilessly slaughtered, splattering blood all around and young girls/women being raped, crying for help shouting, "save us Oh Harnam uncle (*Harnamea chacha, bacha la sannu*)." He was able to save many of the Muslim young girls from sexual assault and kidnapping by pretending that there was no girl in the house targeted by the hooligans. At long last, the law and order agencies effectively intervened and escorted the badly mauled Muslims to a camp established by the authorities that be, for those eager to migrate to Pakistan, then a newly carved Sovereign State, out of British India. As soon as peace was restored in village Burj, all non-Muslim families who had evacuated their homes and hearths in the village, returned and resumed their routine domestic affairs. My wife was taken back to their village by my father-in-law.

Our village Sakruli had predominantly non- Muslim population. All the Muslim families were given due protection and were escorted out safely to the camp set up for such people, uprooted in the wake of creation of Pakistan. Our schools had continued functioning normally. My marriage had not affected my psyche in any way, so far as my schooling was concerned. I had continued my studies with full devotion and passed Matriculation Examination in 1949 with Distinction. With all the excitement around, I had joined the College at Mahilpur, for my FSc Course.

Family

Nasib Kaur my wife

She has been a very dutiful and lovable daughter-in-law, highly affectionate and caring mother to nurse the family and on the top my devoted, sincere life companion, standing by my side, as a great pillar of my strength through thick and thin of life. It is mutual love, faith, trust, and understanding and caring, that the wonderful boat of our married life has blissfully sailed through sweet and sour days, which we have spent, with blissfully during, the last 63 years in sweet togetherness.

Since our marriage had taken place in July 1947, my in-laws started persuading my parents in 1949 that their daughter should start living with her in-laws. I had already joined the college for my FSc Course after passing the Matriculation. My wife joined me at our village on 12th July 1949. My mother would often give me and my wife valuable advice that we were both then grown up and we should both understand our respective responsibilities as husband and wife particularly, I still being a student. Since we were both entirely dependent financially, nay for all intends and purpuses on our parents, we both conducted ourselves with utmost responsibility. I remained fully devoted to my studies and extended helping hand, to the extent possible, to my father in his farming profession, my wife very dutifully shared responsibility with my mother in taking care of the household affairs. I used to feel very happy and relaxed that my mother and wife had developed mutual understanding of love and affection with each other. My mother treated her daughters in-law like her own daughters who had already gone to their in-laws after their marriage. I passed my FSc Examination in April 1951 and took up Arts for my Graduation. On 3rd December 1951, we were blessed with a daughter Vanita. After Graduation in 1953, I shifted to Delhi for Post-Graduation in Political Science. I joined Punjab University Camp College, evening session and got a day time government job with a view to become self-supporting. On 3rd September 1955, we were blessed with another daughter Nisha and on 25th November 1956, we were blessed with a son Raj Kamal. Having been selected in the IPS, I had joined Police Training College, Mount Abu on 26th October 1957, for basic training. I was then 27 years old and father of three children. After one-year basic training at Mount Abu, I joined Punjab State IPS Cadre. I had a little more than 4 years service in the IPS when on 18th May 1962 we were blessed with another son Rupinder Kumar at Ferozepur.

Daughter Vanita

She was born when I had just passed my FSc and was pursuing First Year of my Degree Course. She had seen both of us struggling for progressing in life, fighting against all odds and ultimately achieving the success in being selected in the coveted Indian Police Service. As an adolescent girl, she was brimful with self-confidence and wisdom of a mature woman. She would not feel shy of telling her mother and me the do's and don'ts of life as if she were our grand mother. The Almighty Creator had blessed her with a razor-sharp intellect and a beautiful physique. Vanita was married to Gurdial Singh IPS-1969 (RR), Punjab State IPS Cadre on 7th May 1972. Gurdial Singh retired as Additional Director General of Police, Punjab State in February 2002. The family is settled in Panchkula in their own house. They had two sons– Vikram Singh born on 12th of December 1974 and Gaurav Singh born on 8th December 1976; they both got their Post Graduation and qualified in the written test for the posts of Assistant Commandants, Gazatted Class-I Post, in the Para-Military Forces. Vikram Singh did not attend the interview call but Gaurav Singh took it to a logical conclusion. On selection, he joined Border Security Force on 30th September 2000. Gaurav Singh excelled in his batch during his basic training and during his subsequent training as a Commando. He is married to Simaranjit Kaur daughter of Darshan Singh Shivalik and Paramjit Kaur of Ludhiana in Punjab. They both are in active politics. Gaurav Singh is posted as Deputy Commandant in Khemkaran Sector (Amritsar District) of Indo-Pak Border.

Vikram Singh was a very handsome, brilliant, studious and hard working boy. A keen lover of books, authored by renowned intellectuals and magazines of varied types, he had an admirable collection of about 100 books in his personal library. Turn over any page of any book, one would find his imprints in the margins showing how attentively and with deep interest he had read every book. Vikram Singh had persisted to pursue his set goal of competing for All India Services/Central Services Examination, being conducted by the UPSC every year. Unfortunately, he narrowly missed the merit list in a few attempts. He refused to confuse his repeated failures with the final defeat and vowed to make a determined last bid. His study-cum–bedroom was on the first floor of their house-a beautiful Bungalow equipped with all conceivable comforts. He had the habit of continuing his study until mid-night. On a fateful night, he woke-up in the small hours of the morning. While almost half-a-sleep, he wanted to go to the bathroom for urination but unfortunately, the destiny diverted him towards the stairs. As if pushed by some evil spirit, he fell tumbling down the stairs and suffered a spinal injury. It was the saddest day of 17th June 2005 that the competency of the PGI Chandigarh became questionable. During a week's treatment as an indoor patient in the PGI, none in that Premier Institution ever confided in any elder in our families that Vikram could go into eternal sleep quietly. Inevitable happened. The Rosy Bud, which was yet to blossom into a beautiful flower, enriched with sweet fragrance just withered away, leaving all of us in a total gloom, deep despair and utter helplessness.

Daughter Nisha

She has been somewhat reserved and self-centered, introvert by nature. She was married on 12th May, 1979 to SR Lakha. When their engagement was solemnized a year earlier, Lakha was in Central Civil Secretariat Service, Gazetted Class II Officer, recruited through the UPSC's Civil Services Examinations. He was tipped to avail another attempt and had appeared in the All India Services/Central Civil Services Examination held in October-November 1978. It was a happy co-incidence that on 12th May, 1979, the day of their marriage, UPSC declared the results of the All India Services/Central Civil Services Examination held in 1978. Lakha had made it to the IAS. He was allocated to the UP State IAS cadre. They have three charming children – two sons and a daughter. Their elder son after graduating from St. Stephen's College, Delhi, has also done his Post Graduation from Delhi University. Their daughter, after her Graduation from Lady Shriram College, Delhi, is preparing together with his elder brother for competing for All India Services/Civil Services Examination. Lakha, after his retirement from the IAS as Financial Commissioner was appointed as Chairman of the UP State Public Service Commission. Presently, he is Vice Chancellor of Buddhist University, Noida (UP). Their younger son after his graduation from St. Stephen's College, Delhi is pursuing three years Law Degree Course. The family has settled in Gomti Nagar, Lukhnow in their own beautiful house. Lakha's eldest brother has since died but his family is settled in UK Younger to him is Harbhajan Lakha, who has been a member of Lok Sabha twice, from Phillaur Parliamentary Constituency in Punjab State. He is still active in politics. His family however is settled in UK.

Elder Son Raj Kamal

Third in line, among our children Raj Kamal was born on 25th November 1956, when I was in the midst of my All India Services/Central Civil Services Examinations. He was diagnosed as suffering from inflammation of appendicitis when he was 8 years old. He had to undergo appendicectomy when he was about 10 years old. Soon after appendicectomy his growth was very quick and he blossomed into a very handsome youth with robust physique and sweet disposition with cultured mannerism. He graduated from Delhi University and got admission in the Law College, Punjab University, Chandigarh, in 1978. He was a regular doner of blood in the blood bank of PGI Chandigarh for many years. He also loved playing Guitar and had been blessed with enchanting voice to sing melodiously in college functions.

From October 1973 to November 1978, our family was in Delhi because of my Deputation to Central Industrial Security Force, an upcoming Central Police Organization. During his college days in Delhi, Raj Kamal strayed into developing friendship with Ritu daughter of Er O P Verma. She was a 2nd year BA student of Jesus and Mary College in South Delhi. Er O P Verma an Aeronautical Engineer was also the first Engineer of his time holding many licenses on different Aircrafts. He was then working as Chief Engineer, Delhi Flying Club. The friendship between Raj Kamal and Ritu blossomed into an intense love affair with no clue to either family. In the meanwhile, I returned to my parent cadre Haryana in November 1978 and posted as DIG, Hisar Range. Soon we discovered about the love affair between Raj Kamal and Ritu. The fact that they were 250 km apart, that being the distance between Delhi and Chandigarh, was adversely affecting their studies. The Verma family started insisting that Ritu and Raj Kamal should go into marital bond without any delay. Ritu was then just 20 years of age and had passed her Graduation from Delhi University. Raj Kamal about 23 years of age was in his second year of three years Law Degree Course. We all elders in our family had initially viewed this proposal little skeptically, apprehending that Raj Kamal might not complete his Law Degree Course in time. Buckling under Vermas' pressure, I agreed that a formal engagement ceremony should be performed and the actual marriage could come up after a year or so. Accordingly, engagement ceremony was performed towards the end of 1979. This had been done to reassure Ritu and Raj Kamal that their respective families had gracefully accepted their affair as worthy of being converted into a marriage bond so that they could take their studies seriously. However, in due course of time we had to agree with the Verma family to advance their marriage to 16th May 1980.

In the general election to the Lok Sabha, following the collapse of the Janta Party Government headed by Ch. Charan Singh as Prime Minister, who had never faced the Parliament during his tenure of about six month, Congress Party had come to power with Smt. Indira Gandhi once again as the Prime Minister in early 1980. In the new political scenario, Sanjay Gandhi and Swami Dhirendra Brahmchari had become the parallel center of power. Sanjay Gandhi was very fond of flying 'Cessna Aircraft' and used to come to the Delhi Flying Club daily when in station. Er OP Verma the Chief Engineer of the Delhi Flying Club was the incharge to give clearance about the air-worthiness of flight for the Cessna Aircraft of Sanjay Gandhi. Er OP Verma thus had very informal relations with both Sanjay Gandhi and Swami Dhirendra Brahmchari. They both were present as guests of Er. OP Verma when *barat* had reached Delhi Flying Club on the occasion of Raj Kamal-Ritu marriage.

I had a chance meeting with Sanjay Gandhi on 21st June 1980, I happened to be in the Delhi Flying Club with Vermas just for a social call. Er OP Verma got an urgent telephonic message from the hanger that Sanjay Gandhi would soon be arriving at the hanger. He immediately rushed to the hanger. Before he could reach there, Sanjay Gandhi had already arrived. Er OP Verma apologetically explained to him that he was held up in the house because his *Sanwandi* i.e. I had come there unscheduled. Sanjay Gandhi smilingly told him "why don't you call him here". Er OP Verma told him "I would do it now Sir". The message came from the hanger. This raised my rate of palpitation because Sanjay Gandhi was known to be a tough, well meaning, up coming political figure of few words exercising tremendous influence and authority in the governance of the country. When accosted to him, I greeted him with respect "where are you posted" he enquired "DIG at Police Complex Madhuban Sir". "What is your seniority in IPS?" "I come from 1957 IPS batch". "Are you senior to Bhinder?". "Yes Sir". "OK we will bring you to Delhi as Police Commissioner". "Thank you Sir but I am too junior for that job". "Why are you bothered about that". "Still....... Sir". "OK, OK" where else we can utilize you" "Sir, if your good self care you may consider my posting to UT Chandigarh" "But that is DIG's post". "Yes Sir". He asked his Aide to tell the Home Minister to issue order for his posting to UT Chandigarh. After confirming from Er. OP Verma the airworthiness of Cessna, he was getting ready for the flight. I greeted the big authoritative person then and left the hanger. This was my first and the last, face-to-face, a very brief conversation with the then almost top powerful man of the country. A sharp featured person with penetrating eyes, face glowing like the first rays of the rising sun, well-tapered physique, draped in fine snow white cotton Kurta Pajama and Chappal, majestic gait, this prince charming could be the heart throb of many a world fame beauty.

I returned to Madhuban the same evening. Next day, a hush-hush rumour started trickling in that Sanjay Gandhi had died in an air-crash. Apart from being in gloom because of this tragedy, we were also worried about the fate of Er OP Verma. It was he, who used to certify the aircraft for its airworthiness. Sanjay Gandhi often used to take him along on his sorties. However, I learnt that Sanjay, along with the Chief Flying Instructor Captain Subhash Saxena of the Flying Club had together gone on the sortie. It was a two-seater Pushpak Aircraft. I accompanied Raj Kamal and Ritu to Delhi to look up the Vermas. Madam Indira Gandhi, the Prime Minister of India had called OP Verma to know the details. After meeting her and finding that she was satisfied about the airworthiness of the aircraft, he felt somewhat relaxed; otherwise, he was highly tense and worried. Sanjay's tragic death in the air crash caused lot of upheavals in the national political scenario.

Since I had known Giani Zail Singh, then Union Home Minister, I sought an audience with him with a view to apprise him about my relationship with Er. OP Verma, the Chief Engineer of the Flying Club. He told me that the concerned engineer should not worry about this tragedy; Sanjay had an adventurous disposition. He also mentioned that a "Note" had come to him from the Aide of Sanjay Gandhi for my posting as IGP, UT Chandigarh, but Bhajan Lal, CM Haryana was vehemently opposing that proposal. I explained to him briefly the background for his animosity against me and requested the Home Minister to ignore the proposal for my posting as IGP, UT Chandigarh.

Happy days were followed by sad turn of events. On 9th March 1981 Raj Kamal and Ritu were blessed with a handsome lovely male child. He was named Shiraz. Raj Kamal was still a law college student. Ritu had already done her Graduation. My wife and I decided to put Ritu also in Punjab University Chandigarh as regular day scholar for Post Graduation, which she completed in time. She then continued her study for M.phil but did not complete it. Raj Kamal completed his Law degree very late and got himself enrolled as an advocate in Punjab and Haryana High Court Chandigarh. The couple had another lovely male child on 25th May 1986. He was named Sahil later changed to Yuvraj Singh. They were a happy couple by all standards. As Thomas Hardy said, **"Happiness is an occasional episode in the general drama of pains"**, their happiness also started receding. The practice of Raj Kamal, as an Advocate did not shine at all. During his early thirties, he started appearing somewhat lazy and sickly. I had built a house in Delhi on a DDA Plot of 500 sq yds in Ashok Vihar in 1970. I decided to sell off that house and with its sale proceeds, to build a house in Panchkula, Haryana, on a plot of 1350 sq yards, No.33, Sector-6, purchsed in resale. The family shifted to this house in October 1987. On 31st July 1988 I retired from the Service. The area where we had our Farm at Machhiwara, was badly affected by the terrorist's activities. We sold off our said lands. From the sale proceeds, a shop-cum-office site at Chandigarh was purchased. A piece of 10 acres of land was, also purchased near Naraingarh, Haryana.

One late evening, while returning on his motorbike, from the farm at Naraingarh, Raj Kamal escaped narrowly, head on collision with a truck, because of double vision he had suffered from. After detailed investigations by the PGI, to the utter horror of everybody in the family, he was diagnosed to be suffering from Multiple Sclerosis – a dreaded incurable degenerative disease of the nervous system, demyleating the sheath of the nerves, which consumes the body muscles slowly and slowly rendering the patient disabled up to 100%, culminating into painful fatality. Raj Kamal breathed his last on 11th March 2007, thus ending the protracted agony and sufferings, spanning over a long period of 14 years.

Shiraz and Yuvraj got school education from reputed institutions. Shiraz blossomed into a tall handsome youth, very intelligent, obedient and responsible in his conduct. He did his BE Civil, and cleared his GMAT. By getting scholarship in GMAT he did his ME Environment from Punjab Engineering College Chandigarh. He got a befitting job in Satluj Jal Vidyut Nigam, a Hydro-Electric Power Project Corporation of Government of India in the Public Sector. Like his father, he too is a regular blood doner. Music and playing Guitar are both as dear to him as if a gift in inheritance. He was married to Puneet Kaur, M Sc Bio Chemistry, a pretty, cultured and well-mannered daughter of Dr Niranjan Singh and Smt Charan Kaur, on 29th January 2008. The young couple was blessed with a lovely son on 5th October 2008 named Aayaan Raj. Younger to Shiraz is Yuvraj Singh, an equally handsome and intelligent boy. He had joined Punjab University Law College. Human life is a queer combination of benevolent and malevolent events of life. No one is perfect, that is why pencils have erasers. His mother, out of deep affection for Yuvraj and thinking it to be a benevolent gesture, allowed him to use her car for commuting between residence and the College, despite my pronounced disapproval to this gesture of Ritu. The tender mind of the boy, instead of availing this facility to his benefit, proved to be highly malevolent. He missed the chance to become a legal luminary. Frustration has made him short tempered. He might come over this negative trait in his character when he has settled down in some profession. He has since done his three year B.Com degree Course.

Younger Son Rupinder Kumar

He was born at Ferozepur on 18th May 1962. I was then, posted as ASP at Ferozepur. Soon after his birth, I was promoted as Superintendent of Police and posted as SP/Border with Headquarters at Ferozepur. Rupinder Kumar did his Schooling from Delhi Public School in 1978 and MA, Political Science from Punjab University, Chandigarh in 1984. As a college student, he was by nature an adventurous and fun loving boy very fond of hunting, horse riding, playing Tennis, Cricket and Skating. A well-groomed, handsome and smart boy with razor sharp intelligence, he cleared the All India Services/Civil Services Examinations in the first attempt in 1984. In his preferences for various Services, he kept DANI Police at S. No. three, after IAS and IPS. As per his merit, he could get only one of the Class I Services and that he had not chosen. In his second attempt, same position was repeated. He thus joined DANI Police in 1986. He was promoted to the next higher Grade in the DANI Police, in due course of time. After a three years stint as DCP Traffic, Central Range at New Delhi, he was shifted to District North. He has since been inducted into the IPS with ten years elevated seniority. *He was awarded Police Medal for Meritorious Service on Independence Day, 15th August 2010, a befitting recognition of his excellent service record.*

A very sought after eligible bachelor, marriage proposals cropped up from many quarters during the year 1987. One was a senior political figure from Punjab. It did not materialize. The father of the girl has been nursing a grudge against me on this account. Another proposal was about a highly educated, beautiful and promising daughter of a senior political personality from Haryana, who had very good reputation for high integrity and consistency in his political career. Simultaneously, there was another proposal, through a well-placed relation of ours, about a promising and highly educated daughter of a District and Sessions Judge in Punjab. I had personally known both these gentle men and had high regards for them, they both being highly respectable and well reputed persons. For me, it was highly embarrassing to say "No" to either of them. From my son's point of view, both the girls were equally meritorious but I had apprehensions that the girl from Haryana, being from the political family, might get tempted to join active politics, to inherit the legacy of her father, at any time and that situation might not be a welcome thing for congenial and harmonious married life. For the other girl, being daughter of a Senior Judicial Officer, our general perception was that she would prove to be better in compatibility. This very important event in Rupinder's life was ultimately settled accordingly. His marriage with Loveleen, daughter of Sh. M. S. Luna, District and Sessions Judge, Patiala, Punjab was solemnized on 27th December 1987 at Panchkula. Sh Luna was reputed to be a highly religious, thoroughly honest, kind hearted, affable and loveable human being, with sweet smile ever playing on his glowing face. Rupinder and Loveleen started their married life blissfully. They were blessed with a son on 22nd May 1989. He was named Amulya, later rechristened as Varun Kumar. Unfortunately, Loveleen died in a freak accident on 13th September 1992. This tragedy caused an acute pain and sufferings to all of us, much more to Rupinder. What everybody wants from life is a continuous happiness. A good and smooth life is the main argument. However, the tragedy washed it all away.

We persuaded Rupinder to take long leave from his Office and stay with us in the family at Panchkula. My wife and I had got highly worried, seeing Rupinder, smitten with intense grief, slowly withdrawing into a shell, looking often stoically with expressionless gaze, while conversing even to his close friends. My elder son Raj Kamal was not keeping good health and had been diagnosed as patient of Multiple Sclerosis-a dreaded incurable disease. This had further compounded our worries. Such a severe blow of ill luck it was that trapped in a tempest, we were finding no way to navigate out of it. Time is a great healing factor. Rupinder came over to Punjab State on deputation in late 1992 and continued in Punjab in the rank of Superintendent of Police. He went back to his parent cadre UT Delhi in 1995. In due course of time, we had learnt to come to terms to the realities of vicissitudes of life. Rupinder had then just turned 30 and Amulya was only a baby about 3 years old. To take Rupinder out of the acute shock caused by the tragic death of his wife we, the entire family decided to make him understand that the situation demanded that he should think of resurrecting his personal life. Initially he was much averse to any suggestion for going in for another life partner who could mitigate his grief by her tender love. On our persistent goading and persuasion, he agreed to leave things for us to decide. We arranged his new marital bond. A simple ceremony of marriage, attended by a few close relations was performed on 10.04.1993 with Shavinder Kaur. The couple was blessed with a lovely son on 14.3.1994, named Anmol, who has done all of us in the family proud by scoring CGPA-9 in his CBSE Matriculation Examination. Presently he is studying Commerce in his plus two Courses.

Varun Kumar, son of Rupinder–Loveleen, has blossomed into a tall handsome, well-built, well-groomed and well-mannered youth. Having successfully undergone training as a Commercial Pilot in America, he is a Commercial Pilot License (CPL) holder. He is studying in the final year of three years B.Com Degree Course, through correspondence. He got regular job of a Pilot in well-known Airways Kingfisher.

Traditional Values vis-a-vis Modern Culture

My wife and I used to value a lot the advice of our elders. We had experienced our parents listening to the advice of their elders carefully and acting thereon with regards. I have grown up in that mould. I, like my mother, have the habit of giving sermons to the members of our brood to follow the teachings based on *Shastras, Gurbani* and the sayings of godly men of wisdom. "Do you want to know what you are? Do not ask. Act! Action will delineate and define you," said Thomas Jafferson. Bible 133.1 "Behold, how good and how pleasant it is for brethren to dwell together in unity." Atharva Veda says "May we unite in our mind, unite in our purposes, and not fight against the divine spirits within us." The Holy Dalai Lama says, "True happiness comes from a sense of brotherhood and sisterhood. We need to cultivate a universal responsibility for one and another and the planet we share." Guru Nanak said, "In order to be a man of truth, your actions should be pure and pre-conditioned for mental peace and happiness lies in the suppression of ego by moulding one's life in accordance with Hukam and Raza-His will." They always put up attentive ears and such sweet talk does cheer them up. I often feel disappointed that some of them do forget all about it soon. Times have changed fast. The present generation does not feel happy with too frequently given to them sermons on ethics by the elders. Let we elders keep pace with the changed times!

Chapter – 5

Entry into IPS and Basic Training

Appointment to IPS and Commencement of Basic Training

I got appointment letter to the IPS from the Ministry of Home Affairs, Union Government, with directions to join at CPTC, Mount Abu (Rajasthan) on 26th October 1957 for one year Basic Training. Another Punjabi boy Gurmail Mehmi also from a scheduled caste, too got his appointment letter to the IPS. We instantly became good friends. On the eve of our departure to Mount Abu, almost the entire gentry of our community, in government services, at Delhi had assembled at a prestigious Hotel in Connaught Place, to host a high tea to honour and bless us with their best wishes. Such was then euphoria and enthusiasm in the assembled crowd of the community on selection of some ones from amongst them in the IPS, considered then a rare and unique achievement, making proud the entire community. Warmth, affection and expectations writ large on every body's cheerful face left deep imprint on my mind so as to remind me always, throughout my career, to prove worthy of their touching sentiments. While on way to the Railway Station, Delhi for boarding the train to Mount Abu, I was sweetly recalling what Swami Vivekanand said. "When I asked God for strength, He gave me difficult situations to face; When I asked God for brain and brawn, He gave me puzzles in life to solve; When I asked God for happiness, He showed me some unhappy people; When I asked God for wealth, He showed me how to work hard; When I asked God for favours, He showed me opportunities to work hard; When I asked God for peace, He showed me how to help others; God gave me nothing I wanted, He gave me every thing I needed." I was identifying myself with the shadow of Swami Ji as if he had given expression to his inner feelings, in that beautiful composition, for the posterity to emulate.

Within a week of joining at Mount Abu, the training had started in the right earnest. The outdoor syllabus included Physical Training, Infantry Training (including Weapon Training) and Equitation (Horse Riding). All the outdoor training subjects used to be very taxing and toughening. Study of Laws (IPC, CrPC, Indian Evidence Act, Constitutional Laws, Local and Special Laws), Scientific Aid to the detection of crime including Ballistics and Map Reading, all included in the indoor syllabus, were very absorbing and highly interesting. Daily evening games were always a welcome recreation. Every Faculty Member of teaching staff, both for outdoor and indoor subjects, was thoroughly efficient, highly conversant with the intricacies of the concerned subjects and fully committed to the job requirements. The Instructors of PT and Infantry Training, apparently looked harsh in their conduct, but then it was, indeed, the need of the time. The Riding Master was very rough and crude; once the Horse-Riding period was over he would cheer up every trainee with his rural based jokes and anecdotes. The trainee officers, who came from the rural background and those having interest in some sports, used to feel at ease during outdoor training periods. However, the urbanites used to feel little strenuous, particularly during Horse-Riding exercises like jumping over the hurdles and trotting without strips. So much so, that one IPS Probationer from Delhi deserted within one month after the start of the training. On compassionate consideration, he was later permitted to join Central Secretariat Service-B, Gazetted Class-II.

Initially All India Inter-se Seniority was fixed as per merit based on the total marks secured in the UPSC Competitive Examinations. However, the inter-se seniority amongst the batch-mates was ultimately to be determined based on the total marks accruing after adding marks scored in another examination conducted by the UPSC towards the end of the completion of the training period of one year at the Police Training College. Score less than 50% in any subject, both outdoor and indoor would reckon as failure, counting as zero while totaling the score in all the subjects. To keep track of the performance of the Probationers, periodical tests used to be held by the college authority during the training period. The whole system, as above, was in place obviously to ensure that trainee officers continued evincing keen interest all through, in the training syllabi. The trainee officers generally would give pointed attention to their training syllabi.

Bharat Darshan Programme

One very interesting and excitedly awaited item of the Training Syllabi was "Bharat Darshan Programme." It came up during the summer spring days. The entire batch was split into two halves. One group was taken out to visit various places in the Northern and Eastern states and the other group was taken to the Western and Southern states. I opted for the group going to Western and Southern states. Mr. Jayawant, an officer from Madhya Pradesh Cadre, was the Director (then designated as commandant) of the Police Training College, in the rank of Inspector General of Police, that being the top most rank in the Police set up during those days. The Jayawants couple were to lead the Trainees group going on Bharat Darshan to Western and Southern states. A member of the college faculty equivalent to a Senior Scale IPS Officer, designated as Assistant Director, was the incharge of the group.

Our group was taken around various places in the states of Madhya Pradesh, Andhra Pradesh, Tamil Nadu, Kerala, Karnataka, Goa, Maharashtra and Gujarat. The occasion provided, indeed, a very rare opportunity to see on the ground, wonderfully diverse cultural centers, historical monuments, famous temples, mosques and churches, States' capital cities and on the top working systems of the policing in different regions of our vast country. Otherwise, also the trip proved to be highly beneficial for the trainees as many of us had little practical knowledge as to how and where the soul of India pervaded in its actual manifestation.

Obeisance at Rameshwaram

Among the visits to various religious places, our paying obeisance at Rameshwaram Temple was soul soothening for those having faith and curiously amusing for others. Ideally situated at the Eastern Coast amidst almost heavenly environs, it presented an elegant look. Local Dy SP acted as our guide. We were given quite a few do's and don'ts. None of us was to be in uniform. Simple Indian dress like kurta-pyjama, dhoti preferably if available, no headgear, to be barefooted and no socks even, none to carry intoxicant and no loud talking. Since non - Hindus, Sikhs excluding, nor even scheduled castes Hindus were allowed to go inside the temple, we were also told to strictly avoid addressing each other by that part of the name which would reveal the caste or religion.

Our group included the two trainees from Punjab, belonging to the scheduled caste. Both Mr. Jayawant, the Commandant of the CPTC and the Assistant Director, incharge of our group kept studied silence about the inclusion of two scheduled castes in the group being led by the guide, the local Dy SP, inside the temple. It was quite clear that both the CPTC top officers did not approved this particular restriction and their silence meant their approval for the inclusion of us two scheduled castes trainees inside the temple. Anyhow, the entire group including the Jayawant couple and we two scheduled caste trainees were led into the temple.

The head priest, during the course of reciting hymns in Sanskrit first blessed the trainee standing by the right side of Mrs. Jayawant, by applying *chandan* paste *tilak* on his forehead and then sprinkled sacred water drops on all of us. He then did the *aarti* rituals, with a number of small burning *diyas,* placed on a gold-like shining big plate, on Mrs. Jyawant and the trainee officer standing on her right side, taking them as husband and wife. None of us showed even the slightest reaction to this goof up, strictly abiding by the sermons of the do's and don'ts given to us before hand. Finally, our paying obeisance at the sanctum sanctorum of temple was over. It was all in private that later, the trainees used to joke about how the head priest had showered blessings on all of us particularly the *chandan* paste *tilak* on the forehead of a trainee officer and *aarati* rituals performed on Mrs. Jayawant and the trainee officer.

Resuming Training after "Bharat Darshan"

After our return from weeks' long "Bharat Drashan" we all trainees were given a week's holiday break, enabling us to visit our parents back home. It was a very welcome mid-way break to be with our dear ones and share with them our experience on our way to becoming fully trained police officers. Fully relaxed and somewhat rejuvenated and energized with sweet expectation and keenly awaited bright future, our further training programme was resumed in the right earnest. Mr. Jayawant would ensure that the training syllabi were being pursued meticulously. Mr. Stracy, an Australian as second in command closely watched the progress of the trainees, both in outdoor and indoor subjects. He was loved by the trainees for imparting lessons very affectionately with personal touch on dress code for different occasions, table manners, behavioural etiquettes during conversation particularly with ladies, importance of punctuality on all occasions, correct body posture while walking on and off the parade ground, while in uniform or in civil outfits. The basic idea was not to turn the trainees into Westernized Sahibs: it aimed at inculcating into them the good qualities and habits of always presenting themselves as well-groomed Indian citizens, befitting the high ranks they would be holding. Mr. Devonport incharge outdoor training, despite being a strict disciplinarian, would cultivate an instant rapport with every trainee. Because of Geographical location CPTC at Mount Abu, early morning hours during winter used to be very foggy, causing very poor visibility. However, Mr. Devonport had his own amusing ways to ensure that every trainee had come out to attend the early morning PT class after shaving and bathing. All the trainees had fully adapted themselves to the total requirements of training environments and were really enjoying their stay at the CPTC.

Turn of Events

On the turn of events, Mr. Jayawant was replaced by Mr. GK Handoo, IP. He had earlier functioned as Chief Security Officer of Jawaharlal Nehru, Prime Minister of India. A tall, athlctic figured, fair complexioned, he was endowed with a very imposing personality brimming with incisive and penetrating look. However, his pontifical conduct would reflect his innate sense of an aristocrat, egoistic, whimsical and a self-righteous fanatic having strong likes and dislikes, falling in narcissistic love with verbal mirage of his own making. He would have been an ideal cop to carry out the objectives of the British Rule, but in Democratic Republic of India he would, as a Field Officer have made out to be an odd figure. His arrival as replacement of Mr. Jayawant was like a torrential stream violently gushing into a calm ocean, frighteningly disturbing the infinite marine species. He would often unabashedly ridicule the lessons on dress code, table manners behavioral etiquettes etc. imparted by Mr. Stracy, in the presence of Mr. Stracy himself, during the formal dinner gatherings in the Officers' Mess, obviously with the mean intention of slighting Mr. Stracy.

My Interview with GK Handoo, IP

On his arrival in the CPTC, Mr. Handoo interviewed every IPS Probationer individually, obviously to know the background and potential of every one of them. When he interviewed me, I, like other probationers, was also somewhat excited. On entering his office chamber I greeted him and he bid me to sit down. His first question was how and why I, as Hans Raj by name had chosen the suffix Swan which he said, was the English name of the bird called "Hans" in Hindi. When I tried to explain he cut me short commanding not to burden him with all such "Silly details." Then he asked me about my family background. I had just said that I had come from a scheduled caste family he immediately cut me short and said, "How could you manage to get nominated to the IPS." His tone was clearly sarcastic. Unfortunately I could not discern his mood and with haste I said "Sir, there is no system of nomination to the IPS; I have come into the IPS through a competitive examination conducted by the UPSC." He was red with rage and shouted at me saying, "You dirty housefly, how dare you try to teach me the method of IPS recruitment; get up and get lost." I repeatedly said "Sorry sir" and came out of his office room after saluting him. I was highly bewildered and dejected. On returning to my room in the Rajputana Club, I narrated the entire episode to my room-mate Gurmail Mehmi. He cautioned me to be extra careful so that "The flamboyant" man did not create hurdles in my successful completion of training in the CPTC. Pray! In any case this stormy interview with the man who really mattered a lot at that stage of my career in the IPS, just at the threshold, did somewhat shatter my self-confidence. However, I gathered my poise recalling that earlier I had faced much violent storms; this too would not be of much consequence if I continued working hard with keen interest in the training programme. After every set back, I had come out more confident and having full faith in myself. As and when the Commandant would come on the parade ground, he would invariably single me out alleging some fault on my part and would address me as "You double Hans." I got used to such remarks and this would not bother me any more.

Days passed, I continued putting hard work, evincing keener interest in the training Syllabi. My unpleasant interview with Mr. Handoo often haunted me. My comprehension would fail me to conclude whether it was some indiscretion on my part in responding to his queries, which offended him or was it my caste identity that triggered the severe aversion. I determinedly decided to prove G.K.Handoo wrong by my performance and my determination.

Some two month before the completion of our basic training, results about the performance of the trainee officers during the 10 months of training had been compiled, based on the performance in the various periodical tests conducted by the CPTC authorities. My over all performance, as adjudged by the CPTC authorities placed me at much higher pedestal than the majority of my fellow trainee officers. This perhaps was not to the liking of Mr. Handoo. He was to announce the results in the Officers' Mess after the formal dinner. In fact, the idea behind such announcement of the results was to point out if any trainee officers had given poor performance so that they could try to make up the deficiencies during the remaining period of the training. Mr. Handoo, in his usual over awing style, often raised his voice to make his points more effective and very sarcastically raising the pitch of his tone he shouted at trainees gathered in the Mess "You should be ashamed of yourselves, even Swan could beat a majority of you. Go and drown yourself in the Nakki Lake." (Nakki is a vast lake surrounded by hills in the picturesque environs of Mount Abu - a famous place of tourist interest). These remarks blurred my vision and wisdom momentarily. I instantly got up to register my strong protest.

I had just uttered the word "Sir", when he shouted angrily "Would you sit down, else I would get you thrown out of the Mess." A fellow trainee officer sitting by my side started pinching my leg signaling sympathetically in whispering voice to sit down. I sat down without uttering any word but sobbing with agony and pain, which I had suffered mentally during those sad moments. However, a hapless man can do nothing in such a situation except to curse himself for his low caste birth. Many trainee officers who too had felt aggrieved on the excesses of Mr. Handoo would sympathetically reassure me often saying that it was a bad patch in my destiny and I should forget about that and concentrate on my studies to ensure still better results in the Final Examination to be conducted shortly by the UPSC. In any case, I would, often get lost in philosophical thoughts that I needed to awaken to the fact that I was not perfect and that not every one would love, appreciate or approve of who or what I was. That was OK. They were entitled to their own views and opinions.

Result of the IPS Probationers Final Examination

The result of the final examination conducted by the UPSC was declared indicating subject wise score of every probationer and fixing accordingly the revised order of merit. It was circulated to all the IPS Probationers vide GOI, Ministry of Home Affairs, letter dated 20.07.1959. We the five IPS Probationers allocated to Punjab State Cadre were then undergoing five months training at PTC Phillaur, starting from 01.04.1959. On the receipt of the detailed marks of the Final Examination, I was highly disappointed, if not flabbergasted to find that Mr. Handoo from the famous IP, had continued nursing deep-rooted bias against me reflecting meanest aspect of his conduct, by trying to cause damage to my IPS career. The results showed that my performance was better than 49 others in Indian Criminal Laws with 244 marks out of 400; better than 36 others in Basic Principles and main Provisions of the Constitution of India with 28 marks out of 50; better than 20 others in Medical Jurisprudence with 25 marks out of 50; better than 38 others in Scientific Aids to the Detection of Crime, including Ballistics with 61 marks out of 100; better than 38 others in Equitation with 58 marks out of 100; better than 49 others in Physical Training with 34 marks out of 60. However, in Infantry Training, score awarded to me by Mr Handoo, then the Examiner for this particular subject only, was 40 marks out of 90, the lowest in the batch of 67 Probationers. These 40 marks had to be added to 34 marks scored by me in Physical Training. This made 74 marks out of 150, only one mark less than the minimum requirement of 75 pass marks. The score of 74 marks was, reckoned as zero while determining and fixing a revised order of merit list. Mr HRK Talwar, Principal of PTC Philaur, who would rarely open up with any trainee, displayed admirably graceful and affection laden conduct, in encouraging me with his advice that I should forget about what Mr. Handoo had done to me but should try to make up this loss in seniority by better performance, during the long IPS career ahead. Mr. Talwar's advice was, indeed, a potent tonic for regaining my shaken self-confidence.

Practical Training in Police Working at Police Station Level

After the batch dispersed from Mount Abu, on the conclusion of the Basic Training, I had first reported at Sangrur on 24.11.1958. Since, then District SP Sangrur was a SPS Officer, IGP Punjab shifted me to Amritsar where I reported on 29.12.1958. Sardar Ranjit Singh Grewal IPS (1948) and Sardar Tarlochan Singh Sachdeva IPS (1948) were the SSP and SP Hqr at Amritsar. Grewal was related to Surinder Singh Kairon; both were married to real sisters. Surinder Singh was the elder son of Sardar Partap Singh Kairon Chief Minister of Punjab. Due to his political clout, Grewal commanded lot of authority. However, he was very kind and affectionate to me. Under the close supervision and guidance of both Grewal and Sachdeva, I learnt, closely working and discharging practically, the duties of police station clerk called "Munshi", Investigating Officer and SHO of the police station. I also watched the proceedings being conducted during the trial of quite a few heinous crime cases in the Sessions Courts and the roles played by both the Prosecution and Defence Lawyers. I was required to submit weekly report on every Sunday evening to SP Hqr about my practical training. He often used to cross check the depth of Practical Knowledge acquired by me in a question answer session of half an hour and so. All IPS Probationers had to under go such practical training after completing Basic Training at CPTC Mount Abu. The Practical Knowledge acquired by me during my stay at Amritsar stood me in good stead later in my service.

Training at Police Training School Phillaur, Punjab

Training at Police Training School Phillaur started on 01.04.1959. We all the five IPS Probationers allocated to Punjab State IPS Cadre joined this Training. Gulam Jilani Pandit and ON Kaul both Dy SP Probationers and another Dy SP Probationer by the name Chopra of J & K State also joined us at Phillaur. Chopra was the son-in-law of Mr. DWC Mehra, the then IGP J & K state. The Training Syllabi for indoor classes included following subjects:

(i) Local and Special Laws, specific to Punjab State. (ii) Indian Police Act, 1861 and Punjab Police Rules framed there under. (iii) Various Standing Orders and Administrative Orders, issued by the IGP, Punjab State and the Punjab Government, on various subjects like use of force including tear smoke against unlawfully assembled crowds. (iv) Indian Excise Act. (v) Indian Gambling Act.

In the outdoor classes, Syllabi included Physical Training, Infantry Training and Equitation all of much higher standard than that followed at CPTC Mount Abu. Mr. HRK Talwar IPS (1948) the first batch of the IPS was the Principal at the PTS Phillaur. A few days after our joining at Phillaur the Principal called me to his office. He told me that IGP Punjab had received a letter from Mr. GK Handoo Commandant CPTC Mount Abu saying that the performance of Hans Raj Swan in Physical Training and Infantry Training at the CPTC Mount Abu had remained poor. The Principal warned me that I would be retained at the PTS Phillaur for another 5 Months period if my performance in the said outdoor subjects remained poor. Shri Talwar, a strict disciplinarian was known for his non-sparing approach against any complacent or non-serious carefree trainee.

However, during the second month of training, Shri Talwar during a formal dinner in the Officer's Mess, while appreciating the meticulous arrangements made by me as Mess secretary, had formally announced that Swan was as good in outdoor subjects as anybody else among the trainees. This had given me much needed self confidence which had been somewhat shaken on my learning earlier about what Mr. Handoo had written to IGP Punjab, giving adverse comments on my performance in outdoor subjects. Towards the conclusion of the training at PTS Phillaur Departmental Examination had been held. Before our passing out from PTS Phillaur, all the trainee officers, had successfully cleared the said Departmental Examination.

While I was moving out of Phillaur, a kaleidoscopic scene of my interview of March 1956 with revered Dr. B R Ambedkar, the greatest icon of Social Justice was coming to my mind repeatedly and his words "Community needs fighters like you" were ringing in my ears. Another idea coming to my mind was what Gandhi Ji had said, "The best way to find you is to lose yourself in the service of others." I was on the way to serve the humanity as an IPS Officer, a rare opportunity, so benevolently bestowed upon me by the Almighty God and I was highly excited to prove myself worthy of His trust and blessings.

Chapter – 6

As Assistant Superintendent of Police

Posting at Hisar District Headquarter

Since a year's Basic Training at CPTC Mount Abu and subsequent five months' training at PTS Phillaur had been successfully completed, I was due for confirmation in the IPS with effect from 26th October, 1959. A formal order in this regard was issued by the Ministry of Home Affairs Government of India vide order dated 06.02.1960. However, in the meanwhile I was posted as ASP at Hisar where I joined on 09.09.1959. Shri TS Sachdeva IPS (1948) was the District Superintendent of Police, Hisar. This district then extended from Dabwali to Loharu about 150 km apart. Sirsa was the only, both civil and police sub-division in the district. Bhiwani, Loharu, Siwani and Tosham areas were arid having hardly any vegetation except small prickly bushes. Tosham and Siwani areas were dotted with sand dunes. For miles no shady tree was seen. Bhiwani had a civil/criminal court of Magistrate Ist Class. I was assigned the role of a supervisory officer for the Police Stations Bhiwani City, Bhiwani Sadar, Tosham, Siwani and Hansi. Loharu was under the charge of District Inspector. There used to be very little crime. Poverty was pervasive all around. Young people were very keen to join the Army. The system of village touring by all the gazetted police officers in the district during the winter months, introduced by the British was being followed meticulously. Night staying in the villages was an integral part of the system. This provided a very useful opportunity to the police officers to understand by interacting with the rural folks, the village way of life, their grievances if any and well or ill reputed people and the disputes which could lead to commission of heinous crimes. Being a new entrant in the service, I was quite excited to go out on village touring on the horse back, dressed in proper equitation uniform i.e. breaches, shirt, sola hat and knee high riding shoes, reminiscent of system introduced by the British.

Visit to Village Bapoda

It was during the village touring of the area of Police Station Sadar Bhiwani that I happened to visit village Bapoda, 5 km from Bhiwani– a big village overwhelmingly populated by Rajputs community. Majority of them were either ex-army or serving army personnel. The next population in number was that of scheduled castes. When our party reached the outskirts of the village, I was amazed to see that a motley crowd of about 150 people, both genders, had assembled there. They raised a few slogans like "Swan Sahib Zindabad" and a band in high pitch tune accompanied by the beats of drums, started playing. The SHO was a Punjabi refugee from West Punjab. He told me that the crowd was of scheduled castes people and they had organized this welcome programme in my honour. I did not like this idea and sensing that it was a crude attempt of a sycophant, perhaps a mischief on the part of the SHO. I dismounted, talked respectfully and affectionately to the persons leading the "Welcome Procession" and repeatedly saying "Thank you very much", I proceeded on to the village *choupal.*

The *choupal* of the village was located in the area inhabited, all around, by Rajput community. At the *choupal* I found only a few persons assembled and they were all somewhat indifferent. I greeted them saying "Ram-Ram Bhaio" I could sense from their reaction that there was perhaps a serious divide between the rajputs and the depressed class people. It was perhaps their high and low pedigree complex syndrome. By way of placating the rajputs' sentiments, I announced that it was an honour for me to come to village Bapoda that had produced many brave soldiers in the Indian army; I would first pay my regards to the family members at the house of Lt.Col Brij Pal Singh from Rajput Regiment who had been awarded *Vir Chakra* for displaying exceptional bravery in the famous battle of Naushera (J & K State) during 1948; thereafter, I would meet the villagers from all communities together, in the compound of village school. This cheered up the people who had assembled at the *choupal.*

After about 20 minutes, I reached the school. A big crowd of people from all the communities assembled there. I bucked up and induced the elderly rajput men who were ex-army to narrate their success stories of valour and bravery, displayed during their service ventures. I also indulged in some sweet pep talk narrating how the rajput in India were the sword arm of the country during difficult days, before the advent of the alien rulers and how the legendry Rajput Raja Maharana Pratap had waged a relentless war against the Mughals. I also explained in Haryanvi dialect, the famous quotes of the men of wisdom like "True happiness comes from a sense of brotherhood and sisterhood; we need to cultivate a universal responsibility for one another and the planet we share." I also narrated the extreme sacrifices made by Guru Gobind Singh during his determined fights, launched against the tyranny let loose by the Mughals and his unique concept of casteless society. The other story I narrated was that of Swami Dayanand Saraswati. With his unique concept of Arya Samaj, he devoted his entire life to establish an ideal Samaj – a fraternity wherein the worth of an individual is determined by his own status in the society and not according to the status of the parents who gave him/her birth. Equally most important was the contribution made by Dr. B R Ambedkar in giving to the country a constitution, the sum total of which aims at establishing an Indian society where equality, liberty and fraternity have to be ultimate objectives.

Normally my programme used to last maximum for three hours in a village. However, I had spent full four and half hours in Bapoda in an attempt to identify myself with them as one of them. I expressed all happiness on listening to the elderly persons' success stories of their days in the army and the youngsters aspiring to become army/police officers. In the atmosphere laced with humour and anecdotes only a few people came out with any grievance. Finally, it was all very happy ending with the village most respected elderly person from rajput community thanking me for visiting their village and spending more than four hours for interacting with them. They assured me that village people were very peace loving and all disputes or misunderstandings if any would be mutually sorted out. This village inhabited by the majority of a brave clan whose first love has been to join the Indian army and display their valour, has given to the country a great son as the Chief of Army Staff, General Vijay Kumar Singh.

On return to the Rest House at Bhiwani, I severely reprimanded the SHO for his creating a very embarrassing situation for me at Village Bapoda. A sycophant subordinate can prove to be very dangerous, at times, for senior officers; it is more so in the case of IPS officers. "Keep the sycophants at arm's length" should be the motto for the IPS officers.

Threat to Commit Dacoity at Village Devrala - A Big Hoax

Village Devrala situated about 15 km from Bhiwani, was falling under Police Station Tosham. Lala Phool Chand belonging to this village had earned admirable fortune in his business based at Kolkata. He often used to visit Punjab and once in a year he would come to his village Devrala. Because of his flourishing business, he had earned the patronage of high ups in the political circle. His house in village Devrala was a very big *Haveli*. He owned a big car, which used to easily negotiate sandy track from Bhiwani to his village. During his visit to the village in January 1960, he received a hand written letter in Hindi, in an envelop, addressed to him, purportedly from a notorious dacoit at large, asking for a ransom of an amount of Rupees five lacs for sparing his life. The demanded ransom amount was considered to be very high during those days. The money was required to be delivered in the jungle known as "Barh-Barh ki Bani." Lala Phool Chand made a complaint to the Chief Minister of Punjab requesting for police protection. His complaint was received by SP Hisar with the endorsement from Home Secretary Punjab that CM Punjab had desired that a police party under a gazetted officer should station at village Devrala to provide protection to Lala Phool Chand and his family members and to haul up the 'dacoit'. SP Hisar deputed me together with a force comprising Inspector CIA with 20 police personnel for moving to village Devrala for providing necessary protection to the complainant and haul up the dacoit. The police party under my charge stayed in the village for about a fortnight. A cook had been provided with the police party. Lala Phool Chand used to be extra liberal, on his own, to provide plenty of "desi ghee and milk." We had put our camp in the grounds of the village primary school. Inspector CIA and I were all the time worried and deeply concerned about solving the ticklish problem of hauling up the alleged dacoit.

Our initial anxiety was to trace the origin of the threatening letter. The envelop did not carry the stamp of any post office. Obviously, the envelop had not come to Lala Phool Chand through the Post Office. This fact created a strong suspicion in my mind about its genuineness. A list of youngsters from the age group of 15 years to 30 years who had the knowledge of writing Hindi was prepared. A few residents of the village who were not enjoying good reputation were also included in the said list, irrespective of their age and we started taking their sample hand writings and also started finding out whether any of them had been absent from the village for unexplainable reasons after the arrival of the police party in the village. It was discovered that a young boy aged about 17/18 years, a nephew of Lala Phool Chand had gone out of the village on the pretext of meeting some relatives, soon after the arrival of the police party in the village. We requested Lala Phool Chand to call him back to the village. He came back after we had repeatedly insisted and pressurized Lala Phool Chand to make that boy available to us. The boy was highly reluctant to give the sample of his handwriting and appeared to be under acute fear. While giving his sample handwriting, he committed many errors. Needle of suspicion was pointing at him. We decided to interrogate him.

Lala Phool Chand was not cooperating with us saying that we were only harassing his own family members. We were landed in a queer situation. We persuaded Lala Phool Chand to agree for our interrogating the boy in the presence of two elderly respectable persons of the village. I assured Lala Phool Chand very sympathetically that we were camping in his village only to watch his interest and to unearth the mystery of the threatening letter received by him. Finally, Lala Phool Chand agreed. Next day the boy was brought to us at about 8 pm along with two elderly persons of the village of his choice. I along with the Inspector interrogated the boy in their presence for two hours. The boy broke down and prostrating before Lala Phool Chand, started crying and begging his pardon. So the cat was out of the bag. Lala Phool Chand apologizing for his making accusation of harassing his own family members by us, requested me not to let the real fact of his own nephew's mischief known to the villagers as that would cause him a lot of embarrassment. Next day I took Lala Phool Chand, the 2 elderly men of the village and the boy, nephew of Lala Phool Chand, to Hissar and presented them before the SP, after briefing him about the results of our investigation into the matter. The SP talked to them for about an hour and half and after satisfying himself that the mischief of the alleged threatening letter was really committed by the nephew of Lala Phool Chand, SP asked me to prepare a detailed report accordingly and to wind up the camp at Devrala, to be back to Hisar. Later SP Hisar applauded the solving of that naughty problem by Inspector CIA and me, during the monthly meeting of GOs and SHOs of the district.

Social Relations with Civilians

During my short stay at Hissar I had come to know rather closely quite a few respectable citizens with whom my social relations lasted for years. Mani Ram Godara, a bishnoi from a village in Fatehabad area, then a very tall, young, temperamental and heftily built person, was an active member of the Congress Party. He would always, very boldly and fearlessly, point out an accusing finger at the erring district level officers attending the so-called Monthly Grievances Redressing Meetings, generally chaired by a Minister or in his absence by the Deputy Commissioner. For obvious reasons the officers attending such meetings used to be extra alert and careful. Godara had become popular with the common people commanding respect for his high integrity, truthfulness and straight forwardness. He was a breed entirely different from the generally disrepute politicians.

Balwant Rai Tayal, a Baniya from Hisar City was another person well established in his business. He also used to be quite critical of the lapses on the part of officials of various departments. His very long association with politics remained immune to swindle-ridden politics. My social relation with him had developed through Peer Chand a scheduled caste of Hisar. This skinny person always adorned a Gandhian dress. He studiously and intelligently pursued the business of shoe-making and prospered. He had engaged many reputed artisans in the profession of shoe-making. Those were the days when leather business had not been hijacked by the big industrial houses – a present times breed which has highly modernized and revolutionized the shoe-making industry. Peer Chand was a thorough gentleman, hardworking to the core and highly enterprising in his business. He was not much active in politics then. However, he was keen to play clean game while interacting with selected political figures of reputed standing. My social relations with him had continued through out. He was a rare instance of a semi-literate scheduled caste businessperson in shoe-making industry with clean image having very good social relations with many upper caste persons believing in Gandhian philosophy. However, at the core of his heart he was a staunch Ambedkarite. Later Ch Peer Chand became MLA and Chairman of HAFED. For the reputation he had built up for himself in the Samaj, all his daughters got married to the boys holding appointments in All India Services/Central Civil Services. His one pretty daughter got married, in mid-seventies to my cousin, an officer in the Indian Railways Accounts Service. He has since retired after holding a coveted position, equivalent to Additional Secretary to the Government of India. Mahavir Prasad son of Peer Chand has proved to be a very successful businessperson. With all his dynamism, dash and drive, he has taken the legacy of his father to the new heights.

Dalbir Singh was a Deputy Minister attached with Suraj Mal Cabinet Minister holding Irrigation portfolio in the Punjab Government, then a popular jat politician with very clean image. Dalbir Singh was a gentleman politician with whom my social relations, as developed at Hisar, continued throughout. He was a very well educated scheduled caste person in the State politics at the times when adequately educated scheduled caste persons were few in the State politics. He was a staunch Congressman adequately blended with

Amedkar's philosophy. He was a quiet worker avoiding indulgence in unnecessary confrontation of cheap type politics generally played to impress the gullible electorates. He became Member of the Punjab Public Service Commission and in that capacity, he established his reputation of being a man of integrity. Again in politics his steadfastness and stability of character was of high quality through out. He was never carried by the instinct of grabbing pelf and power and remained stuck to his guns during the fast shifting loyalties of the politicians during the late seventies.

As and when any political crisis, resulting in an uncertain state of affairs in Haryana State happened, Dalbir Singh used to be the common choice to hold the reins as Chief Political Executive. However, such opportunities would slip away with political crisis being resolved otherwise. He had, at one point of time, proposed to have a lasting inter families' relationship with me by going in for a marriage between our children. He was very keen in this regard and so was our family. However, the proposed relationship was not destined to be so, to the utter disappointment of both the families. Dalbir Singh left long back this mortal world. However, my often interacting with him on various social problems ailing the Indian society at large would ever remain a sweet memory for me. After his death, I have happily seen his daughter Selja prospering and blossoming, in due course of time, into a seasoned politician, carrying on, as a dutiful and responsible worthy heir of the legacies of her worthy father. May God bless the family with all the happiness in life?

In early April 1960, I was transferred on posting as ASP Incharge sub-division Jind of District Sangrur. I relinquished the charge at Hisar, accordingly.

As Incharge sub-division Jind of District Sangrur

I joined at Jind as ASP Incharge Sub-Div on 12.04.1960. This Sub-Div. of district Sangrur was once a princely state situated about 70 km from the district Hqr. It had 5 Police Stations– Jind, Narwana, Klayat, Safidon and Julana. Being an erstwhile princely state, it was the most backward and undeveloped place, educationally in particular. Civil administration included SDM– a PCS officer and civil/criminal courts at Jind and Narwana and a civil Hospital with SMO Incharge. At the district Hqr. Sangrur, Dalip Singh the District SP, was 1952 IPS (SPS) seniority. He had joined police service as an Inspector during the pre-Independence days and had strong British days' police mind–set. I called on him to seek his advice and guidance. District Magistrate Sardar Mahinder Singh Bedi was an IAS officer, a pre-Independence PCS appointee. He was a good Urdu poet and was a very popular and highly respected bureaucrat. Shri BL Goswami was the District and Sessions Judge. To understand the topography of the Sub-Div, I under took familiarizing tour of all the police stations during the process of settling down in the new environment.

Land Dispute at Village Mohangarh, PS Narwana

During my familiarizing tour of Police Station Narwana area, the SHO briefed me about a long-standing land dispute existing in village Mohangarh. By way of details, I was apprised that quite a few jat families had been in possession of a big piece of land as tenants for the last three generations. Pratap Singh Daulata, an advocate of district Rohtak, together with some of his relations, had purchased the said land. Daulata had been able to obtain decrees from the law court, in favor of the buyers of the land, for ousting the tenants from the land. The Revenue authorities could not execute the warrants of possession, obtained by the decree holders during the first week of April 1960 because of furious resistance made by the decree-debtors. I advised the SHO to keep close watch for taking timely preventive measures against any possible breach of peace.

On 5th June 1960, a murder case was reported from the area of Police Station Jind. On 6th June, I spent entire day in supervising the investigation of that case at the scene of crime. I returned to Jind late in the evening. On 7th June 1960, early morning KC Grover SDM Jind whose residence was just near by, came to my place still in his night dress. Grover had many years' standing in the PCS. He appeared to be quite tense. He told me that previous evening, he was given instructions, on telephone, by District Magistrate Sangrur to personally go to village Mohangarh Police Station Narwana along with other Revenue Officials like Tehsildar, Kanoongo and Patwari etc. to execute the warrants for delivery of possession of agricultural land purchased by Pratap Singh Daulata and others. He also told me that I, with adequate force was required to accompany them to the village to take care of law and order situation and any breach of peace. I told the SDM that I would proceed further only after taking instructions from the District Superintendent of Police. However, I requested the SDM to acquaint me with the detailed background of the case.

As I learnt from SDM, a big piece of land owned by a few jat families had been under cultivation by many tenants of the same village, also belonging to the jat community; the said land had been in the possession of the tenants for three successive generations. For many years, the tenants would neither give any share in the produce nor pay any rent to the owners of the land, nor pay even the land revenue to the Government. Therefore, the tenants had ceased to be entitled to any right or privilege legally available to the tenants under the law of the land. Civil litigation, spanning over years, did not provide any relief to the original landowners. Therefore, they wanted to sell out the land if there were any buyers. Pratap Singh Daulata, a leading lawyer himself and a communist leader of Punjab state exploited the situation to his advantage. He, together with his several associates, purchased the entire piece of land at a throw away price. Since the tenants had ceased to fall under the legal definitions of tenants, due to their own fault, Pratap Singh Daulata et al succeeded in obtaining decrees in their favour, from the law court, for the eviction of the tenants. Decree holders were issued warrants for delivery of possession, by the competent legal authority. Revenue authority had made unsuccessful attempts earlier to execute the warrants for delivery of the possession. The district revenue authority was duty bound to execute the warrants for possession of the land. With his political clout Daulta had succeeded in pressurizing the district administration to execute the warrants at all costs. The SDM, thus explaining the detailed background of the case told me that the District Magistrate had strongly told him that the warrants must be executed with strong hands. As per order of the DM, a strong police force had to accompany the Revenue Officers headed by the SDM himself.

On checking up with the SDM I found that the date specified before which warrants were to be executed had already expired much earlier.

Having learnt all these facts from the SDM, I could visualize the grave complexity of the problem. I therefore requested the SDM to let me check up with SHO Police Station Narwana and seek instructions from the District SP. On checking up with SI Sitaram SHO Narwana, he told me that though the warrants for the delivery of possession, in execution of several decrees, in favour of the decree holders had been issued as back as 5th April 1960, yet these had remained unexecuted despite two attempts. He further told me that on the previous day he had been summoned by Dalip Singh the District SP to Sangrur and told strictly that warrants of possession in favour of decree holders must be executed at all costs and any laxity on his part would result in his transfer to the police lines. SHO further read out to me order no.1058/DC dated 06.06.1960 sent by DC Sangrur to SP Sangrur for making adequate arrangements to avoid any breach of peace and the endorsement made on the order by District SP in his own hand "Copy to SHO Narwana for strict compliance. One Police guard consisting of NGO/1, HCs/2 and constables/20 are given to him from Police line Sangrur, if needed additional force may be taken from PS Narwana." He also told me that police party as above under Inspector Jagroop Singh had already arrived at Police Station Narwana late night of 06.06.1960. SHO also told me that he had been to village Mohangarh a number of times earlier because the relations between the families of the original landowners and the tenant had remained very tense. The tenants would violently resist any attempt to execute warrants for delivery of possessions to the decree holders.

I talked to Dalip Singh the District SP on telephone and tried to place before him my point of view in the matter. Without allowing me to speak anything, he commanded in a typical rural dialect, "Listen I have deputed Inspector Jagroop Singh with 23 policemen and have already instructed SHO Narwana to detail maximum number of policemen from his Police Station. You mobilize 15-20 policemen from Jind and go with the SDM and see that nobody comes in the way of execution of warrants of possessions in favour of the decree holders." On my persistently pleading with him to give me a chance to submit to him my difficulties, he agreed to listen to me. I submitted: (i) that situation in the village was highly volatile and the tenants were determined to resist any attempt to dispossess them from the land. (ii) That last date for execution of warrants had expired. (iii) That fresh warrants should be got issued from the competent court. (iv) That the District Revenue Administration should make efforts to persuade the tenants to abide by the law of the land. (v) That adequate preventive measures would be taken well before the date fixed for execution of fresh warrants. I also mentioned to him that in the present volatile situation using sledgehammer to kill a fly would not be the best course of acumen.

District SP did hear me quietly and then said "You are two and a half year old in service but you have the audacity to deliver a long useless lecture to me – listen if there remains any laxity on your part in this case, you will suffer its consequences." Interrupting him, I strongly pleaded with him that at least tear smoke squad should be provided with some extra force.

Thundering, "You are shirking to perform duty by raising such silly demands," he disconnected the telephone line. The SDM on his part had also tried to plead with the DM Sangrur to postpone the date of execution of the warrants on the plea that last date for the execution of warrants had already expired, therefore the decree holders should approach the court for fresh issue of warrants. DM had insisted like the district SP that warrants must be executed as already decided in consultation with district SP. In any case, both SDM and I could not comprehend the sanctity of 7th July fixed for the execution of the warrants, except to speculate that Pratap Singh Daulata, being an active politician, might have managed some very strong pressure on the DM and the SP. In such a peculiar situation, we decided to mobilize as much police force as could be raised from within the resources of the Sub-Division. We did not want to lose much time as the task of execution of warrants had to be accomplished well before sun set.

Tragic Scene at Village Mohangarh

KC Grover, SDM Jind together with Mehar Singh Naib Tehsildar, area Kanoongo and concerned Patwari with relevant Revenue records set out for village Mohangarh. I mobilized a police party of some 20 personnel from Jind Police Station. 14 of them were armed with muskets and 0.410 bore *golidar* ammunition; rest of the force carried *lathies* only. A police party consisting of NGO/1, HCs/2 and 20 Constables, all armed with *lathies* under Inspector Jagroop Singh had already arrived at PS Narwana from Sangrur. SHO, Narwana had also mobilized 15 police personnel, all armed with *lathies*. We, together with Revenue officials and SDM Jind, reached village Mohangarh at about 5:30 pm. Naib Tehsildar Mehar Singh suggested to SI Sitaram, SHO PS Narwana to take along some civilians to witness the transfer of possession. Three civilians, that is Iqbal Singh, a gun licensee of village Rashidan, Diwan Singh, numberdar of village Bithmara and Munshi Ram from a close by village were, taken along. Rattan Singh brother of Pratap Singh Daulata, Dharam Singh, Abhey Ram, Bharat Singh and Nihal Singh were to take possession of the land, on behalf of the decree holders. On reaching village Mohangarh Revenue officers and the police party accompanying them, proceeded to settle down in the open, on the village panchayat land, some 200 meters from the village. The land in question was adjoining the panchayat land. Revenue officials asked Rattan Singh and his companions to fetch bullocks and ploughs from their friendly persons in the village so that formality of delivery of the possession of the land to them, at the site, could be gone through. They themselves became busy in consulting the relevant revenue record. I organized the police parties. Fourteen musket men were constituted into a firing squad to function under my direct control, supervision and direction. On checking their weapons and ammunitions, it was found that two constables possessed ammunition which included two charges loaded with five buck-shots each. Since buck shots were not to be used on the crowd under the Rules, I withdrew these buck shots loaded charges and handed over to my Reader for depositing in the *Malkhana* on his return to the Police Station Jind. The rest of the force was organized into two *lathi* squads. One squad with ASI Gurdial Singh as incharge was placed under

SI Sitaram SHO Narwana. The second squad was placed under Inspector Jagroop Singh. Almost the entire village folks were seen standing/sitting on the rooftop of their houses.

After about 15 minutes, Rattan Singh and his four companions were seen fetching two ploughs yoked to two teams of bullocks. They had just entered the field of Prabhu, one of the Judgment debtors, about 200 men and women armed with pointed and sharp edged agriculture tools, came rushing, like a flash storm, towards Rattan Singh and his four companions, shouting "Kill Rattan Singh and do not allow possession to be taken." Rattan Singh and his companions tried to run for their lives towards us. Finding that situation was flaring up and turning into serious violence, SDM standing by my side declared the assembly as unlawful and ordered *lathi* charge, which proved to be ineffective due to openness of the area. Still *lathi* squads tried to chase away the crowd. A large number out of the mob however, managed to reach Rattan Singh and his companions. Rattan Singh and three others were trapped and attacked by the rioters. Nihal Singh was able to get away. The mob also counter attacked the *lathi* wielding policemen. In the course of their attack, ASI Gurdial Singh received some injuries and some of the rioters were seen dragging him away. A couple of gunshots were also heard from the side of the rioters. In an attempt to save the situation, SI Sitaram fired two shots in the air from his service revolver. Almost within seconds on my strongly pleading with him, the SDM ordered to open fire. The police party of four fired two volleys under my orders. The rioters were advancing menacingly shouting "Police is firing crackers only to frighten-attack them." I then ordered all the fourteen musket men to fire a volley. This made real impact. Men and women were seen dispersing away, running helter-skelter in desperation, to escape from any further likely firing from the Police. Within a few minutes the whole crowd melted away leaving behind the dead or injured only. Some had suffered fatal injuries, some were seriously injured and from amongst the injured some had run away to the village, as it appeared from the trails of blood. Rattan Singh, Dharam Singh, Abhey Ram and Bharat Singh were lying seriously injured. It was indeed, a highly ghastly scene. I was smitten with deep anguish and pain and was intensely sad. I was wondering how these poor people had suffered because of harshness of the Tenancy Law and mischievously misguided by some politicians, serving their own interest.

I looked around. The revenue staff including the SDM were all hiding and lying prostrated under the police bus - the only hiding place they could find. On my shouting at them they came out. SDM started accusing me of firing excessively on the crowd saying that he would not support me on this point. Thinking that it was not the time to argue with him, I only told him to tell his staff to assist the Police in taking care of the injured who had been collected at one place and buckets of water were brought from the near by village pond to serve to the moaning and crying injured persons. By 6:30 pm, there were 11 grievously injured persons appearing to be dead and 12 injured persons of whom two had suffered serious injuries from amongst the rioters. Out of the five persons representing the decree holders Rattan Singh and Dharam Singh were dead. Abhey Singh and Bharat Singh were seriously injured. ASI Gurdial Singh had suffered serious injuries at the hands of the rioters. Some Police personnel from amongst the two *lathi* squads had also suffered injuries but no injury seemed to be serious in nature.

After consultation with Inspector Jagroop Singh I left for Narwana at about 7:00 pm with all the injured, to take them to Civil Hospital Narwana for early medical treatment. SHO Narwana with 15 police personnel also left with me for Narwana. Inspector Jagroop Singh was left behind with major part of the police personnel including armed personnel. He was instructed to take up the investigation part including the recovery of the injured rioters, who had run away to the village so that they could also be provided medical aid lest the injuries suffered by them could prove fatal due to excessive hemorrhage or delayed medical care. Iqbal Singh, Diwan Singh and Munshi Ram the respectable persons who had witnessed the entire happening also remained at the spot with Inspector Jagroop Singh. The revenue staff had also left.

KC Grover the SDM had accompanied me in my official Jeep. On the way there was some unpleasant exchange of arguments between us. My point was that he should have stood by my side while each one of the police personnel was furiously engaged in the task of saving the decree holders and dispersing the rioters. He was arguing that he himself being unarmed could become the target of the rioters and hence had to save himself by taking shelter wherever it was available. In any case he was totally averse to the idea to swim or sink together with me in the likely aftermath of the episode. From his strange mannerism, it appeared that he would not own that he gave any order to use force against the tenants, their friends and sympathizers, who had constituted into furious unlawful assembly.

Having reached Narwana, best possible medical care was arranged for the injured in the Government Civil Hospital. Doctors from Civil Hospital Jind and private medical practitioners from Jind and Narwana were also mobilized. SDM reported his own version of the episode to DM Sangrur. I reported the matter to district SP and gave him full details asking him to arrange medical care from Sangrur as well. I also requested him that law and order situation might worsen due to the likely strong reaction from the public in view of the ghastly nature of the episode. I had to stand quietly and patiently his all sorts of diatribes and invectives. Without giving me any instructions, he disconnected the telephone. Pray! The SP could ever have come across what is ordained in *Yajurveda* "May the Lord of Speech make our voice sweet and soft. We should always be soft spoken; doing so would attract all. On the contrary, vitriolic speech keeps people away. This is why one should always be soft spoken so that it enhances brotherhood and affection." To reinforce the police party left at Mohangarh, SHO Jind was told to take with him 10 police personnel with some cooked food for assisting Inspector Jagroop Singh there. I in the meanwhile prepared the FIR.

During house-to-house thorough combing conducted by the Police under Inspector Jagroop Singh at village Mohangarh, 10 persons with multiple injuries and 1 dead body had been recovered. Inspector Jagroop Singh had sent the injured and the dead body to Narwana. By the morning of 8th June, injured/

dead brought to Narwana Hospital included 15 dead and 19 injured out of the tenants group. From the decree holders' side Rattan Singh and Dharam Singh both were dead; Abhey Ram and Bharat Singh were seriously injured.

DM Sangrur accompanied by district SP, Civil Surgeon and a few doctors arrived at Narwana by 11:30 pm. District SP improved upon the FIR prepared by me by introducing two false stories. One was that the Police party mobilized from Jind Police station had also been issued buckshots ammunition chargers. The second was that while dragging ASI Gurdial Singh the rioters had snatched his service revolver. SDM orchestrated a ridiculous drama before the District Magistrate. Weeping and sobbing, he alleged that he had not given any orders to the ASP to open fire on the crowd and that the ASP had threatened him to sign a self prepared note, purportedly an order from me, to open fire and that on his refusal to do that he had further threatened him with dire consequences. On his still refusing to oblige the ASP, he had threatened him with dreadful fate. The district SP started snubbing me. The behaviour of the SDM and the district SP dawned on me a new kind of awakening that I needed to learn to stand on my own and to take care of myself and in the process the sense of safety and security grew in me to become self reliant. I stopped finding fault in the others' shortcomings and human frailties. The utterances of both the SDM and district SP provoked the DM. He immediately intervened asking the SDM to wait in the adjoining room.

The DM in the presence of the district SP asked me to explain the sequence of events. Having heard me, he called Naib Tehsildar Mehar Singh and inquired from him what he had observed at the scene. He told the DM that having seen a large number of villagers armed with *jailies* and *gandasa* etc. coming toward them, the entire Revenue staff had hurriedly collected the revenue records and had taken shelter behind the police bus. The SDM was standing by the side of the ASP. After the Police had started firing the SDM also came running and joined them to take shelter behind the police bus. The DM then called the SDM and warned him in strong words that he should not utter a single word in the matter. His part of the story would be considered next morning when the Chief Secretary, Home Secretary, Divisional Commissioner and IGP would all reach Narwana by then. District SP told me that a large number of police personnel from the adjoining districts would be arriving at Narwana and I should start arranging for their lodging and boarding. During the whole night, I with the help of SHO Narwana, local revenue/BDO staff and some respectable and influential persons of Narwana town, made adequate arrangements.

Senior officers from Divisional/State Hqr arrived in the morning of 8th July. They held a marathon meeting. SDM and I both were called in the meeting later. After hearing us, one by one the Divisional Commissioner told K C Grover, the SDM that he would have to be placed under suspension and legally proceeded against for dereliction of duty. He started crying that his daughters were approaching marriageable age; he would be ruined if such a drastic action was taken against him. He readily agreed to own that he had given orders to the Police to the opening of fire. Ashwni Kumar IP, highly dynamic and strong willed officer was then officiating as State IGP in the absence of the regular State IGP who happened to be on leave. It was he, who was guiding all Police operations after his arrival. He had very strongly snubbed the district SP for introducing into the FIR the story of buck shot ammunition as that ammunition had not been used at all during the firing. He had also strongly advised the district SP to conduct himself sympathetically while communicating any orders etc. to the ASP. The attitude of the IGP and DM Sangrur was highly reassuring and morale boosting for me. At least the district SP from then onwards stopped using rough language while conveying to me any of his orders of dos and don'ts.

By mid-day of 8th June, a large crowd of people from the adjoining area had built up at village Mohangarh. Inder Singh, a communist leader from the area, bitterly opposed to the communist faction led by Pratap Singh Daulata, had given a call to organize a huge demonstration against the Sangrur district Administration on 9th June. By the evening of 8th June, a team of doctors under Dr. Ram Gopal, SMO Incharge Civil Hospital Jind had conducted the postmortem of all the dead bodies. The plan was to cremate the dead at village Mohangarh, on 9th June as no body from village Mohangarh was coming forward to claim and receive the dead bodies. The relations had taken the dead bodies of Rattan Singh and Dharam Singh to their village. On 9th June, the demonstrators came up with the demand that post mortems should be re-conducted by senior doctors totally unconcerned with district Sangrur.

Later in the afternoon, the Home Secretary issued a press note that Government of Punjab had decided to appoint a Judicial Commission of Inquiry and the Government would take strong action against those Civil or Police functionaries indicted by the Commission. The Civil Surgeon of district Ferozepur would conduct the post mortem afresh. On 10th June, a team of Doctors under Civil Surgeon Ferozepur conducted the postmortem afresh at Tarkha Kothi Rest House. By then putrefaction had set in and almost the entire area up to 500 meters, all around was filled with foul smell. I assisted by some 20 police personnel had been deputed by the district SP to guard the area against any attempt by the agitators to grab the dead bodies in pursuit of their declared threat to take the dead bodies to Delhi after the second post mortems was over. However, the dead bodies were taken to village Mohangarh, escorted by a strong Police party, under DSP Malerkotla and cremated there without any significant opposition by the villagers. Punjab Government appointed B L Goswami, District and Sessions Judge Sangrur as one man Commission of Inquiry. He started his job immediately by holding day-to-day proceedings at Sangrur. Investigation of the criminal case FIR No.55 dated 07.06.1960 U/s 302/307/148/149 IPC registered at PS Narwana, was simultaneously taken up by Inspector Jagroop Singh, assisted by SI Sitaram, under my personal supervision.

Agitation launched by the Communists in the wake of this episode, in fact, was to promote their own agenda. It had spread wide, all over Punjab though its main thrust remained confined to district Sangrur only. Akali Party under the leadership of Master Tara Singh also started flexing their muscles to fish in the troubled water and threatened to launch "Punjabi Subba" agitation. Neki Ram of village Dumarkha, a son-in-law of late Sir Chhotu Ram, was a highly respected person of the area. He counselled the villagers to remain peaceful and wait patiently for the outcome of the Inquiry by the Goswami Commission. His sane advice had good effect on the villagers and they became somewhat indifferent to the provocative measures advocated by Inder Singh, the Communist Leader. This was, indeed, a very welcome development.

Sardar Gurdial Singh IP, a Punjab cadre officer then a Joint Director in the Intelligence Bureau, Government of India was drafted to take over as IGP Punjab. He was reputed to be a hard taskmaster. Unfortunately, the new IGP had a preconceived notion that Sangrur District Administration had seriously faulted in dealing with the situation at Mohangarh. I was often conveyed by many police officers that IGP while addressing meetings of District SPs, Range wise, had been saying that officers like Swan who faulted in handling situation at Mohangarh would be severely punished after receipt of the Commission's Inquiry Report. However, I mentioned to a senior IPS Officer my apprehension that such utterance by the IGP might prove to be detrimental to my interest because of the pending inquiry by the Commission. On his advice, I sought an interview with Giani Kartar Singh, then Revenue Minister Punjab and explained to him my apprehension. This worked. The Minister assured me that neither I would be transferred nor any action would be taken against me till the outcome of not only the Inquiry Report of Goswami Commission but also after the final verdict of the trial court, in the criminal case against the rioters. I felt relieved and relaxed.

The Punjab Government appointed a senior advocate practicing in the Punjab High Court to represent the State Government and Sangrur District Administration et al, before the Goswami Inquiry Commission. He was assisted by local Government pleaders. The Judgment debtors i.e. the tenants group had engaged a battery of senior advocates. The decree holders headed by Pratap Singh Daulata, himself an advocate, had also come up with a battery of advocates as Third Party. My examination-in-chief lasted for two days followed by the cross examinations for three days by the battery of advocates representing the Judgment debtors and the decree holders. I had to discharge twin duty of mobilizing adequate evidence in support of our stand before the Goswami Commission of Inquiry and also to ensure that the Investigation of the case FIR No.55 dated 07.06.1960 was conducted speedily, in a fool proof way.

Report of Goswami Commission of Inquiry

The Commission presented its Report of Inquiry to the Government some time in September 1960. Investigation into the case FIR No.55 dated 07.06.1960 was also completed in due course of time and 39 accused persons were sent up to face trial by the District and Session Judge Sangrur. Shri BR Dhameja Additional Session Judge Sangrur conducted the trial. The Goswami Commission of Inquiry made the following observations regarding the use of force by the police:

Page 236 *(Para No. 537)* "In the instant case, I find that the rioters had adopted a very defiant posture and paid no heed either to the presence of a large police force, heavily armed with lathies, muskets and rifles, and the show of their force or to the lathi charge or even to the firing opened by the police until the firing became heavy and they felt that the police actually meant business. There is nothing to show that the firing done by the police was more than the exigencies of the matter required. There is no evidence that the mob started melting away before the last firing of 14 rounds. It cannot be said that the firing was either unjustified or excessive. But what I would like to say in this connection is that if the district authorities had been in possession of a tear smoke squad and had taken the same to the spot and used it, in all probability they would have been able to avoid the use of force by lathi charge or opening of fire. It is however on the record that the district authorities had no tear gas equipment with them and that is why it was not taken to the spot."

Page 236 *(Para No. 538)* "The learned counsel for the State argued that there is no requirement of law or the rules that tear gas must be employed in the first instance. There is certainly no mention of any tear gas in Rule No.14.56 of the Punjab Police Rules. My attention has not been invited to any statutory provisions of law or of any statutory rule or even of any departmental instructions on the point. It would, of course, be plain common sense that the tear gas squad should be used, if it can be made available, because that is a harmless and effective way of dispersing a crowd."

Trial of Accused in Case FIR No.55 Dated 07.06.1960

During the trial the prosecution presented the same facts and the same State witnesses before the trial court, to prove the State case, as presented before the Goswami Commission of Inquiry. On consideration of the evidence, Shri BR Dhameja Additional Session Judge Sangrur who tried the case found the prosecution case substantially proved and rejected the plea of the accused of their right of private defence. He held that there was an unlawful assembly with common object of murdering Rattan Singh and others, that in prosecution of this common object, offences U/s 304 part-II read with section 149 were committed by members of the assembly by causing the death of Rattan Singh and Dharam Singh and that offences U/s 326, 324 and 323 IPC were also committed in pursuance of the common object. He further found proved that 10 accused who were members of that assembly and had committed rioting having been armed with dangerous weapons. These 10 accused had been found lying at the scene of crime and being injured, could not run away. Accordingly he convicted all of them, for the offences U/s 148 IPC and also two offences U/s 304 part-II read with section 149 and U/s 326/149, 324/149 and 323/149. For each of the offences U/s 304 part-II, read with section 149, he sentenced these 10 accused to rigorous imprisonments for seven years each. Lesser sentences were passed under the other offences and all the sentences were directed to run concurrently. As regards the other 29 accused the Additional Session Judge held that their membership of the unlawful assembly had not been proved beyond doubt and accordingly acquitted them. Regarding the prosecution story about snatching away the revolver of ASI Gurdial Singh by the rioters the defence counsel had posed a position as to why the revolver from ASI Gurdial Singh was snatched, if it was not to be used at all by the rioters. The trial court held that the use of the snatched revolver by the rioters could not be the only object behind their snatching. The ASI might as well have been relieved of this weapon to deprive him of its use against the rioters. Concerning the recovery of the revolver on the next morning, it was argued by the defence counsel that it was difficult to believe that when the police and other witnesses had been within a few feet of the place of recovery on the evening of the occurrence, they were not able to spot it out then. The court observed that there was nothing to suggest that it was visible from the place, to which they had been on the preceding evening. Moreover there was nothing to be gained by the prosecution in putting forth the story of snatching the revolver and its subsequent recovery. Regarding the quality of the investigation, the trial court remarked, "There is, therefore, nothing inherent in the FIR to suggest that the prosecution story is concocted one." Regarding the non-official state witnesses named Iqbal Singh, Munshi Ram and Diwan Singh the trial court described Iqbal Singh and Diwan Singh as category-4 witnesses and remarked that "The two witnesses comprised in the fourth set are truly independent and at the same time respectable. The father of Iqbal Singh PW-9 is a numberdar and he is his attorney. Diwan Singh PW-10 is himself a numbardar of Bithmara village. The former is also a gun license holder. There is nothing improbable in the two of them having been joined by the police party before starting from Narwana. The possibility of some thing untoward happening was there and the presence of some responsible non-official was therefore, highly desirable. It was argued by the learned counsel for the accused that in view of the position they held, pressure could be put on these two non-official witnesses. However, there was hardly any room for that. The witnesses had already been named in the FIR, which was lodged at latest by midnight falling the evening of the occurrence. ——— The attestation by these witnesses and the memos concerning recovery of weapon of offence prepared at the spot immediately after the occurrence and of the memos by means of which ASP took into custody the empties from the musket men amply established that these two witnesses were present at the scene of occurrence when it took place. ——— neither of them in spite of their official position was shown to be a stock witnesses ——— the two witnesses belong to two different villages which are nowhere near to the accused." The trial court had not accepted the plea of the defence counsel that the warrants issued by the court for delivery of the possession of the lands to the decree holders had ceased to be executable on 7th June, 1960 as date of execution had expired in early April, 1960. However, the court did not find this plea of the defence to justify their forming unlawful assembly duly armed with weapons and attacking the decree holders.

These 10 convicted accused persons appealed against their conviction and sentence to the High Court of Punjab. The State of Punjab also filed an appeal against them on the ground that they should have been convicted U/s 302 read with section 149 and not merely U/s 304 Part-II, read with section 149. The High Court agreed with the Session Judge's findings and dismissed the appeal of the accused and the appeal of the State of Punjab.

The 10 convicted accused persons presented their appeal (Cr. Appeal No. 93 of 1962) to the Supreme Court of India, by special leave of that Court. State of Punjab also filed an appeal to the Supreme Court of India, by special leave (Cr. Appeal No. 142 of 1962), against the decision of the High Court that offences U/s 302 read with section 149 had not been proved. The main contention raised before the Supreme Court in support of the appeal of the 10 convicted accused person was that in law no unlawful assembly was formed in as much as Rattan Singh and others who went to the field were guilty of criminal trespass and it would be reasonable to hold that the villagers who had assembled there had only the object of defending their property against such trespass and no object to commit the offences as alleged. In contending that the acts of Rattan Singh and others amounted to criminal trespass, the learned counsel for the 10 convicted accused persons had stressed the fact that the last date for execution of the warrants for delivery of possession was some time in April, 1960 so on June 07, 1960 they were not executable by law. The trial court had also not accepted the contention of the defence that the warrants had ceased to be executable before June 07, 1960 and Punjab High Court had agreed with it. The Supreme Court also held that there was no doubt about the correctness of the view taken by the courts below as that was supported by a long line of decisions of all the High Courts in India.

The above view notwithstanding, the Supreme Court of India decided to examine this contentious issue in depth in the light of the provisions of rule 24 and 25 of order 21 of the Code of Civil Procedure. The question before the court was whether Rattan Singh and others, while entering the lands of which possession was to be taken under the warrants, were committing the offence of criminal trespass, as this was the main point being stressed by the defence counsel. In the course of detailed examination of the defence plea, the Supreme Court finally held that in order to establish that the entry on the property by the decree holders was with the intent to annoyances, intimidation or insult, it is necessary for the court to be satisfied that causing such annoyances, intimidation or insult was the aim of the entry, that it was not sufficient for that purpose to show merely that the natural consequences of the entry was likely to be annoyances, intimidation or insult and that this likely consequence was known to the persons entering, that in deciding whether the aim of the entry was the causing of such annoyances etc., the court has to consider all the relevant circumstances including the presence of knowledge that its natural consequences would be such annoyances etc., being the dominant intention which prompted the entry. Applying these principles to the facts of the case under their examination the Apex Court held "We are satisfied that the courts below are right in holding that Rattan Singh and others have not been shown to have had the intention to annoyance. It may be true that they knew that annoyances would result. Armed as they were with the warrants of execution it is reasonable to think however that the intention, which prompted and dominated their action, was to execute the warrants. We think also that the courts below were right to their view that Rattan Singh and others could not be reasonably expected to know that the warrants had ceased to be executable in law. Taking all the circumstances into consideration we have come to the conclusion that the courts below were right in their view that criminal trespass was not committed or apprehended from the acts of Rattan Singh and others who entered the property and rightly rejected the defence plea that the object of those who assembled was to defend the property against trespass. There was therefore no difficulty in holding that the assembly of the villagers was an unlawful assembly with the common object of killing Rattan Singh and others who wanted to dispossess them."

The apex court did not agree with the contention raised on behalf of the State that offences U/s 302 IPC were committed by causing the death of Rattan Singh and Dharam Singh. Their conclusion was that the appellants had been rightly convicted U/s 304 part-II, read with section 149, section 326/ 149, 324/149 IPC. Regarding the submission by the appellants that the sentences passed were too severe, the apex court held that "The question of sentences is in the discretion of the Trial Court and would not ordinarily be disturbed by the High Court in appeal if it has been exercised judicially. There is still less reason ordinarily for this court to interfere with sentences passed by the Trial Court and confirmed by the High Court. It is difficult to say however, that in the present case the discretion on the question of sentences has been exercised judicially. It cannot be over looked that of these 10 appellants, 6 are women and 4 men. No specific part has been allotted to these women. It is reasonable to think in all the circumstances of the case that they did not take a leading part in the occurrence but came into the fields to save their men, when they came out to save their fields." In the peculiar circumstances of the case, the Apex Court thought it proper to interfere on the quantum of sentences passed against the women who had already served out more than two years and nine months of the sentences and thus reduce the sentences on the women appellants to the period of imprisonment already undergone. Regarding 4 male appellants, 2 of them being in their sixties and seventies, the court thought that the interest of Justice would be served if their sentences were also reduced to the period of imprisonment already undergone and ordered accordingly. Regarding the other two male appellants the Apex Court did not find any reason to interfere with the sentences passed on them by the Trial Court and confirmed by the High Court.

Action Taken on the Report of Goswami Commission of Inquiry

The Goswami Commission submitted its Inquiry Report to the government some time in September 1960. The Punjab Government presented the said report in the State Assembly during late 1964. The State Assembly duly discussed the Report and found that the action taken by the State Government was satisfactory.

It needs to be reiterated here that it was all because of the egoistic approach of Dalip Singh, the District SP that he had introduced the stories of police party coming from Jind, carrying some chargers of buckshot ammunition and the snatching away of the revolver of ASI Gurdial Singh by the members of the mob; it was because of his evil intention to harm my interest somehow, embedded deep into his psyche, that I got a warning from the Government, for no fault on my part. I was satisfied that even at the threshold of my career I handled the entire very complex episode, including investigation and successful prosecution of the case, in a reasonably creditable manner.

Epilogue of Mohangarh Chhapra Episode

All that has been stated in connection with this episode notwithstanding at the end of the day whenever this episode has ever come to my mind, during my entire service career, even after retirement, until date, I feel sad that so many people were killed and injured. Because of my background and bringing up, I have got deeply ingrained in my mind that poor and hapless people should always be helped to get justice in this vile world. The tenants involved in the episode were poor and hapless. Because of the harshness of the law, I had to perform my duty as per the Law Book. As a commoner, however, I sincerely have been feeling throughout that even if the law was against the tenants who were in possession of the land for three generations, they should not have been dispossessed of the lands. Ours is a welfare State, therefore, the State should have come forward to acquire the lands in question and then hand over with ownership possession to the tenants on easy payment of installments of the expended amount. Alas! It did not happen, not even thought of by anybody.

Rape Case against Relatives of Dalip Singh, the Distt SP, Sangrur

I had received a complaint from Surta, son of Chandgi, caste Dhanak (scheduled caste) of village Bhimeva, PS Safidon. He had alleged in the complaint that his wife Shanti, aged about 20 years had been kidnapped and raped by four persons, residents of village Kila Zaffargarh, PS Julana. He pinpointed the accused as Ramdia son of Devidas, Sudhun son of Harnam both Dhanak by caste, Bhim Singh son of Sis Ram and Sube Singh son of Bhim Singh, both Jat by caste. He also accused Manohar constable of PS Julana as their accomplice. Bhim Singh and Sube Singh were in the liquor business and were notorious for indulging in malpractices linked with this business. Surta had also sent telegraphic complaint to state IGP and district SP Sangrur in this regard. Complaints received by state IGP and district SP Sangrur had come to me for inquiry.

During the course of village touring, I happened to be in village Bhimeva, PS Safidon, on 08.11.1960. In connection with the complaint of Surta, both he and his wife Shanti were summoned to the village school where I had called various persons including the respectable of the village, for interaction with them. The statements of Surta and his wife Shanti were recorded in the presence of village respectable persons. Both of them reiterated the allegations of kidnapping and raping of Shanti by the persons as mentioned in their earlier complaints. Since I had also received Surta's telegraphic complaint addressed to state IGP and district SP Sangrur for inquiry I did not straight away register the FIR against the accused persons. I thought it appropriate to send my inquiry report to the district SP Sangrur, particularly in view of the fact that two alleged accused Bhim Singh and Sube Singh happened to be close relatives of a real brother of district SP Sangrur. I had concluded my inquiry report with specific comments that criminal case U/s 366/376 IPC was made out from the statements of Surta and his wife Shanti. My inquiry report dated 08.11.1960 submitted to district SP Sangrur was received back by me with his hand written endorsement dated 16.11.1960 "Please register a case and investigate personally." Accordingly a criminal case FIR No. 64 dated 18.11.1960 U/s 366/368/376 IPC was registered.

The investigation of this case was started by me personally as per order of SP. Though the SP had ordered for the registration of the criminal case, yet he got conveyed to me his strong annoyance through Sunder Lal Malik Inspector CIA, alleging manipulation on my part in booking his own relatives

– Bhim Singh and Sube Singh, in a serious sex crime with a biased mind. Let it not be skipped that Sunder Lal Malik Inspector CIA, a Punjabi displaced person from West Punjab used to enjoy extra patronage of the district SP. At least two SHOs of Police Stations falling in Jind Sub-Division had told me that Sunder Lal Malik would come to them in the first week of every month and pressurize them to give him money for purposes stated by him, which appeared to be dubious. I had called Inspector Malik and had reprimanded him. I had strongly told him that as and when he ever visited any Police Station in Jind Sub-Division, he would invariably come and discuss with me the purpose of his visit. Despite the annoyance of the SP, I continued with the investigation of the case quite unruffled, to complete it at the earliest.

All the accused persons were arrested and after two days custodial investigation, the local Court at Jind remanded them to judicial custody for a fortnight. Shri J B Garg, Judicial Magistrate, Jind lived in a house opposite to that of mine. District SP thought that the Magistrate being my immediate neighbour and having friendly relation with me would, perhaps, honour my personal request and grant bail to the accused persons. He, therefore, was extra friendly while asking me to prevail upon the Magistrate to grant bail to Bhim Singh and Sube Singh. Honestly speaking, I made a strong personal request to the Magistrate. However, he smilingly put me off telling me that every official high and low in the Sub-Division had known well, how crudely and rudely, the district SP had been behaving to harm the ASP during Mohangarh firing episode. Regarding granting bail to Bhim Singh and Sube Singh, he said that let them apply for the bail and he would consider their plea keeping in view the facts of the case as emerged from the investigation carried out till then. I told the district SP that I had played my part honestly in talking to the Magistrate and he did not make any encouraging commitment. District SP wrongly thought that I had cheated him. He used abusive language while talking to me on the telephone. "Silence is the best eloquence" and "Silence is deep as Eternity, speech is shallow at times." Therefore, my silence perhaps further disturbed his blood pressure. He raised the pitch of his bitter yelling. I remained unruffled. Perhaps completely exhausted he banged the telephone, thus, stopping his vituperative howling. From 17th November to 23rd November, 1960, I had prepared 6 case diaries and the facts brought on the file reflected strong case against all the accused persons. Soon rumours started floating that ASP was likely to be transferred shortly. However, I continued with the task of completing the investigation of this case and attending to my other duties as Sub-Divisional Police Officer with a cool mind. Within next two days, I almost completed the investigation. In all, I had prepared 8 case diaries. Lo! I got order from IGP Punjab, transferring me from Jind and posting me as ASP Sub-Division Sirsa of District Hisar. I relinquished the charge as ASP Sub-Division Jind on 02.12.1960 quietly and felt highly relieved and relaxed. At least there will not be any more mental agony, which I had to face often because of the ungentlemanly nay, uncouth language of the boss. It has not been in my nature, at any stage of my life to accept unchallenged, any excesses and injustice. I have always liked to play with fire while fighting for justice. However, in every day life, a time comes when the eloquence of silence and quietly letting the storm pass over, are used as effective weapons. Leaving

Jind was one such occasion which I thought to be the most welcome riddance. However, before leaving Jind I put a call to Dalip Singh the district SP to say just for formality sake "Thank you Sir for all the guidance given to me. However, my instinct of self-respect did force me also to say, "Sir, I have learnt while working with you, not to lose poise even in the face of worst provocation."

After I left Jind, Inspector Jagroop Singh was ordered by the district SP to take over the investigation of the rape case. One can easily imagine what sort of fate this crime and its victim would have met, with district SP himself being deeply interested in the two accused who happened to be the close relations of his real brother. Poor depressed class people, like Surta and Shanti, have been crying hoarse for centuries to get Justice, which has been eluding them in this vile world, dominated by the rogues, as in the instant case.

As Incharge Sub-Division Sirsa of District Hisar

I joined at Sirsa on 5th December 1960. Sub-Division Sirsa of District Hisar was the largest in Composite Punjab State. It had six Police Stations- Fatehabad (Fatehabad has since become the headquarter of a full-fledged district.), Sirsa, Rania, Badaguda, City Dawbali and Sadar Dawbali. Sirsa town was of medium size. After Independence, it had become the abode of quite a few *Raees* (aristocratic) families. They were allotted big chunks of agricultural land, earlier owned by Muslims who had migrated to Pakistan. These *Raees* families had come from West Punjab after leaving behind similar big agricultural farms. The Office-cum-residence of the Sub-Divisional Police Officer used to be an old big residential building owned by the Railways. Since I had earlier served as ASP at Hisar for about five months, I was quite familiar with the district level administration. T S Sachdeva IPS 1948-RR was still the district SP. Prem Kumar IAS, earlier the Deputy Commissioner at Hisar had been replaced by Iqbal Singh IAS. I paid courtesy calls to all the senior officers at the district level. After getting instructions from the district SP, I settled down to attend to the routine affairs of the sub-division.

Village Chautala, a Centre of Politics

The biggest village in the sub-division, Chautala had acquired significant political importance. Devi Lal who at the peak of his political career had reached almost the highest position in the political ladder as Deputy Prime Minister of India, belonged to this village. He was, during those days still on the threshold of his tumultuous political career, though he had already carved out an important niche for himself, in the political scenario of the Punjab State. He had held the assignment as Chief Parliamentary Secretary in the Kairon Government of Punjab. He had later fallen out with Pratap Singh Kairon, the Chief Minister of Punjab, on some political issues. He had thus become estranged and a rebel leader in the State Congress Party. A very tall, over-awing personality, he was reputed in the area to be a very big landlord, somewhat egoistic, highly self respecting and still holding radically socialistic views for which reasons he seemed to be in the making of an icon of the State peasantry. His estrangement with Pratap Singh Kairon had in fact, added to his political stature, earning for him the reputation of being a fearless fighter for a public cause. His elder brother Sahib Ram, apparently a mild mannered person was a seasoned politician and a well-known political figure of the area. He used to visit me often. Due to his sweet nature, he would instantly develop a good rapport with any officer. Village Chautala was considered to be a synonym of the brood of the father of Sahib Ram-Devi Lal.

Rape Case in Village Chautala

A case FIR No 148 dated 20.11.1960 U/s 376 IPC, PS Dabwali, from village Chautala was pending under investigation, before my taking over charge of this sub-division. The accused in this case was a young man named Om Prakash son of Mani Ram Jat, a collateral of Sahib Ram-Devi Lal. I found that the local police had been avoiding arresting the accused person because of his high links. Exactly similar was the situation in case FIR No.64 dated 17.11.1960 U/s 376, 366 and 368 IPC PS Safidon of sub-division Jind in which I had to incur the wrath of district SP Sangrur for following the Rule of Law, because accused persons happened to be related to district SP.

A few days after I settled down, Sahib Ram came to me and pleaded that the allegations of rape were baseless and rape story had been falsely concocted against Om Parkash. I, therefore, decided to look into the matter. I found that the allegation of rape was very true and in fact, the accused person accompanied by some goons carrying firearms, had been threatening the kith and kin of the rape victim with dire consequences if the complaint of rape allegation was not withdrawn. I had to tell the SHO to affect immediately, the arrest of the accused and put up a report recommending the suspension of firearms licenses granted to all persons friendly to the accused. The SHO came into swift action. Sahib Ram came to me and pleaded that the accused person would surrender before me. In the meanwhile, SHO submitted his recommendation for the suspension of the firearms licenses of about half a dozen persons including the accused. Their weapons were got deposited in the Police Station. A report was, sent to district SP Hisar for taking up the matter with DC Hisar. Sahib Ram approached SP Hisar and DC Hisar, but they declined to restore the firearms.

It was during those days that Devi Lal a stormy petrel of Punjab politics came to meet me. I was then playing Badminton, in the Railway Officers' Club, in sports dress after office hours. I met Chaudhary Sahib in the club lawn. He seemed to be in hurry. He told me during his brief meeting with me that "Sahib Ram was impressed with your straight forward and strong willed nature and therefore, I had thought it appropriate to see you in person." Then in a stance of self-importance, he said, "I have never gone to meet any sub-divisional officer and it was in your case only that I had made any exception." Then moving to go away, he said "*Achha bhai, mazbooti se kam karo*." He had gone away before I could pick up any word to say anything. He neither asked for any favour nor made even an oblique reference to the police action in the rape case and seizing of weapons of all persons connected with the accused. The incident left me guessing that the purpose of his meeting me was, perhaps, to make me to realize that he was of too high a stature to make any direct reference to the rape case and that I should remember that there was some body very big related to the accused person. In any case, I was highly impressed with his body language and the plethora of ideas conveyed to me in his surprisingly brief solo talk. Sahib Ram had also not shown any sign of annoyance for the strong police action in the rape case and its follow on. When he met me next after Devi Lal's brief meeting with me in the Railways Officers Club, he only told me that, "Devi Lal never goes to any officer even at the district headquarter and he is always very brief in his talk." These two stalwarts of village Chautala, despite being very big land holders of the area did not flaunt any feudal disposition. Meeting them left a deep healthy mark on my mind.

In the rape case, the law had taken its own course. The accused had been sent up for trial by the court on 13.01.1961. Their licenced weapons were later restored to them under the order of Divisional Commissioner, except that of Om Prakash, the accused in the rape case. Sahib Ram had continued meeting me often, as cheerfully as ever before, with no sign of any annoyance against me for my role while dealing with rape case against his collateral Om Prakash.

In the Criminal Justice System, the investigating officer is the pace maker of Justice that is delivered by the courts. The job of the investigating officer is to probe a case diligently and impartially and ward off pressure from various quarters to present a watertight case and bring guilty to the book. However, whenever an investigating officer nets a big fish, there is sure to be a drama. Exactly I saw a drama staged in this case but this drama was different from the one, which I had seen in the rape case of Police Station Safidon of Jind sub-division, discussed earlier. In both the cases, the accused persons coming from jat community had strong links and the victims were poor women from the depressed caste. I disappointedly observed that in both the cases the accused had successfully manipulated pressure on the victims to back track from their stands as reported in the FIR and as stated before the investigating officer. Thus, the Justice was, throttled at the delivery stage of the Criminal Justice System. There have been an infinite number of rape cases in India, in which the victims coming from depressed poor classes have failed to get justice because of the accused persons having muscle power and the money power to manipulate the things in their favour. It would not be incorrect to say that ours is still an uncivilized society.

My Sufferings for Faith in Superstition

I had two daughters while still struggling to acquire a foothold during my "Learning and Earning" days. My wife was again expecting. My mother had then solemnly prayed to pay obeisance at Harmandir Sahib Amritsar and Dera Baba Vadbhag Singh, together with all family members, if my wife were blessed with the male child. It was during my posting at Sirsa that my mother planned to take the family members to Dera Baba Vadbhag Singh. Our son born after our two daughters was then about 4 years old. This Dera in fact is Gurudwara Manji Sahib located on Una-Hamirpur (Himachal Pradesh) Road 30 km from Una. It was founded by Baba Vadbhag Singh who moved to this place after Mughal invasions destroyed his traditional seat at Kartarpur Sahib (Punjab). As per the myth, Baba Vadbhag Singh controlled the powerful spirits in the area. The most powerful spirit of the area was believed to be Nahar Singh. A large number of people from rural Punjab visit the Gurudwara to ward off the effect of evil spirits on their near and dear ones. Those with faith believed that bath under the fall (known as Dhauli Dhar) at the Dera would cure all ailments. A stream was also flowing there in which the pilgrims used to undergo a dip and would drink some draughts of flowing water. I was averse to drink from the flowing stream water taking it to be unhygienic. However, my mother's decision being final I had to take many sips.

Next day in the morning, I had suffered severe infection in my throat and other parts of the body. I had to return to Sirsa together with my family as my casual leave was expiring. On reaching Sirsa the infection had further spread over my entire body. Doctor in the Government Civil Dispensary at Sirsa gave me penicillin injection. During those times penicillin used to be the panacea for all sorts of infection. However, I was allergic to the drug called penicillin. My condition deteriorated. My face had swollen, accompanied by acute pain, rendering me unable to speak and even sip any liquid, much less to swallow any solid. Food is the fuel of life. From it comes energy, which sustains life. Since being unable to sip and swallow anything, loss of energy in the body started affecting very adversely my general state of health. There was a panic in my family. A rumour was afloat in Sirsa town that ASP was poisoned by some body. District SP and DC Hisar accompanied by Civil Surgeon and SMO from Hisar Civil Hospital came to my place to take care of me. The doctor who had given injection to me had gone to Shimla for holidaying. Being unable to speak and writhing in pain, I could not convey that the doctor had given penicillin injection to me. The doctor holidaying in Shimla was called back by DC Hissar with the help of DC Shimla. Civil Surgeon Hisar having talked to the doctor at Shimla on telephone started treating me with anti-allergy drugs. It took me a fortnight to be out of the woods. Since I had become speechless for about a week, my beard had remained unshaven and my face was laden with scars caused by rashes, my little son had started fearing my look. Mr. Pathania PCS was SDM Sirsa. This sweet couple persuaded my wife to take me along with them to see a movie in the city as that would have cheering effect on me. We all four were in the cinema hall. Then a very popular movie "Devdas" with equally popular actor Dilip Kumar in the lead role was being screened. The movie being screened was a tragedy. Dilip Kumar with ruffled hair on the head and unshaven face embraced death at the door steps of his love. As this scene appeared on the screen, my wife, who was then five months' pregnant shrieked in panic and fainted, making the Pathanias and me highly panicky and worried. However, she soon recovered. By the time we reached back our residence, she suffered profuse bleeding leading to aborting a five-month-old still male fetus. She remained on the sick bed for more than a month. According to my mother's faith all the sufferings caused to the family were due to my displaying aversion to drink water from the flowing stream at Dera Vadbhag Singh. I did not question her wisdom, but vowed never to take chance of consuming anything under any circumstances, which I would believe to be unhygienic.

Towards the close of May 1961, I was transferred and posted as ASP Hqr District Ferozepur.

As ASP Hqrs, District Ferozepur

Police setup of District Ferozepur

I joined as ASP Hqrs District Ferozepur on 30.05.1961. District Ferozepur Police Chief was designated as Senior Superintendent of Police (SSP). Geographically very large, having long borders with Pakistan, this border district was very important from crime point of view. It had two very big sub-divisions– Fazilka and Moga, each having an SDM on the civil side and a Dy SP as sub-divisional police officer. Muktsar was only a civil sub-division. Only one Dy SP at the district Hqr was functioning as officer-in-charge of two Police Stations, apart from doing some office work. My charter of duties included charge of the police lines, assisting SP Hqrs in looking after English branch and Accounts branch, apart from supervisory charge of Police Stations Ghal Khurd, Zira and Makhu. SP Hqrs had also supervisory charge of PS City Ferozepur. Three Police stations, Ferozepur Cantonment, Muktsar and Lambi were under the direct supervision of the SSP. However, in all heinous crime cases in these Police Stations, I was assigned the task of supervising the investigation at the initial stages by visiting the scene of crime.

S N Mathur IPS (1948-RR) was the SSP. An upright, honest and highly professional in dealing with crime, criminals and the public at large, S N Mathur was a highly respected officer. I owe a lot to him in developing requisite taste for getting into the minor details of everything coming in my way, in the discharge of official responsibilities. Shri Mathur reached the pinnacle of his career as Director Intelligence Bureau – a highly coveted post and a sweet dream of every IPS Officer. Shri Mathur held this apex post in the police hierarchy during the days of Emergency of 1975-76 and the Janata Party rule of 1977-79. Baljit Rai (1954-RR) was Superintendent of Police looking after the long Indo-Pak border from the point touching Amritsar district on one side and Rajasthan on the other side. Baljit Rai, a very upright, honest and straightforward police officer, was reputed to be fearlessly calling spade a spade. He used to treat the junior IPS Officers like younger brothers with profound affection. He was later transferred and posted as Superintendent of Police District Hisar, an important charge by all standards. His place as SP Border Ferozepur was taken by V K Kalia, IPS, a batch mate of Baljit Rai. Balwant Singh, an ex-PEPSU police officer was SP Hqrs. A thorough gentle man and kindhearted person, he had very amiable disposition. SJB Ohri a young spirited and boisterous Probationary Dy SP was often, detailed by the SSP to accompany me during my supervisory visits to scene of heinous crime cases for initial investigation. Bhim Singh IAS (PCS) was Deputy Commissioner and Gurdev Singh, PCS was Additional Deputy Commissioner; both of them were gentle men par excellence.

Later Kuldip Singh Virk, PCS, a very resourceful person replaced Gurdev Singh. Virk was later inducted into the IAS and after retirement was made Chairman, Punjab Public Service Commission. Bhim Singh was a fatherly figure and was very affectionate to the junior officers. His wife, a typical Haryanavi grand old lady would shower all love and affection on us whenever I and my wife went to their residence for social calls. I sweetly remember the

Holi festival of 1962 when she and her young married daughter drenched me with coloured water and rained on me lashes of wet whip improvised from jute string. I had to run for my life seeking shelter behind Bhim Singh. The old man was a great lover of bottle. He promised me protection provided I took half a glass of neat whisky in one go. Under duress, which in fact was a sweet and affectionate gesture in celebration of festival of colours, I submitted to his sweet dictate and escaped from further lashes at the hand of sweet and affectionate woman. Soon I got drunk and started staggering in my gait. It was a moment of great fun and hilarious laughter in unison by everybody amongst the Holi revelers. I have always sweetly remembered Bhim Singh couple with high regard. I thoroughly enjoyed my duty in very congenial and affable environment around, during my entire stay at Ferozepur and learnt many an innovative skill in the realm of professionalism.

Murder Case in Village Phoolewala, PS Muktsar

A murder case was reported from village Phoolewala, PS Muktsar. This was an interesting episode – a complex riddle requiring extra professional skill. Village Phoolewala was notorious for two very hostile warring groups of jat sikhs. Sham Singh Brar led one such group and Balwant Singh was patronizing the other. There was a history of committing murders and counter murders in retaliation between these two groups. Sham Singh the ringleader of one group, had earlier been murdered while present in Muktsar town on an errand. His dead body continued lying at the scene of crime for quite some time, such was the terror created by the perpetrators of crime. After Sham Singh's murder, his son Bharpur Singh, the only one in the family who had studied up to Matriculation, had become the group leader. Both Balwant Singh and Bharpur Singh would not themselves participate in the crime. Instead, they would cleverly use their supporters including Mazhbi Sikhs (scheduled caste) to commit the crime. While lodging FIR, both warring groups would introduce some innocent persons who mattered in the opposite group so that they remained confined to the Jail and the real culprits left out to quench the thirst for wreaking revenge. Indeed a maliciously mischievous tactic designed to mislead the Police from the time of lodging the FIR itself.

A person from the group of Balwant Singh had been murdered by the group led by Bharpur Singh. After committing the murder, the dead body was tied with a rope and pulled with the help of a tractor through the main streets of the village abusing, threatening and terrorizing the people by the armed goons. The village streets presented horrible scene of blood trails and pieces of human flesh were scattered all around. The dead body had been later set on fire in the main chowk of the village. As usual, in this case also, one innocent person had been introduced while lodging FIR. When I reached the village, the SHO with adequate Police force was already camping in the village and the scene of crime had been guarded for my inspection. I found that the village presented a scene of utter silence of the grave. In fact, the villagers were so terrified that they had shut themselves inside their houses. Combing of every house of the village was undertaken with a view to seize licenced/illicit firearms.

As a confidence building measure, all the male persons present in the village were collected at one place and open investigation was conducted including the recording of statements U/s 161 Cr PC. The witnesses either supporting the FIR or describing it as a pack of distorted facts were examined in the open. Most of the prominent persons from the accused party had disappeared from the village. However, I got convinced that one person mentioned in the FIR, as an accused, had been falsely implicated; this was however, subject to the verification of the alibi plea advanced by the accused party. I spent the whole day in the village. Balwant Singh and Bharpur Singh appeared, one after the other, after three hours of my reaching the village. They both had their own excuses, claiming that they were not in the village when the murder took place. I sternly told both of them that they would be put behind the bars if they did not stop indulging in lawlessness. I also warned all the persons present there that a permanent punitive police post would be set up at village Phoolewala soon to keep the wayward conduct of anti-social elements in check and that the punitive police post shall be entirely at the cost of the residents of the village.

The SHO had informed me that one accused person, as per the FIR was stated to be with Sardar Harcharan Singh Brar of village Sarai Naga. Brar was the son-in-law of Sardar Jaswant Singh an elder brother of Sardar Pratap Singh Kairon, the then Chief Minister of Punjab. Despite his high political influence Brar, a very big landholder of Ferozepur district was reputed to be a thorough gentle man with no feudal ego. (Harcharan Singh Brar had later become the Chief Minister of Punjab and Governor of Orissa and of Haryana for some time).

Leaving SHO to continue with the investigation at village Phoolewala, I went to village Sarai Naga to meet Sardar Harcharan Singh Brar. He was living in royal style in his palatial bungalow. There was a long queue of visitors to see him because of his high political status. As soon as he learnt about my arrival at his residence to meet him, he immediately came out to receive me as if I was an honoured guest. He entertained me lavishly with all sorts of evening delicacies. I told him that I was returning from village Phoolewala whereto I had gone in connection with the investigation of a murder case and thought of paying a courtesy call to him. Intervening immediately, he said, "Swan Sahib a person accused in that murder case was with me at the time of commission of murder." Feigning surprise, I told him that one word from a highly respectable person like him would save the innocent person from the gallows. He promptly said that he would not go to any court to depose as a witness. I changed the topic and after staying with him for half an hour, I left for Ferozepur.

As per the orders of the then IGP, Gurdial Singh IP, every gazzetted officer visiting the scene of any heinous crime like murder, dacoity and robbery et al was required to record a detailed case diary of the investigation conducted by him. A copy of such a case diary was to be sent to the IGP for his perusal. Therefore, I had recorded a detail case diary and handed over its two copies to the SSP next morning. The SSP having thoroughly perused the case diary called me. Appreciating the labour put in by me, he advised me to convert the conversation that had taken place between Sardar Harcharan Singh Brar and me into his statement U/s 161 Cr PC. I did the same. Next day Sardar Harcharan Singh Brar came down to Ferozepur, met the SSP and anxiously inquired from him if the ASP had actually avoided any mention of his telling the ASP that one person accused in the FIR was with him at the time of commission of the murder. The SSP smilingly told him that there could be no wrong if the ASP had mentioned that fact in the case diary. Brar Sahib pleaded with the SSP that he would not depose in any court as witness for any party as that would tarnish his image as an impartial person in the area. However, the SSP put him off in his usual known style of a non-committal officer. Brar Sahib then came to my room and told me smilingly that I was unfair to him by recording his informal conversation with me during my visit to his residence. I very politely told him that I had to do that only to uphold the Rule of Law. However, the SSP later assured me that he would himself take care of that matter.

In the said murder case, the person whom I had described as falsely implicated was so described while putting the case in the court. The name of said accused person was however, mentioned in column no. 2 of the challan form. The Sessions Court acquitted him honourably. The real accused persons were also acquitted by giving them benefit of doubt as the Court disbelieved the story given in the FIR. I personally felt very happy that at least I could save an innocent person from going to the gallows. In the process, I earned applause from the SSP. But, I was sad that real culprits escaped punishment because of the foolishness of the people who gave twist to the true facts while lodging FIR.

A punitive police force was established at village Phoolewala. After the murder case, the rivalry between the two warring group in the village stopped persisting. Both Bharpur Singh and Balwant Singh, the ringleaders of the warring factions would often come to me to express their gratitude for being instrumental in bringing about peace and harmony in the erstwhile faction ridden village.

This episode demonstrated that investigating officer should go deep down the real facts and put them on record. It is certainly not a desirable practice to support the concoction as reported and recorded in the FIR. Resorting to padding, apprehending that the falsehood introduced in the FIR, if not supported by the Police during investigation, shall lose its sheen as an important piece of evidence and in the process, even the real accused getting the benefit of doubt would escape punishment, is a malpractice calling for severe condemnation. The object of police investigation should be to place only facts, duly supported by unassailable evidence on record and ensuring conviction of the accused, as an ultimate objective, but not at all the first priority objective. The peace loving and respectable people avoid deposing as witnesses in the court. A concerted campaign would need to be launched to motivate such people to assist the court by willingly coming forward to discharge such duties as responsible citizens of the state. Fear psychosis created by goons in the society, needs to be carefully taken care of by the state through law enforcement agencies. Firmness displayed in a few cases would send right signals and the required change would be brought about by consistent positive efforts. This was all a laudable philosophy advocated by S N Mathur, SSP Ferozepur and I did my best through out my police career to emulate it. It never failed me, though some embarrassing and harsh situations did arise. However, that was a part of the game, nothing less and nothing more. "Justice is conscience, not a personal conscience but the conscience of the whole of humanity. Those who clearly recognized the voice of their own conscience usually recognized also the voice of justice"– Alexander Solzhenitsn.

Punjabi Suba Agitation

The post independence Punjab state comprised the districts of Amritsar, Gurdaspur, Hoshiarpur, Jalandhar, Ludhiana, Ferozepur, Shimla, Solan, Kangra, Lahul Spiti, Ambala, Karnal, Rohtak, Hissar, Gurgaon and Narnaul. The princely states of the British era falling in the then Punjab state were constituted into a union called Punjab and East Punjab States Union (PEPSU). When the States were reorganized on linguistic basis, in 1956, PEPSU was merged into Punjab. The state of Punjab, thus formed, had two distinct regions – Punjabi speaking and Hindi speaking. The population of the Sikh community was in minority. The Sikh community in the then Composite Punjab was divided politically into three distinct groups. The majority of them were with the Congress Party. Second in number, having Sikh community's support was the Communist Party. The third group was of the Akali Dal. This third group thought that a Sikh always becoming the Chief Minister of the state would remain an uncertain proposition. They, therefore, floated an idea that in the then Composite Punjab, Punjabi language would never be the first language of the State. Thus, they believed that injustice had been done to the Punjabi language while reorganizing Punjab State on linguistic basis. Therefore, they threw up strong demand for the creation of new State of Punjab from out of the then Composite Punjab state, wherein only Punjabi speaking areas should be included. To press their demand, the Akali Dal launched an agitation called the Punjabi Subba agitation. Master Tara Singh was the leading light of the said agitation.

Punjab Vidhan Sabha Elections were scheduled for early 1962. Master Tara Singh, the chief of the Akali Dal, with an eye on mobilizing maximum support of the Sikh voters, announced the launching of agitation. Generally, Amritsar used to be the epicenter of the Punjabi Subba agitation. However, the local Akali Dal leaders, at every Punjabi speaking district hqrs, used to act as "dictators" of the agitation. In Ferozepur district, Muktsar is a place where a famous historical Sikh gurdwara is located. During the time when Guru Gobind Singh was in the midst of war for fighting against the tyranny of the Mughals, some of his followers had deserted him. It was at Muktsar that those followers tendered their apology to the Guru and rejoined his ranks. Whenever Master Tara Singh announced the launching of Punjabi Subba agitation, Muktsar also used to be an important centre of agitation in the Malwa region. When the agitation was announced during the pre-election days of 1962, SSP Ferozepr shifted my hqr, temporarily to Muktsar to deal with the situation arising out of the said agitation. Thousands of Sikh agitators used to court arrest voluntarily. However, soon after the announcement made by Master Tara Singh for launching the agitation, prominent Akali Dal leaders used to be rounded up as preventive measures, under the order of State Government.

One Baj Singh Baj was a self-styled dictator of the agitation using famous gurdwara Muktsar as his retreat. Throughout the day, he would blurt out from the precincts of the gurdwara, on amplifier, virulent propaganda using highly uncivilized and provocative language. He was a marked Akali leader and was to be rounded up as a preventive measure. It was not at all appropriate to enter the gurdwara precincts to affect his arrest. I was getting repeated orders from the district hqrs for his early arrest. Accompanied by some police personnel, all in civil dress, I went to the gurdwara to pay obeisance. I found that a drinking water well was located close to the gurdwara, within the vast walled area of the gurdwara. The boundary wall had a number of small entry gates. Many middle aged and young women had assembled at the well to collect drinking water. Baj Singh Baj seemed to be enjoying the fun of the presence of so many women gathered there. I learnt that it was a daily evening scene there. It just occurred to me that Baj Singh Baj might have weakness for fair sex. I put the Intelligence boys to find out if Baj Singh had any romantic fun with any woman. Soon a report trickled down that Baj Singh almost daily visited the house of a woman, getting out of the gurdwara area, through a particular entry/exit gate during the late hours of the night. A close watch was kept on that particular gate. The strategy worked and Baj Singh Baj was nabbed to my great relief, while he had just come out of the gurdwara gate.

Another very important marked Akali Dal leader was Kirpal Singh Chakk Sherewala. He was a very big landholder in the area and was reputed as a gentleman and respected Akali leader. He was also to be put under preventive arrest. I was finding it somewhat embarrassing to effect his arrest as that could, as per intelligence report trigger off sharp reaction from Akali supporters in the area. I thought of taking him into confidence and called him to Muktsar Rest House where I had set up my camp office. On his arrival, I treated him with respect and told him gently that he was required to be put under preventive arrest and if he had any urgent work elsewhere, he might take a day and come back to surrender voluntarily. Apparently, he tried to give me the impression that he was grateful to me for that courtesy. However, I could discern from his facial expression and body language that he was getting tense and nervous. He asked me to permit him to attend to his urgent work in the Muktsar SDM's office. He returned after half an hour and to my utter surprise, he produced Muktsar SDM's order granting him anticipatory bail against any likely arrest by the police. Judiciary was not separate from the Executive at the Lower Court level. Both were under the District Magistrate. I had early morning on that day, given the information to the SSP Ferozepur about the arrest of Baj Singh Baj and had reported that general situation was peaceful. He was happy. However, my reposing trust in Kirpal Singh due to his reputation, as a gentle man Akali leader, had put me in highly embarrassing situation.

I talked to the SDM. He was a senior PCS officer approaching retirement. He curtly told me that he had passed order of granting anticipatory bail to Kirpal Singh as per the power vested in him. I immediately placed all the facts before the SSP and was apologetic for my showing extra courtesy to Kirpal Singh. SSP however, told me that I had not done any wrong and I should wait for some time for his fresh message. In the meanwhile, he advised me not to allow Kirpal Singh to slip away. After half an hour, the Reader of the SDM came to me at the Rest House and handed over to me another order of the SDM cancelling his earlier order of granting anticipatory bail to Kirpal Singh. I later learnt that district Magistrate Ferozepur had snubbed the SDM telling him to immediately rectify the wrong done by him and fully co-operate with the ASP. Kirpal Singh was put under preventive arrest and was produced before the SDM at his residence, as his office had already been closed by then. I did not consider it appropriate to keep Kirpal Singh in the police station during the night as that could perhaps, have sent a wrong message that he was kept in the police station out of any sense of vengeance. The SDM ordered that Kirpal Singh be lodged in Central Jail Ferozepur and that was done without any loss of time. This incident was a wake up call for me. A political figure, no matter deserves to be treated with courtesy, the Samuel Johnson's saying that "Politics is the last resort of a scoundrel" remains ingrained deep in every politician in varied degrees, some honourable exceptions apart. This fact should always be kept in mind by the civil/police officers while enforcing the law of the land. It is however, to his credit that Kirpal Singh during my entire tenure in Ferozepur district gave me lot of regard whenever he met me, always showing his regrets for manipulating anticipatory bail.

Trade in Illicit Liquor

Makhu Bridge was the only link between Ferozepur and Amritsar districts. River Beas merges into river Satluj at Makhu. A vast marshy area short of the confluence point is dotted with variety of wild growth bushes forming shifting islands due to check in the velocity of water during rainy and dry seasons. Distillation of illicit liquor was rampant in these floating islands. The illicit liquor so distilled, used to be smuggled under the cover of dark nights, into Ferozepur and Amritsar cities and the adjoining villages on both sides of Makhu Bridge. It has been an uphill task for the police to curb this crime. The liquor contractors would extensively utilize the illicit liquor for preparing their own spurious liquor brand and sell it from their retail counters, as genuine government distillery liquor. In one interesting case, a big cache of such spurious XXX Rum was unearthed from the premises of the store of liquor contractors having various retail outlets in Ferozepur city and Cantonment area. An innocuous looking person met the SSP Ferozepur in his office and produced four half-bottle packs, together with his affidavit, alleging that he had purchased that spurious liquor from a particular retail shop, in the Cantonment area. SSP told me to conduct raid personally. Inspector SHO Police Station Cantt joined me with requisite force. Raid was conducted on the retail outlet and quite a few samples were taken. Adjoining the retail outlet there was a big store belonging to the contractor, for stocking the liquor bottles. We saw lot of activities going on inside that building. The door, opening into the street, was locked from inside. It was not opened despite our repeated knocking. It was therefore broken open and we discovered huge stock of illicit liquor contained in scores of tin boxes.

There were about a dozen workers, who having seen us entering the premises, had tried to hide themselves here and there, leaving unfinished task of preparing spurious XXX rum, by adulterating distillery made liquor with illicit liquor. Hundreds of empty bottles with genuine distillery labels and corks were found there. When asked, they prepared three bottles of spurious XXX rum and three bottles of spurious country liquor in our presence. Six samples were taken one each from the three spurious XXX rum bottles prepared in my presence and one each from the three bottles of XXX rum displayed at the same outlet counter. Similarly six samples were taken out, one each from the three bottles of spurious country liquor and one each from the three country liquor bottles, displayed at the sale outlet counter. The matter was reported to the SSP. During the investigation, all the twelve samples were sent to the laboratory at Patiala for test and analysis. In the meanwhile, it transpired that it was the son of a top political executive of Punjab state, who was the actual owner of the contract for sale of liquor in the entire district of Ferozepur. During the investigation, it was revealed that illegally prepared XXX rum used to be supplied to the Army Canteen, in very large quantity. The criminal case registered in the matter could not even be filed in the Court because the report from Patiala laboratory had testified that all the twelve samples received by the laboratory were found on analysis, to be of genuine XXX rum and country liquor made from the government distillery. This case was a good wake up call to me that even scientific aid in the investigation of crime can be manoeuvered by the criminals to their own advantage and how the politically linked people can play, with impunity, havoc with the health of the innocent people, with no fear of law.

In July 1962, I was promoted to the Senior Scale of the IPS and posted as SP, Border Ferozepur.

Chapter – 7

Promotion to Senior Scale of the IPS

Posting as Battalion Commandant on Indo-Pak Border at Rajauri, J&K State

On promotion to the Senior Scale of the IPS, I joined as SP Border Ferozepur on 18th July, 1962, later on transferred and posted as Commandant, Punjab Armed Police Battalion No.01, deployed in Jammu & Kashmir State, where I joined on 12th December, 1962. This Battalion deployed on Indo-Pak cease fire line (CFL) was to man forward pickets from Naushehra to Mehndher about 40 km apart. The Battalion hqr was at Rajauri, a sub-division of district Jammu, located about 100 km from Jammu, on Jammu-Poonchh Road. Rajauri was also the Indian Army's hqr of 25 Division. Maj Gen Chopra was the Div Commander with Lt Col Gurbachan Singh Butch, (who later rose to the rank of Lt Gen) as G-1 and Lt Col Chopra as AQ. Lt Col Singh, father-in-law of my batch-mate Gurdial Singh Mander was from the ASC, the supplier of all ration items. The three senior staff officers were very friendly with me. However, the system of putting on badges of rank-National Emblem, with a star, by the Commandants of PAP Battalions, used to create some heart burning to the Lt Cols of the Army. In Army, it would need at least 15 years Commissioned Service to reach the rank of Lt Col. But in IPS, an officer with 5 years service would get promotion to the rank of SP/Commandant and become entitled to put on the badges of rank like that of Lt Col.

The administrative control of the PAP Battalions, irrespective of place of deployment, remained with the State Police hierarchy through DIG/PAP hqr at Jalandhar. The operational control of the PAP Battalions deployed in J & K vested with the local Army Command. As per the cease fire terms, only police personnel could be deployed to staff the forward pickets on both sides of the CFL. However, Army could be deployed in the rear to give back up support, in the event of any flare up. The UNO observers were deployed to ensure that there were no violations of the CFL terms. The UNO observers were Australians. On Pakistan side of the border, their force called Pakistan Rangers with back up support from Pakistan Army in the rear only theoretically staffed forward pickets. In fact, Pakistan Authority had plans, in place, to play dirty tricks and cheat the vigilant eyes of the UNO observers. The Pakistan Rangers were laced with Pakistan Army personnel. The goons with criminal background and trans-border smugglers were settled in border villages amongst civil population. They had been provided with firearms. The Pak Rangers used to let loose the leashes of these criminals to commit all sorts of crimes on Indian side. Approach to every forward picket involved negotiating difficult rocky steeps, at some places dangerously exposed to the evil designs of Pak Rangers. Unprovoked firing and violations of CFL terms by the Pak Rangers was very common. I as Commandant was required to visit forward pickets very often to ensure the efficiency of the force personnel deployed there and to boost their morale by attending to their problems if any. Ration items were generally carried to forward pickets by the Army mules or the locally deployed coolies. The antecedents of the coolies were got verified through local Police. Still their trust-worthiness was always suspect. Therefore, their deployment had to be done very carefully. Extreme alertness on every body's part, particularly while moving in the forward area and for those deployed on the forward pickets was very necessary, both for personal safety and to keep vigil on the attempted infiltration of Pak criminals and spies.

Soon after my posting to this Battalion, I had motivated each police personnel of the Battalion to contribute voluntarily one-day's pay to build up a sizeable amount. These funds were to be used for providing financial help to the next of kin of our fellowmen in the Battalion, expiring while in service. This scheme was highly applauded by all the battalion personnel. It had infused spirit of comradeship amongst them.

Rajauri was a non-family station, both for the army and the police Battalion personnel. I had arranged rented accommodation at Jammu for my family. The force personnel stationed at the Battalion hqr had been provided tented accommodation with big bunkers raised all around. The only DSP in the Battalion and I, stationed at Bn Hqr had improvised bunker accommodation as our residences. However, there was a good officers' mess built with stones. Life was, indeed, very tough and taxing. Still it was enjoyable, with the entire thrill around, particularly with army officers posted at Divisional Headquarter often joining us in evening games and all types of social intermingling, in stag parties held boisterously on every other day. Free ration items at army scale, was available to all the Bn personnel. Rum in plenty for the NGOs and Jawans was provided free of cost. Scotch whisky for the officers was available at very nominal price.

Shifting of Battalion from Rajauri to Ranbirsinghpura

In early June 1963, Lt Gen Kashmira Singh Katoch, Corps Commander visited hqr of 25 Division, at Rajauri. During my courtesy call on him, he inquired if there were any problems in performing the operational duties by the PAP Bn personnel. I pointed out that the Bn had been operating in the difficult area continuously for the last over 3 years and if some sort of rotation could be fixed in the deployment of all the three PAP Bns, then deployed in the Corps Area, that would help every Bn to remain deployed in the peace area for some time. Indo-Pak International border between Jammu district of J&K State and Sialkot district in the West Punjab of Pakistan was considered to be a peace area, from the point of view of deployment of the PAP Bns. The Corps Commander assured me to give due consideration to my proposal. A few days after his return to the Corps hqr, orders were received regarding reshuffling the deployment of the three PAP Bns.

As per the new deployment order, PAP Bn No.1 was to shift from Rajauri, the Hqr of 25 Div of the Army to 26 Div of the Army to man Indo-Pak International Border, between Jammu and Sialkot with Hqr at Ranbirsinghpura. In July 1963, I shifted the Bn, lock, stock and barrel to Ranbirsinghpura border. The Bn personnel became very happy because this border was not only a plain area, the Bn personnel could bring their families also to stay with them, with prior permission. Improvised accommodation had been arranged for the officers' mess, as also for the families of the officers down to the level of Inspector. I allowed 60 NGOs/ORs at a time, to bring their families to RS Pura to stay with them, in their privately arranged rented accommodation. I was able to establish a very good rapport with the Commandant of the Pak Rangers deployed on Pakistan side of the border. Unauthorized Infiltration of Pak civilians including the activities of Pak cattle lifters from the villages on our side and surreptitious entry of Pak spies were effectively curbed. 162-Brigade under the command of Brig Manmohan Singh, headquartered at Meeran Sahib, a place between Jammu and RS Pura, was guiding our operational activities. Both the Brig Commander and the Div Commander were very happy with the performance of my Bn and they often complimented me for that. I thoroughly enjoyed my posting in this Bn, both at Rajauri, which was highly thrilling and at Ranbirsingpura where I had the opportunity to keep my family with me at the Bn hqr.

During my posting in this Bn for over 2 years, I had known all the personnel by name. The Jawans were liberally permitted to avail short spells of leave to meet their kith and kin back in Punjab. There was no instance of anybody overstaying or absenting. Every Bn personnel, after return from leave, was required to meet me in my office. I would affectionately inquire from them if there were any problem at their home and every body in the family was in good health. With all such gestures, I had developed a very good rapport with the force personnel who always looked to me as Head of the family. The training aspect of the force was always kept in mind. At least one platoon at a time was always doing one month's intensive re-orientation training.

Political Turmoil in Punjab

Political leaders from various opposition parties had launched a concerted tirade against Sardar Pratap Singh Kairon, the Chief Minister Punjab, alleging large-scale corruption. The intensity of the pressure of these leaders had become so severe that the Prime Minister had to concede their demand for constituting a Commission of Inquiry for investigating into the charges of corruption against Kairon. Justice Das was appointed as the Chairman of the Commission of Enquiry. The Das Commission submitted its report wherein Kairon had been indicted on certain points. The Chief Minister had to resign. With his resignation, the political equations in the Congress Party had undergone drastic changes. Comrade Ram Kishan became the Chief Minister. Sardar Darbara Singh, a very senior Congress leader who was aspiring to succeed Kairon had to remain contented with the important portfolios including the Home Department.

Later Sardar Kairon while returning from Delhi was waylaid near village Rai on Delhi-Ambala-Jalandhar Highway, some 20 km from Delhi border by a band of antisocial persons who had been nursing deep animosity against him for their own reasons. Kairon was assassinated with firearms. After committing this ghastly crime, the culprits fled away from the scene of crime. The investigation of this crime was assigned to a special team headed by Mr. Ashwini Kumar, IP. The king pin of the crime was one Sucha Singh by name. He had fled to Nepal. It was due to the highly commendable courage and capability displayed by the investigation team headed by Mr. Kumar that Sucha Singh was nabbed in Nepal. His accomplices in the crime were also arrested in due course of time. All the accused were tried on the charge of murder by a specially designated court of a District Sessions Judge, at Rohtak. During the trial of the case, I happened to be the District Superintendent of Police at Rohtak and the prosecution of the accused persons took place under my guidance and supervision.

Visit of Home Minister, IGP Punjab and DIG PAP & Border Range to Ranbirsingpura Border

During first week of January 1965 Gurdial Singh IP, IGP Punjab and Ashwini Kumar IP, DIG/PAP & Border Range, accompanied by Darbara Singh, then Home Minister, Punjab visited the Bn hqr at Ranbirsingpura. Darbara Singh later became the Chief Minister of Punjab. These VIPs were taken around to some border pickets also. The Div Commander and the Brig Commander applauded my performance as Bn Commandant when the IGP and the DIG interacted with them. I had arranged *Bada Khana* in honour of the Punjab dignitaries at Bn hqr. Both the Div Commander and Brig Commander, together with a couple of Lt Cols and Majors, had also joined, on my request. The boys had organized wonderful cultural show including famous Punjabi bhangra, very befitting to the occasion. It was highly appreciated by both the Home Minister and the Div Commander. During his brief address to the Bn personnel, the Home Minister very kindly, used highly complimentary words for me. I also amusingly overheard the Div Commander asking the IGP not to shift the Commandant of this Bn., at least for another six months, as the Division would be organizing army exercise shortly. When I was seeing off the Punjab dignitaries, the Home Minister said "Thank you very much Swan; well done and keep it up." Shri Ashwini Kumar complimented me a lot in his own style. The IGP whisperingly told me "It is high time you get experience of working as District Superintendent of Police." With all the excitement and happiness, I said, "Thank you very much Sir for your kind visit, we all the Bn personnel feel highly motivated and honoured."

I was soon expecting my posting order as District Superintendent of Police, somewhere in Punjab. However, mysterious was the working style of Sardar Gurdial Singh IP, then IGP Punjab. He did not bother about what the

Div Commander had recommended for not shifting me from RS Pura, at least for six months. He did not post me to any place in Punjab, as District Superintendent of Police as told by him while departing from RS Pura. I got orders for attending Senior Officers' Course at Mount Abu. Bakhtawar Singh IPS (SPS) replaced me at RS Pura on my proceeding to CPTC Mount Abu for the Training Course.

My posting on J&K Borders was reckoned as a difficult area posting. I was therefore, awarded POLICE (SPECIAL DUTY) MEDAL, 1962 with a BAR.

Senior Officers Course at CPTC, Mount Abu

This in-service course from 18th January to 8th July 1965 was very interesting and professionally very beneficial. About 16 IPS Officers from different State IPS Cadres, in the Senior Scale of the IPS, with 5-8 years service attended this course. Lectures by experts on varied subjects and discussions on important issues projected in such lectures, with active participation of the officers attending the course, proved to be very fruitful. Every officer attending the course had some interesting episodes, as experienced during their postings at different places, to share with other officers. Therefore, it was a useful platform to learn from each other's experiences of facing the challenging situations successfully. Every officer was asked to write an article on an interesting subject relating to crime, criminals and general law and order. The subject allotted to me was captioned "Habitual Offenders – How to deal with them." Apart from individual wise allotted subjects, there were four burning topics of those days. Every such topic was allotted to a syndicate, each of four officers. The senior most among every syndicate was nominated as chairperson. I was chairperson of the syndicate to whom the topic allotted was captioned "Armed Police Battalions–Their Role and Training."

In between the course duration, every syndicate had been detailed under a Faculty Member of the rank of the DIG to visit different states in the country to study their police systems, interact with the senior officers, collect and collate relevant material, enlist varied useful points on the subject's allotted individual wise, and syndicate wise. My syndicate had visited the states of J&K, Composite Punjab, West Bengal and the bunch of Eastern states. The visits to various states proved to be highly knowledgeable professionally, for every officer, apart from providing opportunity to meet batch-mates at different places. After return from our visit to various states, all of us submitted papers on the subjects allotted individual wise and syndicate wise, within a specified timeframe. Every article written individually and by the syndicate was thoroughly discussed in the open house. Those were the days when Border Security Force had not yet come into existence. Indian borders with Pakistan were being manned by the Armed Police of various Indian states, raised haphazardly with inadequate training. My syndicate had made very pragmatic suggestions regarding the system of raising, re-organizing, training, man management, deployment and role, both for staffing the borders of the country with Pakistan and deployment in the states, in aid to the civil police for internal security. Later, the BSF, the CRPF and the state's Armed Police Battalion had been raised/re-organized more or less on the lines suggested by my syndicate.

The training syllabus had been so designed as to induce every officer to participate spiritedly and enthusiastically in the discussion of the introduced subject. There was no occasion to get bored or feel stale. Except light PT in the morning, there were no other compulsory outdoor activities in the training programme. Those of us interested in equitation used to enjoy the pleasure of Horse-Riding exercises. Everyone of us was, however, required to come out to the playground in sports kit. However, playing any game was not compulsory. The games like Badminton and Tennis were very popular with almost everyone of us. Evenings used to be very enjoyable and relaxing. Some of us had also taken along our families to Mount Abu. We had to arrange our own rented accommodation. This had given a very welcome opportunity to our families to develop new relations, particularly to our spouses to learn from each other the recipes of various delicacies peculiar to varied regions. Overall, the entire period of our stay at Mount Abu, remained very enjoyable and very free from any sort of professional tension. On the conclusion of our training, we left Mount Abu to resume our professional duties, in our respective State IPS Cadre, carrying sweet memories of our unique togetherness for a little over five month.

As Superintendent of Police Indo-Pak Border, Gurdaspur

On return from Mount Abu, I joined at Gurdaspur as Commandant of the PAP Battalion No.5 deployed on Indo-Pak International Border between District Gurdaspur of East Punjab (India) and District Sialkot of West Punjab (Pakistan) in July 1965. In addition to managing the said border, all the Police Stations of District Gurdaspur, falling in the border area, were under my supervisory charge. This border was known to be calm and peaceful as compared to RS Pura border of J&K State. However, soon after my taking over charge at Gurdaspur, the relations between India and Pakistan had started getting tense. I had hardly settled down in the new set up that reports of alarming situation developing in Kashmir Valley of J&K State had also started pouring in. According to Union Government's Intelligence Agencies, Pakistan had planned to push a large number of intensively trained armed guerillas into Kashmir Valley of J&K State, for causing internal disturbances.

A Challenging Assignment in Srinagar Valley

In the first week of August, 1965 Pakistan had started para dropping scores of guerillas in the Kashmir Valley. Pakistan had also installed strong broadcasting system at some vantage points under the misnomer "Azad Kashmir Radio." Through this system, Pakistan had launched a virulent propaganda: "Freedom fighters of Kashmir Valley have arisen up with arms to liberate the Valley". Ninth August of 1942 was the day when Mahatma Gandhi had given a "Quit India Call" to the British Rulers. Aping the same, "Azad Kashmir Radio" started repeating false announcements that "Kashmir freedom fighters had already captured and liberated major part of Kashmir Valley." Indian Government had definite reports that Pak guerillas in large number, would attempt to gatecrash into the All India Radio Station Srinagar on 09.08.1965 and announce from there that Kashmir Valley had fallen under the control of Kashmir Freedom fighters and that Indian forces had been driven out of the Valley. On 8th August early morning, Ashwini Kumar IP, DIG/PAP & Border Range told me telephonically about a challenging assignment. As per the decision of the State IGP, I was to head a contingent of 500 Punjab Armed Police personnel constituting 5 companies with a Dy SP. This contingent was to be air lifted from Pathankot to Srinagar by Indian Airforce planes where IGP, J&K state would receive the said force at Srinagar Airport for deployment against the onslaught of Pak guerillas. I was given two telephone numbers of Indian Airforce authorities at New Delhi to get in touch with them, for arranging requisite number of Aircrafts. He also told me that he too was trying to get in touch with IAF authorities.

I immediately started preparing to handle the new challenging assignment. My wife set to packing my clothings including a few sets of my uniform articles. We had already prepared a few Bunkers outside the residential bungalow for the family members to take shelter, in case of any Pak Air attack. I gave some Do's and Don'ts to the family members about the use of Bunkers in case of any Pak air strick. My mother, then 66 years old was staying with us at Gurdaspur. Her first reaction to my highly risky assignment was somewhat saddening but then she regained her poise and assured me that she would take care of the children and I should take cheerfully and bravely the new challenging assignment. My wife had grouse against IGP Punjab that he was harassing us with all sorts of new ideas. In any case, I was just about to leave for Pathankot when a telephone call came from Kumar Sahib. He advised me that IAF authorities had detailed three Aircrafts, each with a capacity to carry 50 persons with their luggage and the fleet shall be reporting at Pathankot by 9.00 am. I reached Pathankot well before 9.00 am. Jagjit Singh Khattar Dy SP with 6 Inspectors and 500 NGOs/ORs had already arrived at Pathankot. IAF aircrafts were to ferry the force from Pathankot to Srinagar in as many sorties as necessary. The first sortie was to carry 150 personnel. I told the Dy SP that he would go with 150 personnel in the first sortie and I would come to Srinagar in the last flight. I also asked the Dy SP that having reached Srinagar Airport he would wait along with the force until I reached there in the last sortie.

The Dy SP took me aside and to my utter bewilderment told me curtly that he would not go to Srinagar, at any cost, and would not care less if any disciplinary action was taken against him for disobedience of order and that he would go back and report at PAP hqr Jalandhar. All the NGOs/ORs constituting five companies were very robust and spirited lot coming from sikh community of Punjab and non-sikh personnel mainly coming from Rohtak/Narnaul districts. Jagjit Singh Khattar had earlier remained posted along with me at Rajauri. That was not the time to tell him anything, which would harden his attitude. I also did not want that any other force personnel should know the intention of the Dy SP as conveyed by him to me. My fear was that howsoever the force personnel were spirited, the Dy SP's sudden decision might encourage desertion by the weaklings in the force. Therefore, sympathizing with the Dy SP, I told him that he being on the wrong side of 55, should not have been detailed for the up coming challenging job. I assured him for taking up the matter with the DIG PAP for his replacement in due course. I pleaded with him to go with the first flight and I, on reaching Srinagar with the last flight, would send him back in the returning aircraft. After getting a solemn promise from me, he agreed to go with the first flight. I felt highly relieved that ticklish problem had been solved for the time being. I boarded the last sortie. The philosopical words of John David Bartoe came to my mind, "As I looked down, I saw a large river meandering slowly along for miles, passing from one country to another without stopping. I also saw huge forests, extending along several borders... Two words leaped to mind as I looked down on all this commonality and interdependence. We are one world". It is unfortunate that humans do not understand that there is no distinction between East and West. People create distinctions out of their own minds and then believe them to be true.

By about 3.00 pm, we all were at Srinagar Airport. Mr. Thakur, then IGP J&K State was also present there. Our force personnel had been treated lavishly to variety of Kashmiri delicacies, on reaching the Airport. The IAF aircraft's pilot came to me to take leave for return flight. I called Khattar and thanking him for co-operation asked him to go back by the IAF aircraft on its return flight. However, he was so delighted, relaxed and cheerfully enthusiastic, having experienced the respect, affection and lavish hospitality of the top brass of J&K Police that he very spiritedly saluted me and said "Sir I will swim and sink with you; I wouldn't go back like this." Very happy ending of the tense drama staged at Pathankot!

We all the Battalion personnel were first taken to the Tourist Reception Centre, a vast structure. That was our lodging place. We were advised to remain in readiness by 7:30 pm for deployment. I reported to my DIG at Jalandhar about the details of our having reached Srinagar and the plans to deploy us somewhere. He asked me to keep him informed about all developments from time to time. It was perhaps under Government instructions that PAP Commandants were assigned top priority to the telephone calls made by them to Punjab. I was told to keep four companies in proper formation, each with an Inspector in charge. I was to go with this force, while the Dy SP was to remain with the rest of the force to ensure adequate arrangements of all sorts of wherewithal for the force.

At about 7.00 pm IGP, accompanied by a couple of Senior Police Officers, arrived at the Tourist Reception Centre. They had brought packed foodstuff for 500 persons. I was told that Pak guerilla infiltrators, as per intelligence report, would attempt to enter Srinagar city from the side of Jehlum River, and we were to block their entry into the city by laying strong invincible Nakas. A local Dy SP with two constables was detailed as our guiding party. The route to the place of proposed site of deployment was through the narrow lanes of the city. Therefore, the force had to march through the city lanes, in columns of two. It was strategically very wrong, rather risky. Many people were watching us from the rooftops of their houses. Almost every second house was seen flying a Pakistan National Flag. I strongly protested to the Dy SP. He told me that there was no other route to the proposed site of deployment. For me, taking the force back to lodging place in the Tourist Reception Centre, at that point of time, was an option, which seemed to be fraught with serious consequences. Proceeding ahead also seemed to be equally risky. I was thus confronted with a serious dilemma of to be or not to be. The call for duty to save the city from the onslaught of the Pak guerilla infiltrators seemed to me a better option even though very risky. My conscience goaded me to play with fire courageously. The force marched on. By 8:30 pm the force was deployed on a stretch of about 1000 mtrs on the bank of River Jehlum.

The local Dy SP wanted to go back saying that he was only to guide us upto that place. I did not allow him and firmly told him to stay with us. Jhelum bank was marshy. Situation demanded that the force should remain either in lying position and crawl only for making movements or at the best in crouching position, if very necessary. I remained with the force until half an hour past midnight. Accompanied by the local Dy SP and a personal security of five men from our own force, we left for our lodging place in the Tourist Reception Centre at the wee hours of 9th August, thinking that perhaps the show of force had made the Pak guerilla infiltrators to change their plan of entering the city from that side of the river. At about 1.30 am we were still in the lanes of the city. Loud thuds of heavy firing started echoing the city as if full-fledged war had started. The entire city seemed to have lost in the silence of the graveyard. People had switched off all domestic lights and the streetlights had also been switched off. We had to take shelter in the city lanes only, huddled together. By 3.00 am the firing stopped. We waited for half an hour. It was all calm and quiet.

I decided to go back to the site where I had left my force deployed on the bank of Jehlum River. Local Dy SP was reluctant to accompany me. Looking at my aggressive stance and equally rough mood of my personal security personnel, the Dy SP meekly submitted; we quickly marched back. I was extremely worried and all sorts of frightening thoughts about the likely fate of my force personnel were haunting me. At about 4.00 am I was with my men. I heaved the most welcome sigh of relief to find that every one of them was safe. However, they were all drenched in muddy water, as they had remained in lying position throughout, on the marshy bank of Jehlum River. I was told that at about 1.30 am movements were discerned as if some persons were coming towards the site, which was blocked by our force. Someone from our force foolishly shouted, "Who are you bastards?" Response to this was shouts in a dialect not understandable by our force and simultaneously came bursts of rapid firing as if from stenguns. In retaliation, our force opened fire. There was no more firing from the side of so-called "bastards." It looked as if the armed guerilla infiltrators, in the face of huge firing in reply to their stenguns bursts, retreated to some safe resort. However, from the other side of the Jehlum bank, there was uninterrupted heavy firing which had continued for more than two hours. Our men thought that they were entrapped from two sides, therefore they too continued with intermittent firing. Our men remained in constant tense situation. However, calm was restored a bit when firing from the other side of the bank of the Jehlum River too had stopped. Local Dy SP, our guide told me that Kashmir Armed Police Battalion had been deployed on that side of the River. That solved the mystery. However, I was unhappy that we were not taken earlier into confidence and not apprised of the fact of deployment of KAP Battalions on the other side of the bank. I advised my men to continue holding to their position up to 5.30 am and stand down by 6.00 am when our Dy SP would come to them with instructions for next course of action. I accompanied by the local Dy SP and my personal security, left for Tourist Reception Centre by 5.00 am.

There were already two PAP Battalions in the city commanded by Mr. Jaiji and Mr. NS Phoolka. These two Battalions were looking after the security of various strategically sensitive areas in the city. Phoolka was staying in the Tourist Reception Centre. The adjoining room had been allotted to me. On approaching my room, I found that there were 4-5 PAP officers including my Dy SP Jagjit Singh Khattar, absorbed in mutual talk. When I entered that room, all of them jumped out of their seats exclaiming in unison "Oh Swan Saaa—hib—." Then Phoolka asked me in depressed tone, to talk to Kumar Sahib immediately. I was highly startled by their unusual behaviour. Phoolka did not disclose anything except exhorting me repeatedly to talk to Kumar Sahib immediately. While dialing telephone to connect Kumar Sahib, safety of my family left behind at Gurdaspur started agitating my mind. Within minutes, I got in touch with Kumar Sahib. When I said "Good morning Sir, I am HR Swan speaking from Srinagar", Kumar Sahib in a very affectionate tone exclaimed "Oh Swan how happy I am to hear your voice, you will live hundred lives." Then he inquired about our deployment that night. I gave him all the details. He was very anxious to know about the safety of the force personnel. I assured him that everyone of them was safe until 5.00 am when I left them. He repeatedly exhorted me to keep him informed very frequently.

Later, I learnt that Jaiji Sahib had apprised Mr. Kumar about deployment of my force to face the likely infiltration of Pak guerillas from Jehlum River side and that heavy exchange of fire had continued for about two hours followed by the silence of the graveyard. Everybody had apprehended that the entire force including the Commandant had perhaps been wiped out. Mr. Kumar spent a sleepless night under the prevailing situation. On getting this information from Jaiji Sahib, he had been trying hard to get a confirmed piece of information through the channels of Government of India, Ministry of Home Affairs, Director Intelligence Bureau and IGP/DIG-CID J&K. However, none could give him any authentic information as no system of communication was in place between my forces from its place of deployment to the J&K State Control Room. Therefore, all sorts of rumours based on the alarming thuds of heavy exchange of fire were in circulation. Mr. Kumar had got my family shifted to my village. My mother was then staying with the family at Gurdaspur. Their shifting from Gurdaspur to my village in Hoshiarpur District during the early hours of 9th August had caused lot of tension to the family, particularly my mother. Mr. Kumar had instructed SP Hoshiarpur to keep him informed about the welfare of my family and to attend to all calls from Srinagar with priority. As advised by Mr. Kumar, I talked to SP Hoshiarpur and requested him to inform my family at my village that I was quite safe. He deputed Dy SP to go to my village and meet my mother and my wife, to apprise them about my personally conveyed message from Srinagar.

Mr. Khattar the Dy SP brought the force back to Tourist Reception Centre at about 8.00 am. I had by then, learnt that the Armed Police Battalion of KAP deployed on the other side of Jehlum River had fired around ten thousand rounds, towards the opposite side of the River, making an umbrella of firing over the heads of the force personnel, assuming that they were facing from that side the onslaught of Pak guerillas. They were not aware that PAP Battalion had been deployed on the opposite bank of the River. Similarly, the force was also ignorant about the deployment of KAP on the other side of the River. In that situation both the forces were trying to hit like the legendary Arjun hitting the eye of a fish blind folded, thanks to lack of planning on the part of J&K Police top brass for ensuring any co-ordination in the deployment of different forces. When IGP, J&K state came to Tourist Reception Centre at about 8.30 am, I strongly protested against the careless and thoughtless way of deployment of two different wings of the force. I demanded immediate disarming of the KAP. The IGP was much apologetic. I, therefore, retreated from demanding the disarming of the KAP, in deference to the senior position of the IGP. For next 48 hours, my force remained on rest. There was a general sense of happiness that the declared plan of the Pak guerillas to seize Srinagar All India Broadcasting Station, on 9th August and make declaration that Valley had been liberated by throwing out the Indian Forces, had been foiled. In the process, the role of my force was highly applauded.

Soon after, a strong Control Centre with the name "Siri Force" was established under the direct supervision of Maj Gen Amrao Singh. A number of Armed Police Battalions from Punjab and Rajasthan started pouring in. Army under the command of Maj Gen Amrao Singh assumed over all operational control, for utilizing the Armed Police Battalions as well as the Army troops to face the situation squarely and effectively. There used to be daily briefing and debriefing of the Army/Police Commanders in the meetings, chaired by Maj Gen Amrao Singh, at 8.00 am and 8.00 pm respectively. From 11th August to 15th August my Battalion remained deployed in Dal Lake area. Dusk to dawn curfew remained enforced in the entire city area. There used to be a lot of movement of the VIPs in that area because of the approaching Independence Day. It was to be celebrated with usual fanfare to send a strong message to Pakistan of our complete sense of self-confidence and full preparedness to effectively spatter their vile plan of causing internal disturbance in the J&K state, by pushing their guerillas into the Valley.

Shri DP Dhar, Home Minister of J&K State had a very close proximity with Nehru family. He was a very active VIP to move about to check the Police Bandobust. One late night he, accompanied by two plain-clothed security personnel, was moving in an unnumbered car in the Dal Lake area. My men on duty stopped his car and asked its occupants to come out. He asked his security men to leave their weapons in the car and they all came out of the vehicle. Shri Dhar shouted that he was the Home Minister of the state. My men did not bother about what identity he had disclosed. He was requested not to shout. All the three occupants of the car and its driver were detained. The car was searched and my men took their weapons into possession. After about 10 minutes, our Inspector on his routine checking round reached that point. He also refused to release the party and respectfully told Shri Dhar that he would take order from the Commandant. Neither Shri Dhar, nor the men accompanying him had shown any identity card or passes issued by the competent authority for moving in the curfew area. I reached there around

1.30 am in the course of my checking round. I immediately recognized DP Dhar and showed him due respect. However, I told him firmly that he and his security men should have carried the requisite VIP Pass, issued by the "Siri Force" for moving out in the curfew area. Shri Dhar then not only showed me his VIP pass, he also told me that he was moving out only to personally check the efficiency of PAP personnel in guarding the sensitive curfew area of the Dal Lake and that he had intentionally not showed the VIP pass to my men and even the Inspector. He profusely congratulated me on the firmness of my men in dealing with the situation. He also offered to entertain my men to a lavish dinner at a prestigious Hotel. Next day, when I attended usual morning meeting at the "Siri Force" taken by Maj Gen Amrao Singh, he narrated this incident in the meeting, asking all the Commanders to emulate what Swan's men had done, the previous night in detaining even the Home Minister of the state. He then handed over to me an envelop containing Rs.5,000/- (a very big amount by all standards during those days) saying that this was the reward sanctioned by the Home Minister to my men who were on duty at the time of his visit. Saying "well done and keep it up Mr. Swan." General took up the other points on the agenda of the meeting. This was, indeed, a proud moment of elation for me and my men.

From 16th August onwards, I was detailed to deploy my Battalion on a number of strategic points to guard the safety of various bridges on the road linking Srinagar with Sonamarg. Srinagar-Sonamarg-Ladakh Road has always been an important highway for the movements of Army Troops. There is a vast plain area surrounded by low hills near Sonamarg. Pak guerillas were generally airdropped in that area during the night hours. Lt Col Chadha, a renowned UK Para Trained Army Officer was stationed with his troops at Sonamarg. I had also put up the temporary hqr of the detachment of my Battalion personnel deployed on Srinagar-Sonamarg road. I used to remain on Srinagar-Sonamarg road from 10.00 am to 8.00 pm for ensuring effective safety of the road, with my men deployed on dozens of points on this road. Dy SP Khattar used to take care of providing cooked food to men at their duty points during his checking rounds. During this period, I had developed a very close and affectionate rapport with Lt Col Chadha. We often used to move together in that area. During the period from 16th to 26th August, scores of Pak guerillas were killed by the security forces and those caught alive remained with the Army's Intelligence Wing for their interrogation etc.

On the morning of 26th August, my DIG telephonically instructed me to come to Gurdaspur for a few days to attend to important pending matters including the pay bills for the Battalion personnel for the month of August 1965. Gen Amrao Singh allowed me to move on 28th August only.

Miraculous Escape from the Planned Ambush by the Pak Guerilla Infiltrators

On the evening of 27th August, before starting from Sonamarg, I met Lt Col Chadha and told him that I would come back from Gurdaspur on 2nd or 3rd September. He asked me to stay on for evening of 28th August to attend his wedding anniversary celebration, at his place at Srinagar. He also told me that travelling at that hour of late evening would be risky for me. Congratulating him on the wedding anniversary, I requested him to excuse me for my absence from the celebrations as I had decided to travel immediately to reach Srinagar before it was too late. I had reached the outskirts of Srinagar by about 8.00 pm. I was moving on the road passing through the huge apple orchards of the city. I heard heavy exchange of fire just a couple of miles back away from that place. Soon I reached the hqr of "Siri Force" and joined the debriefing meeting taken by Maj Gen Amrao Singh. After half an hour, a company of Gorkha Battalion also reached there. They had brought with them a truckload of about two dozen dead bodies of Pak guerilla infiltrators. It dawned on me then that the Gorkha Company was following the small convoy of three vehicles wherein my escort personnel and I were travelling.

The infiltrators had planned to lay an ambush, to waylay my security personnel and me. However, they miscalculated and instead tried to entrap, in an ambush with the Gorkha Company. The Gorkhas too were travelling in three vehicles. The Gorkhas proved to be too smart for the infiltrators. Instead of entrapping the Gorkhas, Pak infiltrators themselves fell flat like the wall of sand, in the face of powerful counter blast by the Gorkhas. Three cheers for their alertness and bravery! The dead bodies of the infiltrators remained on display for quite some time for the public to see for themselves what fate the Pak infiltrators had to face at the hands of vigilant, alert and gallant security personnel of Indian Army. I was quietly thanking the Almighty for my and my security personnel's miraculous escape from the evil plans of the Pak infiltrators. Frankly speaking, if we were entrapped in the ambush, we would have been easily outnumbered and killed in no time by the powerful-trained Pak guerilla infiltrators. My security personnel comprising only NGO/1, HC/1 and Constable/ 10 were no match for the infiltrators. Maj Gen Amrao Singh, in a light vein told me "Swan you owe us all a sumptuous party." Any way 27th August was a day of celebration for the "Siri Force" for the truck load of 24 Pak guerilla infiltrators dead, despite being equipped with all sorts of deadly small arms weapons and hand grenades.

Tragic Death of Lt Col Chadha

I boarded the morning flight from Srinagar Airport on 28th August, and reached Gurdaspur by lunch time. I attended the office, disposed of pending papers, and reported my arrival in Gurdaspur to my DIG. He very kindly told me to take a day or two off and visit my family at my village, in District Hoshiarpur. Inderjit Singh, Dy SP, who was looking after the routine affairs of the Battalion had specially gone to my village, as advised by Mr. Kumar to inquire about the welfare of my family where he had found everybody hale and hearty. On 29th morning, Jagjit Singh Khattar conveyed to me the sad news of tragic death of Lt Col Chadha, by a stray bullet coming, nobody knows from where, while he was on his way to Srinagar on the afternoon of 28th August to participate in his wedding anniversary celebration. His wife had made all preparations and guests had just started arriving when this sad news reached her. Celebration party turned into a mourning assembly. Dead body of Chadha was brought to his residence at about 8.30 pm. Army's entire top brass and that of Police had assembled there; Khattar too represented our PAP Bn. This was indeed, a great tragedy, as Chadha himself was advising me on 27th evening not to travel from Sonamarg to Srinagar late in the evening. What an irony! His own destiny had been scripted by the Almighty to leave this mortal world on his wedding anniversary day. Mysterious are Thy ways Oh Almighty Supreme Lord! We mortals in our helplessness pray for your mercifulness!

Declaration of Indo-Pak War, 1965

I went to my village on August 30th evening, stayed there on 31st and returned to Gurdaspur on 1st September afternoon. As advised by our DIG, I left for Jammu on 3rd September morning by jeep and was to catch the flight for Srinagar from Jammu. I saw en-route extra ordinary movements of Army troops between Sambha and Jammu. On the outskirts of Jammu, I was stopped by the Army troops and was refused permission to go beyond that point. I was in my uniform and made them known my identity and the purpose of my going to Jammu. A Major was called in. He talked to me and told me to wait until he sought orders from the Higher Formation. It was then, after all sorts of hassles of verification etc that I was allowed to proceed further. That Major expressed his surprise that I, as a Senior Police Officer, Commanding a Battalion, did not know, by then, that Indo-Pak War had been declared. This information worried me a lot. On reaching Jammu Airport, I learnt that all civilian flight from Jammu to Srinagar had been cancelled. Thanks to local Army Command, I got lift in an IAF aircraft after two hours hassle. I reached Srinagar very late and was with my Hqr company in the Tourist Reception Centre, at about 10.00 pm during the curfew hours.

On 4th morning, I attended the meeting at "Siri Force" hqr. Gen Amrao Singh was in a hurry. He briefly explained that right in the start of Indo-Pak War on 3rd September, Pak troops had snatched the initiative and had registered their superiority in their preparation for War, in Khem Karan Sector of Punjab and Chhamb-Jaurian sector in Jammu area. In Amritsar sector, they had prepared almost invincible bunkers on their side of Ichhogil Canal. Both sides had commandeered their air sorties. Situation in the Valley was very tense, because of the likely presence of Pak guerilla infiltrators, in large number. The main job for the security forces in J&K was to launch concerted mop up operation to catch these Infiltrators, dead or alive. Police Bns from then onwards were to take care of security of various vulnerable points with greater alertness. The deployments of Armed Police Bns, duly reorganized and reshuffled were ordered afresh, to spare maximum number of troops for strengthening the borders against any onslaught of Pak troops. On getting a telephon call, Gen Amrao Singh abruptly ended the meeting saying good luck and goodbye.

In reassignment of duties, my men were to ensure the safety of Srinagar-Sonamarg-Ladakh Road only up to a distance of 15 km from Srinagar, by strengthening the force at every vulnerable point. Army troops were to ensure the safety of that road beyond 15 km. Srinagar-Sonamarg road was considered an important highway for the unhindered movement of the troops. The rest of my force was deployed for guarding the Hqr of "Siri Force", Dal Lake area, Telephone exchange, AIR Broadcasting station, main city's power station. Curfew remained enforced during the night hours. Streetlights were kept switched off. All civil population strictly avoided to switch on the lights.

The fear and apprehension of bombardment by Pak Airforce was so imminent that this fear psychosis had in a way instilled a lot of discipline amongst the citizenry at large, forgetting any individual or collective grievances. My men discharged their duties with admirable sense of responsibility. A radiostation installed by Pakistan somewhere near the border by the name 'Azad Kashmir Radio' used to broadcast totally false news claiming that various important Indian cities like Srinagar, Jammu, Poonch, Amritsar and Firozepur had already fallen and seized by the Pakistani troops. Trunk calls from Srinagar to other cities in India were restricted only to the selected persons. Though AIR Srinagar and also other stations of AIR in India were functioning efficiently and countered the canards spread by the so called 'Azad Kashmir Radio' Station, yet the weaklings amongst the citizenry were prone to believe even the false propaganda made by Pakistanis amidst the confusion created in their mind. Govt of India did their best to block the dissemination of news by Pakistan managed Radio Stations.

Round about 18th September, it started dawning on the top managers, both in Pakistan and India that neither party was losing or gaining much, in the fiercely fought war for about a fortnight. However, one stark truth certainly was the blunting, nay completely fracturing the jaws of claim of Ayub Khan, Pak dictator, who used to unabashedly boast from every platform that his Patton Tanks would not be halted anywhere short of Delhi. His Patton Tanks were reduced to scrap, useful only to the *Kabadis,* by our Artillery, manned by our brave soldiers and commanded by able and fearless top leaders. Sorties piloted by our spirited IAF officers who loved to play with fire, smashed many important Pak army installations thus wrecking all plans of Pak infantry to advance forward on the Indian soil. It was on 23rd September 1965 that Indo-Pak War came to an end when both sides formally declared cease-fire. Soviet Socialist Republic, then a very strong and top World Power had played very vital role, right from the day when relations between India and Pakistan had started taking ugly turn in early August. Top leaders of Pakistan, led by its Dictator Ayub Khan, and that of India led by Prime Minister Lal Bahadur Shastri were to meet at Tashkent, the Capital of the Uzbek State in Union of Soviet Socialist Republics (USSR).

I was awarded SAMAR SEVA STAR – 1965 for my serving in the war theatre during 1965. I was also awarded RAKSHA MEDAL for my participation in Indo-Pak war of 1965.

Back to Gurdaspur

On the eve of cessation of war, Armed Police Bns specially deployed in the valley started returning to their states. My men too came back to Jalandhar PAP Hqr on 23rd September. I got back to Gurdaspur, the place of my regular posting. During the war days, border pickets manned by Pakistan Rangers in the Shakargarh area of District Sialkot, Pakistan had been deserted. These deserted pickets were ransacked and in some cases badly damaged by the civilians of both sides of the border.

Normalcy was soon restored. Joginder Singh IAS, my old friend was the Deputy Commissioner, District Gurdaspur. Our two families enjoyed each other's company and hospitality. Gurdaspur town had not yet seen any developmental activities. Both Batala and Pathankot towns were much better developed after Independence because of some industries coming up there. Pathankot was also important because of the Army Units stationed there. Dhariwal, a nearby small town had acquired importance because of a spinning mill manufacturing quality blankets by the then standards. New construction had not come up much at Gurdaspur. Civil Lines area was the only place having a number of new houses, which had come up for the officers after Independence. A civil club had also come up with skeleton facilities. I used to enjoy playing games of badminton and tennis at this club. General Sparrow, a popular figure for his heroic performance in the Army belonged to Gurdaspur. After retirement, he had become a leading political leader of Punjab and had graduated, in due course of time, to become the President of the Punjab Pradesh Congress Committee.

After the War was over, Pakistan Rangers who earlier used to be always in aggressive stance and would indulge in undesirable activities, without any provocation, remained largely subdued. Total peace prevailed in the border area. Illegal border crossing and all types of the Trans-border crime had become negligible. Both sides were eagerly waiting for the outcome of Tashkent Talk. Finally, Tashkent Agreement was signed and both countries were to revert to the positions of status-quo-ante. However, a very unfortunate tragedy struck at Tashkent. Lal Bahadur Shastri, a highly respected leader and the darling of everyone, suffered fatal heart attack at Tashkent. He had succeeded Pandit Jawaharlal Nehru, our first Prime Minister for 17 years who had died in harness. Lal Bahadur Shastri's popularity index during his short period of Prime Ministership had surpassed even Nehru's Prime Ministership of 17 years; such was the love and respect he had earned from the Indian citizenry. After Shastri's death, it was Smt. Indira Gandhi who became the unanimous choice of the Congress Party to become the Prime Minister of India. Morarji Desai, a contemporary of Jawaharlal Nehru had strongly laid his claim for the Prime Ministership, based on his seniority. He had to remain contented with the Dy Prime Ministership, in the face of a large majority in the Congress Parliamentary Party favouring Indira Gandhi.

The entire country, as one nation, had solidly supported the government of the day to give very befitting reply to the all time belligerent stance of Pakistan under their dictator Ayub Khan. Indira Gandhi, the new Prime Minister of India was highly appreciative of this fact and had often said so in public speeches. The wily politicians in the Akali Party thought that the iron was hot to strike. They threatened with their usual agitation for pressing the demand for 'Punjabi Suba'.

Strong Protest against Posting as SP, Agitation at Amritsar

Sardar Gurdial Singh, IGP Punjab once again had the opportunity to test my endurance as to how long and safely I could tread on burning coal. He managed to obtain government approval for my posting as SP, Agitation with Hqr at Amritsar. I was playing tennis in the club when at about 6 pm a wireless message was delivered to me for my posting as SP Agitation. The order further stipulated that I should move immediately to Amritsar without waiting for my successor and without availing any joining time. I decided not to obey these orders this time, because I never had a chance to be posted at Amritsar on any regular assignment and was not fully familiar with the topography of the area. The Akali agitators were in very volatile mood and even the Sikh peasantry was to participate actively in the agitation. Additional SP Amritsar, who had already been stationed there, should have been designated as SP Agitation and if his replacement were required, I would have welcomed that posting. I immediately left for Amritsar on a mission to meet Ashwini Kumar who was convalescing in the hospital there, after undergoing operation for minor ailment. I met him at 9.00 pm. He sympathized with me and advised me to meet the IGP. By the time I reached Chandigarh, next day, the offices had already been closed. I went to the residence of JS Bawa, the then AIG Administration, which used to be a very important assignment during those days. Shri Bawa, an excellent human being and a fine officer, known for high integrity and proven efficiency, gave me a very sympathetic hearing. He could have easily put me off by telling me to come to the office during working hours, next day. However, he rang up IGP at his residence and asked him that Swan from Gurdaspur wanted to meet him urgently. IGP told him to direct me to come to his residence immediately.

I reached IGP's residence in Sector-10. His orderly head constable asked me to wait in the lawn. IG came out soon. I greeted him and he enquired about the situation at Amritsar. I told him that I had gone to Amritsar last evening only to take permission form Shri Kumar for meeting the IGP. He said "For what?" I said, "To protest against my posting as SP Agitation at Amritsar". He said, "It is government order and whatever you have to say against that, put it in writing and I would send it to the government. Listen, this is indiscipline unworthy of an IPS officer to disobey government orders when the situation is getting so tense in the face of threat of agitation." I requested him to let me have a sheet of paper and I would put in writing whatever I had to say. He gave me a queer look and went inside his house and brought two sheets of paper and said "Write down whatever you have to say quickly as I have to attend to some other urgent work". My mind was highly agitated. I wrote down whatever occurred to me as correct at that time and handed over my 'Representation' to the IGP. In the last para of my 'Representation' I had written that I would not join at Amritsar at any cost even if that was considered to be an act of indiscipline. Saying that I was extremely sorry to bother him at his residence, I took his leave and went straight to Gurdaspur reaching there by about midnight.

After two days, I got a telephone call from Chandigarh that Home Minister Punjab wanted to talk to me. I was apprehending a severe reprimand at the hands of the Home Minister, but it was just the opposite. On my greeting him, the Home Minister said, "How come you went away without meeting me while the purpose of your visit to Chandigarh was important". I apologized for that. Then he told me that IGP had sent my 'representation' to him saying "This officer is trying to wriggle out of this difficult posting; it is an act of indiscipline on his part". The Home Minister further told me that he had written on the file that Swan would continue at Gurdaspur and it was thoughtless to propose his name for posting as SP Agitation. IGP should propose the name of some other officer who should have earlier remained posted in Amritsar in some capacity. Meanwhile, in the month of July 1966, Ram Kishan Ministry was dissolved and Governor's Rule was enforced.

Creation of Border Security Force (BSF)

As per provisions in the Constitution of India the proposal to have a well organized and well trained Central Force, under the unified command, to man the Indian borders common with Pakistan, was already under the consideration of the Home Ministry of the Government of India. However, the Indo-Pak war of 1965 accelerated the process. Even during the war days, a nucleus staff headed by KF Rustamji IP assisted by a couple of senior police officers had come into existence. Soon after the cessation of war, Border Security Force was constituted by merging, on ad-hoc basis, Armed Police Battalions of various border states then deployed to staff their respective borders. I was then, posted as Commandant PAP Battalion No. 5 deployed on Indo-Pak border with Hqr at Gurdaspur. That Battalion, likewise, was merged into the BSF, lock, stock and barrel. I was treated as a deputationist to the said force.

Demand for Creation of "Punjabi Suba"

Smt Indira Gandhi who had been an apprentice politician under the immediate stewardship of her worthy father Pandit Jawaharlal Nehru, had by then graduated into a very seasoned politician and administrator. She correctly felt the pulse of the Sikh community, particularly the Sikh soldiery and peasantry who were basking in the glory of part played by them during the war with Pakistan. She surely did not want to fill the Punjab jails with 'Punjabi Suba' agitators from Sikh peasantry so soon after the Indo-Pak war. She, therefore, very gracefully conceded the demand of the Akali leaders to carve out a predominantly Punjabi speaking area, as a new Punjab State, from the existing all embracing large bilingual state of Punjab. Akali Dal, who was planning to launch 'Punjabi Suba' agitation, started instead celebrating the fulfillment of their demand, eulogizing the decision of the Prime Minister.

The Indian Government set up a Parliamentary Committee for reorganization of Punjab state on 23rd September 1965 headed by Sardar Hukum Singh, a prominent Sikh leader. All the legislators coming from Haryana region discussed the issue of the new State in a meeting at Rohtak on 17th October 1965. The following three Resolutions were passed.

(i) A new Hindi-Speaking State should be formed which should include, in addition to the Hindi-speaking areas of Punjab, some areas of Delhi, Rajasthan and Uttar Pradesh.

(ii) If the States of Rajasthan and Uttar Pradesh do not agree, then the new State should be formed comprising Hindi-speaking areas of Punjab.

(iii) The People of Haryana would not tolerate any division of the Hindi-speaking areas and whole of this area should constitute the new State of Haryana.

The Hukum Singh Committee recommended on 23rd April 1966 that a Boundary Commission may be set up to facilitate the division and reorganization of Punjab State. Accordingly, the Government set up the Boundary Commission with Justice JC Shah as Chairman. The Commission gave its reports on 31st May 1966. After receiving report of Shah Commission, the Parliament passed

"The Punjab Reorganization Act, 1966" on 18th September 1966. In the meanwhile, the Ram Kishan Government of Punjab was dismissed in July 1966 and Governor's Rule was enforced. "The Punjab State Reorganization Act, 1966" came into force on 1st November 1966 and a new State of Haryana came into existence.

With the Punjab Reorganization Act of 1966 coming into force with effect from 1st November 1966, Composite Punjab State IPS Cadre was split into three parts. Allocation of every IPS officer to a particular State Cadre, right from the beginning had throughout, been done based on a thoughtfully laid down policy. However, it was extremely unfortunate that splitting up of the Composite Punjab State IPS Cadre and allocation of officers to the three newly created State Cadres was done as per the whims of a couple of top officers of the Cadre, without laying down any rational policy. I had been allocated to the IPS Cadre of the newly created State of Haryana with effect from 1st November 1966. Though I was deemed to be on deputation to the BSF, yet I was advised by the Punjab Police Headquarters to report at Central Police Office, Chandigarh, on 1st November 1966 forenoon, after relinquishing charge at Gurdaspur.

Chapter – 8

As Director Special Inquiry Agency in the new State of Haryana

In the sky, there is no distinction of East and West, North and South; people create distinctions out of their own minds to promote their own interest at stake. 'Punjabi Suba' that is the new State of Punjab, with pre-dominatingly Punjabi-speaking area, was created to appease the Akali Dal leaders who were forcefully agitating for over a decade, to have an area, wherein the Sikh population should be in majority so that only a Sikh, particularly from the Akali Dal, could easily become the Chief Minister of the State. The political leaders coming from Hindi-speaking areas of Punjab never seriously demanded the creation of a new State of Haryana. Truly speaking the new State of Haryana resulted, as a sort of by-product of conceding the demand of the Akali Dal, for creation of their dream state 'Punjabi-Suba'.

Territorial Limits of Haryana State

Under the provisions of the Punjab State Re-organization Act, 1966, enacted by the Indian Parliament, the new State of Haryana came into existence on 1st November, 1966. All the existing movable and immovable assets of the Composite Punjab State had fallen to the shares of the new States of Punjab and Haryana, in 60:40 ratios. Four big districts – Karnal, Gurgaon, Rohtak and Hisar and a small district Narnaul, without disturbing their territorial boundaries, were included in the new State of Haryana. Ambala district also used to be very large in area, in Composite Punjab State. Its Ropar sub-division was taken out of it and included in the new state of Punjab, as a full-fledged district. The remaining part of Ambala district, still quite large in area, came over to Haryana State as Ambala district. Jind, an erstwhile princely state, was a sub-division of district Sangrur. This sub-division came over to Haryana state and was made a full-fledged district. The remaining part of district Sangrur continued to be in the new state of Punjab. In all, there were 90 Police Stations in the Composite Punjab State. In the new State of Haryana consisting of only seven districts, Ambala Cantt was an important Civil Divisional Hqr and the

Hqr of a Police Range. It continued to be so with its territorial jurisdiction concurrent with the State area. In the area constituting Haryana state having 61 cities and 6690 villages, with total population of 91 lacs, there were 52 Assembly Constituencies. With these 52 MLAs, Pandit Bhagwat Dayal Sharma became the first Chief Minister of the state with about two dozen Ministries.

The Commission appointed to identify Hindi and Punjabi speaking areas had awarded Fazilka sub-div of district Ferozepur to Punjab state. Most of this area was in fact Hindi speaking. Chandigarh, which was developed as an ideally located new City as Capital of East Punjab State (India), as conceptualized after Independence, was awarded to Haryana State. The Punjabis had developed an emotional attachment with Chandigarh City. The Akali Dal leaders, the pioneers of 'Punjabi Suba' could never think that Chandigarh could ever be included in Haryana state. However, that did happen. Further, there could not be any mutually agreed formula for sharing the River water between the two States. All these issues were kept unresolved by the Commission.

The Government of India decided to convert Chandigarh into a Union Territory, to be governed directly through the Union Ministry of Home Affairs, pending final decision on this issue. The other unresolved issues were also to be sorted out later on. Both the states were to continue to have their State Hqrs i.e. Capital at Chandigarh, sharing the Secretariat Building and other various residential buildings, on 60:40 ratio. The High Court was to remain common for both the states. All these unresolved issues were naturally to become very contentious but providing, incidentally, very welcome opportunities for the wily and crafty politicians of both the States to launch all types of *morchas*, rallies and agitations, arousing the sentiments and emotions of the gullible people of the states, to win their support for strengthening their political base. The obvious result was acute bitterness between the two states.

Haryana State Police Force

It came into existence, as a sequel to the creation of Haryana state with a total strength of 12165 personnel. The IPS Cadre of the Composite Punjab state was shared by the two new states. The Haryana State IPS Cadre consisted of 35 IPS Officers. HC Saxena, IPS 1943 – ER was the seniormost IPS officer in the Cadre. He was on deputation with the Government of India at that time. Bhagwan Singh Rosha 1944 IPS (SPS-ER) was the next seniormost IPS Officer. Therefore he had the distinction of donning the hat of the first Inspector General of Police of the State. JC Vachher 1946 IPS-ER, being third in order of seniority in the Cadre, became the first state DIG/CID. Next to him, Kanwar Randip Singh 1946-IPS-ER was, made DIG -Ambala Range. The only other IPS Officer, in the Super Time Scale, then available in the state, was HRK Talwar 1948 IPS-RR. He became the first DIG/HAP and Home Guards-cum-Director Civil Defence.

On allocation to Haryana Cadre of IPS, I reported at the Central Police Office, Chandigarh on 01.11.1966. After my appointment in the IPS, I had initially been allocated to Punjab State Cadre of IPS because of my Punjab domiciled status as per the laid down policy of the Ministry of Home Affairs of the Union Government. My allocation from Punjab State IPS Cadre to Haryana

State IPS Cadre was therefore, not in accordance with the said laid down policy. I was not quite happy with my allocation to Haryana State IPS Cadre. Nevertheless, I reported at Central Police Office.

I had earlier served as ASP in Hindi speaking region of Composite Punjab State, at District Hqr Hisar, Incharge-Sub-Division Jind of the then District Sangrur and Sub-Division Sirsa of District Hisar. I had not then seen much of the core area of the famous jat-hinterland of the newly created Haryana State. However, I had heard inspiring success stories of daredevil War Heroes and brave Freedom Fighters of this land. Therefore, I was keenly looking forward to have first hand knowledge of the culture, traditions, social life, customs and general life style of these people. A number of Haryanvi Jawans had been in the Punjab Armed Police Battalions, which I had the chance to command. I had seen their very good performance, from very close quarters. Memories of unpleasant happenings during the land dispute of village Mohangarh Police Station Narwana of Jind Sub-Division and the diatribes and invectives of Dalip Singh, then SP Sangrur, which I had to suffer, were also very fresh in my mind. With all such mixed feelings, I was curiously waiting for orders for my new assignment in the new State.

Working as Director Special Inquiry Agency (SIA), Haryana State

My first posting in the new set up was Director Special Inquiry Agency, with Hqr at Chandigarh. In the Composite Punjab State, the Agency, by this nomenclature was headed by an officer of the rank of DIG, assisted by two officers of the rank of Superintendent of Police. However, with the splitting of Composite Punjab State Police IPS Cadre, the post of DIG, with one SP's Post, remained with Punjab State and one post of SP came to the share of the new State of Haryana. The office of the Agency was earlier housed in a residential building in Sector-9. Some space, out of the said premises, was provided for the office of Haryana Agency having modest establishment, consisting of 1 Director (in the rank of SP), 5 Inspectors, 1 Prosecuting Inspector, 1 Head Constable, 8 Constables and 7 Ministerial staff. Justice Tek Chand (Retd.) was the Vigilance Commissioner for supervising the working of the Agency, in Composite Punjab State. He continued to play that role for Agencies of both the States of Punjab and Haryana, even after 31st Oct. 1966.

The prevalent system of working of the Agencies involved five stages. On receipt of any complaint of corruption/irregularity against any government official, the government in the Vigilance Department would decide whether a thorough probe into the allegations, contained in the complaint, was required. The complaint would then be sent to the Director of the Agency through the State Vigilance Commissioner. The Director of the Agency would conduct inquiry and send his report to the State Vigilance Secretary through the State Vigilance Commissioner. The State government in the Administrative Vigilance Department, after examining the report of the Director of the Agency and the comments of the State Vigilance Commissioner, would decide about the next course of action. If the government considered that criminal action was warranted against the accused, criminal case under the Prevention of Corruption Act would be registered in the concerned Police Station and the Director of the Agency would undertake investigation thereof.

It soon dawned on me that Special Inquiry Agency was a toothless organization. On my pointing it out to the Secretary to the Government, Vigilance Department, he advised me not to be overenthusiastic about curbing the evil of corruption. I sought advice of the IGP and DIG/CID. I then learnt that SIA was the brainchild of a smart Political Advisor to the Chief Minister, to provide him, a ready instrument for making the belligerent political figures and the bureaucrats to fall in line; curbing evil of corruption was just incidental to the main agenda. This position notwithstanding, I initiated and submitted a detailed proposal to the Administrative Secretary of the Vigilance Department of the State, through the State Vigilance Commissioner for reorganizing the State Anti-Corruption Machinery, with a view to streamlining the system and making the SIA as an effective tool to deal with complaints of corruption. State government effected only a few organizational changes and made some cosmetic improvements by issuing instructions on 17th June 1967.

On the creation of new State of Haryana with effect from 1st November 1966, the complaints pending inquiry with the Agency, concerning the areas which had been included in the new State, were transferred to the Haryana Agency, irrespective of the fact whether the concerned officials/officers were allocated to Haryana or Punjab States. All these pending inquiries were promptly finalized by the Agency with commendable diligence, industry and thoroughness, as observed by Justice Tek Chand, the State Vigilance Commissioner.

In the Punjab State Agency, housed in the same building, Shri Ajaib Singh IPS 1945 SPS-ER was the DIG as its head. The said officer had been earlier DIG/CID, for a number of years and in that capacity, he was considered to be a very powerful big boss. As head of the Punjab SIA, it was no wonder that he was the most disgruntled and disinterested in the job. He would often, call me to his chamber and ventilate his feelings in informal chit-chat *(Gup-Shup)* sessions. I had developed a very close rapport with him and from the narration of his own success stories, during his hey days. I really learnt various aspects of professional hazards. That way, my *'Gup-Shup'* sessions with him stood me in good stead, in my future career. On his retiring from service, he was replaced by Sh. Ranjit Singh Grewal IPS 1948 list II. I knew him when he was SSP Amritsar district and was doing training in Practical Police Working as IPS Probationer. Grewal too had enjoyed enviable political influence. He also used to involve me in *'Gup-Shup'* sessions. He was still to serve for many years. Overall, he was very kind hearted and used to give me lot of affection and regard. My social relations continued with him even after his retirement. My short period of stay as Director SIA, Haryana was quite enjoyable. This posting provided me many opportunities to cultivate good mutual social relations, with officers of different departments of the state.

Chapter – 9

As Superintendent of Police, District Rohtak

Political Scenario in Haryana State

General elections for Vidhan Sabha were due in Feb-March, 1967. By that time, the number of Assembly constituencies had been increased from 52 to 80. Accordingly, elections were held on 3rd March, 1967. Congress Party won the majority of seats. Pandit Bhagwat Dayal Sharma again became the Chief Minister on 11.03.1967, heading about two dozen Ministers. During his earlier short tenure as Chief Minister, he had not played his political cards like a seasoned politician. In the new State of Haryana, every politician of some reckoning was considering himself to be worthy of becoming the Chief Minister of the State. Pandit ji had wasted most of his time in suppressing his opponents in a questionable manner and thus antagonizing the senior fellow-Congress leaders. The ultimate results, therefore, had to be disastrous for him.

All India Congress Party was ridden with acute factionalism following the unfortunate death in harness of Prime Minister Lal Bahadur Shastri at Tashkent. Though Smt Indira Gandhi had become the Prime Minister, yet the faction led by Morarji Desai, who had to remain contented with the Dy Prime Ministership was equally strong. Pt. Bhagwat Dayal Sharma had aligned himself with the Desai faction. Though he had become the first Chief Minister of newly created State of Haryana, yet the factionalism in the All India Congress Party had badly affected the Haryana Pradesh Congress Party. The faction lead by Panditji was very strong. Therefore, instead of carrying with him the leaders of the rival faction, he had attempted to further weakening their position. Antagonism between the two factions had come in the open when Congress candidates were to be selected for contesting elections to Vidhan Sabha. Panditji had managed Congress tickets for his loyalists, in an overwhelming majority. However, he had lost the element of that popularity which was very necessary to establish himself as an undisputed leader of the Congress Party in the State. Thus, despite his becoming Chief Minister of the State second time in March

1967, about a dozen top disgruntled Congress leaders, not only formed a ginger group in the Congress Legislature Party, but also staged a revolt against the Chief Minister and joined hands with the non-Congress Party MLAs. Sharma's Government was reduced to a minority and thus, eating a humble pie, he had to resign on 22.03.1967. The rebels garnered a majority with the help of Jan Sangh MLAs, who were in sizeable strength. A new political formation by the name United Front (Samyukat Vidhayak Dal) was formed. Rao Birender Singh, an erstwhile senior leader of the Congress Party and speaker in the Sharma's Ministry, was a unanimous choice to become the Chief Minister.

Rao Birender Singh was the undisputed 'lord' of Ahirwal. His style of functioning was very dignified. He was a Cabinet Minister in Composite Punjab and had fallen out with Partap Singh Kairon on certain issues. Out of political vengeance, some inquiries were initiated against Rao through Special Inquiry Agency. He was harassed to the hilt by the police officials during the course of inquiry conducted against him. Rao had a rich heritage. Rao Tula Ram, an ancestor of Rao Birender Singh had led a rebellion against the British in 1857 in Haryana. On May 17th, 1857, Rao Tula Ram marched to Tehsil Hqr of Bhiwani leading about 500 strong followers. They dislodged the tehsildar and thanedar and took command of all the Government buildings. However, British Forces chased them away and a fierce battle ensued in Naseebpur village in Rewari. Afterwards Rao Tula Ram had moved to Rajasthan and joined Tantya Tope's forces for one year. He never surrendered to the British and laid down his life for the freedom of the country. He died a hero's death at the young age of 36. The tales of his great sacrifices have become folklores in Haryana. Haryanvis remember him for his unique martyrdom. With such an enviable glorious heritage, Rao Birender Singh commanded a dignified and respected social and political stature.

After becoming the Chief Minister of first Non-Congress Government, on 26th March, 1967, it was, indeed, an up-hill task for him to constitute the Cabinet. Loyalty to the newly found Samyukat Vidhayak Dal (SVD) was only skin-deep. Poaching in the SVD was seriously apprehended at the hands of crafty politician in Panditji. Therefore, in a bid to please everybody, Rao Sahib had to opt for a Jumbo size Cabinet. Sh. Hardwari Lal, Education Minister had been elected MLA from Bahadurgarh constituency. He was a very clever and foxy politician. He used the "moral" credentials as his trump card and resigned from the Cabinet to seek a fresh mandate from the electorates of his old constituency to prove that he was morally on the high ground to desert the Congress Party.

During the by-election from Bahadurgarh Vidhan Sabha constituency held on 21st May 1967, stakes both for Sh. Hardwari Lal with his SVD and Pt. B D Sharma were very high. Both sides put in all their might, in the electioneering. Sh. Hardwari Lal wanted to win with larger majority this time. He mobilized his own jat clan, which formed a big majority of electorate. The non-jat electorate were made to fall in line in the entire rural area with muscle power. In the process, quite a number of unpleasant incidents of aggression took place at places in which the jats had allegedly committed atrocities on weaker sections. Many scheduled caste families had to leave their homes and hearths.

They fled away to save themselves from the sporadic attacks from supporters of Sh Hardwari Lal. By-election was held with Election Commission closely monitoring the day-to-day happenings.

Hardwari Lal, after winning the election, had again become the Education Minister in the Rao Cabinet. Bhagwat Dayal Sharma and Ranbir Singh Ex-Minister, like ferocious injured tigers, were pursuing the complaints of scheduled caste families, lodged with Election Commission. Rao Sahib, the Chief Minister of Haryana was in a dilemma. On one side, there was a lurking serious apprehension of poaching by Bhagawat Dayal Sharma in his flock of SVD MLAs and on the other side, he did not want any stigma on his fair name for atrocities allegedly committed on scheduled caste families during his Chief Ministership. Chand Ram, a senior scheduled caste leader from Rohtak, holding an important portfolio in the Rao Ministry, was also very keen that no blame should come to him from his community that during the days of his ministership, atrocities had been committed on the scheduled castes families in Rohtak district. It was under such a highly surcharged and volatile situation of politics of Rohtak District that I was posted as District Superintendent of Police Rohtak in May 1967.

After receiving my transfer and posting order as District Superintendent of Police Rohtak, I called on the State IGP, Sh. Bhagwan Singh Rosha. He gave me few tips rather briefly. However, he emphatically advised me to proceed cautiously as the people of the area he said, were highly conscious politically and were temperamental in their reaction. J C Vachher DIG/CID gave me numerous do's and don'ts, in his typical slow-marching style, laced with words of wisdom. He, particularly told me to try to assuage the injured feelings of Dr Mangal Sein, Jan Sangh leader, mentioning in passing that he was genuinely aggrieved because of Rohtak Police treating him, as if he was a rogue and hardened criminal. I also called on Ajaib Singh who had been DIG/CID for very long period, during Composite Punjab days. He, inter-alia, advised me to meet and hold longer sittings with Siri Ram Sharma of Rohtak City, Ranbir Singh of Sanghi, Lehri Singh and Rizak Ram, both from Sonepat– all these four leaders had been Cabinet Ministers in Composite Punjab. I also sought an interview with the Chief Minister Rao Birender Singh. He told me in chaste Urdu that he wanted to post me as District SP Karnal but Chand Ram, his Cabinet colleague, pressed him to post me at Rohtak. These words of the Chief Minister were meaningfully loaded. He perhaps wanted to convey to me that I carried the tag of being a scheduled caste and extra-friendly to Chand Ram. Though there are no permanent friends and foes in politics as they often swap positions to suit their political interests, yet I had to be extra careful to ensure that the Chief Minister, in no case should carry impression doubting my complete impartiality and neutrality. As an IPS Officer, I had to remain committed to uphold the Rule of Law and nothing else. However, this was a wake up call for me to be on my guard against any bad impression being nurtured.

Joining at Rohtak

I took charge of the District Superintendent of Police Rohtak, on May 22nd 1967. L. Isa Das IAS (SCS) was the Deputy Commissioner and Gurnam Singh was the District and Session Judge. My predecessor was Surinder Nath Chopra, 1955 IPS (SPS). He did not vacate the earmarked residence of the District SP for three weeks due to marriage ceremony of his daughter. I had to stay put in the Rest House for that period. As per advice of Ajaib Singh IPS, DIG (Retd.), I availed the earliest possible opportunity to hold long interacting sessions with Siri Ram Sharma of Rohtak City, Ranbir Singh of Sanghi, Rizak Ram of Sonepat and Lehri Singh, then a practicing advocate at Rohtak. Lehri Singh appeared to me somewhat of eccentric mind. He was blowing his own trumpet. In addition to developing good rapport with the other three respectable leaders of district Rohtak, I learnt a lot about the history and nature of the people, from their narration of numerous past stories.

Ranbir Singh briefed me in detail about the atrocities that were committed unabashedly by the supporters Hardwari Lal against the non-jats, during the electioneering of just held by-election. He had then approached VC Shukla, Union Minister of State for Home Affairs with a request to visit the sensitive villages in the constituency, which bore enough testimony of the lawlessness then prevailing during that period. Shri Shukla along with B S Moorthy and Prof Sher Singh, both Ministers of State in the Union Government, agreed to visit the constituency. Ranbir Singh conducted their visit to the most sensitive villages. Both the Deputy Commissioner and the Superintendent of Police also accompanied them. In village Bopania, the jat supporters of Hardwari Lal had assaulted Brahmins, Banias, some other backward class people and the scheduled castes. The Ministers heard their woeful tales of sufferings, at the hands of the jats, the supporters of Hardwari Lal. The jats gheraoed them in village Mandauthi and made a determined bid to assault Ranbir Singh. But for the timely intervention of the police, he would have been badly assaulted.

On return to Delhi, Shri Shukla gave a press statement, depicting the lawlessness prevailing in village Mandauthi. Since Hardwari Lal was the Cabinet Minister at the time of contesting the by-election, even the district administration, much more the district police had failed to provide necessary protection to the weaker sections, in the village. On the election day of 21st May 1967, the non-jat voters were threatened and harassed. Secrecy of voting was thrown to the winds and impersonation became the order of the day. Many horror-struck people fled away from the village to save themselves from the jat fury. The victims submitted their complaints to the higher authorities but nothing was done to haul up the culprits. L Isa Das the Deputy Commissioner, explaining to me the state of affairs which had prevailed during the electioneering and also on the by-election day, expressed his extreme unhappiness against the district police, specially the attitude of the then District SP, for their inaction and remaining mute spectators to the atrocious attacks by the jats on the scheduled castes. Both, Dy SP Harinder Singh and SHO Bahadurgarh, confirmed to me what Ranbir Singh and the Deputy Commissioner had told me about the happenings during and on the day of by-election of 21st May 1967. All these startling and hair raising revelations made me deeply concerned and determined to restore law and order in the constituency at the earliest.

Soon after my taking over the charge, Chand Ram and Hardwari Lal, both Cabinet Ministers held a Public meeting at Bahadurgarh, from where Hardwari Lal had won the by-election, causing acute bitterness between the jat supporters of Hardwari Lal and the scheduled caste electorates. I had to be personally present at Bahadurgarh to ensure proper law and order. Hardwari Lal was the star speaker at the public meeting. On his suggestion, whispered to Chand Ram, the latter asked me to address the gathering and announce that my inquiries revealed that the allegations of atrocities, committed by the jat supporters of Hardwari Lal, against the scheduled caste community, were baseless.

Without offering my detailed comments on the suggestion of Chand Ram, I simply informed him that addressing any political meeting, by the District Superintendent of Police or for that matter by any district level government officer, would be against the Service Conduct Rules. Chand Ram conveyed my views accordingly to Hardwari Lal who got very annoyed and told Chand Ram, within my hearing "This scheduled caste District SP is very arrogant and useless to us; this will have to be brought to the notice of the Chief Minister." This incident unfortunately turned out to be the basis for hardening an utterly biased attitude of Hardwari Lal against me. I was only a few days old as Rohtak District SP. I brought this matter to the notice of the Range DIG. His advice was that I should learn to swim with the current. Feeling sad on this advice, I decided to meet the IGP. During my audience with Bhagwan Singh Rosha, the IGP, he appreciated my stand and assured me that he would bring it to the notice of the Chief Minister. He also advised me to have an audience with the Chief Minister and explain to him my viewpoint. Accordingly, I sought an interview with CM and narrated, not only the said incident to him, but also explained to him as to how the law of jungle had prevailed, during the electioneering and the election day. The CM advised me in very dignified manner that I should try to uphold the rule of law and not bother about any threats from any quarter. I felt elated by the very encouraging and morale boosting words of the CM and started taking up my job as District SP in the right earnest.

During initial two months' period, I undertook extensive touring of the district to familiarize myself with its topography, historical background, prevailing state of crime in every police station, socio-cultural fabric and the people that mattered. In fact, Rohtak was the nerve centre of politics of Hindi speaking area in the Composite Punjab State. Anybody coming from Hindi speaking region of Composite Punjab State was known as "Rohtaki" in common parlance in Punjabi speaking areas. The district was also known as nursery of Indian soldiery and many army officers of the district earned the distinction of displaying gallantry of exceptionally high order in the army. The people of Rohtak had also displayed nerves of steel during the 1857 Mutiny by creating difficult situation for the British Rulers. The district had the distinction of producing front ranking freedom fighters.

The non-Congress Government of Haryana had jumbo Ministry of 34 persons, headed by Rao Birender Singh. Ten ministers including the Speaker and Deputy Speaker were from this district alone. Every politician of the district, with some standing, considered himself capable for the top political executive post. The Bhartiya Jan Sangh (BJS) the only well organized political outfit opposing the Congress Party had its command centre at Rohtak, with its fire brand leader Dr Mangal Sein, heading the Haryana Unit. For all these reasons, I thought it imperative to acquaint thoroughly myself with every aspects of this, all-important geographical and political unit of the new State of Haryana.

When Dr. Mangal Sein came to see me for the first time, I was reminded of the words of DIG/CID that this Jan Sangh leader had not been fairly treated by the police. Therefore, I found it to be a good opportunity to get first hand information about his grievances against the police. He was utterly bitter in criticizing the district police administration. I could guess that something very unusual must have happened to him, at the hands of the police. With moist eyes and emotionally surcharged temper, he almost broke down while narrating his woeful tales of inhuman treatment meted out by the police. He told me that he was victimized and hauled up by Surinder Nath Chopra, the then District SP, at the behest of Bhagwat Dayal Sharma, the then CM. He was tortured and beaten blue during night hours by two constables in the city police station. Crying incessantly, he narrated the horrendous tales of police excesses and atrocities against him. Feeling sad, I tried to sympathize with him and clam him down. However, my conscience was badly pricked on the thought that as successor of Chopra, I would be heading a force with rogues like those two constables and the then SHO of city police station. When I suggested to Dr. Mangal Sein that "forget and forgive" approach would give him peace of mind, he shot back saying that if ever he comes across Chopra dying and asking for a draught of water, he would not even spit on his foul mouth. The meeting with Dr. Mangal Sein kept me always on the guard to ensure that no police personnel of the district ever misbehaved with any public man.

Historical Background of District Rohtak

From the old records, available in different sources including *Rohtak District Gazetteer Volume-III* compiled and published under the authority of Punjab Government in 1910, and my interaction with some old people, I found the physical aspects of district Rohtak to be quite fascinating. Rohtak, as name of the district, as it is often pronounced, is said to be a corruption of Rohtasgarh, a name applied to the ruined sites of two older cities, one lying immediately north of the town and the other about 12 km to the east. Traditionally, it was named after Raja Rohtas, during whose reigns the city was built. In 1824, Rohtak district comprised four tehsils of Gohana, Kharkhauda-Mandauthi, Rohtak-Beri and Mehm-Bhiwani. The whole Delhi territory including Rohtak was administered by a political agent, under the Resident at Delhi till 1832. The district was abolished in 1824, Gohana going to Panipat and the rest of the tehsils to Delhi. The district was recreated soon after. Rohtak district contained four tehsils- Gohana, Jhajjar, Sampla and Rohtak up to 1910. Sampla tehsil was abolished in 1910 and only the remaining three tehsils formed the part of the District, on redistribution of its territory. However, on the eve of Independence of India in 1947, the district had four sub-divisions– Sonepat, both, civil and police sub-div, Gohana, Jhajjar and Rohtak only civil sub-divisions. When I joined as District SP Rohtak in May 1967, the ibid position was still standing.

A huge road-roller is on public display in a park in Sonepat town, as a proof of the absolute repressive tactics unleashed by the British during the Mutiny of 1857. This road-roller is known as Khooni Kolhari. According to Dr. Mahender Kumar, a historian, one Udhmi Ram and his group, waylaid some Britishers on Sher Shah Suri Road (Grand Trunk Road). British forces laid siege of Libaspur village and directed the villagers to either hand over Udhmi Ram and his companions to them or they would kill the entire population of the village. The road-roller had then rolled over around 20 youths of the village, who along with their leader and local hero Udhmi Ram, had earlier assassinated some Britishers and had held their women hostage in Chaupal of the village. The women folk of the village even today sing songs glorifying the sacrifice of Udhmi and others.

Priority Activities During First Two Months

My activities during the first two months were very hectic and absorbing. I studied in depth, the physical aspects of district Rohtak, its early history, nature, customs, characteristics and social life of its people and political standing of various politicians of all parties. I had the complex problem of rehabilitating the scheduled castes families who had deserted their home and hearth to save themselves from the atrocious attacks by the supporters of Hardwari Lal, during the just concluded by-election in Bahadurgarh Assembly constituency. For this purpose, I constituted a team of three officers – Harinder Singh Dy SP, District Inspector and SI SHO of Police Station Bahadurgarh. Through this team, I ensured concrete confidence building measures, to encourage the terror-stricken scheduled castes families, who had been up-rooted, to return to their homes in their respective villages.

In every sensitive village, Peace Committees of all caste respectable elderly persons were constituted. All the mischief mongers were identified. A number of complaints had already been received in the District Police Office against many persons from various villages of Bahadurgarh Assembly constituency for grave acts of violence committed against those persons whom Hardwari Lal and his supporters had suspected for not voting in his favour. Based on inquiries conducted by Dy SP's team, criminal cases were registered against the concerned offenders. Those who were found not guilty of committing grave violence by the Dy SP's team, were let off with stern warning, on assurance of the Peace Committees. However, the hard-liners were proceeded against as per law. Soon the displaced scheduled castes families returned to their respective villages. In some cases, their cattle heads had died of hunger and thirst, having remained tethered and unattended for many days. The District Magistrate sanctioned financial help very liberally to such sufferers from the District Relief Fund.

The role of the All-Castes-Peace Committees was highly appreciated in all quarters. Complete peace and harmony was restored. However, in the process, many of the hard-liner supporters of Hardwari Lal had naturally to suffer, for their misdeeds. This was not to the liking of Hardwari Lal. He was already annoyed with me for my not agreeing to address the political public gathering, earlier convened by him together with his Cabinet colleague

Chand Ram at Bahadurgarh. Strong and effective measures taken by the District Administration, particularly the District Police further hardened antagonism of Hardwari Lal against me. I not only remained unruffled against Hardwari Lal's added animosity towards me, I was rather feeling happy that the Range DIG, DIG/CID, the State IGP and the State Chief Minister applauded my role in rehabilitating the suffering and uprooted people of scheduled castes community. Chand Ram also took the credit for himself rightly or wrongly for this. For me, he became my admirer to the point of my embarrassment, at times.

I was reminded of what Swami Vivekanand had said "We are responsible for what we are, and whatever we wish ourselves to be, we have the power to make ourselves. If what we are now has been the result of our own past actions, it certainly follows that whatever we wish to be in future, can be produced by our own present actions, so we have to know how to act." It was my daily routine, when to welcome everybody and anybody coming to meet me in the office, during the working hours. This was my priority number one. I availed of the opportunity at the earliest, to interact in question-answer sessions with the lawyers in bar rooms at Rohtak, Jhajjar, Gohana and Sonepat. I requested the lawyers to refrain from accompanying any complainant coming to meet me seeking redressal of his grievances. They agreed grudgingly that appearing before the Police of a lawyer was not within the ambit of their professional rules. Having studied in depth the state and trend of crime, Police Station wise for the last three years and close interaction with the Dy SPs, Inspectors and SHOs, I worked out a policy to tackle the problems concerning crime, criminals, police efficiency and public-police relations. During my visits to various police stations and also to the police lines at the District Hqr, I repeatedly exhorted and impressed upon the police personnel neither to use intemperate language while conversing with any public man nor to manipulate any political interference in the matters of their posting and transfer. I called upon them to put in their written requests if they had any difficulty in this regard and to feel free even meeting me any time during the working hours in the office with the prior permission of their seniors.

From day one of my innings as District SP, I maintained a register to record the gist of conversation with all important persons visiting me in the office or residence, in my own hand. It was exclusively for my personal information and remaind under my personal custody. It had 99 such entries during the first five months of my tenure. Entry no. 41 of dated 17.07.1967 is about Pratap Singh Daulata, a Cabinet Minister, in the Rao Government who called me to Canal Rest House. He recommended the posting of some police personnel at certain places at first. Thereafter he said that Chand Ram-Devi Lal axis was trying to consolidate the Congress Party to dislodge the Rao Ministry, with Chand Ram despite being in the Ministry, clandestinely playing active role. He told me to break this nexus. Entry no. 43, dated 20.07.1967, is regarding my meeting with the Chief Minister at his residence on the evening of 20.07.1967. I explained to him, as to how his Cabinet colleagues were pressurizing me not to take action as warranted by law against the accused involved in assaulting a constable in village Mendipore. I also explained as to how Hardwari Lal, while presiding over the District Grievances Redress

Committee meeting, had accused me of encouraging the scheduled castes people against the jats on caste consideration and that in such eventuality the aggressive jats would crush the scheduled castes. Such aggressive and humiliating posture of Hardwari Lal was intended to degrade the District SP in the presence of the district level officers in the meeting. Having heard me patiently, the Chief Minister told me that I was doing quite well but I should also try to take into confidence, Hardwari Lal and Pratap Singh Daulata, as they were typical jat leaders of Rohtak.

As per Entry no. 47 of 24th July, 1967, I met Hardwari Lal in the Rest House at Bahadurgarh and tried to explain the factual ground position and informed him that the criminal cases were registered after holding discussions with Range DIG and State IGP and that the complainant was Ranbir Singh, an eminent jat Congress leader. Hardwari Lal was not at all impressed. He rather raised the pitch of his voice and said, "The scheduled cates were dependant on jats and they had acquired false notion that they could live peacefully while at daggers drawn with jats and that within next two years, there would be caste war between the jats and the scheduled castes and in that scheduled castes would suffer heavily." He further demanded that I should give proof of my being favourable to jats by hushing up all criminal cases registered against them. I explained to him that all the cases, had been put up in the Courts after due investigation, and his Government, if so desired, could withdraw those cases, as the District Police could do nothing in the matter. He shouted furiously "Here you are." In the same tone, he said "Samyukt Vidhayak Dal (SVD) would soon show Chand Ram his place, as inquiries against him would soon be initiated for his bungling in Cooperative Department." Despite his bullying behaviour, I kept my composure. Writhen with self-inflicted pain caused by his loss of temper that raised his blood pressure also, he commanded me to leave. Saying "Thank you Sir", I saluted him and quietly left his room.

Entry No.49, dated 28.07.1967 is regarding my meeting with DIG Range in Rai Rest House. I narrated to him the details of the shouts hurled on me by Hardwari Lal, on 24.07.1967 at Bahadurgarh. He appreciated my stand and told me that Hardwari Lal wanted to get Dalip Singh posted as District SP Rohtak as a scheduled caste would not suit him as District SP Rohtak. He also wanted to teach a lesson to Chand Ram for lodging criminal complaints against the Jats. The DIG further told me that he not only refused to toe his line but also made it clear that if honest officers were to suffer and corrupt officers encouraged for serving the politicians' ill-conceived motives, he would rather prefer to be transferred. The Range DIG advised me to remain vigilant and he on his part, would keep the IGP and the CM posted with the dubious designs of Hardwari Lal. Tirade against me by Hardwari Lal continued unabated. However, the Chief Minister did not agree to oblige him and I continued functioning uninterrupted. Finding that the Chief Minister was not inclined to transfer me from the District, Pratap Singh Daulata changed his stance and started getting friendly with me. There was another reason also for Daulata's changed attitude. He did not want Dalip Singh to become District SP Rohtak as desired by Hardwari Lal, because Daulata had not liked Dalip Singh for his role in the episode at village Mohangarh, PS Narwana of Jind, in 1960, as mentioned earlier.

Among the other politicians, meeting me often, with all types of recommendations, Mangal Sein of the Jan Sangh met me eighteen times during this period. He either recommended favour to be done to his people involved in grain smuggling/hoarding cases or for transfer and posting of police personnel. Mukhtiar Singh, MP from Sonepat, who was the State President of Jan Sangh, met me six times for the transfer and posting of some police personnel. One very funny instance of his interference in the Police Administration was his repeated insistence that SI Mangat Ram already posted as SHO Sonepat should not be transferred, while two other politicians of Sonepat were alleging SI Mangat Ram to be a corrupt police officer. I called the SHO and snubbed him for manipulating political interference by Mukhtiar Singh for continuation of his stay at Sonepat. It was during his fifth visit to my office on 08.10.1967 that Mukhtiar Singh spoke bitterly against SI Mangat Ram and regretted for his earlier recommendation. I had a hearty laugh at that summersault of Mukhtiar Singh. Another politician of the SVD was Manphool Singh, the Deputy Speaker in Rao Government, who made many recommendations regarding posting and transfer of police personnel. One of his repeated recommendations was to help one Jai Narain, an accused in a robbery case. I had to convey him respectfully that it was not worthy of his position to plead the case of an accused of robbery. He however, expressed his unhappiness over this.

Pratap Singh Daulata, Cabinet Minister, was generally very egoistic and unnecessarily over assertive in making his point. Once he went unannounced to Police Station Kalanaur. He went straight to the SHO, who had laid his office out in the winter sun. Two chairs with worn-out cane seats were placed opposite to his table. The SHO looked at the tall, hefty built, turbaned, white clad Chaudhary and offered him a seat. The SHO was not aware of the visitor's status, nor had he seen him earlier. The Minister took an offence to the offer of chair with worn-out cane seat. Losing his cool, he shouted at the SHO. To placate the visitor, SHO offered his own chair, which was no better than the one already offered. Daulata's temper shot up and he shouted at the SHO saying that he was making fool of him. On knowing the identity of the visitor, SHO regretted his lack of knowledge about the status of the visitor and extended due courtesy.

However, the Minister did not calm down. He asked the SHO to connect him to the State IGP on telephone but he himself instantly connected the telephone. He told the IGP that he was insulted very badly by the SHO, therefore he should be placed under suspension forthwith. The IGP informed me of the incident and asked to tackle the issue tactfully at my level. I rushed to Police Station only to find that the Minister had already left for the Rest House. Getting the first hand information of the incident from the SHO, I met Daulata Sahib at the Rest House. He asked me not only to place the SHO under suspension but also to punish him severely by dismissing him from the service. I very respectfully explained to Daulata that SHO was not at fault at all and that his suspension was not warranted, much less his dismissal. Arguing vehemently, he tried to overawe me. Informing him that I would report the matter to the IGP to take his instructions, I saluted the Minister and took his leave.

I briefed the IGP on telephone about my meeting and Minister's desire to take severe action against the SHO. The IGP suggested considering the suspension of the SHO and reinstatement after a few days to appease the Minister. However, I declined the suggestion, as the action would have demoralized the Police Force. Daulata on the other hand remained adamant. Despite all sorts of pressure from different quarters, I refused to suspend the SHO. I compromised only in asking the SHO to proceed on a few days leave, which he did. On return from leave, he resumed his duty as SHO Kalanaur. This episode became an amusing talking point amongst the lawyers at the Bar Room. Daulata did not, even once, agitate thereafter and perhaps thought it to be appropriate to forget all about this incident.

During the Rao's Government of Samyukt Vidhayak Dal(SVD), I had found many non gazetted officers (NGOs) and other ranks (ORs) indulging in malpractices and blatant corruption under the patronage of politicians. Since I was very busy with restoration of deteriorating law and order situation, I could not devote adequate time to tame the wayward police force personnel. Almost every non-gazetted police officer (NGO) and other rank (OR) had a godfather in one or the other politician.

Fall of Rao Government and Subsequent Development

Samyukat Vidhayak Dal was a loose conglomeration of political leaders with no commonality of views, ideas and objectives, much less any common political ideology; their only commonality of objectives was to hold on to power by hook or by crook. Samyukat Vidhayak Dal, as political party, had not at all gone down to the masses. Every political leader claiming to be a Dal leader had his own pack of followers, who would follow him like sheep to whatever political party the leader would switch over. Thus, every Dal leader of some reckoning used to promote his own interest, as also the interest of his followers. Jan Sangh led by its top leader Dr Mangal Sein, had its own agenda to pursue for getting maximum political mileage while clinging on to Samyukat Dal. Therefore, serious cracks in the top SVD leadership surfaced soon. Hardwari Lal, who was extremely crafty and cunning, started hobnobbing with the Swatantra Party leadership. Devi Lal a strong jat leader of the Congress Party could not develop adequate equation with Congress High Command after falling out with Pratap Singh Kairon, the then Chief Minister of Composite Punjab. In fact, Bhagwat Dayal Sharma, who became the first Chief Minister of Haryana State, left no stone unturned to slight all Congress leaders in the state, who could challenge his leadership. Thus, Devi Lal had lost his moorings in the Congress High Command. After the fall of Congress Government led by Bhagwat Dayal Sharma, Devi Lal was won over by Rao Birender Singh, an Ex-Congress leader. Chand Ram, the top scheduled caste Congress leader, had already joined Rao's camp as a Cabinet Minister. The top jat leaders in the Dal were manoeuvering to sideline Chand Ram. He therefore, joined hands with Devi Lal and shortly Devi Lal-Chand Ram axis became very strong. Devi Lal got Chand Ram elevated to the position of Deputy Chief Minister. Still Devi Lal-Chand Ram axis visualized that the future of the Dal was very bleak and they wanted, some how to revert to Congress fold. On the other hand, Bhagwat Dayal Sharma was ferociously fighting back like an injured tiger to pull down the Rao Government.

Defections from one political group to the other became the order of the day. One MLA changed sides three times and another five times within a span of a fortnight. While addressing a public meeting at Jhajjar, Rao Sahib sarcastically remarked that no time was left for him to launch any developmental scheme in the state, because his entire time is consumed in taking care of "jumping frogs." He said this when an MLA from the Dal came to meet him and introduced his name as Gaya Ram. Rao Sahib remarked that he was sick of hearing every day the reports of *'Gaya Rams*. Would anybody inform him whether there were any *"Aaya Rams"* also? The saying of *'Aaya Rams'* and *'Gaya Rams'*, meaning the frequent to and fro defections, became very popular not only in Haryana but in other states as well. Money power and muscle power played the dirty role in this ugly game of *'Aaya Rams'* and *'Gaya Rams'*. SVD Government came crumbling down like a sandy wall. In the face of utter confusion and political uncertainty when Rao's Government fell, the Union Government imposed President Rule on 22.11.1967.

B N Chakraverty, ICS with proven Administrative competence, was made the Governor of the State. All powers to administer the State and cleanse the Augean stable came to be vested in the very experienced Governor. The politicians changed their style, while dealing with the district officers. The Congress leaders, who earlier used to behave like lambs, all of a sudden started snarling like wolves and those in all opposite camps, mellowed down presenting very amusingly dejected colours. Rao Birender Singh, Ex-Chief Minister must have felt highly relieved, at the fall of his Government as it was a very good riddance from all the unprincipled politicians surrounding him, as his Cabinet colleagues. The politicians in the district had experienced by then that their uncalled for interference and illogical recommendations, regarding the postings and transfers of police personnel and their efforts to influence the course of investigations of criminal cases had found no favour with the District SP even throughout Rao Government. Therefore, they changed their stance and completely stopped pestering me with any recommendations.

The general thinking with the people was to bring back the Congress Party to form the Government. Therefore, the politicians, who had gone in hibernation and were aspiring to get Congress Party ticket, became active and started making requests respectfully to accommodate the police personnel of their choice in their respective constituencies; this however, did not have any effect on my approach of keeping in mind only the best interest of the administration in all matters. By way of my respectful tribute to Rao Sahib, I must make a mention that true to his reputation, he never made any recommendation either to influence the course of any investigation or for posting or transfer of any police personnel. He announced the formation of a new Political Party by the name 'Vishal Haryana Party' after the fall of his Government. The political leaders, who flocked to this new political party, were of comparatively clean image.

Administration During Governor's Rule

Political leaders in the district kept very low profile during the six months' period of Governor's Rule in the State. This gave me ample time to successfully revamp the police administration and tame the wayward police personnel in the district. The district police made many achievements during this period in maintaining law and order and developing excellent police–public relations.

Four political figures came to my mind who had shown magnanimity of being less of playing throughout fair game and were helpful to me in many ways. Prof Sher Singh, a senior Congress leader from Jhajjar area of the district was a State Minister in the Union Government. A true Gandhian and well cultured by all standards, he never played dirty politics. Amenable to reason, I never found him losing his temper. I always gave high regard to his advice and was immensely benefited. The second person was a very young comely scheduled caste girl, Ms Kartar Devi. The cause of justice to scheduled castes was very dear to her heart. Despite her humble origin and modest resources, she was a one person army, to fight against oppression and injustice to any scheduled caste person. She had once resorted to fast unto death in Delhi, at the Samadhi of Mahatma Gandhi – the Father of the Nation. I had deep regard for her mission and her person, dedicated to the social cause. I could then see in her the making of an important leader in the days to come. No wonder, she remained a Cabinet Minister in many Congress ministries in the state. She remained a dignified unmarried woman throughout her life. She expired in 2009 after brief ailment.

The third person was Charanji Lal Sharma, an upcoming dignified figure in politics. A leading advocate, mainly practising at Sonepat, he used to play principled politics and seemed to be on the way to become a popular face as a non–jat leader, in the wake of waning popularity of Bhagwat Dayal Sharma, who was in the amidst of various self created controversies. I used to take advice of Charanji Lal Sharma in complicated matters, particularly legal matters emanating from vile conduct of some rogue politicians. The fourth person, in fact, very important of all was Rizak Ram, a Congress leader, from Sonepat. He was honest, straightforward and a man of principles. An advocate by profession, he pursued politics like a gentleman. I remember an interesting incident about him. There were restrictions on the unauthorized movement of foodgrains during sixties. There have been many instances of people indulging in smuggling of foodgrains from Haryana to UP by crossing Yamuna River, falling between Sonepat area and Baghpat area of UP. Rai police hauled up many persons of a particular village in Rai constituency on the charge of smuggling foodgrains to UP. As the number of persons involved in the crime was very large, Rizak Ram got upset over it. He talk to me on the telephone and instead of introducing himself, started shouting, "You as District SP, consider yourself a dictator like Ayub Khan of Pakistan; this would not be allowed to happen." Shouting back at him, I said, "You imposter, how dare you impersonate Rizak Ram, who is a highly respectable soft spoken and cultured gentleman politician." I dramatized the incident knowing well that it was really Ch. Rizak Ram on the telephone. He immediately disconnected the telephone line without uttering a single word. After about three hours, he came to my office and apologized for his 'utterances' saying that he was under tension. He further told me to do whatever I considered appropriate as per law. He remained very friendly with me and warmly extended helping hand to me whenever I sought his advice on law and order matters; he never made any unnecessary recommendation throughout my tenure at Rohtak. Even after my transfer from the district, he continued to maintain very cordial relations with me. Rizak Ram was indeed an honest and straightforward man of high values.

Annual Police Administration Report of the District for the year 1967

Detailed Annual Police Administration Report of the district, for year ending on 31st December, is prepared by the District Superintendent of Police and submitted to the higher authorities, through the District Magistrate. Accordingly, I prepared a detailed and comprehensive report and submitted it to the District Magistrate, on 21st January 1968. L. Isa Dass, the District Magistrate forwarded my said report to the DIG Ambala Range and Commissioner Ambala Division on 29.02.1968 with the following comments:-

"3.(i) there were 23 cases of murder, during the year under report, as against 22 during the previous year. It is pertinent to point out that out of these 23 cases, as many as 20 were such, which could not be anticipated as they were neither pre-meditated nor the outcome of any apparent party faction. There was not a single case of dacoity during the year."

"(ii) The district police acquitted itself with credit, particularly in the prevention and detection of serious crime, anti-smuggling measures and liquidation of proclaimed offenders and military deserters. The vigilance exercised by the Superintendent of Police, in particular and other senior police officers, in general, in the prevention of corruption and prompt disposal of public grievances deserve special mention. Satta gambling has almost been eradicated, since the present Superintendent of Police took over charge of the district."

"(iii) There had generally been a persistent complaint of lack of proper co-ordination and co-operation by the police, with other departments. This has altogether disappeared, in the district. The Supdt of Police takes special pains to ensure perfect co-operation and co-ordination of the police, with all departments, in genuine cases, at all levels. This has considerably enhanced the prestige of the administration, as a whole and has resulted in better enforcement and implementation of laws, rules and government policy by all agencies of government."

"(iv) Prompt and effective action taken by the Supdt of Police against unscrupulous police officers has restored confidence of the public, in police administration of the district. Appropriate action, on all genuine and specific complaints, is very much applauded, by all sections of the community, particularly those, who have no political support or influence."

"4. In the end, I may state that Shri H R Swan, the Superintendent of Police, since his taking over, has altogether transformed the police administration of the district with his upright humanitarian approach, sympathetic dealings, and sincerity of purpose and prompt and effective action. Notwithstanding inherent difficulties and hurdles in his way, he has been able to imbibe a spirit of sacrifice in a considerable portion of all ranks of the police force. I have no hesitation in stating that the present Supdt of Police Shri H R Swan is really a model police officer, in a welfare state, like ours, where even the police are expected to lay more stress on the moral, social and welfare aspects of the society, rather than mere prevention, detection and prosecution of crime. I wish there were more officers like him."

The Most Eventful Year of My Police Career

During the year 1968, I had to grapple with a number of important situations and events, some of which are narrated here.

Students Agitation

There had been widespread unrest in the student community, all over the country during the year. My timely and appropriate measures, including close interaction with the principals and staff members of various colleges and educational institutions kept the students unrest under check. The students studying in Delhi colleges, used to commute by Railways, without ticket, between Rohtak and Delhi. The Railway Authorities had reconciled to the situation. However, of late the students while returning from Delhi would halt the trains at will at any place of their convenience, by pulling the emergency chain. This had caused a lot of discomfort and inconvenience to other travellers on the trains. I organized and deployed strong police squads at various sensitive places to check and curb this nuisance. This produced good results.

In another incident, the students of Medical College Rohtak put up a strong demand for the transfer of Dr. Inderjit Dewan, the Principal of the College. Mahant Shreyo Nath of Bohar Monastery, who had been Health Minister in the Rao Government, instigated the students to demand the removal of the Principal, who was a well-known figure in the medical profession. The Mahant was heading the famous Bohar Monastery, which had a considerable following and had highly valuable immovable assets. He was less of a socio-religious person and more of a politician playing very cheap politics. As a Minister in the Rao Ministry, he had even more nuisance value. He had his own axe to grind against the Principal. Some members of college faculties were also clandestinely instigating the students.

The students organized a long march from the college to the residence of the Deputy Commissioner in the Civil Lines area. I got the procession stopped much short of the residence of the Deputy Commissioner and asked the students to go, as a delegation of five of them, for presenting the memorandum of their demands to the DC. However, students became restless and violent. I had to suppress their evil designs of causing damage to public property by resorting to strong-arm tactics. They dispersed without causing much damage to the public property. As per the intelligence reports they were soon to organize a violent agitation. I, along with the Deputy Commissioner prevailed upon the Principal and also had straight talk with the mischievous senior members of the college faculty to close down the hostels, for indefinite period and to issue instructions requiring the students to vacate the hostels immediately. Adequate police arrangements were made in and around the college premises to prevent any untoward incident. Rikshas were not allowed to operate between the college hostels and the city bus-stand. The students had to carry the heavy loads of their belongings on foot to the city bus-stand. The parents of the students, who had spent lots of money for their studies, naturally got worried and upset. They approached the district authorities, to have the college re-opened, assuring good behaviour, conduct and discipline of their wards. The strategy worked very well and peace was restored in the college. With all such measures by the district administration, the district remained completely unaffected from student unrest, which was endemic in other parts of the country.

Essex Farm Kundli

An enterprising industrialist of Delhi had set up Essex Farm on Delhi-Ambala Grand Trunk Road at Kundli in Police Station Rai of sub-div Sonepat of the district. In fact, the idea to set up this farm was conceived during early sixties and the state government of Composite Punjab had then sanctioned the setting up of this factory in the private sector. The products of this factory comprised the processing of pork and preparing various types of sausages for supply to the Indian army. The hygiene and cleanliness of this unit could match any International standard. Manual handling of the product involved only the initial cleansing of the pigs. All other processing right from the entry of the pigs in the mechanical cleaning chamber, upto the stage of canning the finished product, was automatic.

The factory reached the operation stage in early January 1968. Haryana people being generally vegetarian were resenting the setting up of this factory from the very beginning. When the factory reached the production stage, some unscrupulous politicians found it to be an opportunity to extort money from the factory owner by exploiting the public sentiments. Sensing the trouble, the owner approached the Governor of Haryana for ensuring proper law and order. The Governor called the Deputy Commissioner and the Superintendent of Police to get their views before taking the final decision whether the factory should start their production operations. Both the Deputy Commissioner and I studied the situation in depth. We concluded that the owner of the factory was entitled to adequate law and order arrangements and necessary support of the district administration as the apprehended public resistance was only the result of instigation by some wily politicians and as such no serious law and order situation was likely to develop. We reported our views accordingly to the Governor. The factory was thus, allowed to start production operations.

However, a few days later, a local politician from Sonepat manipulated an agitation by some people led by a 'Baba' from Gurukul at Jhajjar, a place far away from Sonepat. The district administration planned adequate security arrangements at the factory site to forestall any untoward situation because of violent posture of the agitators. I along with the Deputy Commissioner camped at a place some 500 yards from the factory. A police party under Inspector Narula was deployed at the factory. A few hundred agitating people assembled and tried to *gherao* the factory. However, they were driven away by the police. They reassembled and were again chased away. Such hide and seek games continued for about a week. Ultimately, we had to make some preventive arrests of the leading troublemakers. The political leader, who was behind all this trouble as also the Gurukul Baba of Jhajjar, were given a very stern warning. They understood that we were serious and it was futile to put any further resistance. The agitation thus fizzled out.

After the mid-term poll of 14th May 1968, some political leaders thought that their prestige suffered a setback in this incident during Governor's Rule. Therefore, they made a determined bid to teach the factory owner a lesson for not falling in line to meet their demands. They approached the newly elected Chief Minister Ch. Bansi Lal and pressurized him to order closure of the factory. The Chief Minister did not want to start his innings with any sort of trouble. It is unfortunate that instead of taking the decision on merit he succumbed to the pressure of the politicians and directed the district administration to ask the proprietor to close down the factory voluntarily. Thus, the helpless industrialist who had invested then a huge amount of Rupees Twenty five lacs in setting up the factory had to close it down. Resultantly, he went into coma and suffered a fatal massive heart attack. This was a very painful ending of the episode indeed!

Garib Dassi Monastery of Jhajjar

Like the Bohar Monastery, there was another very famous Monastery of district Rohtak at Jhajjar. A Dhankar jat saint by the name of Garib Dass had established this monastery around 1724. He produced his own Granth (Holy Book) titled *"Garib Dass Ka Granth Sahib."* It contained 7000 verses of the celebrated Saint Bhagat Kabir, followed by his own 17000 verses. This monastery had its followers spread almost all over the Composite Punjab State. The Mahant (Spiritual Leader) of this monastery used to be hereditary. The presiding head of the monastery was Mahant Ganga Sagar since 1968. This Mahant too, like many of his predecessors did not have much religious commitment as per the "Granth." There has been a long drawn-out feud, turned into rivalry, between Mahant Ganga Sagar and his co-laterals. The enmity between the two warring groups was so severe that the members of both the groups would lock themselves inside their respective 'forts' immediately after the sunset. The situation was so volatile that it could result into serious violence at any time. The district administration had sanctioned firearms for self-defence to both the groups. I felt that the district administration was definitely required to do some thing more, very concrete and positive, to restore normalcy, as merely providing the firearms was not a very wise step.

I worked out my own strategy to end the rivalry as a permanent measure. Accordingly, I spent two full days in Jhajjar and enlisted the active support of the elderly persons to bring about a permanent rapprochement between the hostile groups. Both the groups did not show amenability to my reasoning and persuasion, as they were adamant on their own terms and conditions. The elderly persons intervening in the matter also felt sick of their rigid stand. Finding no other way, I had to announce, as the last resort that the fire arms of both the groups would be confiscated, their licences cancelled and all the adult members put under preventive arrest, ensuring that none of them was released on bail. This threat worked. Both the groups came to terms and a complete rapprochement followed. This was followed by warm embraces and distribution of sweets. It was highly gratifying when at the end of the day, every body paid rich compliments to me for arranging rapprochement between the two warring groups who were at daggers drawn for years. Mahant Ganga Sagar got the Congress ticket to contest the forthcoming mid-term polls of May 1968. The members of his erstwhile enemy group had campaigned vigorously for his success. No wonder, Mahant Ganga Sagar won the Election.

Mid-Term Polls for State Vidhan Sabha

The Election Commission of India decided to hold mid-term polls for the State Vidhan Sabha on 12th and 14th May 1968 after holding meetings with the prominent political leaders. The kind of violence and disorder resorted to by the supporters of Hardwari Lal in the by-election held on 21st May 1967 in Bahadurgarh constituency had many lessons to be learnt by the district administration. The extent of violence and atrocities committed by the supporters of Hardwari Lal, on the weaker sections of the society during the by-election held on 21st May 1967 have already been described. Going by the past experience, it was indeed, an uphill task to ensure peaceful conduct of elections. It required a lot of planning and effective strategy, much ahead of the polling days.

I undertook intensive touring of all the villages falling in Bahadurgarh constituency and also the villages considered to be sensitive in other constituencies of the district, had close interaction with various people from all communities and held meetings with prominent likely contestants from all major parties. After holding detailed discussions with the gazetted police officers including Dy SP, CID, Police Inspectors, and SHOs, I finalized my contingency plan for making adequate arrangements. Thereafter, I held detailed discussions with the Deputy Commissioner in the meeting held by him with all the SDMs of the district. Demand for extra police force was projected to the higher authorities after holding discussions with the Range DIG, DIG/CID and State IGP. Since all the high-ups in the state administration had bitter experience of the happenings during the by-elections of May 1967, the plans drawn up by me were appreciated and adequate additional police force was provided to the district.

While the district administration remained busy with drawing up plans for making effective arrangements to tackle any foreseen or unforeseen contingency, the political scenario in the district underwent comprehensive changes. The SVD completely disintegrated and vanished, Rao Birender Singh, the Chief Architect of SVD had floated a new political party by the name Vishal Haryana Party. Hardwari Lal had joined Swatantra Party. The old Congress leaders having earlier revolted against the party for the sake of pelf and power were again hobnobbing with the Congress High Command. The Jan Sangh, while holding position of power in Rao Government, had lost much of its sheen. The general public mood appeared to be inclined to give mandate to the Congress Party. Bhagwat Dayal Sharma still having firm hold on the Congress Party as a result of his very close rapport with the High Command thanks to Morarji Desai, the then Deputy Prime Minister patronizing him. He seemed to have the last word in the selection of candidates to contest the mid-term poll on Congress ticket.

Devi Lal-Chand Ram axis was no longer welcome in the Congress fold. Devi Lal continued his efforts to find favour with the Congress High Command. Though he was denied the Congress ticket, yet he continued as a senior leader and a Congressman. Chand Ram having lost all hopes to get the Congress ticket decided to contest as Independent candidate from two places – Baroda constituency of district Rohtak and Babain constituency of district Karnal. Ramdhari Balmiki, a staunch follower of Bhagwat Dayal Sharma, was picked up as Congress candidate from Baroda constituency. Shyam Chand, a well-educated scheduled caste was new entrant in politics. Rao Birender Singh patronized him as Vishal Haryana Party candidate, from Baroda constituency. Shyam Chand had earlier missed narrowly his selection for class-I post in the All India/Central Civil Services Examination held by the UPSC in 1960 being overage. He was offered Central Secretariat Service class-II. He did not join that service and instead went to UK where he had three years stint in British Civil Service. Simultaneously by attending evening classes, he did two years' course in Journalism from London School of Journalism. He being very cultured, well mannered and well educated, soon became very popular with the electorates of Baroda constituency. Ramdhari Balmiki had unfortunately acquired notoriety for heavy drinking. He was semi-educated. Chand Ram, despite his being a well-established and highly respected scheduled caste leader had lost much of his charm after becoming Deputy Chief Minister in the Rao Government. This was because of his being in the company of jat leaders like Hardwari Lal and Pratap Singh Daulata.

Apprehending defeat during the electioneering, Ramdhari Balmiki indulged in levelling all types of allegations against me for manoeuvering his defeat and success of Shyam Chand. He created an ugly scene at the Canal Rest House when Morarji Desai and Bhagwat Dayal Sharma were staying there. I along with the Deputy Commissioner was sitting with them to explain the state of law and order in the district. Ramdhari Balmiki gate crashed into the room and started pointing his accusing finger at me alleging that the SP would get him defeated. Bhagwat Dayal Sharma endorsing his plea started accusing me for working against a Congress candidate who was so dear to him. Very cool mindedly, I requested him not to raise his voice and be a party to baseless accusations against me. I also requested Sh. Desai to permit me to put across my viewpoint. I explained to him the real face and the quality of character of Ramdhari Balmiki as a human being, who I said, was a slur on the fair name of Mahatma Gandhi and his Congress Party. After listening to my view point, Sh. Desai told Bhagwat Dayal Sharma very strongly that it was wrong on his part to patronize a person like Ramdhari Balmiki. He told me to carry on my duties in the best interest of the rule of law.

As the electioneering picked up, the law and order agencies in the district fully geared up to meet any possible eventuality. The centre of focus for the Union Home Ministry, the State Administration and the Chief Election Commissioner was Bahadurgarh constituency, where Hardwari Lal and his supporters had indulged in large-scale violence during the by-election of 1967. Hardwari Lal was contesting as a Swatantra Party candidate this time. The jats are known to be hard-liners by nature. They do not adopt a leader easily and once they do so they go all out to back him. However, if the things come to a pass where the community feels its political dominance at stake, they do not hesitate to dump their leader without second thought. Hardwari Lal had been the darling of Dalal jats of Bahadurgarh constituency. However, he had been changing political colours quickly like chameleon within the last 18 months period. Therefore, barring his die-hard supporters from Dalal Jats, the others were feeling sick of his political somersaults. On the other hand, Congress Party had selected Pratap Singh Chhikara a young jat leader of the area, with very clean image to contest the elections.

The non-jats were determined to vote against Hardwari Lal provided the district administration could effectively prevent violence by his die-hard supporters. Their apprehension of violence was confirmed when a strong jat group of 14 persons attacked Pratap Singh Chhikara armed with *lathis* and sharp edged agriculture tools during canvassing on 3rd May 1968 in Mandothi village. Chhikara was lucky to escape unhurt from Hardwari Lal's goons. However, two of his companions Amir Singh and Hoshiara were injured. Case FIR No.170 dated 03.05.1968 u/s 452/506/147/148 IPC was registered at Police Station Bahadurgarh. A strong police party was therefore, stationed at village Mandothi to restore and keep in check proper law and order situation in the village. The police action proved to be an ulcer in the throat of Hardwari Lal and his die-hard supporters. They started conspiring to obstruct all attempts by the Police to a free and fair election.

The fateful polling day of 14th May 1968 arrived. Fearing his defeat, Hardwari Lal was determined to create serious law and order problems so that the election in Bahadurgarh constituency could be cancelled. *The Hindustan Times,* Delhi dated 16.05.1968 described the situation under the caption "Drastic steps suggested for fair election" in the words "The Haryana mid-term poll has high-lighted the fact that the weaker sections of the community, particularly the Harijans, are not able to exercise their franchise freely, if the more powerful section is bent upon imposing its will. The police have limited utility because the extra force on election day disappears the next day and cannot afford requisite protection indefinitely. In the case of at least one constituency, Bahadurgarh in Rohtak district, it was, found that even the police were on defensive on the polling day. When some police officers tried to intervene to make it possible for the Harijans to go to the polling centre, they were, beaten by a section of the jats, who had earlier asked the Harijans, not to stir out of their houses. The Chief Election Commissioner went to inspect the polling and saw the injured police officers. Finding the situation getting out of control, extra police force had to be summoned from Delhi." A case FIR No.180 dated 14.05.1968, u/s 364/332/353/506/147/148/341/188/149/115/117 and 109 of IPC, Police Station Bahadurgarh was registered regarding the violence caused by Hardwari Lal and his supporters at village Mandothi on the polling day. The exact situation which prevailed in the constituency on the polling day can best be gauged from the statement dated 29.06.1968 of S P Sen Verma, Chief Election Commissioner of India, given by him to the Investigating Officer u/s 161 of Cr. PC His verbatim statement as recorded by the Investigating Officer is at Annexure-1.

The other prominent prosecution witnesses were P N Bhalla, Chief Electoral Officer-cum-Home Secretary, L. Isa Dass, DC Rohtak, V S Allahavadi, IAS, Chief Supervising Officer, Kanwar Randip Singh, DIG, Ambala Range, RR Singh IPS, Commandant HAP Bn and myself the District Superintendent of Police. Hardwari Lal had lost the election because he was not democratic by disposition and believed that might was right. He could not reconcile to his defeat at the husting. Heavy pressure started building up on his mind for preparing election petition against the winning candidate and for saving himself and his accomplice accused in the criminal case. It all adversely affected his psyche giving the impression as if he was losing mental balance. I got 'caution reports' from various sources including the State IGP, DIG/CID and DIG Range, that Hardwari Lal was hatching a conspiracy to physically eliminate the District SP, by raising a gang of hatchet men from his rabid supporters, notorious goons and army deserters. All these threats notwithstanding, I remained unruffled, with my firm belief that Hardwari Lal was behaving like a mad dog because of his cowardice to face the reality. What I only did was to direct the SHO PS Bahadurgarh, to arrest Hardwari Lal and the co-accused, in the above said criminal case. This unnerved him a lot. After the completion of the investigation, the case was sent to the court in July 1968, for the trial of the 30 accused persons. Hardwari Lal and his rabid accomplice Uday Singh were arraigned as abettors u/s 115 and 117 IPC for offences u/s 506 and 109 of IPC 28 other accused were made liable for offences u/s 364/332/353/341/188/147/148 and 149 of IPC. The trial continued for about a decade. Hardwari Lal and other accused persons used all sorts of tactics to delay the completion of trial. At long last, Hardwari Lal like a tamed and ashamed fellow yielded in 1978, before Devi Lal, the then Chief Minister and begged for pardon.

Devi Lal had become the Chief Minister of the state for the first time and was very liberal in approach. At the end of the day, the state government withdrew the case against Hardwari Lal and all his 29 co-accused persons on 27th April 1978, absolutely on political consideration. In the words of Sarvapalli Radhakrishnan "The aim of education is not acquisition of information, although important, or acquisition of technical skill, though essential in modern society but the development of that bent of mind, that attitude of reason, that spirit of democracy will make us responsible citizens." However, I had many encounters with Hardwari Lal. This led me to believe that behind all the posturing of being a highly educated "Sant" from St Stephen's College, a premier institution and claiming to be a prolific writer with defiance as his virtue, laid a primordial man, a narcissist with violence and litigation in his blood, who thought he could get away with anything. Few powerful men are able to balance their committed love for playing castiest politics with educational novelty. This may hold them with passing success but they are exposed soon. Hardwari Lal is no more alive. May his soul rest in peace!

Chand Ram, contesting as an Independent candidate lost at the hustings from Baroda constituency. However, he had won from Babain constituency of district Karnal. Shyam Chand, Vishal Haryana Party candidate, trounced Ramdhari Balmiki, Congress candidate from Baroda constituency. Chand Ram, a well-educated scheduled caste leader was reputed for fearlessly pursuing his agenda. He remained in active politics for more than four decades. Many opportunities came his way to hold high positions in politics, with promise to attain greater heights. Still he could not establish himself firmly in politics. He had the potential to become a Pan-India scheduled castes leader like Jagjivan Ram. Unfortunately, his heart guided him more than his head. Knowing well that perseverance, steadfastness, consistency and vision are the qualities which a politician, aspiring to go high in that profession, like the horse of a long race, must acquire. Chand Ram did not bother much to inculcate these qualities. Then his often-changing political colours impulsively, amounted to his acquiring self-inflicted setback. His ultimate failure in active politics has been a great loss to the depressed class communities all over and in Haryana particularly.

Mid-Term Poll threw up Bansi Lal as the Chief Minister

In the mid-term poll, Congress Party got mandate with thumping majority to rule the state. In fact, Bhagwat Dayal Sharma was the star campaigner for the Congress Party and it was generally believed by the electorate that he would become the Chief Minister. However, that was not to be. He had not himself contested the election because he too was denied the Congress ticket by the High Command, hence he was not the member of the Vidhan Sabha. There was an old resolution passed by the AICC that a non-member of the Vidhan Sabha would not become the leader of the Legislature Party. Due to the acute factionalism in the party, the leaders unhappy with Bhagwat Dayal Sharma invoked the said resolution. Therefore, he was told by the Congress High Command to wait, till he became the MLA in any by-election in future and in the meanwhile one of the elected MLAs should be elected as the leader of the party to become the Chief Minister. Because of the patronage of Morarji Desai, the Deputy Prime Minister, Congress High Command deputed Gulzari Lal Nanda and Bhagwat Dayal Sharma to select jointly a suitable Congress MLA, to lead the Congress Legislature Party and become the Chief Minister.

Bansi Lal, a very non-partisan Congress MLA, was very close to Gulzari Lal Nanda, who himself commanded enviable reputation for honesty, high integrity and truthfulness. Nandaji was immensely inclined to choose Bansi Lal. However, Panditji had inherent disliking for the jats. However, finding Bansi Lal as the most non-controversial and junior in politics, Sharma Sahib endorsed the preference of Nanda Sahib, despite Bansi Lal being a jat. Bansi Lal, born in 1927, had become a Member of the Rajya Sabha, in 1960 at the age of 33 years, thanks to Devi Lal, then the stormy petrel of Composite Punjab State politics. He had earlier successfully contested, as a Congress candidate, in the General Election, held for Haryana State Vidhan Sabha in Feb-March, 1967. This time, Ranbir Singh of Sanghi village, a renowned freedom fighter and ex-member of the Constituent Assembly, was a very strong claimant for the Chief Ministership being a very senior Congress leader. He made lot of efforts to register his claim with the Congress High Command and was among the top hopefuls. When it became known that Bansi Lal, a dark horse had become man of the day, Ranbir Singh felt slighted. I did discern, during the ensuing days that this incident had adversely affected his psyche, as he had to suppress compulsively his rebellious spirit. After Bansi Lal became the Chief Minister, hush-hush talk continued for quite a few days in the political circle and in the bureaucracy to know the detailed profile of this "Hero of the mid-term poll."

During my posting as ASP at Hisar in 1959-60, I had met on a few occasions Bansi Lal, then a non-descript lawyer. He used to be very respectful and very well behaved, while interacting with the officers. I had also met him when I was Director Special Inquiry Agency (SIA) in 1966-67. He was then playing a second fiddle to Devi Lal who, even then was considered one of the top political figures. An inquiry was pending with the SIA against a lecturer, posted in the Government College at Sirsa, who had allegedly embezzled funds, granted for the NCC wing of the college students. Bansi Lal had then come to me to recommend for doing some favour in the inquiry, saying that the accused person was close to Devi Lal. However, nothing favourable was done. Bansi Lal, on his first visit to the district as Chief Minister, gave me a warm hand-shake and publicly said, "Happy to find you Swan Sahib here, it was because of your deft and tough handling of the situation that free and fair polling could be conducted in Rohtak District; my congratulations to you."

During the first two months of his Chief Ministership, Bansi Lal kept very low profile. He would publicly announce that Gulzari Lal Nanda was his top patron and next to him was Bhagwat Dayal Sharma and that it was because of their grace that he had become the Chief Minister of the state. The senior administrators, at all levels, could easily discern that his such announcements, were only political gimmicks and his playing, as a 'sycophant' was just to appease and soften the egoistic disposition of Bhagwat Dayal Sharma. He in fact, had his own plans to successfully steer through every storm, created by Bhagwat Dayal Sharma to dethrone him. As an administrator, he started off admirably. He appointed S K Mishra, IAS, as his Principal Secretary. Sh. Mishra was an experienced bureaucrat, gifted with innovative ideas. To call him a "Modern Chanakya" would be very apt because of his understanding the complexities of administration and politics. He had very thoughtfully worked out plans, to bring the new state of Haryana, on the world map, by creating some "wonders."

Bansi Lal very correctly understood the dictum coined by Mahatma Gandhi "India can't prosper if rural India lags behind and I think rural electrification is the first step towards this." In addition, linking every village with a metalled road and promoting tourism by exploiting the geographical location of the state, were his other ambitious plans. Bansi Lal was very keen to display something very extra-ordinary, he therefore adopted in letter and spirit all the above said plans, for giving them practical shape and very determinedly set on to realize in reality all these plans. Bansi Lal would brook no delay or lethargy at any level in the state administration. His reputation was registered very well with all and sundry. No wonder, that he caught the attention of the Prime Minister of India, Smt. Indira Gandhi, who liberally extended her patronage to "The Man of Action", governing the new state of Haryana.

The CM during his visits to Rohtak would take me into confidence and often talk to me, rather informally, on issues concerning the state and the police department. On more than one occasion, he told me "If my father ever comes to your residence with any recommendation, make him sit only in the *Varandah,* not at all in your drawing room and don't offer him any cold drink; listen to his recommendation but act only as per law." Regarding his elder son, ever coming to me, he said, "Don't encourage him to come to your residence, meet him only in your office; treat his recommendation as the law permits.' I served for a number of years in Haryana state, but never any politician of some standing ever gave me advice like that of Bansi Lal about his kith and kin. Bansi Lal's style of governing the state as the Chief Minister annoyed many a shallow type politician. The brand of Hardwari Lal et al having been cut to size in politics, made vain efforts to tarnish his name. Hardwari Lal's one pamphlet "A CM Runs Amuck" and another publication running into 128 pages entitled "Emergence of Rough and Corrupt Politics in India -Anatomy of a Chief Minister" are two such instances in point. He used all type of invectives and diatribes against Bansi Lal, senior politicians and senior officers, whom he thought to be close to Bansi Lal. Hardwari Lal claimed to be a learned person, apparently based on his academic degrees. According to Sathya Sai Baba, "Learning is related to the *budhi*, intellect. It is not mere scholarship. Familiarity with books is not knowledge. One's entire life is a continuous process of learning. Any process of inquiry is related to learning. But basically, our inquiry should be concerned with finding out, what is transient and what is permanent. This is true knowledge." Hardwari Lal, holding impressive educational degrees, calling himself "Sant", had a perverse intellect, which he tried to conceal, under the mask of saffron dress. He was, perversely in blind love, with his desire to acquire political power by hook or crook. His madly pursuing his base desire to acquire political power with dubious means, got him entrapped in the web of spinnerets of politics and was swallowed by it, ending thus, his vicious desire to acquire political power for the rest of his life.

Notoriously Corrupt and Incorrigible Extortionist Police Sub Inspector

"Do not fear the thorns in your path, for they draw only corrupt blood." When Governor's Rule was clamped in November 1967, the police personnel stopped behaving waywardly. I was able to cleanse the Augean Stable to a considerable degree. However, on the eve of the mid-term polls, the aspiring politicians started influencing the transfers and postings of police personnel of their choice in their constituencies. It was during that time that Ajmer Singh a sikh Sub Inspector came to district Rohtak, on 2nd April, 1968. He had joined police department as a constable in 1935. Between the period from 1948 to 1961, he remained posted in district Rohtak for 13 years. He served outside this district only for one year and came back again in 1962. He was transferred out of this district in 1967 and again managed to return in April 1968.

During his very long stay in district Rohtak, he had earned notoriety for developing connections with undesirable characters. He staged some fake encounters and was a dreaded extortionist. With the blessings of my predecessor, he had given a foreign made revolver to his tout Sube Singh, a notorious character of village Rukhi, who used to display this weapon, posing as a man of great standing, with no fear of law. Bhagwat Dayal Sharma was aspiring to become the Chief Minister again. There was every possibility of that eventuality becoming a fact. He told me on 20th April 1968 that the said Sub Inspector was his old trusted man and he should be posted as SHO PS Gohana. I ignored his recommendation in view of very bad reputation of this Sub Inspector. I continued receiving recommendations from various politicians, for getting the SHOs of their choice posted to police stations of their respective constituencies. I had a ready excuse to put off their recommendations under the plea that transfers and postings of SHOs were not permissible after the dates for the mid-term polls had been announced. After the mid-term polls of May 1968 were concluded peacefully, entirely a new set of politicians came into power. Raj Singh Dalal had won from Meham constituency as a Congress candidate. Immediately after the election results were announced, he came to my office and expressed his deep gratitude saying that "But for police arrangements made by you, Harijan voters would not have been allowed by the jats to vote for him and he would have lost the election." Again on 24th June 1968, Raj Singh Dalal came to my office, with a long list of recommendations, including his demand for the posting of above said SI as SHO, Police Station Meham. I explained to him that the said Sub Inspector was incorrigibly corrupt and a man like him, should not patronize such a notorious police officer. However, persisting with his demand, the MLA said that he had to oblige his voters and the said SI would be useful to him and should, therefore, be posted at Meham, as SHO. Same day the Deputy Commissioner told me in the evening that the CM, during his visit to Kathura Block on 16.06.1968, had told him to ask the SP to post SHO Meham as per the choice of Raj Singh Dalal. Unwillingly, I issued the orders posting the said Sub Inspector as SHO Meham and endorsed a copy thereof to the Deputy Commissioner, apropos his talk to me.

Ram Chander Sharma was a very close confidante of Bhagwat Dayal Sharma, who had assumed to himself the role of a king maker, after installing Bansi Lal as Chief Minister. On 7th July, 1968, Ram Chander Sharma came to my office, with a long list of recommendations including that of the said Sub Inspector about whom he told me that the said Sub Inspector should not be discouraged when he suppressed the opponents of their group with iron hand. He concluded his recommendations saying egoistically that Panditji had asked him to impress upon the Superintendent of Police to attend meticulously to all the recommendations made by him. CM was camping at Bhiwani on 3rd August 1968. He summoned me to discuss law and order affairs. I availed the opportunity to mention to the Chief Minister that SI/SHO Meham was indulging in blatant corrupt practices and high handedness in behaving, not only with public, but also with his senior police officers. The Ruling Party patronizing him would be disgraced. CM assured me that the said Sub Inspector would soon be transferred out of the Rohtak district.

On 21st August 1968, one Kehri Singh, Municipal Councilor owning a retail outlet of liquor at Meham, complained to me that SHO Meham had been taking from him monthly bribe money, ever since his posting as SHO and that he had been harassing him to enhance the amount of bribe money. He also complained that the SHO had been sending his constables, frequently to fetch from him, crates of liquor without making any payment. He also expressed his utter apprehension that if the SHO had ever learnt that he had made any complaint to the Superintendent of Police against him; he would have to face his wrath. On 9th September 1968 Raj Singh Dalal, MLA, met me in my office, with a deputation of about 50 persons. Their complaint was that a revolver, allegedly recovered, from a person of village Saman, was planted by a stooge of SHO Meham with ulterior motive of extorting huge bribe money from the victim. It was also complained that the SHO was indulging in vulgar corruption and his high-handedness with the public was unbearable. The MLA expressed his deep regrets for getting him posted as SHO at Meham. While demanding his immediate transfer, the MLA made a humble request that it should not be made known to the public that the said Sub Inspector had been posted as SHO, PS Meham, on his recommendation, as that would put him in an awkward position.

A complaint dated 8th September, containing serious allegations of corruption against the said Sub Inspector, during the period from 10th August to 15th August 1968, was received in my office. I marked this complaint on 12th September, 1968 to Harinder Singh, Dy SP, to inquire personally and report urgently. Harinder Singh's inquiry report disclosed serious allegations of corruption against the said Sub Inspector. The Dy SP concluding his inquiry report, had suggested that the matter should be referred to District Magistrate Rohtak for decision under Police Rule 16.38(1). Under this Rule, the District Magistrate has to decide, whether a matter like the instant one, should be disposed of by the Superintendent of Police by taking disciplinary action, after holding departmental inquiry or the matter has to be disposed of by initiating criminal proceedings. In this case, the District Magistrate decided on 21st September 1968 that "A regular criminal case be registered against the said SHO and others at PS Meham." Accordingly case FIR No.138 dated 21st September, 1968 was registered at Police Station Meham, U/s 5/2/47, Prevention of Corruption Act and its investigation was entrusted to Gurbuksh Singh, Dy SP Sonepat sub-division. The SHO Meham and his two co-accused police officers were arrested. Their plea for bail was rejected by the local Court. However, in due course of time, they managed to get bail under the orders of the High Court. In the meanwhile, after the completion of the investigation, the case was sent up to the Court for trial of the accused persons. The accused Sub Inspector got the case transferred from the Court of Sessions Judge Rohtak to the Court of Sessions Judge Gurgaon under the plea that the District Superintendent of Police would influence the Court at Rohtak. The Sub Inspector, while under suspension, remained attached to Police Line Rohtak. He indulged in various nefarious activities to enlist the support of some politicians and notorious smugglers.

I was amazed when Ram Chander Sharma came to me with a strong message from Bhagwat Dayal Sharma that the said Sub Inspector had to be somehow, saved in the corruption case pending trial against him. I felt very upset, but without giving expression to my feelings, I told Sharma rather bluntly to go away and allow me to attend to other important official work. Sharma understood the meaning of my ticking him off. Intelligence reports started pouring in that Hardwari Lal, nursing extreme grudge against me, had started using the Sub Inspector accused in corruption case to mobilize a gang of goondas, military deserters and proclaimed offenders known to him, to accomplish the task of assassinating the Superintendent of Police assuring that his own musclemen would help him with money. DIG Range, DIG/CID, IGP and the Chief Minister, all cautioned me, to remain extra vigilant regarding my own security. A few good-natured senior Congress politicians also cautioned me similarly. There were various instances other than the criminal case of corruption pending investigation against the said Sub Inspector regarding serious indiscipline and irregularities committed by him.

Departmental action was initiated against the Sub Inspector and a Dy SP of another district was appointed as the Inquiry Officer. The Sub Inspector, under suspension was shifted on transfer to that district, for facing the departmental inquiry. He did not attend the proceedings, which had to be continued ex-party. High Court, on technical grounds annulled the ex-party proceedings, ordering the Sub Inspector to attend the proceedings, if initiated afresh. Therefore, Departmental action was initiated afresh. This time he attended. However, when show cause notice dated 9th January, 1969, for the penalty of dismissal was issued to him, he again went to the High Court. This time he did not get any relief from the High Court. He was directed by the High Court vide judgment dated 18th March, 1970 to reply to the show cause notice. He was due for retirement on 2nd April, 1970. Finally, he was dismissed from service. He was quick to realize that the arms of the administration, as usual, had to be very strong. He also rightly realized that the CIA of district Rohtak, would haul him up, for his having close contacts with the military deserters and proclaimed offenders at large, if he ever was seen lurking around district Rohtak.

The way this notorious Sub Inspector was subdued, sent out a strong message to the fence sitter police personnel, itching for making easy money and indulging in indiscipline. Various senior advocates at the Bar and elderly respectable citizens of the district, applauded my strong armed measures against the Sub Inspector, who was notorious all over the state for his wayward activities.

Fresh Political Turmoil in the State

Bhagwat Dayal Sharma was determined to dethrone Bansi Lal and to assume for himself the coveted position of Chief Minister. He resorted to all sort of tactics. The only option left for him was to win over a large number of MLAs, both from the Congress and opposition parties, to his camp and thus, dislodge Bansi Lal's government. Therefore, shameful game of horse-trading commenced. Bansi Lal was no less than a "Man of iron will" an epithet used generally with the name of Sardar Patel, the first Home Minister of India, who was instrumental in making six hundred princely states of British India accede to the Indian Union.

The CM knew my friendly relations with Shyam Chand, a Vishal Haryana Party MLA from Baroda constituency. He asked me to persuade Shyam Chand to defect and join Congress Party and in that eventuality, he promised to give a Ministerial berth to him, with portfolios of his choice. Shyam Chand was reputed to be a man of principles, believing firmly in high moral value system. I knew he would not defect from Vishal Haryana Party. Still, being obliged to convey CM's sentiments, I talked to Shyam Chand. He very politely declined the CM's proposal, saying that he had lot of regards for Bansi Lal, but would consider joining the Congress Party only when Haryana Assembly elections were held next time provided Rao Birender Singh, president of HVP also decided by then to dissolve his party. I highly appreciated this stance of Shyam Chand. I accordingly, conveyed his views to Bansi Lal, the Chief Minister, who said "Shyam Chand is a talented boy; he would be wasting his five years for nothing." With the matter ending there I felt relieved of the tension, as CM did not show any ill will against Shyam Chand.

During the General Elections, held in 1972, Shyam Chand won as a Congress candidate, from Baroda constituency. He was made Cabinet Minister in the Bansi Lal Government with seven portfolios, including Excise & Taxation Department, Urban Development, Food & Supply Department, Social Welfare, and Welfare of SCs/STs. Shyam Chand, throughout, kept up his reputation as an honest politician with high integrity. His son, Justice Jatinder Chauhan a worthy progeny of a worthy father, is presently a reputed Judge on the Bench of Punjab & Haryana High Court at Chandigarh. Shyam Chand has a flair for writing. He has authored two books- "Seeds of Slavery" and "Saffron Fascism" apart from several articles on political and economic affairs in the country.

The competitive game of winning over maximum number of MLAs to either side with money power became a pet pursuit for politicians. Known businessmen/industrialists were targeted. Bansi Lal, who had become known as a clean man apart from being an excellent administrator and a seasoned politician, soon lost the sheen of epithet as a clean man. Circumstances forced him to be bracketed with Bhagwat Dayal Sharma in playing wicked games of using money power and muscle power. Those were really the very tough and challenging days for the administration, both at the state and the district levels. It was with great farsightedness, perseverance and patience that I fortunately came out of the complex situation unblemished. The CM had at times told me to take stern action against some senior politicians, opposed to him to make them fall in line. However, I ignored his recommendations tactfully. The CM, on his part also never inquired from me anything in this regard.

In due course of time, Bhagwat Dayal Sharma was almost eclipsed in Haryana politics, thanks to the political and administrative acumen of Bansi Lal.

Ranbir Singh of Sanghi village, a very senior jat politician of the Congress then in his fifties had become MLA in mid-term poll of May 1968. He was a freedom fighter and ex-member of Constituent Assembly. In Composite Punjab State, he was a Cabinet Minister. He was a top claimant for the top position in the event of Bhagwat Dayal Sharma being denied the same. However, when Bansi Lal bagged the top honour, he strongly felt that the Congress High Command had done injustice to him. He was perturbed on this account and was not reconciling to accept the leadership of Bansi Lal whom he considered to be a junior jat politician. There were instances galore when Ranbir Singh, otherwise reputed to be a gentleman, behaved strangely while projecting his recommendations to me.

With due respect to him and without malice at any rate, I would quote only two such instances. On 20th June 1968 he told me on telephone, using very rough and threatening language that Godha harijan of Sanghi, his staunch supporter, was stripped of his arms licence by the police and if it was not immediately restored, serious consequences for me as District Superintendent of Police would follow. When I tried to explain to him the reasons for the said police action, he used even more insulting language adding that he was not inferior in any way to the CM. He continued shouting as if his blood pressure had gone very high. I had to disconnect the telephone. Late in the evening, he forced his entry into my residence, despite the security constable on duty stopping him at the entry gate of my residence. I received him and made him seated comfortably in my drawing room, extending normal courtesy and hospitality. He told me in a very soft tone that Godha was sitting with him when he was talking to me on telephone and that he had used some undesirable words out of excitement without any ill will to me. He said he was rather grateful for the pains taken by me personally to give him moral and other support during the pre-poll days. He felt sorry for what all he had said on telephone. I told him that I take it in my strides whatever the elderly respectable person like him would say and that he should forget all about that. Giving me kind compliments, he left my residence quite relaxed and cheerful. "We should always be soft spoken. Sweet speech has the ability to attract everyone. On the contrary, vitriolic speech keeps people away. That is why one should always be soft spoken so that it enhances brotherhood and affection"— **Yajurveda.**

On another occasion, Ranbir Singh, accompanied by one Ved Prakash, came to my office on 21st June 1968 and talked about a case in which someone had suffered some injuries. I told him that Inspector Narula was specially deputed to personally investigate to find out the truth. He doubted the integrity of the Inspector. I called the Inspector and asked him to explain the facts as found by him, to Chaudhary Sahib. Without allowing the Inspector to speak even a word, Ranbir Singh started shouting at the Inspector, stroking his chest and proclaiming in rage that he would see to it that all such police officers were properly fixed up. He continued his unusual drama using very obscene and insulting language as if he was a possessed person. I told the Inspector to go out and tried to calm down Ranbir Singh, but all in vain. Then I had to be little rough and tell him that he had committed criminal offence, by his uncalled for and offensive behaviour in my office and that I would have to report the matter to the Government. He at once softened up and became apologetic. I called Inspector Narula again and asked him to narrate the facts as found by him in the investigation. He did not let him speak anything and started instead pampering him saying that he was one like his own children. He spent more than one hour in my office showering all type of sweet words, praising me for excellent arrangement made during the mid-term polls, my patience and still very firm dealings et al. He went to the Deputy Commissioner in the evening and pleaded with him to ask me not to take to heart what he had said in fits of rage and that I should not make any report to the higher authorities. As per ejainism.com, "To ask for forgiveness is a great quality of brave ones and if I have committed any mistake, knowingly or unknowingly, I ask for your forgiveness– The quality of forgiveness requires humility that is Vinay or absence of ego and suppression of anger." At the end of the day Ranbir Singh, a Gandhian largely, had earned my respect and regard. Throughout my stay in the district, I kept him in good humour and he in turn was very helpful to me in tackling some difficult law and order situations.

Clash of Interest between Two High Profile Politicians

Raj Singh Dalal MLA, was related to Bansi Lal. He had lost his right arm in some accident long back. Highly temperamental by nature, he was very ambitious to go high in politics. He was nominated as a Congress candidate to contest mid-term polls of May 1968, from Meham constituency. During the electioneering days, he used to be very humble and respectful to the officers of the district. Meham constituency had been a pocket borough of non-Congress people. The jats of this constituency would follow the dictates of the "Chaubisi Panchayat", a supreme body to oversee all their social affairs. Like elsewhere, "Chaubisi Panchayat" seldom allowed the weaker sections of the electorate to vote for any candidate except the one of their choice. This time, "Chaubisi Panchayat' had sponsored Maha Singh, as their candidate against the Congress nominee. The district administration had made very effective arrangements to ensure fair and free election. The weaker sections of the electorate, therefore, exercised their right of franchise without any fear. Raj Singh Dalal reaped the benefit and won the election. Soon after the results were announced, he expressed his deep gratitude to the Deputy Commissioner and myself saying that but for the meticulous arrangements made by the administration, he would not have won the election. He forgot all this soon and started asserting that his demands of postings of civil and police official of his choice to Meham must be honoured. It was on his insistence that Ajmer Singh, an undesirable Sub Inspector was posted as SHO PS, Meham, much against my wishes. Being a Dalal jat, he also started openly criticizing the district administration for the criminal case registered at Police Station Bahadurgarh, against Hardwari Lal and his accomplices - all Dalal jats, merely because of his clan/caste fraternity. He further made the situation worse by his undesirable activities. On 23rd October, he met the Governor of Haryana and demanded my transfer.

District Public Grievances Committee meeting was held in the Zila Parisad Hall On 11th November, under the Chairperson of Smt Om Prabha Jain, state Finance Minister. All the district level officers, a few MLAs, including Raj Singh Dalal and some respectable citizens of the District, attended it. During the course of the meeting, Raj Singh Dalal got up and sarcastically levelled many allegations against me, using highly derogatory language. When the Chairperson told him not to use abusive language, he shouted at her, asking her not to stop him for what he had to say. The Deputy Commissioner took exception to the highly objectionable conduct of the MLA. He sternly told him to stop insulting the Chairperson and using abusive language against the District SP, otherwise he would be forcibly removed from the meeting hall. I reported the incident in details, vide letter dated 12th November to the IGP, with the request to take up the matter with the state government. The IGP brought the matter to the notice of the Chief Secretary and the Chief Minister. Bansi Lal summoned the MLA and gave him a good dressing down. This made Raj Singh Dalal tender apology to me saying that whatever he had uttered against the administration was all because of some misunderstanding. I was informed by the office of the IGP vide letter dated 31st January 1969 that in view of the Dalal's apology the state government had decided to close the matter.

Raj Singh Dalal and K L Poswal, then a Cabinet Minister were holding major shares in a cinema hall by the name Raj Talkies at Rohtak, owned by a Private Limited Company. Its management vested in the Board of Directors. Majority of the directors were on the side of Sh. Poswal. Due to strained relations between Dalal and Poswal over the management of the Raj Talkies, litigation between the two groups had gone even up to the High Court. Both the groups had planned to force their entry with the help of their musclemen, to take over the management. The situation assumed serious proportions. There was imminent apprehension of serious clash between the two groups. To save the situation, from getting worse, police force under Dy SP Hqr was deployed at the Raj Talkies, with the city Magistrate overseeing the police arrangements.

No amount of persuasion by the city Magistrate and the Dy SP could avert the clash between the two groups. The city Magistrate, finally announced that proceedings u/s 145 CrPC would be initiated and if in the meanwhile both the groups did not stop the forced entry in the Raj Talkies, the Police would have to use force. A major tragedy was thus, averted. Persons from both the groups had sustained some injuries for which criminal cases were registered on the complaints of both the sides. The group of Sh. Poswal had alleged in a written complaint that Dalal was carrying a firearm, which he had used against the opposite group. Dalal on his part was adamant that his group was legally entitled to hold the management of the Talkies and the forced entry by the muscleman of the opposite group was criminal trespass. Dalal was also very much annoyed with me for initiating proceedings u/s 145 CrPC alleging that the police had taken to this recourse only to damage his interest. Sh Poswal was equally annoyed with me alleging that criminal case under the Indian Arms Act was not registered and illicit weapon was not being recovered from Dalal, only to help him. In view of the sensitive nature of the case, I personally looked into the allegation and counter allegations of both the groups. No person from either side suffered any serious injury nor did any firing incident take place. Unmindful of all the allegations against me, the investigations in all the criminal cases were carried out impartially and objectively. I had to face the wrath of both the parties. Sh Poswal had become the Home Minister in due course. Nursing grudge against me, he tried in vain, to harm my career. Some times a police officer is placed in such an awkward situation that for his straight forwardness and honest approach to uphold the rule of law, he has to suffer unnecessarily.

Political Turmoil Tamed

In the tug of war between Bhagwat Dayal Sharma and Bansi Lal, the politics of the state touched the lowest ebb of degradation. The former was leaving no chance to destabilize the Bansi Lal government. The latter was determined to foil all such desperate attempts of the former. MLAs had become a saleable commodity. Horse-trading had become the order of the day. Bansi Lal, during that short period as Chief Minister had put in place many schemes for the development of the state. Governor B N Chakarvarty, himself a very experienced administrator, was very much impressed with the way Bansi Lal had started as Chief Minister. In the meanwhile, Smt Indira Gandhi had gained tremendous strength at the centre as Prime Minister. The Central leadership was very closely monitoring all the developments taking place in Haryana. The Congress High Command was also impressed with Bansi Lal's working. The advice of Governor Sh Chakravarty to the Union Government, strengthened the position of Bansi Lal. Mahatma Gandhi had said, "Keep your thoughts positive because your thoughts become your words. Keep your words positive because your words become your behaviour. Keep your behaviour positive because your behaviour becomes your habits. Keep your habits positive because your habits become your values. Keep your values positive because your values become your destiny." Barring a few exceptions, majority of the Congress MLAs in the state were nowhere near this message of Gandhiji. Instead they all fitted well in the definition given by Samuel Johnson "Politics is the last resort of a scoundrel". In the circumstances, the Congress High Command intervened in a big way to cleanse the Augean Stable, created by the foul games played by the politicians in the state. Bhagwat Dayal Sharma was summoned by the High Command and was told very firmly that he would be expelled from the party if he did not desist from his undesirable activities to dislodge Bansi Lal's government. This message of the High Command worked well when percolated down to all MLAs and other Congress leaders aligned with Bhagwat Dayal Sharma. The political turmoil, which at one stage had created a very uncertain situation in the state was thus, brought under control, bringing about normalcy in no time.

Rohtak District Bar Council - Role of Lehri Singh, Advocate

The district Bar Council comprised of 153 members. The approach of the senior advocates was generally professional. The new entrants were struggling to learn the tricks of the trade. Some of the middle rung advocates, who had quite a few years' standing in the profession, but still not very successful in the career, were creating lot of nuisance for the police. There modus operandi for making easy money was to charge heavy fees from the rural folks and come to me or the other police officer including the SHOs, with their complaints, either for taking preventive action against their opponents or asking for changing the course of investigation in criminal cases in favour of their clients. Often these advocates, while accompanying their clients to the police officers would try to overawe them to impress upon their clients so that still fatter fees could be fleeced from them. During my interaction with the advocates in the bar room, I tried to impress upon them that the way some of them were approaching the police officers in person, to plead the cases of their clients, after charging heavy fees, was not in accordance with section 30 of the Advocate Act, 1961. According to this provision, the right of the advocates to practice extended only to their appearance in the Courts, Tribunals or persons, legally authorized to take evidence or before any authority that the law entitled them to practice. The saner element among them appreciated my viewpoint and assured me to go by the legal provisions.

Lehri Singh of Sonepat, an Ex-Cabinet Minister in pre-Independence Punjab, was practicing law at Rohtak. He strongly opposed my viewpoint. In fact, his practice prospered only because some people innocently believed that he would exercise effective influence on the police and even on the lower judiciary, due to his political stature. There were dozens of instances in which he or his kins, had scandalously interfered, in the working of the police at various levels in the district. In May 1968, Lehri Singh became the president of the Rohtak Bar Association. During one of his professional trips to my office, he very emphatically stressed that the lawyers had the right to plead the cases of their clients in their representative capacity before the police officers in all matters. I told him that I had conveyed my views during my interaction with the lawyers, in the bar room and I stood by that. On 6th June he sent a letter to me, in his capacity as president of the Bar Association, reiterating what he had been telling me earlier, during his visits to my office. In my reply dated 25th June to his letter, I explained in detail, the legal position on the subject. He with a few other lawyers, toeing his viewpoint, indulged in whispering campaign casting aspersion and commenting adversely on the conduct of the police officers.

The Deputy Commissioner called Lehri Singh and told him that the district administration including the police, had tried to accommodate him out of respect to the extent possible, but it would be wrong on his part to resort to undesirable activities and that he must desist from such activities in the interest of public-administration relations. This did not have the desired effect on him. Out of 153 members of the Bar Association, he collected about 16 members and declared a resolution as if passed by the Bar Association, in the presence of 26 members. In that resolution, the working and conduct of the police, particularly the District Superintendent of Police was criticized. Many a senior advocate personally conveyed to me that the resolution was only the brainchild of Lehri Singh and very big majority of the members of the Bar, did not endorse its contents. In any case, when I discussed this matter with the Deputy Commissioner, his view was that the said resolution should be ignored as a perverted thinking of its sponsors. Because of this uncalled for resolution, the police at all levels in the district started ignoring Lehri Singh and his kins. It was then that the reaction to the said resolution by the police started pinching him. Lehri Singh, accompanied by another advocate Ishwar Chander Jain, came to my office and expressed his deep regrets saying that in fact, it was his son-in-law, a practicing fellow advocate, who had under some misunderstanding, prompted him to have the resolution passed from the Bar Association and that I should not take any notice thereof.

Since a copy of the said resolution had come to the notice of DIG/CID, he called for my comments. I submitted to DIG/CID demi-officially, vide letter dated 5th May 1969, my 14 page report, explaining in detail, how in dozens of cases, Lehri Singh or his kins had interfered in the normal functioning of the police, after charging exorbitant fees from the innocent people. In any case Lehri Singh and his ilks stopped this unlawful practice.

Controversy Regarding Initiation of SPs ACR by DM; Change of Guards at the Higher Echelon of State Police

Bansi Lal having settled down firmly, pursued his innovative plans of linking every village with a metalled road and also to provide every village with domestic electric supply. In his priorities to improve the law and order situation in the state, he was advised by some over ambitious bureaucrats that the state police should be brought under control of the civil administration. Bansi Lal got convinced, somehow, that the district administration would become more effective if some sort of powers were vested in the Deputy Commissioner to effectively oversee the working of the District SP. Accordingly the Bansi Lal government issued the orders that Annual Confidential Reports (ACRs) of the District Superintendents of police would be initiated by the respective Deputy Commissioners. No prior consultations were held with the top brass of the state police. This order of the government therefore, was not received well by all the directly recruited IPS Officers of the rank of Superintendent of Police and above. Bhagwan Singh Rosha, the State IGP and Kanwar Randip Singh, DIG Ambala Range, strongly resented this order. During CM's visit to Rohtak, I submitted to him that the said order was a regressive step in reforming of the policing system in tune with the changing times after Independence. Finding him a little responsive to my submission, I narrated to him briefly, the historical background of the posts of DM and District SP as these existed during the British Rule. He told me "there is some force in your view point". He advised me to send to him a detailed note in this regard.

This subject had been spiritedly discussed in depth during Senior Officers Advance Course at CPTC, Mount Abu, in 1965. I had attended that course. Based on the material then gathered by me, I prepared a detailed note (Annexure-3) within a week and handed it over to the CM, who was camping at Gurgaon.

When I handed over the above-mentioned note to the Hon'ble Chief Minister, he very kindly spared time to go through its contents in my presence. Having gone through the note he said "You have taken pains to produce this detailed note; I would discuss this issue with the Chief Secretary." I also gave a copy of my above note to DIG/AR, DIG/CID, and State IGP.

In the meanwhile, DIG/AR and State IGP, on their part, tried their level best to convince the Chief Secretary that the state government order would neither be confidence building nor improve the efficiency of the police at the district level. Rather it would promote indiscipline in the force. No arguments would cut any ice with the Chief Secretary. Thanks to the strong lobby of the senior bureaucrats, the Chief Minister toughened his stance and strongly disfavoured the stand of the police top brass against the said government order, taking wrongly as a sort of challenge to the government authority. All the pains taken by me in preparing the above said exhaustive note also went in vain. The CM was not prepared to review his order. When DIG Ambala Range, in resentment against the new order of the Government, proposed to proceed on leave, he was told to put in his leave application immediately. In the wake of his proceeding on leave, Dalip Singh was appointed on promotion, as DIG Ambala Range, on 30th October 1968. Bhagwan Singh Rosha, the State IGP, was shifted on 18th December 1968 to head the Home Guards and Civil Defence Department. In his place J C Vachher, then DIG/CID was posted on promotion, as State IGP. HRK Talwar was made DIG/CID. Later, towards the end of July 1969, Talwar was shifted to Ambala, as Range DIG and his place was, taken by Dalip Singh. This entire reshuffle at the higher level, in the police department, had demoralizing effect on the middle level IPS officers in the state.

Wickedness and Revengeful Conduct of the Range DIG

During my posting as ASP Incharge Sub-Division Jind of district Sangrur, Dalip Singh, the District Superintendent of Police had developed serious animosity against me, particularly in view of my role to uphold the rule of law in the rape case, in which the accused persons were his close relations. Since it was well known that Bansi Lal, the then Chief Minister had been appreciative of my maintaining proper law and order in the district, Dalip Singh, maintained cordial approach for a few months, while dealing with me and Rohtak district law and order affairs. When he found that he was firmly entrenched in the saddle as DIG Ambala Range, he started pinpricking me, even on trivial matters. He found in the Sub Inspector, who was facing trial in a corruption case, a ready tool to provide fabricated material to satisfy his instinct of revenge against me.

A pseudonymous complaint, purported to be from one Chhotu Ram, Editor of a newspaper called "Jat Gazette", containing over a dozen allegations of corruption and irregularities against me, was manoeuvered. This undated complaint was addressed to the Chief Minister, IGP, DIG/CID and DIG Ambala Range. Copies of the complaint, from all quarters, came down to the DIG Ambala Range during first week of May 1969. He did not ask for my comments in the matter and started the enquiry. He submitted his report of enquiry regarding 10 allegations to the IGP, with his nine-page letter dated 2nd December 1969. In the opening para he mentioned, "Chottu Ram, when examined, has stated that he did not submit such a complaint. As such it is a pseudonymous complaint". Despite this, he continued holding the enquiry without obtaining my comments. On his posting as DIG/CID, his place as Range DIG was taken by H R K Talwar. He submitted his enquiry report regarding the remaining allegations to the IGP with his letter dated 31st March 1972. Dalip Singh had made some very adverse remarks in my ACRs for the period from 1st November 1968 to 29th July 1969 on account of personal vendetta, on the excuse of pending inquiry into the allegations made in the said pseudonymous complaints. My representation against such adverse remarks remained pending with the state government for long. It was only on 10th January 1977 that the adverse remarks were expunged. Similarly the reports of inquiries made by the two Range DIGs in the pseudonymous complaints, were dealt with by the government on 29th May 1976, after considering my detailed comments dated 22nd May 1976. The state government closed the matter on 3rd September 1976, with a "simple warning", in a trivial matter. Thanks to the foul and vile game played by Dalip Singh, I had to suffer mental agony for years. If the IGP had applied his mind in the matter, he should have, in all fairness, called for my comments on the allegations contained in the complaint, before asking the Range DIG to hold any inquiry, particularly when the IGP was well aware that Dalip Singh, the Range DIG, was totally, biased against me.

While functioning as State Police Chief during the years 1986-88, I once came across ACR file of Dalip Singh. I found that he had joined the police department as a directly recruited Inspector during forties. His initial probation period was extended. He was awarded the punishment of censure even during his training period. As Inspector, he was described as having poor ability, thick headed, stupid and poor stuff. For the period from 1st July 1947 to 31st December 1947, he was found being casual and perfunctory in approach, showed communal bias against sikhs; there were serious allegations of corruption against his subordinates that reflected adversely against him; corrupt himself and allowed his SHOs to collect money possibly to share with him. IGP remarked "Disgraceful that this officer has lost character". In April 1951, State Public Service Commission considered him not fit for substantive promotion as Dy SP. For the years 1951-52, IGP remarked "Temperamentally not fit as he gets fits typical of a jat". For 1957-58, IGP remarked, "Yet to overcome feelings of vindictiveness". For 1960-61, IGP seriously doubted his integrity as he was inclined to misuse his power and authority. For the years 1961-62 and 1962-63, he was given adverse comments. It was a travesty that he managed to get into the IPS and Bansi Lal, the Chief Minister found him "useful" to function as DIG of Police Range and subsequently as DIG/CID.

Circumstantial Evidence and Forensic Report Enough to Nail the Accused in Murder Case

Detection of crime is the foremost duty of the police. There is no difficulty in booking a culprit where one or more reliable and independent persons have witnessed the commission of crime. The perpetrators of a heinous crime however, exercise considerable preplanning on their intended crime and take precautions to obliterate the stamp of their identity. Such cases are a few but only in such cases, the police officers are required to match their experience and talent with the perverted genius of criminals. Perseverance and keen observation produce indeed, fruitful results. I came across a murder case in which no direct evidence was available. On 19th November 1967 one Dhaja Ram uncle of Manphool Singh reported that some four months ago, Daya Krishan and Jai Krishan, residents of different villages had contacted his nephew Manphool Singh in the village, in connection with the purchase of a tractor. After taking the trial of the tractor all the three had some confidential talk and Dharam Singh, Sher Singh and Shivji of the village witnessed this incident. On that very day Manphool Singh left the village with said Daya Krishan and Jai Krishan and was not seen thereafter. It was also reported that after three days of the said incident, Daya Krishan alone returned to the village and contacted Dharam Singh brother of Manphool Singh and took away the tractor with him saying that Manphool Singh had sent him to collect the same. Based on this information, a case FIR No.150 u/s 364 IPC was registered at Police Station Gohana on 19th November 1967. I specially deputed ASI Chandgi Ram to take up the investigation under my direct day-to-day supervision. Jai Krishan was hauled up and put to intensive interrogation. He broke down on 23rd November 1967 and confessed to ASI Chandgi Ram that he had buried the dead body of Manphool Singh three feet deep in the compound of a *Kotha*.

I personally talked to Jai Krishan for two hours and I was convinced that he had not made the confession to the ASI under duress. His confessional statement was recorded in the presence of two respectable persons and he was taken, together with the said two persons, to the said *Kotha*. There he pointed out the place where he had buried the dead body of Manphool Singh. On digging at his instance, a skeleton, few pieces of decomposed flesh, a torn out *Kurta* and a *Dhoti* were recovered from the spot. The sealed skeleton was sent to the professor of Anatomy Department, Medical College Rohtak and it was opined that the age of the deceased, a male, was ranging between 18 to 40 years. Five injuries were seen on the bones. One such injury was described as caused by a revolver shot. The sealed *Kurta* and *Dhoti* were identified by the relations of Manphool Singh. These torn out garments had bloodstains which were reported to be of human blood by the serologist. Further investigation revealed that one Raj Pal Singh had asked Govardhan to purchase for him a tractor. Govardhan referred him to one Murari, a tractor dealer. Jai Krishan and Daya Krishan, both met Murari for the repair of the tractor and ultimately they sold off the tractor to Raj Pal Singh through Govardhan. Raj Pal Singh paid a sum of Rupees two thousand to Daya Krishan and Jai Krishan vide receipt dated 13.08.1967, duly signed and thumb marked by Daya Krishan as the vendor. This receipt was attested by Govardhan and Risal Singh.

There also existed an entry in the register of Puran Chand, documents writer. Daya Krishan approached Rattan Singh to get him a duplicate insurance certificate. However, this could not be arranged unless the original owner was produced. Daya Krishan and Jai Krishan went to Delhi and approached Ram Lal, an insurance agent, to get an insurance certificate. Ram Lal gave them a fictitious certificate, which was so found later. No direct evidence was available in the case and we had to build up the case entirely based on circumstantial and forensic evidence. All different links were pieced together to make out a complete and coherent case. The case was sent up for trial and Jai Krishan was sentenced to life imprisonment u/s 302 IPC by Additional Sessions Judge, Rohtak. Daya Krishan, his co-accused absconded and declared a proclaimed offender. He was still at large when the Court gave its verdict.

A False Story Concocted by State Vigilance Agency, Linking Me with an Imaginary Murder Case

I would herein describe how a mafia gang of rogue police officers with malicious intentions, made vain efforts to link me with an imaginary murder case. The investigating officer was put in the dock to explain his conduct and severely condemned by the District and Sessions Judge by passing serious strictures against him. Briefly stated a case FIR No.42, dated 26.04.1967, was registered u/s 364 IPC at Police Station Sadar Rohtak, on the statement of Smt. Chandro, alleging that Jagat Singh, Ram Kumar, Ram Sanehi and Umed Singh kidnapped her son Ram Kumar, on 27th October 1966 from her village Jassia. She suspected that the said four accused persons murdered her son. There was a delay of full six months in the registration of this case. The investigation of this case was taken up and an 'untraced' report was prepared by the then investigating officer. I joined as District SP, Rohtak, on 23rd May 1967 that is one month after the registration of this case and seven months after the alleged incident of kidnapping. Various police officers pursued the investigation of this case, after my arrival in the district and all the accused persons were thoroughly interrogated. Since the investigation agency could not find any clue to link the accused persons with the alleged crime, the case was reported as untraced in due course of time. I was transferred from district Rohtak towards the end of July 1969. Kalyan Rudra, my successor, reopened the investigation of the case and deputed Inspector CIA, Rohtak to re-interrogate the accused persons thoroughly to find out their complicity in the alleged crime. The re-investigation of the case, as ordered by Kalyan Rudra, was also closed after it was pursued for many months, as no evidence was forthcoming. Years passed and in course of time the case file was destroyed on 20th March 1974 and an appropriate entry to this effect was made in the *Talfi* Register. Kalyan Rudra was then continuing as District Superintendent of Police, Rohtak.

The investigation of this case was reopened once again on 2nd December 1974, under the orders of the Haryana government, on receipt of a report from Dharam Singh IPS, then a DIG posted as Director Special Inquiry Agency. The Director had made a calculated move, with malicious intentions to link me, some how, with the alleged crime and had deliberately presented a false report to the state government to seek their approval to reopen the investigation of the case. Raj Singh then posted as Superintendent of Police in the said Agency was specially deputed as an investigating officer. With the backing of the Director of the Agency, he cooked up and fabricated false evidence, arrested the alleged accused persons and sent them for trial u/s 302, 364, 201 and 34 IPC, to the Court of Sh. A N Aggarwal, District and Sessions Judge Rohtak, where it was registered as Sessions case no.18 of 1975 and Session trial no.37 of 1975. The Court pronounced the Judgment on April 1st 1976, acquitting all the accused persons and passing serious strictures against Raj Singh, Superintendent of Police in the Special Inquiry Agency, the investigating officer in this case. These strictures *inter alia* included the observations by the court that Mr Swan was not Superintendent of Police District Rohtak at the time of the commission of the offence of this case i.e. in October 1966. There could be no mention of the accused approaching Mr. Swan, SP, in the tape recorded version, when he was not there at the station and the fact that Mr. Swan is very much there in the alleged version of the accused shows that somehow the investigation officer was inclined to rope in Mr Swan.

I represented to the government to take disciplinary action against Raj Singh SP, the investigating officer, for his maliciously building up a false case, to link me in the case discussed above. When the Home Secretary informally asked for my firm opinion, I simply told him that as a person, I would prefer to forgive him and let he be punished by the Almighty for his sins. However, as a senior police officer, I would insist that the police department should be purged of such a rogue police officer including the Director SIA who was privy to the misdeeds committed by Raj Singh. Thanks to their political links and clan affinity with some persons in authority, they escaped any major punishment.

I will be a failing on my part if I do not place on record here my deep gratitude and high appreciation of the most commendable role played by A C Shehrawat, then a young advocate from Sonepat. He visited me at Delhi, a number of times to understand the implications involved in the above-mentioned case. I was then posted at Delhi on deputation with the Government of India. He laboured hard to find out the exact links and relationship between Raj Singh, the investigating officer and various PWs cited by him. It was the feedback provided by Shehrawat to the defence lawyers that armed them with full facts, they were able to demolish the story fabricated by Raj Singh during the cross examination of the PWs. This episode apart, AC Shehrawat, a staunch Ambedkarite, was a man of principles, honest, straightforward and committed social worker.

During the infamous Emergency of 1975, when Chand Ram was under preventive detention, Shehrawat used to raise funds from sympathetic friends for helping Smt. Durga Devi, wife of Chand Ram, in running her family kitchen. He also used to meet Chand Ram secretly to carry messages of Smt Durga Devi to Chand Ram and vice versa. The eagle eyes of the Intelligence Agencies had spotted the activities of Shehrawat and he too was likely to be put under preventive detention. He remained underground for many months. When General Elections were held during 1977, after the Emergency was lifted, Janata Party, trouncing the Congress Party, assumed power at the Centre. Chand Ram became an all-powerful Union Minister. He did not even include Shehrawat's name in the list of likely Janata Party candidates selected to contest Election for Haryana Assembly, much less to help him to get any position of some reckoning in the Janata Party government formed in Haryana state. AC Shehrawat and his wife, a noble woman, who had retired as a senior officer from Education Department Delhi are together involved in social service. Their son is a senior Judicial Magistrate in Delhi. My best wishes for this noble family!

Police Investigation Means Sifting out the Truth Concealed Wickedly in Falsehood

The object of police investigation is to place on record only the true facts, duly supported by unassailable evidence, ensuring conviction of the accused. Therefore, the investigating officer should go deep into the real facts and put them on record. It is certainly not a desirable practice to support the concocted story as reported and recorded in the FIR, by resorting to padding, in order to cover up the falsehood introduced in the FIR. In that case, an important piece of evidence may go overboard and even the real accused, getting the benefit of doubt, might escape punishment. I would herein describe briefly, case FIR No.35, dated 16.03.1968, u/s 302/452/149 IPC, Police Station Gohana. In this case one Ujjala of village Jasrana, had suffered grievous injuries during a brawl in the village at about 5.00 pm on 15th March 1968 and had been shifted to Government Medical College & Hospital Rohtak, where he succumbed to the injuries in the morning of 16th March 1968. At about 9.00 am, one Ram Narain gave a story to the SHO, based on which the said case was registered. Ram Narain had cited Surjan, Ompati, Chandro and Jot Ram as eyewitnesses and seven persons - Gordhan, Jai Narain, Mehar Singh, Raghbir, Gorkha, Darya and Risala, as the accused. Sub Inspector Rameshwar Das, the SHO and Gurbux Singh Dy SP Sonepat sub-division, the Supervisory Officer, during the initial stage of the investigation held the story given by Ram Narain, as recorded in the FIR, as correct. The case diaries written by the SHO and the Dy SP in this case and case FIR No.34, dated 16.03.1968, relating to the same village Jasrana revealed that there were glaring discrepancies in the statements of Surjan given on two different occasions. The Dy SP had gone to village Jasrana by about mid-day on 17th March 1968 to supervise the investigation and had left the village same evening. Seven persons were set on the way to gallows in this episode. Dy SP's flying visit to the scene of crime did not inspire confidence. All this raised doubts in my mind about the correctness of the FIR's contents, so far as the names of some accused mentioned in the FIR were concerned. I therefore, directed the Dy SP vide official letter dated 26.03.1968 to carry out the investigation of the case afresh at the spot, in view of the discrepancies in the two different versions given by Surjan. He came to my office and explained that my observations were correct, but to record anything about the identity of the accused, contrary to what was contained in the FIR, was difficult for him, as that would have put a question mark on his integrity unnecessarily and that he would not risk that sort of situation. "If a gentleman has courage but neglects justice, he becomes insurgent. If an inferior man has courage but neglects justice, he becomes a thief." Confucius. I was unhappy to listen to a foolish explanation as above, from a gazetted police officer and I snubbed him. On my prodding, the Dy SP once again visited the village. I did not receive any case diary regarding his second visit to the village. I therefore, issued another order asking both the SHO and the Dy SP to complete on their part, the investigation of the case and put up the file to me so that I could personally verify, by holding investigation at the spot, the correct version of the incident, so far as it related to the identity of the accused. The police file came to me towards the end of June 1968. I could visit the village only on 16th August 1968 to verify the facts of the case. The delay of about six weeks to take up the investigation at the spot by me was caused due to the explosive situation, which had prevailed in Rohtak district, right from the beginning of April 1968 till the third week of June 1968, because of the mid-term polls held on 12-14 May, 1968. There were some other unavoidable factors including the fracture of my right arm in an accident while travelling on duty in the official Jeep. For all these reasons, I had to perforce, delay the matter. I spent the entire day in village Jasrana, looking into the investigation of the murder case. I found that there existed a standing feud between the family of Gordhan, one of the accused as per the FIR and the family of Ujjala, the deceased.

The version as recorded in the FIR No.35, on the report of Ram Narain, contained twisted and tainted story. Surjan, Ompati and Chandro cited as eyewitnesses, were not at all truthful and trustworthy. I recorded a detailed case diary No.31 dated 16.08.1968 concluding that four accused that is Gordhan, Jai Narain son of Gordhan, Mehar Singh and Raghbir were innocent and falsely implicated. The trial was conducted by Gurnam Singh, Distt. and Session Judge Rohtak (he later was elevated to the Bench of Punjab and Haryana High Court).

Opening his arguments, the public prosecutor submitted that he had placed both the versions of the prosecution story before the Court for adjudication. However, he asserted that the prosecution story as discovered by the Superintendent of Police by investigation conducted by him, was unacceptable, as he did not act with vigil and promptitude, but he had acted only under some wrong impression and under the influence of mighty persons such as MLAs and MPs. The District and Sessions Judge, agreeing with the arguments of the PP accepted the story given out by Ram Narain as recorded in the FIR and supported by PWs Surjan, and Om Pati, whom I as Distt. Superintendent of Police had described untruthful and untrustworthy. The Court held all the seven persons as mentioned in the FIR guilty u/s 304 IPC and sentenced them to 10 years rigorous imprisonment.

The convicted accused had gone in appeal to the High Court against their conviction by the Sessions Court. Ram Narain at whose instance the FIR was registered had also filed criminal revision appeal in the High Court for enhancing the punishment u/s 302 IPC.

Both the appeals were heard together by the High Court and judgment was announced on 12th December 1969. The High Court dismissed the Criminal Revision Appeal filed by Ram Narian and allowed the appeal filed by the seven accused against their conviction.

Epilogue of the Episode

The real villain in this entire episode was the Public Prosecutor (PP), who conducted the case in the Trial Court in a most irresponsible manner. He was fully competent to decide as to which of the two versions of the episode was to be pleaded by him as the true one when the trial started. If he was not convinced about the bonafide of investigation done by the District Superintendent of Police, he had no business to examine Mange Ram, Risal, and Bakhtawar as PWs because the story advanced by the District Superintendent of Police based entirely on the statements of these PWs, read together with the versions given by Jot Ram, PW, and Surjan PW. Once he had examined these three PWs, he was nobody to disbelieve their versions and cast aspersions on the District Superintendent of Police. By his "vacillating" stand, he "enfeebled and impaired" the prosecution case. In this murder case, seven persons including the village Sarpanch, his young son a law graduate and his young nephew-M.Sc. (Agriculture), were on the way to the gallows. Had I blindly acquiesced in the blatantly false story of the FIR and the statements of the so called eye witnesses, all the seven persons named as accused in the FIR, might have, in all probability, been convicted. To seek conviction of the persons named in the FIR, may be an important objective for the investigating officer, but it is never the only objective. The real onus on the part of the investigating officer is to bring the true facts on record so that the Court may dispense Justice and only Justice. Though I felt extremely harassed because of the aspersions cast on my investigation by the Trial Court, yet at the end of the day I felt very satisfied that I boldly discharged my duties by calling spade a spade and, thus, holding the All India Services (Conduct) Rules in full regard. My acting in any way other than the manner I did in this case would have been a grave sin and immoral act, beyond any exculpation. As long as the villains like the Public Prosecutor and the Dy SP Sonepat sub-division continue sneaking into the Criminal Justice System on consideration other than merit, the real perpetrators of heinous crime would continue escaping punishments and the innocent persons falsely accused, would continue suffering all sorts of harassments and indignities even going to the gallows. The authorities that be, may take notice that the Criminal Justice Delivery System requires not only the purging it of such villains, their sneaking into the system would need to be very carefully blocked. The most important constituents of the Criminal Justice System, which are interdependent and closely interrelated, are: (i) The independent and committed to truthfulness investigation agency, (ii) Meritorious and well trained prosecution lawyers, and government pleaders committed to ensure only justice and (iii) The flawless judiciary. The moral of this episode would be well learnt by these three constituents of the Criminal Justice Delivery System by following what Gautam Budha beautifully summarized as the way of life, "Know Truth as Truth, And Untruth as Untruth". Galileo Galilei said, "All truths are easy to understand once they are discovered; the point is to discover them".

Decision to Press for Transfer from District Rohtak

Dalip Singh, the Range DIG, scandalized the issue while conducting inquiry in the pseudonymous complaint against me. The way he started making inquiries about the investigation of case FIR No.35, while it was subjudice, was all a matter of serious concern for me as District Superintendent of Police. The action of the DIG had not only amounted to lowering the image of the District Superintendent of Police in the eyes of the intelligentsia and the general public, it also started breeding indiscipline in the Force. I, therefore, thought it appropriate to withdraw myself from the scene. Accordingly, I made a fervent request to the Chief Minister to shift me out of Rohtak district. It was Chief Minster's kind grace that he strongly reassured me that he would sternly warn the DIG not to create any hurdles in my working as District Superintendent of Police Rohtak. Days passed. I started feeling uncomfortable and therefore emphatically reiterated my request to the Chief Minister. Thus followed order of my transfer from Rohtak district and posting as District Superintendent of Police Narnaul. I made yet another request to the Chief Minister that even as District Superintendent of Police Narnaul, I would have to face the whims of the same DIG, therefore, I may be posted to any place outside Ambala Range. Conceding my request, I was posted as Superintendent of Police Enforcement, with Headquarters at Chandigarh. Thus, I relinquished the charge as District SP Rohtak, on 30th July 1969 and moved to Chandigarh to take up my new assignment. "Life is difficult. It is a great truth, because once we truly see this truth, we transcend it. Once we truly know that life is difficult, once we truly understand and accept it – and then life is no longer difficult" – M Scott Peck.

Chapter – 10

As Superintendent of Police Enforcement (Traffic)

I took up the new assignment as Superintendent of Police Enforcement on 5th August 1969 and continued to hold it till 27th August 1970. This post had been placed under the supervision and control of the Transport Department, Haryana. The immediate supervisory and controlling authority of SP Enforcement was the State Transport Commissioner. Thus, as SP Enforcement I had nothing to do with the Police Department except to maintain some sort of liaison with the District SPs for smooth flow of motor vehicles on the National and state highways.

The entire road transport system in the country is governed under the Indian Motor Vehicles Act and the Rules framed thereunder. The designated Civil Authority in the Transport Department of the concerned state issues the permits and the licences for all types of mechanical vehicles registered in a particular state. However, driving licences are issued by the civil officers at the sub-division levels. The responsibility to ensure smooth flow of traffic on the roads falls on the shoulders of police department. This department is also responsible to ensure that the motorists plying on the roads possess valid permits or licences and they do not commit any violation of the Indian Motor Vehicle Act and the Rules. Thus, there is multiplicity of authorities accountable for the enforcement of the Indian Motor Vehicles Act and the Rules. Despite this, the common average person believes that for any type of violation of the Indian Motor Vehicles Act and the concerned Rules, the fault is laid only with the police department. For no fault of theirs, the police personnel on traffic duty have to face the wrath of the people flowing from the misconception of the real facts. Unfortunately, the authorities that be, had not bothered to correct such misconceived blame game.

In the new state of Haryana, the post of AIG Railways and Traffic, held by a senior SP Rank Officer, had been created. A Deputy SP had been provided in this set up to exclusively function on the traffic side. However, soon the state bureaucratic game came in play to have control over the police, in every possible way. The police force deployed on the traffic side under the supervision and control of AIG Railways and Traffic was thus, named Police Enforcement Staff and was brought under the control of the State Transport Commissioner. That was the state of affairs when I joined as SP Enforcement. The duties and responsibilities of the staff placed under me were to ensure the smooth flow of vehicular traffic on the National Highways falling within the state and the state roads by ensuring that the Indian Motor Vehicle Act and the relevant Rules were not violated. The District Superintendents of Police had their own traffic staff to perform duties within the Municipal limits of respective towns/ cities. The entire police staff placed under SP Enforcement was considered to be on deputation from police department to the transport department. Soon after my taking over this assignment, I found that almost every one in the police staff had been taken on the recommendation of either some police officers or some bureaucrats or some politicians and even the ministers.

Two days after my taking over I went out on the Ambala-Delhi National Highway (NH-1) for checking the state of affairs during the night hours. Some 5 km short of Murthal, district Rohtak I found a very long queue of trucks parked on the left side of the highway. No truck was seen coming from Delhi side. One head constable, working as my Reader and head constable - car driver in uniform, were accompanying me. It was a black colour car with deeply tinted windowpanes. I was not in uniform. I got the car parked on the left side and got out alone to talk to a group of half a dozen persons, engaged in conversation on the roadside. I inquired from them casually as to why the traffic was not flowing. One of them told me "*Babu, agey policewale maame khade han, jeb dhilli karni han, te tusi agey jao.*" (Gentleman, our 'maternal uncles' in police are standing ahead, if you have enough money to shell off, you may go ahead). I proceeded ahead. After crossing about 50-60 trucks, parked on the roadside, I found a Constable in uniform, standing in the middle of the road. He was signalling the trucks to move on after extorting ten to fifty rupees per truck. Pockets of his trouser and shirt were bulging out with currency notes. A police Sub Inspector was standing by the side of the motorcycle, parked off the road. The constable signalled me to move on in my car and not to block the road. I inquired from my Reader about the identity of the constable and the police Sub Inspector. He told me that they both were from the Enforcement Staff. I along with my Reader and the car driver pounced upon the constable and hauled him up red handed, extorting bribe money from the truck drivers. The police Sub Inspector tried to flee away on the motorcycle. Since the road at that particular point was blocked, he too was hauled up. On search, about rupees three thousand were recovered from the pockets of both the police Sub Inspector and the constable. The amount so recovered was in the denomination of rupees ten to fifty. After recording the statements of a dozen truck drivers/owners, and ensuring smooth flow of the traffic of parked trucks. I took the two culprit policemen to Rai Police Station and a criminal case under the Prevention of Corruption Act was registered. Both the accused policemen were put in the Police Station lock up. The accused Sub Inspector, begging pardon, took the plea that they were collecting money to pay as charges to the truck owners for transporting the sugar cane from the farm of the State Transport Commissioner to the sugar mills.

Next day, in the afternoon, the Transport Commissioner asked me to meet him in his office urgently. He disclosed to me that the Sub Inspector was a relation of the Transport Minister and it was on his recommendation that the Sub Inspector had been taken on deputation in the Enforcement Staff. He also told me that the Minister was very upset and had complained to the Chief Minister that the Sub Inspector had been hauled up falsely by the SP Enforcement. That was the beginning that both the Transport Commissioner and the Transport Minister started manipulating my transfer from the Enforcement Staff. On my meeting the Chief Minister, I explained to him the quality and the manner of the working of all the Enforcement Staff police personnel and pleaded that I be allowed to purge the staff of notorious police personnel. The Chief Minister advised me not to move radically but try to go slowly and cautiously to improve the things. In any case, the above incident had its salutary effect and the Enforcement Staff became cautious; at least there was no blatant and naked show of corrupt dealings for quite some time.

A police Sub Inspector with a motorcycle had been provided for every district. I meticulously ensured that no head constable, much less any constable would go out on the roads for checking the vehicles unless they were led by the Sub Inspector himself. Every Sub Inspector accompanied by one or two ORs, was required to go out on the roads for six hours daily, from sunrise to sunset. For checking during the sunset to sunrise, I used to specify, every day three hours period for holding checking by the party of the Sub Inspector, only in specified area. I personally used to go out daily on the roads to ensure that Police Enforcement staff held checking strictly according to the above-prescribed plan which I had introduced, only to curb the wayward activities on the part of any personnel of the Enforcement Staff.

During six months period the replacement of the entire Police Enforcement staff was complete. I had selected, unmindful of any recommendations, only those police personnel as the replacements, whose integrity had never been doubted and none had faced any departmental action for any indiscipline etc. It was really amusing that some politicians and both senior police and civil officers recommended certain names for the reasons that the poor fellows had acute financial liabilities to discharge relating to the marriages of their daughters/sisters, as if the Enforcement Staff was a sort of mint to make money. In any case in the process some politicians and officers got annoyed with me, often dubbing me as "stubborn character."

National permit holders from Punjab used to operate their trucks in large number between Punjab cities and far off places like Bombay, Calcutta etc. Since, I was originally from Punjab state, some of these truck operators started misusing my name to escape from being challaned by the Enforcement Staff. The normal ploy used by them was to say that the truck being checked by the Enforcement Staff belonged to Swan Sahib. I had to curb this evil very firmly by ensuring that no truck from Punjab, plying on the highway, between the cities of Punjab and Delhi or any destination beyond Delhi escaped unchecked. Both the State Transport Commissioner and the Transport Secretary did appreciate that the Enforcement Staff was able to curb considerably the corrupt practices as prevalent earlier. However, the Transport Minister never reconciled to the incident in which his close relation had been put behind bars in a corruption case. As and when I tried to call on the Minister, I got standard reply from his staff that the Minister was busy.

Union Territory Chandigarh has been a highly explosive contentious issue between the states of Punjab and Haryana. The politicians of both the States used to raise this issue very vocally, as and when they thought it appropriate to divert the attention of the people from agitation against some failures on the part of the administration. Bansi Lal had been in power for about two years and there was some simmering resentment among the people of the state against certain decisions taken by the government. Therefore, during the month of October 1970, when the peasantry was generally free, having harvested the *Kharif* crops and still it was little early to sow *Rabi* crops, it was considered the most opportune time to raise the bogie of Chandigarh issue. It was decided by the Congress Party to hold a huge rally at Delhi to project the demand for merger of Chandigarh into Haryana State. Every Congress leader of some standing became busy to mobilize maximum number of people to attend the rally at Delhi. Every available commercial transport was almost "impounded" for carrying the people to Delhi. The entire Police Enforcement Staff was engaged for facilitating the successful holding of the rally. I was asked to liaise with SP Traffic, Delhi, to ensure that tractor trolleys/buses/trucks, carrying the people to participate in the rally did not face any harassment at the hands of Delhi Police Traffic Staff. I was able to enlist full cooperation of SP Traffic, Delhi and Superintendents of Police of various districts of Delhi, through which the vehicles carrying the people to attend the rally were to pass. A massive rally was held in the open area on the rear of Red Fort and dispersal of the people was peaceful and without any major incident. The Resident Commissioner of Haryana, at Delhi, conveyed to me that the Chief Minister wanted that the National Press should carry the news that at least three lac persons had attended the rally. A Press conference was held in the office of SP, North District Delhi, who was my batch mate. I requested him to exercise his rapport with the Press correspondents and persuade them to post the news as desired by Chief Minister, Haryana. According to the Press correspondents, not more than fifty thousand people had attended the rally. They had reached this figure, on counting the number of tractor trolleys/ buses/trucks in the parking area. After long persuasion, thanks to SP, North District Delhi, that the Press correspondents agreed to reflect the presence of one to one and a half lac people in the rally. Chief Minister was not quite happy. It was with great difficulty that I had to convince the Chief Minister that the figure given by the Press was even inflated.

Over the time, I experienced that violation of traffic laws was blatant and the problem was very acute but very little thought was given to meet it. On studying the subject in depth, I found that during the period from 1959 to 1964, 1008 vehicles were involved in the road accidents, killing 443 and injuring 926 persons. Further, during the period from 1965 to 1969, vehicles involved in the accidents went up to 2095, killing 881 and injuring 1546 persons. During the calendar year 1969, 78722 traffic violation cases were instituted by both the Enforcement staff and Police staff of various districts. Fine to the tune of Rs. 9,74,047/- was realized. Even such large-scale prosecution of the defaulting motorists did not deter them from indulging in the violation of traffic laws.

The rapid industrialization, urbanization and keenly implemented rural development schemes, had ushered in an era of automobiles. I was shocked to find that the increase in the fleet of automobiles had turned the roads into graveyards. As on 31st March 1969, there were roughly 30,000 automobiles on the roads in Haryana. This fleet included 9000 heavy vehicles, 15,000 light vehicles, and 6000 tractors. A couple of year back, this fleet was perhaps not even half of it. In addition to this large fleet of the State of Haryana, the motorists of states of Punjab, J&K, Himachal Pradesh and UT Chandigarh, passed through the National Highway for their journey to Delhi and beyond. Similarly, the vehicular traffic from other states on Delhi-Mathura road and from Rajasthan to Delhi was very heavy. There was variety of factors, which were playing in causing accidents. The three main elements coming in play were the human beings, the vehicles and the roads. The typical causes of disruption of smooth flow of traffic and the road accidents were found to be as follows:

(a) Driving automobiles by persons having inadequate knowledge of driving and lacking requisite psychological and physiological make up.

(b) Drunkard motorists: Provisions available u/s 117 of the Motor Vehicle Act was found to be inadequate to curb this nuisance.

(c) Rash and negligent driving: To curb the problem, the provision u/s 116 of the Motor Vehicle Act required to be made more stringent by providing the quantum of minimum punishment, which must be inflicted in proven cases.

(d) General lack of Road Sense in the Public: The road users other than the motorist, needed to imbibe adequate road sense. Jaywalking had become fashion with the pedestrians and the cyclists. The bullock/mule carts plying during dark hours without having any light to indicate their presence on the road, was additional menace. There seemed to be urgent need to educate the public in this regard.

(e) Overloading of Vehicles: The practice of heavily overloading of vehicles and the loading of bulky articles, protruding both vertically and laterally, was a potential danger to road users. Carrying of chaff and sugarcane in bigger bulk were typical instances. Such types of overloading of trucks, causing instability for the vehicles, posed potential threats for road accidents. There was serious lacuna in the traffic laws, to curb such dangerous menace.

(f) Vehicles without backlights and stoplights: The provision of improved type of cat's eye, which would reflect lights needed to be essentially fitted with every vehicle.

(g) Defective dipper or its non-use.

(h) Using mechanically defective vehicles.

(i) Lack of proper road engineering.

Having studied the problem in depth, I drew up a detailed proposal for putting in place a regular cell in the Transport Department, with the role of carrying out Research and Planning to ensure the safe flow of vehicular traffic on the National Highways and the state roads. I submitted this proposal on 30th January 1970, to the State Transport Controller Haryana and also to the IGP Haryana.

The Transport Minister, Haryana, had not reconciled to my tough stand to curb the corruption, earlier being indulged in by the Enforcement Staff, particularly the incident of my nabbing red handed, the Sub Inspector as described earlier above. He succeeded in persuading the CM to transfer me from the assignment of SP Enforcement. For me, it was a good riddance from that highly controversial assignment. I was posted as Assistant Inspector General of Police, Administration, in the office of IGP, Haryana, a prestigious assignment, by all standards.

Chapter – 11

AIG of Police Administration, Haryana

I joined as Assistant Inspector General of Police Administration, Haryana on 27th August 1970 and continued till 1st November 1973. State IGP was assisted in his office by two Assistant Inspectors General of Police. One AIG was to deal with all matters concerning the supply of provision for the police force. I as AIG Administration, as the designation suggests, was to assist the State IGP in all matters concerning the administration of the entire state police force. In certain matters, like recruitment policy, postings, transfers, promotions, disciplinary matters, representations and appeals, concerning all ranks of the state police personnel, only the IGP or the state government, were competent to pass final orders. All these matters had to be thoroughly examined by me and put up to the IGP, with detailed noting on the file, proposing in the concluding para, what kind of final order, the IGP might consider passing.

The job requirements involved long working hours. Haryana being the new state, rapid expansion of the police force had taken place during my tenure spanning over three years as AIG Administration. The state police force has multiplied, several times, in size since then and so has been the status of the State Police Chief upgraded from IGP to DGP. Then the State IGP was assisted only by one senior SP rank officer designated as AIG Administration to deal with Administration of the force. In the present days, the State DGP is assisted, in dealing with the administration of the state police force by an ADGP and IGP each and half a dozen officers of the rank of DIG and SP.

J C Vachher, 1946 IPS–ER, was the State IGP, during those days. He was a very experienced, composed and kindhearted officer. I never heard him raising the pitch of his voice, even when he was to vent his annoyance, in any matter. He would call me to his office chamber for a cup of tea daily at 11.00 am and would engage me in conversation on matters other than official for 15 to 30 minutes and those welcome moments would just slip away in our mutual light-vein talk. Good conversations inspire, entertain and even change the course of life. I had the privilege to have his full trust in me and I in turn extended my unstinted loyalty to him. I thoroughly enjoyed my posting as AIG, Administration, earning total support and confidence of the IGP.

Soon after my taking up this assignment, I had interviewed every Assistant posted in the administration branch, to familiarize myself with the work allotted to each of them. The Assistant dealing with all administrative matters, concerning the IPS, designated as Secret Assistant, was said to be very well conversant with IPS Service Rules. I had earlier learnt that this Assistant used to leak out information to some police officers, relating to confidential matters. During my conversation with him, he boasted that he had helped many IPS Officers of varied seniority and that he had taught the IPS Service Rules to the officers posted as AIG Administration. I did not like his boastful claims. If I were to learn Rules from an Assistant, I would have to give him some latitude. Therefore, I decided to study thoroughly the All India Service Manual, particularly the rules applicable to the IPS, instead of looking up to this Assistant. I was well aware about the IPS Service Rules, but I had only to understand the intricacies in their interpretation. I paid special attention to this aspect. No wonder, my reputation as a knowledgeable officer in all intricate administrative matters was registered in both the police department and the state government. The said Assistant in the meanwhile was allotted some work, other than the administrative matters concerning the IPS officers.

Quite a few IPS (SPS) officers and State Police Service officers including Inspectors were used to take recourse to unethical and questionable means to get their representations about their service matters, dealt with in the Central Police Office, in their favour. Many of them, particularly State Police Service officers (Deputy Superintendents of Police) falling in the zone of consideration of their names for inclusion in the "Select List" for appointments to the IPS got annoyed with me for not obliging them in entertaining their dishonest demands. The exercise for preparing the "Select List" was an annual feature towards the close of every calendar year.

The Haryana State Assembly elections were due in 1973. However, these were advanced to June 1972 at the behest of Bansi Lal, that being the most appropriate time after India's victory in Indo-Pak War of 1971. The political leaders, both in the Congress and the opposition parties, with eye on the coming elections, wanted to raise some issues against Bansi Lal government, by playing on the sentiments of the gullible people. These people raised the bogie of not fulfilling many promises made by the government. An agitation was launched by the opposition parties, in February 1972, on the announcement of the decision on Chandigarh by the Government of India. Soon the agitators took to violence and arson. Serious law and order situation had developed in the state. In Sonepat city of district Rohtak, the agitators caused serious damage to government properties and even the house of Randhir Singh, Member Parliament was torched. The government had to call in the army, in aid of civil authorities. I was specially deputed under orders of the Chief Minister, to take care and restore the law and order situation in Sonepat. With God's kind grace and energy bestowed on me by the Almighty, I was able to enlist the support of all well-meaning people of the city including Rizak Ram and Chiranji Lal, both being in the forefront. The law and order situation was restored to normalcy in no time. When I reported the latest situation to both the IGP and the Chief Minister on the telephone, they profusely applauded my role. The state government's appreciation was, conveyed to me by J C Vachher, the IGP vide his DO letter No.2625, dated 17th February 1972. "I am desired to convey the special appreciation of the Haryana government, for your steadfast devotion to duty and for your untiring efforts, in controlling the serious law and order situation, which had developed throughout the state, on the announcement of decision, on Chandigarh, by the Government of India. You had shown qualities of leadership and had personally substantially contributed, in restoring the law and order situation, so quickly."

Intensive developmental activities of the state government, rapid industrial strides and urbanization had necessitated the reorganization of the state by splitting the bigger districts. In December 1972, new districts of Sonepat and Bhiwani were created by bifurcating existing districts of Rohtak and Hisar respectively. On 23rd January, 1973 another new district of Kurukshetra was created by bifurcating Karnal district. These developments required expansion in the strength of police force at various levels. In fact, during the years 1971 to 1973, various proposals for increase in the police work force continued maturing up by and by. By the close of 1973, the police strength was set to go upto 14828, including 1 IGP, 4 DIGs, 27 SPs, 17 ASPs, 52 Dy SPs, 1274 NGOs and 13453 ORs. This rise during a period of three years when I was AIG/Admn, had tremendously increased the administrative job for me. The IGP had repeatedly applauded my contribution in this regard, on several occasions.

An unfortunate episode happened towards the end of October 1973. An IAS officer proposed to me on the telephone on a Sunday morning that we, together with our families, might enjoy a sunny lunch picnic in the Pinjore Garden. I agreed to this proposal. When I reached Pinjore Garden with my wife and children, I found that the said IAS officer had also invited another IPS officer along with his family to join the picnic party. The Chief Minister was not happily disposed towards that IAS officer and he hated him the most. In any case, we all the three families pooled up our cooked delicacies and started enjoying the picnic. The domestic aide of the IPS officer was named Bansi. As Bansi was at a little distance, the said IPS officer called him by name at the pitch of his voice to render some assistance in laying the food etc. There were some intelligence personnel around the Pinjore Garden who overheard the name Bansi. They cooked up a story that three senior scheduled caste IAS/IPS officers were abusing Bansi Lal, the Chief Minister. A senior IPS officer in DIG Rank took this incident as a welcome opportunity, to win favours with the Chief Minister. By distorting the facts, he villainously told Bansi Lal that these three senior IAS/IPS officers were hatching a conspiracy, to destabilize his government. In the political game of circus, there always remain certain elements, on the look out for destabilizing the government. Naturally, Bansi Lal was always on the guard against such elements.

Bansi Lal, despite being bestowed with admirable skill to tackle the administrative and political affairs, was a normal human being and lent soft ears to sycophancy and backbiting, which mislead even the extra-ordinary human being. He believed the distorted story as told to him as true one. He told his Principal Secretary to ensure my deputation to the Government of India urgently. Government's orders placing my services at the disposal of Government of India, for appointment as AIG Adm, Central Industrial Security Force, Delhi, came to me like a bolt from the blue. IGP was not consulted by the government before issuing such orders. When the IGP talked to the Home Secretary and the Chief Secretary, he was told to relieve me from the post of AIG Administration immediately and if I required any sort of leave, I should get the same sanctioned from IGP, CISF Delhi. All my efforts to seek an interview with the Chief Minister were in vain. I was perplexed not knowing even a bit of the reasons for this sudden development.

My three children were still school going and it was difficult to shift my family to Delhi. However, IGP advised me to take this incident in my stride and proceed to Delhi to take up the new assignment. As the Head of the state police force, he reassured me that there might be some blessings in disguise. On 1st of November 1973, I relinquished the charge as AIG Administration Haryana Police, and proceeded to take up my new assignment in Delhi.

Chapter – 12

On Deputation to Central Industrial Security Force

Posting as AIG Central Industrial Security Force (CISF)

I joined at the CISF Hqr, at New Delhi on a key post, as AIG/Administration on 12th November 1973. Sh. L S Bist, IPS (1943-ER), from Uttar Pradesh IPS Cadre, was the Head of the CISF, in the rank of Inspector General of Police. His earlier posting was Inspector General of Police, UT Delhi State Police Force. Sh. M L Puri, IPS (1946-ER) from Punjab State IPS Cadre, was DIG Headquarter. Sh Tushar Dutt, IPS (1953-RR) was DIG North-Western Zone, with additional charge of administration. Due to my varied experience of sixteen years in the IPS in the states of Punjab and Haryana, particularly my latest assignment as AIG Admn, Haryana Police, for over three years, all the above said three senior officers were happy with my posting and they explicitly expressed so when I called on them. The CISF was comparatively the youngest Central Police Organization with wide scope of its rapid expansion, as there was a big demand for its deployment at various Public Sector Undertakings (PSUs).

CISF was initially raised in 1968 in the wake of a devastating fire in the Heavy Engineering Corporation Ranchi, suspected to be a case of sabotage. The charter of duties of this Force included inter alia providing protection to the selected Public Sector Undertakings against fire hazards, sabotage, pilferage and theft. Until then, the security set up for every PSU used to be maintained independently. Haphazardly raised, ill-trained and inadequately paid, the members of the force in the existing security setup, everywhere was far too below the required standards. The CISF with its strong Hqr at New Delhi comprised three Zones i.e. North Western Zone, Eastern Zone and Southern Zone. For the purpose of command and control in the field, each Zone was headed by a DIG. Large PSUs like Steel Plants at Durgapur, Raurkela, and Bhilai and HEC Ranchi were headed each by a DIG, assisted by one or two Commandants. In due course of time, North Western Zone was bifurcated, with North Zone

Hqr remaining at Delhi and the newly created Western Zone was headquartered at Bombay. Sh SV Singh IPS (1955-RR) from Madhya Pradesh Cadre was appointed as DIG Northern Zone relieving Sh Tushar Dutt to take up as whole time DIG/Admn.

My job as AIG/Admn involved, in-depth examination of all matters of administration, relating to the entire force and submit the files with specific suggestions, to the IG, through DIG/Administration. The army, in the wake of Chinese aggression of 1962 and Indo-Pak War of 1965 had recruited hundreds of Emergency Commissioned Officers (ECOs). Many of these ECOs had been discharged after the cessation of hostilities. Scores of them were recruited as Inspectors in the CISF. Many young graduates had also been recruited as Inspectors as direct recruits. The inter-se seniority of all these Inspectors of both the categories was yet to be determined. The rules for recruitment, training, postings, transfers and promotions and inter-se seniority of force personnel were yet to be formulated. This job was also included in my charter of duties. Further, the requirements of additional force necessary for induction into the PSUs, whose demands were pending, had to be worked out by me, after examining the recommendations of the inspecting officers. The job of preparing and processing the proposals for getting additional force sanctioned from the Union Home Ministry, after the clearance from the Finance Ministry, was also part of my responsibility. I was supposed to pursue these proposals after the clearance at the IGP level and hold discussions with the concerned officers in the said two Ministries. Thus, my job required long working hours. In due course of time, I was able to establish good rapports with the officers of the rank of Deputy Secretary, Director and Joint Secretary, in both the Home and Finance Ministries. Similarly, I had many occasions to hold discussions with AIG/DIG rank officers looking after the administration in other Central Police Organizations like the BSF, CRPF and RPF et al. All such exposure stood me in good stead in my service career to learn many new things and enriching my knowledge, apart from strengthening my self-confidence.

Proposal for My Promotion as DIG

M L Puri, DIG Hqr, was due to superannuate, at the age of 58 years, on 28.02.1975. IG/CISF sent recommendations on 22.02.1975, to the Ministry of Home Affairs, proposing appointment of Tushar Dutt, as DIG Hqr, and my appointment, on promotion, as DIG/Admn. After due examinations, Secretary, Ministry of Home Affairs recommended the said proposal, for the approval of the Appointment Committee of the Cabinet (ACC). In the meanwhile, Haryana government had approved my promotion to the rank of DIG effective from 27th February 1975 under the provision of 'Next Below Rule' which meant that I would have got promotion from that date had I been there in Haryana state. While my promotion case was pending with the Appointment Committee of the Cabinet (ACC), an IPS officer from Haryana, serving with Delhi Police on deputation basis, out of professional rivalry, managed to play the spoilsport. He was a lackey of Sanjay Gandhi and had effective influence in the Prime Minister's Office (PMO). He maliciously concocted some canard and prejudiced the PMO against me. Thus, the ACC withheld its approval of my promotion with the remarks "His work in the CISF should be watched for one more year before his case is considered".

General Elections for the Haryana State Assembly were held in 1972. Congress Party under the leadership of Bansi Lal won the majority seats. Bansi Lal, therefore, became the Chief Minister of Haryana for the second time in a row. He had won the election based on all-round development that took place in Haryana state under his dynamic stewardship. Smt Indira Gandhi, the then Prime Minister of India saw in Bansi Lal, a great potential of becoming a top Congress leader at the National level. He was, therefore, called to the centre by the Prime Minister and inducted in her Cabinet as Defence Minister of India. Banarsi Das Gupta, a crony of Bansi Lal was made the Chief Minister of Haryana. However, it was Bansi Lal as Defence Minister of India, who was ruling Haryana from remote control. He had acquired a very important position in the coterie of the Prime Minister of India.

Emergency of 1975-77

On 12th June 1975, Justice Jagmohan Lal Sinha of the Allahabad High Court declared Smt. Indira Gandhi's election from Rae-Bareli Parliamentary Constituency null and void disqualifying her from contesting any election for 6 years. Opposition Parties clamoured for her resignation. She in her best wisdom decided not to resign and instead, recommended to the President of India to declare a state of Emergency on the basis that "there is an imminent danger to the security of India being threatened by internal disturbances". President Fakhruddin Ali Ahmed declared the state of Emergency on 25th June 1975. All the top leaders of various political parties were put under preventive detention. Vast sections of population welcomed it initially as general administration improved considerably. However, civil rights activists took exception to the curbs on freedom of expression and personal liberties. The Government servants at various levels were cautious enough in their conduct and outbursts lest the eagle eye of intelligence men on prowl would report against them for any inadvertent transgression. The Central Government launched, in good faith, some public welfare schemes, like family planning, slum clearance and promotion of literacy, et al. Sanjay Gandhi, a very dynamic character, soon emerged as a leader of great promise and occupied the centre stage. Due to his over enthusiasm and impatience to get spectacular results, the police and civil servants at all levels, playing as his faithful lackeys, promoted and implemented all these schemes very vigorously but in an arbitrary and authoritarian manner much to the annoyance of the people. Roughshod methods to carry out sterilization operation and forcible clearance of slums, in particular sparked popular anger.

Fresh Proposal of My Promotion as DIG

A new post of DIG was sanctioned by the Government of India for the CISF, in June 1976. IG/CISF again sent his recommendation on 28th June 1976, to the Ministry of Home Affairs, for my promotion and appointment, as DIG, in the CISF. In his recommendation, IG/CISF mentioned, "Sh. Hans Raj

Swan, IPS (HR/1957) has been on deputation with the CISF as AIG/Admn, since 12th November 1973, in which capacity he has functioned very well. He has shown dedication to his job and has rendered extremely valuable assistance in dealing with various administrative and allied matters. Particularly during the last one year, the performance of this officer has been of outstanding quality especially when this force is in the process of re-organization and rapid expansion. With his experience and background, both in the police department and in the CISF, he is eminently suitable for appointment, as DIG in the CISF." This proposal duly processed in the Ministry of Home Affairs was put up by the Home Secretary to Om Mehta, Minister of State, in the Ministry of Home Affairs. The same IPS Officer from Haryana Cadre mentioned earlier had a direct equation with Om Mehta. Taking advantage of his proximity to the Minister, he once again maliciously played a villain to scuttle my promotion. He misinformed the Minister that a vigilance inquiry was pending in Haryana against me. Misled by him, the Minister sent the file back to the Home Secretary, with the remarks dated 6th July 1976, "I understand that there was some vigilance case against him. Has he been cleared?" IG/CISF was accordingly, informed by the MHA. IG/CISF again sent back the case to the MHA saying that his office was not aware of any vigilance inquiry pending against Sh. Hans Raj Swan; however, for the period prior to his deputation to the CISF, clarification might be obtained from Haryana government. The rigmarole of correspondence between the MHA and the state government took time to clarify that there was no vigilance inquiry pending against me even with Haryana Government. My appointment, as DIG in the CISF, duly approved by the ACC, became effective only from 9th December 1976, with a delay of almost two years, thanks to the villainous role played by the Haryana Cadre IPS officer whose animosity against me had poisoned the soft ears of the Minister in the MHA. However, I could not avail of the benefit of actually holding the position as DIG from 27th February 1975 under the "Next Below Rule" because of my being on deputation to the Government of India.

Emergency– The Waterloo of Indira Gandhi

During the days of the Emergency in 1975, most of the senior officers serving in Prime Ministers' Office, had lost all sense of objectivity and had taken easy recourse to sycophancy. Such senior officers included even those at the helm of affairs in the Intelligence Agencies. They conveyed to the Prime Minister that the people at large in the country were happy with the Congress Party in view of various developmental projects launched in the country during the Emergency. They wrongly advised Indira Gandhi that the Congress Party under her leadership had every chance to return to power, if fresh mandate of the people was sought by holding Elections to the Lok Sabha.

In the meanwhile, the top leaders of the Opposition Parties, languishing in jails for 19 months' preventive detention had sunk their ideological differences and an alliance with a common goal of taking on the Congress Party was formed. They floated a new political outfit by the name of Janata Party. Complete eradication of the evil of corruption and bringing about full transparency in the administration was the main plank of this Party. Lok Nayak Jai Prakash Narain was the Chief Patron of this new political outfit.

Indira Gandhi led by the wrong advice of Intelligence Bureau and other senior civil officers and politicians announced fresh Lok Sabha elections to be held on 23rd January 1977. All political leaders under detention were released. In the elections held in February 1977, both Indira Gandhi and her son Sanjay Gandhi lost their seats. Janata Party swept the elections.

Emergency was withdrawn on 21st March 1977. Morarji Desai became the first Non-Congress Prime Minister on 23rd March; thus, ended the Emergency.

With the Janata Party assuming the rein of the country, the police and civil servants at various levels as also the politicians, who had played lackeys to the authoritarian rule during the Emergency and were vying with each other to play sycophants to the top authorities, started quickly withdrawing themselves into their shells. However, the long arms of the law soon reached all those responsible for committing all sorts of excesses on the people. The villain IPS officer from Haryana functioning on deputation with the Delhi Police mentioned earlier was booked for staging a fake encounter. It was, indeed, an amusing scenario to see that the many officers/politicians who used to snarl like tigers, overnight turned into bleating humble and meek lambs.

Police Medal for Meritorious Service

In due course, IG/CISF recommended my name for the award of Police Medal for meritorious service, on Independence Day of 1977. The following are the excerpts from the detailed recommendations made by IG/CISF as duly approved by the Haryana State Government and the Ministry of Home Affairs.

- Sh. Hans Raj Swan joined the IPS on 26th October 1957. In the rank of ASP, he did commendable work, as supervisory officer of various police stations and kept the law and order situation under control. His performance, during Punjabi Suba agitation in 1962 was highly praiseworthy.
- Punjab Armed Police Bn deployed on Indo-Pak Border, in J&K State during the years 1963 and 1964, under his command, close supervision, untiring efforts and able stewardships, maintained high standard of discipline and achieved best results.
- During Senior Officers Course in CPTC Mount Abu, in early 1965, he produced two useful papers.
- He displayed vigour, determination and made very valuable contribution in the mopping up operations against Pakistan guerillas in Kashmir Valley, during 1965.
- As Director Vigilance Bureau Haryana, during 1966-67, his performance amply reflected his qualities; diligence, industry and thoroughness.
- As District Superintendent of Police, Rohtak during 1967-69, he was found to be an officer of integrity, possessing considerable investigating capacity. Because of his cool, astute and firm handling, difficult situations were successfully prevented from assuming serious proportions. Results achieved in the prevention and detection of heinous crime, prevention of corruption and prompt disposal of public grievances were commendable. He proved to be really a model Police Officer, in a welfare State, like ours.

- His work and conduct as Superintendent of Police Enforcement, during 1969-70 remained praiseworthy with noticeable improvement in the Enforcement Branch.
- In January 1970 widespread agitation started in Haryana, on Chandigarh issue. Sh. Swan won special appreciation of the Haryana Government, for immediately restoring the law and order situation, with steadfast devotion to duty, ceaseless efforts and qualities of leadership, in Sonepat area where he had been, specially deputed while posted as AIG/Admn.
- He held the key post of AIG/Police Administration Haryana for over three years (1970-73) with distinction, displaying commendable maturity, dependability, organizing capacity and initiative.
- While on deputation to the Government of India, he remained posted as AIG/Admn, a key post in the CISF, for about three years and was found to be dedicated to his job. He gave outstanding performances and proved to be an asset to the organization.
- As DIG, incharge of a Zone in the CISF, since 9th December 1976, he has been doing extremely well.
- Throughout his service, Sh. Swan has exhibited qualities of leadership, sincerity of purpose and devotion to duty of a very high order. In recognition of the outstanding service rendered by Sh. Hans Raj Swan, he is recommended for the award of Police Medal for meritorious service, on Independence Day, 1977.

As per the Gazette of India, 20th August 1977, Notification No.67-pers/77, the President of India was pleased on the occasion of the Independence Day 1977 to award the Police Medal for meritorious service to Sh. Hans Raj Swan, DIG/CISF.

After promotion as DIG, I was appointed as DIG/CISF Southern Zone in which capacity I looked after the security requirements in the various PSUs, in the states of Tamil Nadu, Kerala, Andhra Pradesh and Karnataka. I was assisted in this assignment by an Assistant Inspector General of Police. This job involved a lot of touring. I had to be on tour to visit various CISF units, in these four states for fifteen to twenty days in a month. Later I was brought back to the CISF Hqr, as DIG Provisions and Accounts. After the superannuation of L S Bist IG/CISF, at the age of 58 years and appointment of R C Gopal, IPS, from UP Cadre, as IG/CISF, I was, appointed, as DIG/Admn, at the CISF Hqr. The CISF by then had expanded to more than forty thousand personnel. As DIG/Admn, I was assisted by three staff officers-AIG/Admn, AIG/Personnel and AIG/Induction & Planning.

Cock Fighting Between Two IPS Officers

An unpleasant situation took place at Durgapur Steel Plant. Both DIG and his Commandant at Durgapur Steel Plant Unit of the CISF, were on deputation from Haryana IPS Cadre. A serious misunderstanding had erupted between the two. The DIG reported to the IG/CISF listing various instances of indiscipline on the part of his Commandant, who on his part, made insinuations against the DIG. The IG appointed a very senior IPS Officer in the CISF to hold a fact-finding inquiry. On receipt of the inquiry report, both the DIG and his Commandant were called upon to clarify on certain points. On receipt of their comments, it was a matter for me as DIG/Admn, to examine in depth and then put up the file to the IG, R C Gopal then holding the charge as both IG/CISF and DG/CRPF. On examining the case, I found that neither the DIG nor his Commandant had committed any grave misconduct and only mud-slinging was involved on the part of both of them. I, therefore, proposed that a notice under Rule 8 of All India Services (Discipline and Appeal) Rules be issued to both of them to explain their conduct for taking appropriate action depending on their explanation. This rule covers the misconduct, warranting only the award of a minor punishment.

R C Gopal, IG/CISF called me to his office chamber and very sarcastically remarked "You have not examined this case objectively; since both these rogue officers come from Haryana IPS Cadre, you have tried to save them from major punishment." I submitted to him that since final decision lay with the Union Home Secretary, therefore he could give his own recommendations as deemed appropriate. Shri Gopal rather lost his cool and started shouting at me. I politely submitted to him that his intemperate remarks were unfair and humiliating. I further submitted to him that he had cast doubts on my integrity and it seemed that I had completely lost his confidence; for these reasons I be allowed to get my posting outside the CISF. Instead of calming down, he retorted that he too was not keen to retain me in the CISF. Saying that I would be happy to honour his feelings, I asked for his permission to leave his office chamber; I got up and after paying my compliments returned to my own chamber. I immediately called my PA, dictated a note and submitted the same to the IG. I mentioned that apropos his impolite remarks about the manner I had dealt with the matter regarding alleged indiscipline on the part of two Haryana Cadre IPS officers, I would like to be posted out of the CISF and for that purpose, I might be permitted to seek an interview with the Union Home Secretary. On receipt of this note, the IG again called me and told me that he did not mean any insult to me. Nor there was any question of lack of his confidence in me. This time the IG was in a very relaxed and cheerful mood. He tore up my said note, in my presence, saying that there was no question of relieving me from the CISF. He talked about many things, in lighter vein, to pacify and cheer me up.

Repatriation to Haryana State Cadre

I was shortly completing my five years deputation with Government of India. The IG had earlier sent up a proposal to the MHA, without taking my consent, to extend my deputation period, for one more year. The MHA asked the IG to obtain written consent from me and then resubmit the proposal. When the file came to me for my report, I asked for my repatriation to the parent cadre, on the completion of deputation period, for personal reasons. IG tried to persuade me to continue in the CISF, for one more year. Since I had some genuine problems because of my father's ailment and crucial stage of education of my children, I requested the IG not to insist on extension of my deputation any more. Finally, the MHA decided to repatriate me to my parent cadre and I was relieved from the CISF on 13th November 1978.

Reverting to the episode involving two Haryana Cadre IPS officers, I learnt later that R C Gopal, IG/CISF had recommended to the Union Home Ministry that the matter called for an in-depth inquiry by the CBI. Accordingly, the CBI took up the inquiry. This Agency after holding inquiry had reported to the MHA that no indiscipline or irregularity against either officer was proved and hence it recommended no further action. The matter was perhaps ultimately disposed of by the MHA accordingly. The entire exercise as initiated by R C Gopal, proved to be futile.

On my return to the parent State Haryana IPS Cadre, I as DIG, Hisar Range, on my official visit to District Faridabad, was passing through Delhi. I thought of calling on R C Gopal who had by then, become Director General of the CRPF, leaving the CISF to the charge of Surinder Nath, IPS, as the new IG/CISF. Shri Gopal extended to me such a warm hospitality when I met him in his office that I felt a little bit embarrassed. He affectionately embraced me and said, "let us go out for a nice lunch at some good hotel." I expressed my sincere thanks to him. He kept me engrossed in happy conversations for about one hour, over coffee and sumptuous snacks, to munch in between. I was very happy to see Shri Gopal in that relaxed and cheerful mood.

As mentioned earlier that CISF had a wide scope of rapid expansion in its role and strength, I have found that the strength of CISF has gone upto 1,10,000 personnel. The CISF became the largest Industrial Security Force in the World by the close of 2010, providing security coverage to 189 PSUs, 57 Airports, 50 government buildings and 33 places of National and commercial importance. Over 100 private firms including those in the strategic sectors of information technology, finance and manufacturing have sought the CISF protection at their establishments.

Chapter – 13

As Dy Inspector General of Police after Repatriation to Haryana State IPS Cadre

Posting as DIG Hisar Range, Haryana State

In the wake of Emergency ending in March 1977, Haryana State Assembly Elections were held in June 1977. Janata Party under the leadership of Devi Lal got resounding mandate of the electorate and he became the Chief Minister on 21st June 1977 for the first time, in his long political career. A stormy petrel in the politics of Punjab-Haryana region for years, he was born in 1914 at Tejakheda village of present district Sirsa. His father Lekh Ram was a wealthy landowner of village Chautala owning nearly 3000 bighas of land. Devi Lal became active in the Freedom Movement at the tender age of 16 years. He was imprisoned in October 1930 for one year for taking part in the Salt movement. He was selected in 1938 as a delegate of All India Congress Committee. His elder brother Sahib Ram was elected in 1938 as a Congress MLA in a by-election and had courted arrest as a *Satyagrahi* in 1940; he was sentenced to nine months imprisonment. Both Devi Lal and Sahib Ram were arrested in 1942 for taking part in the Quit India Movement and were put under detention for two years; they were later, released in 1943.

The legendry jat leader Sir Chhotu Ram, then Revenue Minister in Unionist Party Government, made vain attempts in 1944 to woo both Devi Lal and Sahib Ram, to desert Congress and join Unionist Party. After Independence, Devi Lal launched Farmers' Movement and forced Dr. Gopi Chand Bhargava, the then Chief Minister of Composite Punjab, for amending the Tenancy Act. He was elected as Congress MLA in 1957 and earlier President Punjab Pradesh Congress Committee in 1956. He was also elected as Congress MLA from Sirsa in 1958. He had played active role in the formation of Haryana State. After being member of the Congress Party for nearly four decades, he left this Party in 1971. He was arrested and kept under detention for 19 months along with many top opposition leaders in the Emergency of 1975. The long strenuous and eventful journey of his political career, rightly entitled him to the honour of being elevated to the most coveted position as Chief Minister of Haryana.

On return from central deputation, I got some earned leave. My leave was cut short by the government on 21st December 1978; I was told to take over immediately as DIG Hisar Range. Accordingly, I joined as DIG Hisar Range on 21st December 1978. Haryana state had then two Police Ranges, with Hqrs at Hisar and Ambala. Hisar Range included the districts of Sirsa, Hisar, Bhiwani, Jind, Gurgaon, Faridabad and Mohindergarh at Narnaul.

Discontentment in Police Constabulary

There was simmering discontentment in the constabulary all over the state. A disgruntled constable while on the Quarter Guard duty climbed over the rooftop of the Administrative Block in the Hisar District Police Lines, carrying with him the rifle and the ammunition issued to him. He was shouting that he would not get down until the demands of the constabulary were conceded and that he would shoot down if anybody tried to interfere with his actions. District SP tried his best to persuade the constable to climb down, promising that no action would be taken against him for his act of indiscipline and that his demands would be duly considered, but all in vain. The District SP reported the matter to me over the telephone. After informing the IGP, I reached the police lines to supervise the police operation to calm down the constable. No amount of persuasion worked. No person who would be visible to the constable from the rooftop of the building was allowed to make any movement. His father and mother from his village were summoned to help in solving the knotty problem. They also pleaded with the constable to surrender gracefully. He threatened them with dire consequences if they came in his way.

Everybody was on the toes for nearly six hours. We, therefore, thought of a plan to overpower the constable. He was strategically involved in a conversation about the demands projected by him. Two sturdy Head Constables were deputed to climb up to the rooftop of the building surreptitiously with the help of rain water pipes. They were able to overpower the constable without any injury caused to anybody. They were both, richly rewarded and the rebel constable was sent to his village in a police vehicle, in the company of his parents. In due course of time, the constable was dismissed from the service because of disciplinary action against him.

This very unpleasant episode was a wake up call for the senior police officers, all over the state. I drew up a comprehensive plan after holding detailed discussions with all the District SPs in the Range, for sorting out the genuine grievances of the constabulary. At the state level, the top brass of the police took several welfare measures to redress the genuine grievances of the constabulary.

Highway Robberies and Gallant Act of a Young IPS Officer

Quite a few gangs of highway robbers had been menacingly active on the highway passing through the area under my jurisdiction. Their victims were drivers/owners of the trucks transporting goods by the state highways during night hours. This menace created a lot of panic in the public and the situation assumed serious proportions. Such crimes were mainly confined to the districts of Sirsa, Hisar, Jind and Bhiwani. In consultation with all the District SPs of the Range, I drew up a comprehensive plan for mobile night patrolling by strong police parties. The gazetted police officers, including the District SPs displayed a spirited and enthusiastic response to the plan and undertook the night patrolling on the affected roads with a missionary zeal. Ranjiv Singh Dalal IPS, the present DGP Haryana, was then a very young Superintendent of Police, district Bhiwani, with only four years service at his credit. While on night patrolling, he accosted a stranger who happened to be a notorious highway robber. Instantly pulling out his illicit weapon, the robber fired at the District SP causing serious injury to him. The SP, despite being gravely injured, showed exemplary presence of mind and bravely faced the situation. He fired back from his service revolver at the robber in a twinkle of an eye, affording no reaction time to this criminal to fire another shot at him. The shot fired by the SP at the robber, proved fatal. Ranjiv Singh Dalal was hospitalized for a considerable period. He fully recovered though it took him years to regain normal state of health.

This episode had a very salutary effect on the potential criminals and the incidents of highway robberies became very rare. The exemplary presence of mind and the bravery displayed by Ranjiv Singh Dalal in this incident were indeed, of very high order deserving recognition at the highest level. I, therefore, recommended him for the award of President's Police Medal for Gallantry. The state government accordingly, sent up the recommendations to the Government of India. President of India was pleased to award President's Police Medal for Gallantry to Ranjiv Singh Dalal, when he was very young and just at the threshold of his career – a very inspiring example for the young officers to emulate.

Manav Ekta Sammelan of 14th April 1979

A very challenging situation came up for me and District SP Hisar in mid-April 1979. Nirankari Sect, a socio-religious organization having mass following decided to hold a *Sammelan* at Hisar, under the banner of '*Manav Ekta Sammelan*'. Punjab Akali Dal was highly averse to the activities of this Sect. A very unfortunate incident had happened at Amritsar on 13th April 1978. The over enthusiastic persons from both the Nirankari Sect and Akali Dal clashed using firearms. Some persons from the Akali Dal had been shot dead. A murder case registered against Baba Gurbachan Singh, the Nirankari Sect Chief and others at Amritsar, was pending trial in the Court. Nirankari Sect had taken permission of the Haryana State Government for holding their *Sammelan* at Hisar, on 14th April 1979. Since the *Sammelan* was apparently purported to be held under the banner of "*Manav Ekta Sammelan*", the state government, while granting permission to hold the *Sammelan* did not visualize that it was in fact, the usual Baisakhi Day Annual *Sammelan* of the Nirankari Sect. Further, the fact that previous year a bloody clash had taken place between the Nirankari Sect and the Akali Dal activists at Amritsar, had escaped the notice of the authorities, while permitting the holding of *Sammelan* by the Nirankari Sect at Hisar. On 12th April, the Chief of Akali Dal Punjab spoke to the Chief Minister Haryana that the holding of *Sammelan* by the Nirankari Sect at Hisar would be strongly opposed by the Akali Dal activists, leading to serious law and order problems for the Haryana state. He strongly demanded the cancellation of permission granted by the state government for holding the said *Sammelan.*

The Chief Minister spoke to me on the telephone to know my views in the matter. I explained to him that every socio-religious organization had the right to hold their *Sammelan,* anywhere in the country, with the prior permission of the concerned government. I also submitted to the Chief Minister that Haryana state police generally and Hisar district Police particularly in this case, was fully competent to take care of law and order situation; cancellling the already granted permission to hold the said *Sammelan,* under threats of the Akali Dal, would mean weak-kneed policy of the Haryana state government. The Chief Minister very firmly told me that if any thing went wrong, he would hold me personally responsible. I respectfully submitted to the Chief Minister that I would gladly accept the challenge. On 13th April, Sardar Manmohan Singh IPS (1953-SR), the State IGP almost snubbed me on the telephone for taking such a grave risk, as the Akali Dal activists would seriously disturb the law and order, if the *Sammelan* was held. I always valued his advice. Then my inner conscience was prompting me, not to run away from upholding the rights of the people, howsoever it might amount to playing with fire. I, therefore, assured the IGP that the police of Hisar Range was fully prepared to forestall any ugly situation. The IGP sent one full battalion of the Haryana Armed Police to Hisar, to reinforce the Range Police strength as a precautionary measure. In the meanwhile, the local Sikh community had decided to hold a big *Diwan* at Singh Sabha Gurudwara Hisar, on 14th April 1979, to register their strong protest against the Nirankari Sect.

We planned the arrangement in such a way that no Akali Dal activist from Punjab was allowed to enter the area within a radius of 25 km of Hisar City. Despite our tight arrangements, about a dozen Akali Dal activists travelling by train from Punjab side, managed to reach Hisar railway station on the morning of 14th April 1979. They were immediately apprehended right at the railway station. I had earlier held a meeting of elderly persons from Sikh community of Hisar city and had impressed upon them not to allow any mischief monger to create any problem. They had assured me full co-operation. Still some hardliners among the local sikh community had tried to raise slogans and a few of them attempted to march towards the venue of the *Sammelan.* They were kept in check with adequate police arrangements. The "*Manav Ekta Sammelan*" presided over by the Chief of the Nirankari Sect was held very peacefully as scheduled. No law and order problem, even of minor nature arose in any district of Hisar Range bordering Punjab state. Because of the highly unfortunate happenings at Amritsar a year ago on the previous Baisakhi Day, there was strong apprehension that Akali Dal activists would never allow the peaceful holding of the *Sammelan* at Hisar, so near to Punjab state.

The Chief Minister was profusely congratulated by the top leaders of various political parties, at the National level for ensuring peaceful holding of the *Sammelan* at Hisar. The Chief Minister, the Chief Secretary and the IGP congratulated me on the telephone for making foolproof police arrangements. The State IGP vide his DO letter, dated 14th April 1979, sent to me his deep appreciation of the way, the police arrangements were made ensuring the peaceful holding of the *Nirankari Sammelan.* A. Banerjee, IAS, then Home Secretary conveyed to me, vide his DO letter of 4th May, the appreciation of the Chief Minister. He wrote, "My dear Swan, I have great pleasure in conveying to you the appreciation of the Chief Minister, Haryana, for the outstanding work done by you in connection with the *Nirankari Sammelan,* held at Hisar, on 14th April, 1979. The Police arrangements made by you were excellent with the result that the *Sammelan* concluded peacefully without any untoward incident."

Criminal Cases under the Prevention of Corruption Act against Bansi Lal and his Family Members

During the 21-month long infamous Emergency period of 1975-77, many top leaders of various political parties including Devi Lal and his Cabinet colleagues opposed to the Congress remained under preventive detention in various prisons for 19 months. Haryana police, as elsewhere in the country, had allegedly committed various types of excesses on the people. The general perception had developed with the people of Haryana that Bansi Lal, the then Defence Minister, in the Union Government, was the Chief hatchet man to perpetrate the sufferings on them. After Janata Party came to power in Haryana and Devi Lal became the Chief Minister, the game of vendetta took its turn. Various criminal cases were registered at Faridabad and Bhiwani against Bansi Lal, his family members and public men including those government servants who had been close to him. These cases included FIR No.341 dated 04.04.1977, PS NIT Faridabad FIR No.341 dated 28.09.1977, PS Central Faridabad, FIR No. 358, dated 13.07.1977, PS NIT Faridabad and FIR No.106, dated 01.08.1977, PS Sadar Bhiwani. In the case registered at PS Sadar Bhiwani, the accused persons included Bansi Lal, his wife Smt Vidyawati, his sons Ranbir Singh, and Surinder Singh, Smt Kiran Chaudhary wife of Surinder Singh, and Bansi Lal's daughters Smt Saroj, Smt Savita, Smt Sumitra Devi, and Smt Sunita and minor grand daughters. All these cases were investigated by various officers of the rank of Inspectors, Dy SP and SP. DIG Hisar Range was overseeing and supervising the investigations.

I found that in all these cases, the investigating officers had enjoyed earlier, the bounties showered on them by the Bansi Lal government and the same very officers were equally enjoying the patronage of Devi Lal government. Further, I found that the investigation had almost been finalized and even government sanction had also been obtained in some cases where necessary, for launching the prosecution. However, minutely scrutinizing the files, I found that in most of these cases, there had been only very little documentary evidence and to make up convincing stories lot of padding had been done. The main-stay in these cases was oral evidence. I, therefore, got convinced that these cases would not stand the judicial scrutiny and the whole exercise would prove to be futile.

With regard to the criminal case registered at Bhiwani, involving all the family members of Bansi Lal, it appeared to me to be a blatant case of causing extreme harassment to the female members of the family out of sheer vendetta. I, therefore, wanted to convey my feelings to Devi Lal, the Chief Minister. He might have genuine grievances against Bansi Lal, but as I had observed, Devi

Lal was a kindhearted person always amenable to reason and against playing politics of revenge. I, therefore, picked up the courage and discussed with him in detail during one of his visits to Hisar, the criminal case registered at Bhiwani against Bansi Lal and his family members. On listening to the details from me, he got sentimental and said that nobody until then had ever brought to his notice that in the criminal case registered against Bansi Lal, even his daughters; daughters-in-law and minor grand daughters had been implicated. Appreciating that I had brought the matter to his notice, he advised me to close the case against all the female members of Bansi Lal's family and even in cases where accused persons were the male ones and sufficient documentary evidence was not found. The above advice given by Devi Lal to me was befitting to his reputation as a grand old fatherly figure at the helm of affairs as chief political executive in the state. I personally felt great relief, as I would no longer be made compulsively a party to the undue harassment likely to be caused to the female family members of Bansi Lal. I accordingly set in motion, the process of closing the investigation in all such cases, in which documentary evidence to stand the judicial scrutiny was not adequate.

Ugly Dance of Democracy and Change of Guard at the Top

Bhajan Lal, an MLA from Adampur constituency of Hisar, belonged to Bishnoi sub-caste. He was born on 6th October 1930 at village Koranwall, Bahawalpur District (Pakistan). His family later shifted to village Adampur. As an adolescent boy, he took to selling of cloth on a bicycle in the villages like a small time vendor. He started his political career as Punch/Sarpanch of the village and member Zila Parishad Hisar. Elected as MLA first time in 1968, he remained Minister in Bansi Lal government during the years 1970-72. He boarded the bandwagon of Congress For Democracy (CFD) floated by Babu Jagjivan Ram, who had fallen out of the Congress Party. The CFD later merged into the new political outfit called the Janata Party. Since I remained on deputation to the Government of India from November 1973 to November 1978, I never had the occasion to meet Bhajan Lal. Since he was a Cabinet Minister in the Devi Lal government and Adampur constituency falls in district Hisar, he used to visit Hisar very often. I met him at Hisar during one of his visits and found him very warm and affable person.

In due course, I learnt that Adampur was a pocket borough of Bhajan Lal and it was a hot bed of politics. There were two rival groups in the said town, having number of cross criminal cases against them. One such group was led by Manphool Singh, a brother of Bhajan Lal whereas a person claiming patronage of Devi Lal, the Chief Minister, headed the other group. Some cases relating to both the groups were pending trial and three cases were pending investigation. These were FIR No.250 dated 27.07.1978, FIR No.251 dated 27.07.1978 and FIR No.425 dated 04.12.1978. In these three cases, investigation did not progress due to the political pressure mounted by both the groups to influence the course of investigation. Four additional criminal cases relating to both the groups were registered during my posting as DIG Hisar Range. These were FIR No.145 dated 15.04.1979, FIR No.160, dated 01.05.1979; FIR No.194 dated 30.05.1979 and FIR No. 195 dated 31.05.1979. Bhajan Lal accused the persons from the opposite group as aggressors in all the criminal cases and he wanted police action against the persons of the opposite group. He told me to look into the matter personally. I asked both Deputy Commissioner and SSP Hisar to intervene in the faction–ridden groups of the town and jointly try to resolve the long-standing feud between the two groups. They did try their best and apprised me that both the groups were politically motivated and therefore, their disputes could not be resolved. Bhajan Lal complained repeatedly that in the criminal cases pending investigation Manphool Singh's group was being victimized. Unfortunately, the District SP, when pressurized by Bhajan Lal to help the group led by Manphool Singh, instead of firmly telling that the investigation was being conducted impartially, gave the impression to Bhajan Lal that he was prepared to help his people but the DIG in that case would take him to task. Thus, Bhajan Lal put the entire blame on me. When I told him that the investigation by the local police was being conducted in a very fair and impartial manner he flared up and tried in vain to overawe me. I remained unruffled. However, this incident led to his nursing a grudge against me, so much so that he would not even respond to my greetings during his visits to Hisar.

The feuds in Adampur led to very bitter relations between Devi Lal and Bhajan Lal. The former was one of the main architects of Janata Party. In fact, this Party was a loose conglomeration of top leaders of various political parties. They had come together to form this political outfit for the reason of being co-sufferers, during the days of internal Emergency. This Party did not have any definite common ideology or clear-cut objectives. Therefore, the commitment of the top leaders of various political parties merging into the Janata Party was only skin-deep. There had cropped up a simmering dissidence against the Devi Lal government for a variety of reasons. Bhajan Lal, the estranged Minister jumped into the bandwagon of the dissidents to lead them from the front. A Battle Royal, thus, started between the two "Lals" in early June 1979. The dissidents with Bhajan Lal playing leading role were able to win over a large number of MLAs to their side. The Devi Lal government lost majority in the Assembly. In a way, Adampur, a small town of which Bhajan Lal was an undisputed leader, proved to be waterloo for the Devi Lal government. Dr Sarup Singh, former Vice Chancellor, Kurukshetra University and Balwant Rai Tayal, a dissident MLA from Hisar city, carrying very clean image as a politician, were top favorites with the Janata Party High Command, Delhi as substitute for Devi Lal. However, Bhajan Lal manipulated with the blessings of Kanti Desai. It was an open talk in every quarter in the state that huge moneybags played crucial role in this game of numbers. Finally, Bhajan Lal emerged as the "Hero of the day" and had a meteoric rise. Chosen as the leader of the majority in the State Legislative Assembly, he became the Chief Minister on 29th June 1979. Devi Lal, a stalwart in political arena by all standards, thus, had to eat a humble pie.

Soon after assuming the office of the Chief Minister, Bhajan Lal government, carried out reshuffling of the top brass in the police department. I was transferred from the post of DIG Hisar Range to the post of DIG of Haryana Armed Police (HAP), at Madhuban. I took up this assignment on 2nd July 1979. R S Yadav IPS 1963 (SPS) was posted as DIG Hisar Range. DD Kashyap

IPS 1956-RR was posted as DIG Ambala Range. Manmohan Singh the State IGP, was also transferred and in his place, P C Wadhwa IPS (1952-RR) was appointed, as the State IGP. I could not comprehend what had gone wrong against Manmohan Singh that the state government shifted him from the top position. However, I was very sure that my transfer to Madhuban, so soon after my posting at Hisar was actuated because of my firm stand to uphold the rule of law and not to buckle under pressure while dealing with the Adampur criminal cases cited earlier. I was happy on one count that at least the place of Manmohan Singh was taken by P.C. Wadhwa. He, besides being professional in approach, was reputed to be an IPS officer having commendable knack of comprehending the intricacies and finer points in the interpretation of legal tangles in the service matters. Calling a spade a spade was his notable trait. He would not let go unchallenged any executive orders and practices which he thought, were whimsical and contrary to the law. He had won many legal battles. Further, he would not brook any indiscipline on the part of any subordinate and would bestow all kindness and love on the competent and disciplined ones. During my courtesy call on him, I explained my apprehension that the Adampur criminal cases cited ibid might cast ugly shadow on my career. He assured me that no harm would come to me, so long as he was the Police Chief. He advised me that the HAP force at Madhuban, was in a very bad shape and that I should work hard to bring it back on the rails.

Posting as DIG Haryana Armed Police (HAP), Madhuban

Historical Background of Haryana Armed Police

The HAP had come into existence on 1st November, 1966, consequent to the reorganization of Composite Punjab state, with 5 Bns of the Punjab Armed Police, coming over to Haryana. One more Bn was raised soon. Out of these six Bns, only two were retained in Haryana state and the remaining four were merged into CRPF, Delhi Police, SSB and BSF. A Bn each was stationed at Ambala and Nilokheri. The combined strength of these two Bns was 1636 personnel. As per the law and order requirements, one more Bn was raised in 1969 and stationed at Hisar. In September 1973, another Bn was raised as technical force to meet any eventuality arising in electricity and road transport departments etc in the event of threatened strike by the government employees. The special character of this Bn was maintained only upto 1979 when it became a normal Armed Police Battalion. In 1974, 5th Bn was also raised.

Coming up of Madhuban Police Complex

HRK Talwar was DIG/HAP and Home Guards during the year 1968. It was all due to his vision and untiring efforts, very well supported by J C Vachher DIG/CID, Bhagwan Singh Rosha, State IGP and actively patronized by Bansi Lal the Chief Minister that an excellent idea of having a vast Police Complex at Madhuban (Karnal), on Ambala-Delhi Highway was conceived. A sprawling piece of land measuring 570 acres was acquired, out of which a beautiful Complex was established over an area of 475 acres. When I joined at Madhuban on 2nd July 1979, three Bns were stationed there; the other two Bns were stationed one each at Ambala and Hisar. Besides the HAP, other establishments at the Complex included Police Training College and a very well equipped Forensic Sciences Laboratory, perhaps the best in the country. An impressive Sports Complex with the Stadium, having a four hundred meter cinder track, a Football Field and a Hockey Ground, all beautifully carved out. During the subsequent years, State Crime Records Bureau, Fingerprint Bureau and on the sports side 50 meters Swimming Pool, Wrestling and Judo Arenas and a small Gymnasium were added. The Central Sports Office of Haryana Police is housed in this Complex. At present, this picturesquely sylvan magnificent Complex with a beautifully laid Golf Course, developed by the efforts of successive senior officers, having innovative ideas and pragmatic approach, can boast of being the best in the country.

Proposal to Merge HAP Constabulary into District Police

Soon after my joining at Madhuban, I found that there was a lot of discontentment in the force especially the constabulary. Many acts of indiscipline had been reported. The force personnel were separately recruited and trained to serve, throughout their career, exclusively in the Armed Wing. The Armed Police identity in the prevailing system was the main cause of discontentment and indiscipline, creeping alarmingly into the force. There was urgent need to infuse enthusiasm, espirite de corps and sense of devotion to duty, amongst the personnel of the armed force to restore the requisite discipline. I conceived and implemented many result oriented innovative ideas and plans. Training syllabi for the force personnel, who were available and not committed on any duty, were designed in a manner to ensure their professional efficiency. Their welfare activities were intensified. Sports and cultural events were held frequently and I often delivered pep talks as a 'benevolent' head of family to make them feel at home and inculcate the sense of belonging. In all genuine cases, leave was liberally granted. As and when they were deployed in the districts, in aid of the civil police, I ensured that they were led by their own officers of the HAP instead of leaving them at the disposal of the civil police officers. Their kitchen and messing arrangements were keenly supervised and considerably improved. The Bn Commandants, Dy SPs and the Inspectors took very keen interest with active participation in all these programs.

Another innovative idea, which struck me, was to take care of the tag of "only Armed Police Identity" with the HAP personnel. For this purpose it was necessary to bring them in status at par with the civil police, involving direct public dealing while performing law and order duties instead of only acting as a striking reserve, as has been the practice hither-to-fore. I thought of a plan that after putting them through a tough training cycle, they should be absorbed in the civil police. I discussed this plan with the State IGP P C Wadhwa. Applauding my idea, he asked me to draw up a detailed proposal for seeking the government approval. He got so much enamoured and excited in this regard that he repeatedly asked me to expedite the detailed draft proposal. As advised and guided by him, I drew up the proposal and submitted the same to the IGP. I proposed that initial recruitment for the entire state constabulary should be done for the HAP only. After imparting them intensive training for functioning both as striking reserve and civil police, they should be put in the queue according to their seniority by length of service for absorption in the civil police by and by, as per their turn against the vacancies occurring in the district police all over the state. It was all to the credit of Sh. Wadhwa that this proposal was ultimately approved by the state government. The HAP constabulary boisterously celebrated the occasion. Further, the toilet complex attached with every barrack was renovated and to make up the shortage of family quarters for the other ranks, a proposal was submitted to the State IGP for obtaining government sanction for the construction of additional residential accommodation.

There was no arrangement to ensure quality education for the children of the constabulary. To have a government model school in the Complex seemed to me not an easy proposition. I therefore, mooted an idea that we could make a humble start with a model primary school, built by the police department out of the police welfare fund. This fund is raised from the monthly contribution made by the entire state police force and the state government makes its contribution by liberal annual grant. The IGP commended this idea and advised me to go ahead. The force rightly felt that I as the head of the family was very much concerned with the future of their children. Thus, there remained no semblance of any kind of discontentment and indiscipline in the force. Whereas all these efforts earned me a commendable lasting goodwill with the HAP constabulary, I had won approbation of high order from the IGP. In the beginning of August 1980, I was posted as DIG/Administration & Training in the Central Police Office at Chandigarh.

Posting as DIG–Administration and Training

Controversy Regarding the Authority to Initiate ACR of Police Chief

In the beginning of August 1980 I was posted as DIG Administration and Training in Central Police Office, at Chandigarh. Towards the end of July 1980, PC Wadhwa, the State IGP was transferred and Manmohan Singh was brought back as the State IGP. The transfer of PC Wadhwa was actuated because of his very firm stand that the State Home Secretary had no authority to initiate the Annual Confidential Report (ACR) of the State IGP. The state government buckling under the strong bureaucratic lobby did not endorse the stand of PC Wadhwa. He was not prepared to submit to that situation, which he strongly believed, was not lawful and thus, refused to compromise even at the risk of losing the coveted assignment as State Police Chief. He was left only with the Hobson's choice to knock at the door of the judiciary to seek their verdict, on the issue of competency of the Home Secretary to initiate the ACR of the State Police Chief. He personally argued the case before the Supreme Court. The Apex Court decided Wadhwa's writ petition in April 1987, giving verdict that in future, the Confidential Reports (CRs) of police force would be initiated and processed through police channels only, and that CRs of IGPs and DGPs will be written by the Home Minister of the state and accepted by the Chief Minister. The administrative heads viz: the Home Secretary or even the Chief Secretary, as was the practice till then, were nowhere in the picture. The Supreme Court further ruled, "As the work of the Police is technical in nature, it cannot be supervised by a non-technical administrative authority, although it may form a part of the same administrative setup." However, the Union Home Ministry later amended the All India Service (Confidential Report) Rules 1970, in December 1987, making provision that the Confidential Report of the DGP was to be initiated by the Chief Secretary, reviewed by the Home Minister and accepted by the Chief Minister. In the case of officers holding the rank of Inspector General of Police, the DGP and the Home Secretary were to initiate the Confidential Report, which would be reviewed by the Chief Secretary and accepted by the Home Minister. It goes to the credit of P C Wadhwa that he got the Judicial Verdict, totally excluding the Home Secretary from the system of writing/reviewing/accepting the Confidential Report of the State Police Chief.

Change of Police Brass at the Top

Manmohan Singh had taken over as IGP on 26th July 1980. I joined his team as DIG/Administration and Training on 12th August 1980. Since I had earlier worked as AIG/Administration during the early seventies for about three years, I was thoroughly conversant with the rules, regulations and office practices. Between the periods from 1973 to 1980, lot of developments had taken place in the State. In 1975, district Sirsa had come into existence out of Hisar District. In the same year, Hisar had been made an Administrative Division/ Police Range. In May 1975, a Recruits Training Centre had been, set up in the HAP Campus at Madhuban, with facilities for training 600 recruits in one batch. In January 1976, Police Training College of the Haryana state became functional at Madhuban. In August 1979, district Gurgaon was bifurcated to create Faridabad district. This was the 12th district of Haryana. In 1980, Gurgaon Range came into existence. Thus, by the year 1980, there were 12 districts and 3 Police Ranges namely Ambala, Hisar and Gurgaon. The police force had also been expanded to cater to the larger law and order requirements. Resultantly the administrative work at the Police Hqr also increased substantially. With Manmohan Singh as State IGP, I was thoroughly enjoying my posting because he was always quick in appreciating my performance, inspiring me to keep up my zeal and zest.

Seminar to Identify Organizational Problems and their Solution

Since the administrative work was increasing, there appeared to be an urgent need to identify the organizational problems and solutions thereof, to improve police efficiency and image of police. The IGP, therefore, asked the DIG/CID to organize a seminar on this subject. He told me to examine in depth, all aspects of this subject and produce a working paper under the caption "Police Efficiency and Image", for detailed discussion by all senior police officers in the state in the said seminar. In due course of time, I produced a 33- page article, highlighting the various aspects of police functioning under various headings. These were: (i) Indian Police System- Legacy of British Colonial Rule. (ii) Bonafide of Indian Police- questioned. (iii) Police Structure much behind the time. (iv) Constabulary required to be revamped. (v) Qualitative and Quantitative Improvement in the Civil Police required. (vi) Training syllabi should include the subject 'Attitudinal Change'. (vii) Both Police and Politicians needed to be disciplined to check undue interference in Police Functioning. (viii) Welfare of the Force and Redressal of their Grievances, (ix) Management of IPS Cadre, (x) Strengthening the Hierarchical Level and (xi) Unique Position of the State Police Chief - Needs that it be redetermined. This working paper was highly appreciated by the IGP and it was very enthusiastically discussed in the seminar held in January 1981. I am glad that on various points highlighted by me in the said working paper and fully endorsed after thorough discussion in the seminar, requisite action was initiated and in due course of time, the Police Hierarchical Level was strengthened, more or less on the same lines.

Recommendations of National Police Commission (NCP) of 1977

Janata Party's government at the Centre, constituted National Police Commission on 15th November 1977 under the Chairmanship of Dharmvira, former ICS. The Commission having made in-depth studies of the entire gamut of police system submitted seven reports to the Central Government from February 1979 to May 1981. The core points in the major recommendations made by the Commission became known, unofficially towards the end of 1981. These included:

(i) Mechanism for redressal of grievances of police personnel from district level to state level.

(ii) Mechanism for inquiries into public complaints against police by constituting District Inquiry Agency at district level and Police Complaints Board at state level.

(iii) Establishment of statutory State Security Commission at every State Hqr by way of a strong mechanism to insulate the police against interference with and misuse of police by illegal or improper orders or pressure from political executive or other extraneous sources. The wide range functions of State Security Commission shall include:

  (a) Selection of the State Police Chief with an assured fixed tenure of office.

  (b) Laying down broad policy guidelines and directions for the performance of preventive tasks and service-oriented functions by the police.

  (c) Evaluation of the performance of the state police every year and presenting a report to the state legislature.

  (d) Functioning as a Forum of Appeal for disposing of representations from police officers of the rank of Superintendent of police and above, regarding their being subjected to illegal or irregular orders in the performance of their duties.

  (e) Functioning as a Forum of Appeal for disposing representations from police officers regarding promotion to the rank of Superintendent of Police and above and

  (f) Generally to evaluate and review annually the functioning of the police in the State.

Since NPC had been constituted by Janata Party government, there was strong apprehension that the successor Congress Party government might withhold the implementation of recommendations made by the NCP. However, police officers at various levels felt reassured that the entire gamut of police reforms would be brought about eventually. Alas! The powerful political lobby continued strongly resisting the implementation of police reforms. In mid nineties Prakash Singh IPS, former DGP Uttar Pradesh and later DG Border Security Force filed a PIL petition in the Supreme Court of India requesting for the intervention of the Apex Court for the implementation of the NPC. While disposing of the said PIL petition, the Apex Court issued comprehensive directions on 22nd September 2006 for police reforms and ordered (i) the setting up of State Security Commission to insulate the police from extraneous influence, (ii) a Police Establishment Board to give the force functional autonomy and (iii) a Police Complaints Authority to ensure their accountability. The Court also prescribed a transparent procedure for the selection of the Director General of Police and directed that this person as also officers discharging operational responsibilities, have minimum tenure of two years. The Court further directed that investigation wing and the law and order wing should be separate to improve the quality of investigations. These orders were to be implemented by 31st March 2007. However, the state governments continued dragging their feet over the implementations of these directives. The Committees appointed to monitor the progress of implementation of Apex Court's directions in various states found that no state had fully complied with the said directives in letter and spirit and expressed its dismay over the total indifference to the issue of reforms in the functioning of police. It should be understood that police reforms are not to glorify the police – they are to protect our Democracy, our economy and to uphold the rule of law. In the current scenario, presenting very gloomy picture in the affairs of law and order in the country, it is high time that the Government of India and the governments in the states develop necessary understanding and decide to implement the whole gamut of police reforms debated intensively over the years.

Chapter – 14

Vendetta Game of the Chief Minister Challenged

Ghosts of Adampur Criminal Cases casting shadow on my Career

"If we had no winter, the spring would not be so pleasant; if we did not sometime taste of adversity, prosperity would not be so welcome", said Anne Bradstreet. I had enjoyed the postings as DIG/Hisar Range, DIG/HAP at Madhuban and DIG/Administration and Training at Police Hqr, as if that were the full bloom of spring days. Therefore, some patch of adversity had to follow the blooming spring in tune with the cycle of nature. As and when adversity came in my way, renewed energy had sparked up in me to take it head on. Gloria Gaither had said, "Even in the winter, in midst of storm, the sun is still there. Somewhere above the clouds, it still shines and warms and pulls, at the life buried deep inside the brown branches and frozen earth". While I was getting approbation of the highest order from the State Police Chiefs for my excellent performance, the Bhajan Lal government was seriously contemplating to push me out of Haryana. My meritorious performances consecutively in three different places as DIG had no meaning for the Bhajan Lal government, as if someone, who mattered a lot was possessed by the revengeful spirit. My insistence to uphold the rule of law and not to submit to any political pressure seemed to me as the pretext for pushing me out of the state. The Bhajan Lal government sponsored my name in October 1980 for deputation to the Government of India. I had returned to the state on 13th November 1978 from the Central deputation spanning over five years. As per the 'Tenure Rules' governing the deputation, circulated by the Government of India on 29th December 1976, a "cooling off" period of three years must elapse between the two spells of deputation of an IPS officer to the central government. The Government of India therefore, did not accept the recommendations of the Bhajan Lal government. The state government once again sponsored my name in 1981 for deputation to the central government. This time again the central government did not accept the recommendations of the state government because of the condition of three years "cooling off" period. Further, Rule 6 of the tenure rules lay down that "The total period of deputation spent with a Central Police Organization by an officer and the period spent by him on other central assignments such as in the Central Secretariat, will not exceed eight years". Earlier than my deputation to CISF from 1st November 1973 to 13th November 1978 I had also served for about three years on deputation to J & K State and the Border Security Force. There is no qualm with the system that the central/state governments have inherent absolute powers in the matters of postings and transfers of government servants, keeping in view the administrative exigencies and expediencies. However, it is absolutely unacceptable that the state Chief Minister being the chief political executive, in a democratic set up, should have a free hand to ignore the rules only for political expediency, biased with gratification of his own whim, ego and revengeful spirit, by arbitrarily disregarding the administrative rules and regulations.

In the beginning of the year 1982, the Bhajan Lal government made a third attempt for sending me on deputation to the central government for appointment as DIG, in CRPF. Since I had by then, already entered the zone of promotion and appointment as IG by virtue of my seniority in the IPS, DGP/CRPF turned down the Bhajan Lal government recommendation, saying that there was no vacant post of IG in his organization. The state government then successfully managed to exercise pressure on the central government to take me on deputation as DIG in the CISF. Accordingly, the state government issued orders on 26th March 1982, placing my services at the disposal of the Government of India for appointment as DIG in the CISF. By this time I had put in about 20 years service in the rank of SP/DIG. This 20 years period included 8 years on deputation with the central government.

Distortion in Democratic System

Bhajan Lal had assumed power by toppling his own Janata Party government headed by Devi Lal in June 1979. The Janata Party government at the national level had collapsed by the close of the year 1979 making way for fresh elections for the Lok Sabha. The Congress Party, led by Indira Gandhi won Lok Sabha Elections with big majority. Bhajan Lal enacted an unprecedented drama of en masse defection. In that, the entire ruling Janata Legislative Party of which he was the Chief Minister defected to the Congress Party. This was a highly opportunistic and unethical way to convert lock, stock and barrel the Janata Party government into Congress Party government with Bhajan Lal continuing as Chief Minister. Then the politics is what it is.

In early 1982, General Elections were held for Haryana Assembly. The electorate returned a fractured mandate. Congress Party led by Bhajan Lal won 33 seats out of total 90 Assembly seats. Lok Dal led by Devi Lal won 32 seats. However, both Lok Dal and BJP had pre-poll alliance, which had made near half way mark of 45 seats. Both sides resorted to all sorts of tactics to increase the number in their respective flock. For Bhajan Lal there seemed a bleak chance to form the Government. G D Tapase, the Governor invited Devi Lal to form the government because of the pre-poll alliance with BJP, he carried the support of near simple majority of MLAs. However, the Governor soon changed his decision. Superseding his earlier invitation to Devi Lal, he on second thought invited Bhajan Lal to form the government in view of the Congress Party being the single largest party with 33 MLAs and stipulated the period for proving his majority on the floor of the House. Fumed at his summersault, Devi Lal publicly slapped G D Tapase, something unheard of in Indian politics before and after, though Shri Tapase's revising his own decision was an unprecedented development in the Constitutional history of Indian Republic. Bhajan Lal, an expert in politicking and engineering defection, manoeuvered to prove his majority in the Assembly's First Session within stipulated period. However, the masses at large firmly carried the impression that mandate given by the electorate in favour of Lok Dal-BJP pre-poll alliance was wrongly thrown to winds and democratic traditions were throttled. In any case, the Lok Dal-BJP alliance was left high and dry and Bhajan Lal firmly settled down to rule the State. In the political scenario now totally in his favour, Bhajan Lal had established his credentials in the eyes of Congress High Command as a great strategist in politics.

Deceitful Role of a DIG

I wish to mention here that a wily and highly over ambitious IPS officer had managed to become the DIG/CID in 1977 in the Janata Party government headed by Devi Lal on the recommendation of the Principal Secretary to Charan Singh, the then Union Home Minister. He played the villain when dissidents had raised their banner of revolt against the Devi Lal government. He purposely did not keep the government posted with the factually correct situation. On the contrary, he was hobnobbing, behind the curtain, with the prominent dissident leaders, leaking out the plans of the Devi Lal government for taming the dissident MLAs. On the fall of the Devi Lal government, Bhajan Lal rewarded the said IPS officer not only with favour to retain him as DIG/CID, but he was also allowed to assume the position of an all powerful police officer who used his clout not only overawing the state Police Chief but also the bureaucrats in the state. He played a very dirty role in the game plan of the Bhajan Lal government to push me out of the state.

I had submitted several representations to the state government to reconsider the case of placing my services at the disposal of the Government of India on deputation but I did not get any relief. One such representation dated 07.05.1982 was examined in depth by Manmohan Singh the State IGP. In his letter dated 28.05.1982 forwarding my representation to the home department of the state government, he mentioned in the concluding para: "Justice and fair play demand that officers should be sent on deputation by rotation so that every one has attained the requisite experience of the outside organizations. The request of Sh Swan has force behind. Besides his own illness, his father is under treatment with him. The government may like to reconsider his case in the light of these observations." However, the way, the then Chief Secretary and the Home Secretary from the IAS, a new avatar of the famous ICS, the "Steel Frame" of the British days, played meekly to the dictates of the chief political executive, was highly disgusting. They are the persons in the administration of our democratic set up who are supposed to be well conversant with the rules and regulations. They are supposed to bring on record, the correct position as per rules and regulations and take written orders from the chief political executive, who I am sure, would never commit the folly of passing written orders contrary to the rules and regulations. In my case, both the then Chief Secretary and the Home Secretary became privy to the unjust decision of the chief political executive, to forcibly push me out to central deputation, despite the bar, as per the 'Tenure Rules' about which the position had been very explicitly elucidated by the IGP in his letter dated 28.05.1982 ibid.

Government Order Regarding Central Deputation Challenged

I was on long leave duly sanctioned by the state government, from 15th March 1982, in view of my own bad health, but more so for the treatment of my widower father, suffering from cancer. On 26th March 1982, Bhajan Lal government issued orders, placing my services at the disposal of the central government. I requested for the extension of my leave and in the meanwhile also to reconsider and withdraw the order regarding my deputation to centre. I was told to join at the new place of posting with the Government of India and then ask for sanction of leave from that authority. During the years 1980 to 1982, the Haryana government had deputed seven IPS officers to the central government. As and when the central government asked the Haryana government to relieve these officers for central deputation, the Haryana government withdrew the sponsorship of these officers for central deputation, a dubious game plan indeed. But I was singled out, making it a case of blatant discrimination and injustice. In the meanwhile, M S Bhatnagar IPS (1952-RR), then the seniormost IPS officer in the state was appointed on 4th August 1982 as head of the police department in the rank of DGP. Despite his elevated rank as the state Police Chief, Shri Bhatnagar did not prove helpful to me. I was pushed thus, to the wall. I did not accept the Hobson's choice but went to the law court to seek justice. I filed civil writ petition in the High Court of Punjab and Haryana at Chandigarh on 23rd September 1982, challenging the Haryana Government order, dated 26th March 1982, impleading Central/Haryana state governments and Bhajan Lal by name on the ground of mala-fide, as Respondents. This writ petition was admitted and notice of motion issued for September 27, 1982 to the Respondents. In the meanwhile, operation of the state government order dated 26th March 1982, was stayed. The writ petition was dismissed by the High Court on 4th October 1982. However, the court got a verbal assurance from Advocate General of Haryana, pleading for the Respondents that I could join my assignment in the central government after availing of the leave already granted. I was thus, required to join the central government on 23rd November 1982 before noon. I challenged the decision of the High Court at Chandigarh by filing in the Supreme Court a petition for Special Leave to Appeal together with application for ad-interim ex-parte stay, which came up for hearing before the said Court on 22nd November 1982. The Apex Court was pleased to issue a notice to the Respondents as to why the Special Leave Petition and the stay application be not granted. The petition was directed to be listed for hearing on 29th November 1982. The state government was telegraphically informed on 22nd November 1982, that the Supreme Court had issued notice on my Special Leave Petition with stay application returnable on 29th November 1982. The Haryana state government finding that I had not joined the assignment in the central government on 23rd November 1982, issued orders, placing me under suspension. The suspension order was immediately challenged by me by filing an application in the Supreme Court, where the learned Solicitor General of India, on summons from the Apex Court, gave assurance that the suspension order would be withdrawn. However, the state government reinstated me with effect from 8th December 1982, instead of withdrawing the suspension order. In the meanwhile, my Special Leave Petition which was to come up before the Supreme Court on 29th November 1982 was directed to be listed for hearing on 7th December 1982. And the order then passed was: "Special Leave to Appeal is granted. Filing of statements of the case and furnishing of security are dispensed with, Appeal to be heard in July 1983. Mr. Garg who appears on behalf of the appellant says that the appellant's father is suffering from cancer. If that is so, we expect the Governments of India and Haryana to consider sympathetically his request for withdrawing the orders of deputation. The appellant shall report for duty at Delhi. After he reports at Delhi, he will take charge of the new office and make a request, which shall be considered on the grounds mentioned above. Stay will come up on December 16, 1982."

Since the Supreme Court, in their above mentioned order, had said that "The appellant shall report for duty at Delhi" simultaneously saying "The stay will come up on December 16 1982", I reported for duty at Delhi, instead of waiting till 16th December, 1982. I told my advocate not to press for the grant of stay. Instead, early hearing of the petition was sought for as I was very particular for early adjudication by the Apex Court whether officers from the premier civil services could be forced to silently and meekly submit to the orders smacking deep-rooted personal malice, utter arbitrary and revengeful spirit.

Chapter – 15

As DIG/CISF Western Zone at Bombay

I reported for duty at the CISF Hqr Delhi, in early December 1982. Surinder Nath IPS-1950 (RR) had by then taken over as IG/CISF. His earlier posting was as Chief Secretary of an Eastern state. He was very sympathetic and told me that he would have loved to keep me at the CISF Hqr as DIG/Administration, in view of my earlier five years experience, both as AIG and DIG/Administration, but was constrained under compulsion to post me to a place far away from Delhi.

Setup of Western Zone

I joined as DIG Western Zone at Bombay (Mumbai) in the first week of December 1982. The staff for the office of DIG Western Zone was already in position. Rashtriya Chemicals and Fertilizers Limited (RCFL), a Government of India Public Sector Undertaking was located over a sprawling area in Chambur. The CMD of this PSU provided spacious place for the establishment of Zonal Office of the CISF. Since the AIG for the Zonal Office was an IPS officer from Maharashtra Cadre, I was able to establish the Zonal Office with his assistance in no time. Commandant CISF, RCFL Unit was of great help to provide wherewithal for the Zonal Office. Since I had earlier served at the CISF Hqr as AIG/DIG/Administration and DIG Southern Zone, during my earlier five years deputation to the CISF in the seventies, the CISF personnel of all ranks, all over were quite familiar with my name and reputation. All these situations cumulatively proved to be of great help to me for effectively operating as DIG Western Zone.

The jurisdiction of Western Zone included all the important PSUs located in the states of Maharashtra, Goa, Gujarat, Madhya Pradesh and Rajasthan. The airports security was not with the CISF, nor that of Bombay Port Trust. However, Goa Port Trust was within the purview of CISF. The gazetted staff included about a dozen officers of the rank of Commandant and about fifty Assistant Commandants. For me the task was just like the one, I had earlier experienced as DIG Southern Zone during seventies. A very spacious residential government accommodation from the central pool, in Malabar Hills area, was allotted to me. The duty involved intensive touring for about fifteen days in a month. IG/CISF would often call me to the Hqr for meetings and very liberally grant me 2-3 days casual leave for visiting my family at Chandigarh. My ailing father used to take treatment from Government Hospital, Patiala. My elder son, a law student, used to take care of medical treatment of my father at Patiala Hospital.

Simaranjit Singh Maan

One of the commandants available to me in the Zone was Simaranjit Singh Maan IPS, on deputation with CISF from Punjab IPS Cadre. Shri Maan, an IPS officer turned politician has been viewed by many as a controversial politician. However, while posted in the Western Zone of the CISF, he was Group Commandant with Hqr at Bombay, supervising the working of security arrangements in about a dozen CISF Units, each headed by an Assistant Commandant, in smaller PSUs. As an officer, I found him very efficient, honest and straightforward, having excellent leadership qualities. However, one could discern during informal conversation with him that he had some streak of favouring a particular political ideology but he did not give expression to his views loudly nor I felt his personal views coming in the way of discharge of his official duties. He looked after his subordinates very well and always gave me due regard. During my entire stay at Bombay, my family had continued to stay at Chandigarh. Shri Maan used to pay frequent courtesy visits at my residence. As a human being, he was very warm and affectionate. In January 1984, I had fallen sick. I sent an urgent telephonic message to my wife and son to come over to Bombay immediately. Both Shri Maan and his wife Smt. Geeta Kaur continued nursing me very affectionately and devotedly until the arrival of my wife and son. This sweet couple had thus, earned the deepest gratitude of my family for the noble gesture in taking care of me. After returning to my parent Cadre state of Haryana in early 1984, I lost all links with Shri Maan. I have been sadly learning from the media about the subsequent difficult phases of his life. Strange are the ways of the Nature. Born and brought up in excellent environment, having education in premier institutions and then making to the IPS followed by his controversial role as a politician, committed to a particular ideology so dear to his heart, is the strange turn of events which no body could have predicted. I wish him and his family the best of health and happiness in life.

CISF Declared as Armed Force of the Union

During early 1983, CISF was declared as an Armed Force of the Union, at par with BSF, CRPF and ITBP. Surinder Nath, the IG/CISF had been elevated as DG/CISF. According to the Order of Precedence laid down by the Union Government, all para-military forces declared as the Armed Force of the Union, were to take precedence over the civil/armed police of the states on all ceremonial occasions. During celebration of Independence Day, a ceremonial parade is organized every year at all the state Hqrs. A unit of the CISF had been participating in such ceremonial parade at Bombay with position assigned to it below the civil police unit. That time M G Katre, IPS (1952-RR), IG law and order of Maharashtra state was organizing the show. During the rehearsal, I found that the CISF unit, despite being already declared as an Armed Force of the Union, had not been assigned right position as per the prescribed order of precedence. When I pointed out this anomaly to Shri Katre, he refused to accept my viewpoint. I therefore, sent a letter to DGP Maharashtra with copy to DG/CISF that CISF Unit would participate in the ceremonial parade only if proper place, as per the laid down order of precedence was assigned to it. Shri Katre took exception to my taking up the matter with DGP Maharashtra and DG/CISF. He refused to take up the duty of organizing the ceremonial parade. DGP Maharashtra called me and asked me to co-operate and not to insist on my stand. I was really very surprised that a senior officer of the rank of IG should resist the compliance of Union Government's policy. I respectfully submitted to DGP Maharashtra that if the appeasement of a particular senior officer were to take priority over the laid down policy of the Union Government, I would better withdraw the CISF Unit from participating in the ceremonial parade. DGP Maharashtra requested DG/CISF on telephone to intervene. Surinder Nath DG/CISF asked me to let the ego of Shri Katre be satisfied. I allowed the CISF Unit to participate in the ceremonial parade but to register my protest, I went to the ceremonial pandal after the March Past was over and cultural programme had commenced. During 1986 when I was State Police Chief in the rank of IGP, the Bansi Lal government recommended my name for the Award of President's Police Medal for distinguished service on Independence Day 1986. Sh. Katre had come to the Government of India as DG/CBI. The High Powered Committee at the Centre could not reach unanimity to accept the recommendation of the Haryana State Government because Sh. Katre vetoed it. However, the Bansi Lal government repeated their earlier recommendations and recommended my name for the Award of said Medal on Republic Day 1987. I had already been promoted to the rank of DGP with effect from 3rd November 1986. This time the Central Committee including Shri Katre endorsed the recommendations of Haryana government and I did get the said coveted Medal.

Repatriation to Parent Cadre

The Chambur area, where my office was located within the premises of Rashtriya Chemicals and Fertilizers Limited was worst affected by the pollution generated by this huge factory. It affected my health very adversely. The doctor advised me to take rest for a month or so in some clean and pollution free area. In the meanwhile, my father's health also further deteriorated. I therefore, got six weeks leave in early February 1984, to stay with my family at Chandigarh. My civil writ petition pending before the Supreme Court of India was listed for hearing in March 1984. The Secretary to Government of India, Ministry of Home Affairs, had been called upon to file his affidavit in the Apex Court, in reply to my writ petition. It was then that my case file was perused, for the first time, by the Union Home Secretary and he got convinced that I should not have been forcibly shunted out to Government of India on deputation basis, because of the various factors detailed in my Writ Petition.

He, therefore, recorded his order on the file that I should be immediately repatriated to Haryana state, instead of opposing my writ petition pending in the Supreme Court. Accordingly my repatriation orders were issued by the Union Home Ministry, directing me to report to the Haryana state DGP for duty. Accordingly, I reported for duty to the State DGP. He advised me that the state government decision in the matter would be communicated to me, at my given address. In the meanwhile, I also met the Haryana Chief Secretary and Home Secretary. I also tried to seek an audience with the Chief Minister, but I was every time put off on the pretext that the Chief Minister was busy with some important work and that as and when he would be free, I would be informed on telephone. For two long months, there was neither any intimation about my audience with the Chief Minister, nor were any orders for my posting issued. I therefore, sought for an audience with the Union Home Secretary. He advised me to meet again the Haryana Chief Secretary. On my return to Chandigarh, I immediately met the Chief Secretary. He told me to wait for a couple of days and the government decision would be conveyed to me. Perhaps, in the meanwhile the Union Home Secretary had some straight talk with the Chief Secretary. Soon I got posting orders as DIG Welfare and Rules at the Haryana State Police Hqr. I was, thus, back from central deputation after staying there for a little over one year only, much against the wishes of the Chief Minister, Bhajan Lal. My stand that my forced deputation to the central government was arbitrary and whimsical was fully vindicated. The lesson from the entire episode narrated in this chapter is quite clear. Upholding the rule of law is the first and the only priority of a police officer even if he has to face uncalled for difficulties of any magnitude.

Chapter – 16

Threshold to Reach the Apex

Posting as DIG Welfare and Rules

My repatriation to Haryana State from Central deputation became effective only from 1st May 1984, when I joined this assignment. Though this job was not considered to be of any great significance particularly in view of my seniority, yet I had to remain contended with it in the given circumstances. Otherwise, also, I never considered any job inferior or superior, the incumbent of the job makes it significant or otherwise. "Work is Worship" has throughout been my motto in life. By devotion to one's particular duty, everyone can attain perfection. Taking the work as worship, one can bring such worship to fulfillment. It is always better to perform one's duty perfectly instead of giving any importance to its nature. I organized the welfare machinery so effectively that its effects started percolating down to all the force personnel for whom the welfare measures were devised. Further, the British framed the Punjab Police Rules as applicable to Haryana Police, under the Police Act, 1861 as back as 1934. No pointed attention for the revision of these Rules was paid, though some of these Rules were not at all in tune with the constitutional provisions and the democratic set up adopted by the country, after it was declared a Republic on 26th January 1950. I therefore, considered it to be a privilege to be an important functionary for the revision of these rules which were really warranted. Within a short period, I prepared draft proposals for the revision of four chapters of the Police Rules, submitted the same to the government through the State DGP and continued pestering the concerned authorities for holding early meetings to examine my draft proposals for their finalization. The State DGP and both the State Home Secretary and Chief Secretary were very impressed. I earned their approbation in the words "Shri Swan appreciably organized the welfare machinery to make it more effective. The fact that he is highly conscientious, completely professional, and thoroughly conversant with police working and fully devoted to the duty is amply reflected from the drafts of four important chapters of the Police Rules, he produced in a short spell."

Sad Demise of My Father

While I was feeling rehabilitated and happy with my current job, I had to suffer severe setback at the domestic front because of fast deterioration of my father's health. Since I was not given posting in the State for quite sometime, despite my repatriation orders issued by the Union Home Ministry, my father took to heart my harassment at the hands of the Haryana state government. This adversely affected his health. After my posting as DIG Welfare and Rules in the state, I tried to convince my father that the storm had blown over but he did not believe it. The deterioration in his health continued and on 18th September 1984, he breathed his last. The human being, whosoever takes birth on this Planet, has to go eventually. This is the law of nature and one has to submit to it. However, the most saddening aspect in the tragic death of my father was linked to the bad patch in my service career. I had to bear with it.

Change of heart by erstwhile Foes

The IPS officer, who was still working as DIG/CID and had earlier played dirty role during 1982, the lean period of my career, had come to terms after realizing that my determination to fight against injustice could not be countered. He perhaps got convinced in his heart that even those in the state, not liking me, had to suffer my presence as a senior police officer in the state, particularly when it had become known to everyone who mattered that the higher echelon in the state administration were highly appreciating my conduct and performance. He started changing colour by becoming very respectful and friendly to me. The Chief Minister had also realized that as a police officer, I had proved my mettle in service both in the state and at the centre. His sting of revenge against me had also been considerably mellowed.

Threatened Strike by Police Constabulary

Blooming spring follows the long winter spell. In August 1982, services of nearly 400 constables were dispensed with, dismissing them en masse. The Supreme Court held such en masse dismissal as invalid. These constables had in fact committed serious misconduct by resorting to violent agitation. However, the way they were dismissed was not lawful. In the circumstances, the state government had to reinstate them in service in early 1985. About 150 of them who were considered as hardliners were stationed at a place known as 'Kala Teetar' situated on the intersection of Rajasthan and Bhakhra canal near Punjab, Haryana and Rajasthan borders. They were generally kept engaged in outdoor activities like physical training, parade and sports with no entertainment facilities. Even casual leave was rarely granted to them. In fact, they were confined to miserable conditions. They were the most disgruntled lot. Instead of absorbing them in the mainstream, the treatment meted out to them was certainly not humane, leading them to nurse a strong resentment in the Haryana Armed Police Constabulary.

In the beginning of 1985, acute unrest among the state constabulary had once again raised its ugly head. The epicenter of this unrest was HAP Hqr Madhuban. The situation was reported to be assuming alarming proportions by the threat of the agitating constabulary to block the National Highway at Madhuban. There was panic in the police administration, as also in the state home department. The Chief Minister was reported to be highly worried. The DGP, Home Secretary and the Chief Secretary were searching for a suitable officer who could be effective in dissuading the constabulary from the path of agitation. When they could not spot any officer for this purpose, the Chief Minister asked them to find out if H R Swan (the writer) then DIG Welfare and Rules could be agreeable voluntarily for his posting at Madhuban. I was sounded by the State DGP and the Home Secretary about the viewpoint of the Chief Minister. In the first instance my reaction was that the said proposal was perhaps a trap to push me into a dilemma.

Though both the DGP and the Home Secretary assured me that the proposal was, in a way, recognition of my leadership qualities, yet I decided to seek clarifications on certain points by having an audience with the Chief Minister. It was immediately arranged and Bhajan Lal, the Chief Minister called me. He very gracefully told me, "Some harassment to you was no doubt caused on account of some misunderstanding. However, your reaction to take me even upto the Supreme Court on allegations of mala fide was not proper on your part. In any case the past should be forgotten and I would promote you as IG soon, but in the meanwhile you should take over as DIG/HAP and exercise your expertise as an experienced officer to control the situation at Madhuban." There could not be any better assurance from the Chief Minister. I thankfully agreed to move to Madhuban. On the same day, my posting orders were issued and I instantly took over as DIG/HAP at Madhuban.

My posting orders as DIG/HAP had reached much earlier than my reaching there. There was a mixed feeling with the police administration that the agitating constabulary might block my entry into the Complex and situation might flare up all of a sudden. But, nothing of the kind happened. After taking over the charge, I asked the Commandants to collect as many police personnel off duty as possible, as I wanted to talk to them. I addressed a large gathering of the police personnel assuring them that instead of any one of them acting as their Union Leader, I would myself assume that role and ensure that all their legitimate demands were very sympathetically considered by the authorities and conceded without any delay. Their slogans in appreciation of my talk rented the sky. Thereafter, I went around the Complex and acquainted myself with the visible deficiencies in the various services in the kitchen, bathrooms and the barracks of the constabulary.

I visited 'Kala Teetar' at the earliest and had straight talk with the constabulary 'detained' there. They gave me solemn promise not to indulge in any type of indiscipline and, in turn, I promised to disperse them for their duties. I brought this strategy to the notice of the DGP. He was a little apprehensive that these disgruntled constables might breed indiscipline in the constabulary wherever they were dispersed. He, therefore, advised me to tackle the situation cautiously. However, I dispersed the entire crowd of 150 constables to various districts in the state in small groups, advising the district SPs to ensure that even from these small groups, they were sprinkled in twos or threes all over the district. It was highly gratifying for me that at the end of the day the situation returned to normalcy. The DGP had already learnt the happy developments, which had taken place at Madhuban, through the CID channels. When I telephoned him, he congratulated me and expressed his sincere thanks for my handling the situation to the satisfaction of the constabulary as well as the state authorities. I was very happy to receive "well done" telephonic call from the Chief Minister.

The construction of building for the Model School for the children of the police personnel was started in 1980 during my posting as DIG/HAP. The idea had been mooted by me and construction of a few classrooms out of the total conceived plan, had been started in 1980 as stated earlier. The said school building had nicely come up, particularly with a couple of class rooms. I inaugurated the functioning of the school soon after my joining at Madhuban in 1985 and construction for additional classroom was also started in the right earnest.

The Chief Minister was shortly to go abroad for treatment of his eye. He had assured me that the demands of the constabulary as highlighted by them and recommended by me would be examined after his return from abroad and necessary orders conceding all their genuine demands would be issued. True to his words, he left instructions with the Home Secretary and Chief Secretary to issue my promotion orders to the Rank of IG, against the vacancy, which was to come up soon on the retirement of Dharam Singh. After my promotion as IG, I was made overall incharge of Police Complex Madhuban with effect from 23rd May 1985; my assignment included command and control of the HAP Bns, State Police Training College and State Forensic Sciences Laboratory, a prestigious institution.

My Junior Colleagues proved Asset to me

My team at Madhuban also included A S Bhatotia IPS (1968-RR), M S Malik IPS (1969-RR) and G S Malhi IPS (1974-RR) as Commandants of the HAP Bns. They were excellent and promising officers with remarkable leadership qualities. Shri Bhatotia and Shri Malik were ex-army officers and being pretty seniors were due for promotion as DIG. The Chief Minister, unfortunately, was not favourably disposed towards them, simply because Shri Bhatotia had earlier remained posted as SP Sirsa district during the Devi Lal government and was thus being dubbed as Devi Lal's man. Shri Malik had remained posted as SP Bhiwani district and was therefore, given the tag of being Bansi Lal's man.

During my earlier posting as DIG/HAP in the years 1979-80, a policy had been approved by the authorities for making recruitment of constables, initially in the HAP and the seniors amongst them were to be absorbed against the vacancies occurring in the districts' police. Political pressure for recruiting the favourites of the bigwigs had become very common. However, the top political boss would not exercise any political pressure on Shri Bhatotia and Shri Malhi, the two commandants who were ex-army people. Shri Malhi who had about 11 years IPS service at his credit, was also quite senior and he, like the other two commandants from the ex-army category, was very straight-forward and totally averse to recruiting any ineligible person not deserving recruitment on merit.

I had deputed Shri Malhi for recruiting 50 boys at Hisar. A list of about 60 boys was handed over to him by a person claiming to be representing the top political boss. Very upset on this development, Shri Malhi reported the matter to me on the telephone. I advised him to ignore the list and follow the laid down system. The list finalized by Shri Malhi included only a few boys from the "political list" who had made it only on merit. The top political boss angrily asked me on telephone to pull up Shri Malhi and make him revise the list. I politely explained to him that it would not be appropriate for me to interfere with the functioning of a commandant, if he was following the laid down system. A few days after this incident, I got telephonic message from the Home Secretary that the top political boss was not happy with the way recruitment was conducted by the commandant at Hisar and my failure to persuade the commandant to accommodate the boys recommended by his loyalist. He further told me that the Appeal filed by me in 1982 in the Supreme Court was still pending there and the top political boss wanted that I should withdraw the same so that the matter be taken as closed, after my return to the State and promotion as IGP. Accordingly, I submitted withdrawal application and the Supreme Court were pleased to accept it. Thus, my Appeal was dismissed as withdrawn on 2nd December 1985. The list of candidates selected on merit as finalized by Shri Malhi remained unchanged.

"Nyay Yudh" Movement and drastically winning acceptance of Bhajan Lal as Chief Minister

General Elections to Haryana Assembly were due in June 1987. The opposition parties had started flexing their muscles. There were many factors leading to the various other disgruntled segments of society also to join hands to take on the Congress Party ruling the state continuously since 1980 under the leadership of Bhajan Lal. As mentioned earlier, Bhajan Lal had become Chief Minister of Haryana for the first time on 29th June 1979 by dislodging the Devi Lal government. It was the result of revolt within the Janata Party. The jat community of Haryana had not taken kindly to this political development leading to a discernible political polarization between the jats and the non-jats. Bhajan Lal with his flock had switched over to Congress Party during 1980 converting his Janata Party government into the Congress Party government. This episode further antagonized the jats and polarization between jats and non-jats was further reinforced. As mentioned earlier, in General Elections to Haryana Assembly held in 1982, Congress Party led by Bhajan Lal had won 33 seats out of total 90 seats as against 32 seats won by Lok Dal led by Devi Lal. However, the pre-poll alliance between Devi Lal's Lok Dal and BJP had won near majority seats. The manner in which the Governor invited Bhajan Lal on revising his earlier decision to invite Devi Lal to form the government did not go well with the general public feelings. The masses at large believed that the mandate given to Lok Dal-BJP pre-poll alliance by the electorate was thrown to the winds and democratic traditions were throttled by political manipulation. Thus, the moral right of Bhajan Lal to rule the state carried a question mark in the eyes of the electorate.

Nearly seven lacs of Sikh population, mainly settled in the districts bordering Punjab, were bitterly estranged with Haryana state administration in 1982; Sikhs were checked, searched and frisked at various places to establish their bonafide while travelling on the NH-1 through Haryana territory to Delhi, on the eve of Asiad '82. The object for such checking and frisking, in fact, was to ensure that undesirable elements did not reach the venue of Asiad '82, New Delhi. However, many overzealous police checking parties committed excesses, to the utter humiliation of many genuine Sikh travellers, leading to their nursing a deep-rooted grudge that Sikhs as a community were very badly discriminated against by the Bhajan Lal government. In the aftermath of assassination of Indira Gandhi, on 31st October 1984 by her Sikh bodyguard, serious riots broke out, not only in Delhi, but also in various towns of Haryana adjoining Delhi. Many Sikhs were killed in these riots and huge loss of property was suffered by this community. A strong under-current of hate campaign by the sikhs against the Bhajan Lal government had been built-up in a big way. Sporadic incidents by the Sikh ultras had also been committed, in retaliation of "insult" heaped on Sikh passengers travelling on G T Road.

Tohana (District Hissar) Assembly by-election was held on 5th March 1985 while Bhajan Lal was the Chief Minister. An organized attempt, perhaps for the second time, was made there to rig an election in Haryana. Such an attempt was earlier made in the state when Bahadurgarh (District Rohtak) Assembly by-election was held on 21st May 1967. It was then the first instance of open rigging of an election, as organized by Hardwari Lal. In Tohana Assembly by-election held in 1985 truckloads of men from adjoining constituencies were brought in the early hours of the election day to cast bogus votes. Many polling booths were captured by toughs, hooligans and gangsters. Such a large scale of open rigging of an election was widely believed, rightly or wrongly, to have been organized by the Chief Minister Bhajan Lal to ensure the success of his close relations. This episode enraged leaders of all the major opposition parties.

These factors cumulatively created difficulties for the Bhajan Lal government. All the political parties, like Lok Dal, BJP, Communist Party and the Sikh Organizations et al under the leadership of Devi Lal, a political stalwart of reckoning, with following mainly from the peasantry, launched an agitation under the banner of "Nyay-Yudh" targeting the Congress government led by Bhajan Lal. The issues raised in the "Nyay-Yudh" included inter alia sharing of rivers water, Sutlej-Yamuna Link (SYL) canal, satisfactory solution of Fazilka and Chandigarh problem and uninterrupted power supply in the farming sector. These issues touched the sentiments of the Haryana public at large and therefore, "Nyay-Yudh" movement was able to register the support of very large majority of the people in the state. The Congress government was put in the dock for not grappling with these issues with the desired seriousness during its continued rule of several years in the state.

I would like to elaborate here the importance and complexity of SYL, which was the major issue in the "Nyay-Yudh". The SYL as well as the Hansi - Butana canal, which had been constructed by the state government at a cost of nearly 400 crores were supposed to irrigate the water-starved agriculture fields of South Haryana. However, both these projects had not been commissioned due to inter-state disputes, regional politics and certain other techno-legal factors. Punjab Assembly passed the Punjab Termination of (water) Agreements Act in 2004, unilaterally annulling the tripartite agreement signed between the Chief Ministers of Punjab, Haryana and Rajasthan in 1981. The President of India referred the SYL issue to the Supreme Court after the said Act of 2004 was passed by Punjab State Assembly. The Supreme Court referred the matter pertaining to Hansi-Butana canal to the Central Water Commission. Both these cases have been thus pending with the top legal and administrative authorities for several years now and in the meanwhile the people of South Haryana have continued to be deprived of their due share of irrigation water. However, the irony is that SYL canal issue was thrown up as the major plank of the "Nyay-Yudh" agitation of 1986-87 which led to resounding victory of Devi Lal led opposition parties, in June 1987 Haryana Assembly Election, to almost decimate the Congress Party in Haryana.

The entire police force available in the state was committed to suppress the "Nyay-Yudh" agitation, even at the cost of normal law and order affairs. In the meanwhile, M S Bhatnagar, the State DGP retired on 31st October 1985. Though about two months before his due date of retirement, Shri Bhatnagar had gone into total passivity yet on the eve of his retirement, I organized a grand show including *"Bada-Khana"* in his honour and a decent farewell befitting his rank and 34 years long innings in the Indian Police Service. Manmohan Singh Bawa, IPS (1955-RR) on promotion became the new State DGP on 1st November 1985.

It would be very relevant to mention here that JP Atre IPS (1963-RR), who on his promotion to the super time scale was appointed DIG/CID in 1977, had been still, continuing uninterruptedly on that post till November 1986 when Shri Bawa became the sixth State Police Chief since 1977. The said DIG/CID virtually assumed the role as a *de facto* Police Chief, thanks to his close proximity to Bhajan Lal. State police personnel of all ranks including a majority of IPS officers who lacked self-confidence, self-respect and were not sure of their competency used to swarm him for getting plum postings. The State IPS Cadre was studded with many dynamic and competent officers. They hated playing sycophants to the *de facto* Police Chief and preferred to remain on the sideline postings.

The state had got a wake up call on 9th March 1984 when Ved Pal the then Deputy Speaker of Haryana Vidhan Sabha was attacked by the terrorists while he was travelling in his staff car on Grand Trunk (GT) Road near Karnal. Since then the police strength was steadily increased by SP/1, Dy SP/4, Inspectors/14, Sub Inspectors/23, Assistant Sub Inspector/28, Head Constables/ 206 and Constables/1217 with some additional wireless sets and vehicles during the years 1984-86. However, no special training programme was devised or organized to improve the professional efficiency of the policef to face emerging challenge, in the wake of serious threats of terrorism looming large in the state. I raised this point several times both with Shri Bhatnagar and his successor Shri Bawa, emphasizing the urgency of organizing the training programme for the force by devising special syllabi and ensuring adequate provision of sophisticated weapons for the force. However, I found both of them were concerned only to suppress the "Nyay-Yudh" agitation by using more and more force, not only at the cost of maintenance of general law and order, but also completely ignoring the training aspects. The only new commendable idea mooted by Shri Bawa after assuming charge as State DGP was his proposal for constructing Haryana Police Martyrs Memorial at Police Complex Madhuban. For this purpose he got sanctioned a grant of Rs. 1,23,000/- from the state government. The construction of a grand Memorial started in the right earnest under my close supervision. In the meanwhile, the terrorists had intensified their activities in the neighbouring Punjab state. I continued pressing Shri Bawa to spare in rotation, at least four companies from the HAP and almost similar strength from the district police for undergoing capsule training course of four to six weeks duration at the Police Complex Madhuban. He would put me off saying that he would try to evolve soon a system in consultation with DIG/CID. However, his top priority remained the suppressing of "Nyay-Yudh" agitation by pressing the entire state police force into action.

"*Rasta Roko*" (blocking the state roads and National Highways) and '*Gherao*' became a common feature of the agitation. "*Rasta Roko*" and '*Gherao*' of particular government buildings in the state by the agitators on 23rd January 1986 had created very alarming law and order situation. Terrorism prevalent in the Punjab state had already started casting its ugly shadow in Haryana state. All these factors cumulatively affected very adversely the general morale of the state administration. The duty to keep the National Highway, between Karnal and Delhi, clear of all obstacles created by the supporters of 'Nyay-Yudh', was assigned to HAP under my directions and control. I had to deploy strong armed police parties at various sensitive points on the Highway under the direct supervision of the commandants who very spiritedly and effectively performed the role assigned to them.

In Gohana area of district Rohtak, the supporters of 'Nyay-Yudh' had laid a strong blockade on a state road. SP Sonepat with a police party tried to remove this blockade. The agitators turned violent and in the melee, some police personnel suffered injuries at their hands. Being heavily outnumbered the police had to use force and open fire to handle the grave situation. One agitator was killed in the process. This incident made the agitators all the more violent and the people from the neighbouring villages started coming in droves to the site of the incident. Gohana Police Station was '*gheraoed*' and the agitators threatened to set it on fire. I was directed by the DGP to rush to the troubled spot with adequate police force for restoring the law and order situation. The agitators were demanding that the policeman who killed their comrade, (whom they termed as a martyr) should be handed over to them for "instant Justice" and the government should agree to build a memorial column as a tribute to the "martyr for laying his life for a just cause." It was with great difficulty, perseverance and strategic planning that I was able to bring round the agitators to lift the blockade of the Police Station. I had to tackle many difficult situations created both, by the 'Nyay-Yudh' agitators and the terrorists from Punjab state.

The Commandants of the HAP Bns particularly Shri Bhatotia and Shri Malik always went a step ahead in performance of their duties as assigned by me. If I got any appreciation from the higher authority, it was all because of the unstinted cooperation and unquestionable commitment to duty on the part of these highly motivated officers. Chief Minister Bhajan Lal on various occasions during this period, applauded my role. Shri Bhatnagar the DGP adjudged my performance in the words "An officer with lot of initiative and drive. He is conscientious, has flair for man-management and can handle difficult situations dexterously. Power of expression both in writing and during discussion is very good. He maintained very good relations with all. He appreciably toned up operational capability of the force. He made significant contribution to control law and order situations arising out of extremists' threats. He is an excellent officer in all respects and can be safely entrusted with the higher responsibility in diverse areas."

While the "Nyay-Yudh" agitation by the opposition parties was at its peak, the law and order situation in our neighbouring Punjab started getting further explosive. A very alarming incident occurred at Jalandhar in mid April 1986 in which a gang of terrorists, in a blitzkrieg, not only gunned down six policemen, they also freed three undertrial terrorists and carried away a stengun and a rifle of the dead policemen. This spine chilling ghastly incident exposed the administrative and professional inefficiency of the Punjab police already engaged for over three years in operations against terrorists. The inadequacies and deficiencies of Punjab police were in shocking contrast with the display of skill and planning by the terrorists. Message from Jalandhar for Haryana police was indeed, very ominous. Haryana police, though quite competent and well equipped for taking on effectively the normal law and order affairs, was yet only a pale shadow of Punjab police so far as their training, equipments and weaponry was concerned. Many inter-state disputes between the two neighbouring states had remained unsettled for years. A big chunk of Sikh population settled in Haryana nursed deep antagonism against the Bhajan Lal government for reasons stated earlier. Thus, Haryana was seriously exposed to the fall-out of terrorism prevalent in Punjab.

Under the circumstances, there was an urgent need to pay pointed attention for keeping the law and order machinery in Haryana well oiled, fully geared up and in top state of professional efficiency. I had been earlier crying hoarse all in vain, during discussions held with the DGP to take up the issue of organizing special training for the force and for arranging adequate sophisticated weapons and equipment. Feeling disgusted, I sent a detailed DO letter dated 17the April 1986 to the DGP enlisting all the above mentioned issues pointedly and also availed an opportunity to discuss the matter with Chief Minister who was camping at Sonepat. All this had desired effects. The DGP held a meeting of the senior officers in the state and a strategy for organizing special training for the entire police force, in sizeable groups, was finalized. A group of 4 companies of the HAP and 300 police personnel, 100 from each Range was mobilized at

Police Complex Madhuban for undergoing six weeks intensive training. Requisite syllabus had been specially devised covering new techniques in (i) police public relations and community Policing, (ii) improvement in investigation skills, (iii) security of VIPs and vulnerable points/installations, (iv) dealing with extremists/ terrorists and (v) use of sophisticated weapons.

While there was no respite in the "Nyay-Yudh" agitation, the general law and order situation in the state was deteriorating. There was afloat a strong rumour in the political gallery that Chief Minister Bhajan Lal was on the way out. There was no governance deficit, which could be attributed to Bhajan Lal. He was a very affable person with friendly disposition gifted with excellent acumenship in the art of politicking, as situation warranted, in the context of Indian democracy whatever it is. However, apart from his overt or covert dependence on Brahmin lobby, which misled him often, two milestones in his political career gave him the tag of a leader only of non-jat communities with anti-jat stance. His dethroning Devi Lal in 1979 and again out-witting Devi Lal in 1982 with the help of the then Governor showed his super expertise in the art of politicking. If he was being replaced by the Congress High Command, that too was a political game. In a vibrant democracy, such incidents should not be taken as an adverse reflection on a politician's capability in the art of governance. There have been only very few honourable exceptions in the second-generation politicians who could match the high moral ground, so dear to those committed freedom fighters who took over the governance of the country after Independence in the first instance.

As Bhajan Lal was preparing to move to Delhi to take over his new assignment in the central government as Cabinet Minister, I recalled with no malice my challenging his vendetta game and subsequent developments. I went to his residence and greeted him warmly. Giving me a very warm handshake, he said, "I wish you and your family best of luck and for you particularly glorious career ahead". As his car moved out of the sprawling Chief Minister's bungalow, the philosophical words of Dr B R Ambedkar came to my mind. "Unlike a drop of water that loses its identity when it joins the ocean, man does not lose his being in the society in which he lives. Man's life is independent. He is born not for development of society alone but also for the development of the self".

Chapter – 17

First Tenure as State Police Chief

General Situation in the State

As mentioned earlier, the period between second half of 1985 and first half of 1986 was very troublesome for the Bhajan Lal government. The issues raised by the opposition in their 'Nyay-Yudh' campaign had considerably eroded the credibility of the state government making correspondingly 'Nyay-Yudh' more popular. The people became so disenchanted with the Bhajan Lal government that a stage reached when the 'Nyay-Yudh' supporters started resorting to violent means. At times, even the Cabinet Ministers were not allowed to enter certain villages. The Congress High Command at the centre was monitoring day-to-day developments. They perhaps thought that Bhajan Lal had ceased to carry the people with him and that the situation could still be salvaged if he was withdrawn from the scene, much ahead of the forthcoming General Elections of the Haryana Assembly, due in June 1987 and someone who could retrieve the situation in the state was put in command. Bansi Lal had already proved his mettle, both as the state Chief Minister and Cabinet Minister in the Union Government. The Congress High Command therefore drafted him to take over as the state Chief Minister. Bhajan Lal had played a long inning as Chief Minister and had thus, carved a niche for himself in the Congress High Command. He was therefore, shifted to the centre as Union Cabinet Minister in June 1986. Bansi Lal took over as Chief Minister on 5th June 1986.

Bansi Lal, during his first tenure as Chief Minister of the state had issued orders, as mentioned in detail earlier that the confidential report on the performance of the District Superintendents of Police would be initiated by the respective Deputy Commissioners. During the Bhajan Lal government, *status quo ante* had been restored to making only the range DIG as initiating officers for the ACRs of the District Superintendents of Police. However, the Bansi Lal government revived the system of initiating the ACRs of the District

SPs by the Deputy Commissioners, in June 1986.

To restore the lost credibility of the Congress government and to bring the governance back on the rails, Bansi Lal made some administrative reshuffling in the state administrative set up. In the police department M S Bawa IPS (1955-RR) who had been the Director General of Police Haryana since 1st November 1985, proceeded on leave and I was then elevated and posted as State Police Chief vide state government order dated 4th July 1986. Besides MS Bawa, three other IPS officers senior to me were PC Wadhwa IPS (1952-RR) posted as Director General Prisons Department, DD Kashyap IPS (1956-RR) and K L Dewan IPS (1957-RR) both in the rank of IG, were posted as Commandant General Home Guards and Director Prosecution respectively. JP Atrey IPS (1963-RR) who had been DIG/CID for very long time, both in the Devi Lal government and the Bhajan Lal government, was given a fringe posting. M S Malik IPS (1969-RR) on promotion was appointed as DIG/CID. VN Negi, IPS was posted in the CID as DIG Crime.

The news of my appointment as State Police Chief was first conveyed to me on telephone to my pleasant surprise by M L Jain IAS Commissioner and Secretary to Government of Haryana, Home Department. In his first attempt of competing for All India Services Shri Jain had been selected in the IPS. However, he was selected in the IAS in the second attempt. He was a thorough gentleman of few words, devoid of any ego, which is a common characteristic of the people holding high status in government service. An officer of proven efficiency and honesty, he was respected for his innate qualities of head and heart. I took over the charge of my challenging assignment on 6th July 1986. During my first audience with the Chief Minister, I found him deeply concerned with the unhappy state of law and order in the state, caused due to the role of the 'Nyay-Yudh' activists and the shadow of terrorism in Punjab looming large on Haryana. He advised me to devise an effective strategic action plan for early restoring the situation to normalcy.

Toning up the Governance by the Chief Minister

Bansi Lal had earned the reputation of being a strong and tough administrator. Both the public and the state administration at all levels, were well aware that he was a no-nonsense politician with proven administrative acumen who would brook no delay on anybody's part in dealing with official matters. In his first meeting with the top senior officers of the state, he unfolded his agenda and fixed hundred days time to achieve the given targets. Not only the state's senior administrators but also the government servants at all levels, were on their toes to discharge their assigned duties and responsibilities with the desired urgency and efficiency. Punctuality in 'attendance' had become the norm to the point of scientific precision and the government servants would strictly observe the lunch break only for half an hour.

The effectiveness of the overall governance in the state started showing good results. The 'Nyay-Yudh' activists, who were targeting Bhajan Lal rightly or wrongly as the villain for ignoring the various issues highlighted by them, had considerably mellowed down. They were left with nothing much to blame or malign Bansi Lal. The Congress workers who had gone in hibernation got very much encouraged and Congress Party came on the recovery path. It appeared as if the entire opposition to the Congress Party was mesmerized by Bansi Lal with his dynamic leadership and administrative abilities. The Congress High Command was obviously happy with its decision in sending Bansi Lal to the state to take the prevailing difficult situation head on.

My Efforts to revamp the Police Administration

To revamp the police administration and for meeting the law and order situation squarely, a well thoughtout strategy was evolved in consultation with all the senior officers of the rank of SP and above. To tackle the problem of terrorism, a Special Task Force was created by selecting young and robustly built spirited constables, head constables and non-gazetted officers from the Armed Police Battalions. Special pay and ration allowance to arrange free nutritive food for them were sanctioned by the government. In the meanwhile the government also sanctioned additional post of one Sub Inspector, six Assistant Sub Inspectors, twenty Head Constables and eighty Constables, besides additional fleet of four wheeler vehicles and motorbikes, to ensure better mobility and effectiveness of the police. M S Malik IPS, DIG/CID, an Ex-Emergency Commissioned Officer had intensive training as a commando, during his service in the army. He was put on the job to organize effective intelligence network in consultation with his counterpart in the Punjab state. The Special Task Force so raised was put through intensive commando training by devising a capsule syllabus. Apart from normal duties as DIG/CID, the services of Shri Malik were utilized to direct, coordinate and oversee the anti-terrorist operations. The results were encouraging as no terrorist related incident occurred anywhere in the state.

General law and order situation required the toning up of the police administration particularly, in the context of potential threat to the communal harmony, due to mistrust developed between the Sikh population and the Hindus who having suffered at the hands of the terrorist in Punjab had migrated to Haryana. Intensely aggressive attitude adopted lately by the 'Nyay-Yudh' agitators and near failure of the police to check the alarming violence, arson, looting and hooliganism earlier unleashed by them during the Haryana *Bandh* calls on 23rd January and 21st June 1986, had a very demoralizing effect on the police. As on 30th June 1986, there were 1137 proclaimed offenders and 65 military deserters at large. Special campaign was launched, by creating a strong cell, under the charge of Inspector, Central Investigating Agency (CIA) in every district to arrest these criminals, as their continued remaining underground activities were a potential threat to law and order. All standing schemes like anti-riot measures for all towns as provided in the Internal Security Scheme, Railway Security Scheme and Jail Alarm System were brushed up. Contingency plan for security of banks in isolated area was put in place. Sixty four criminal cases were pending investigation over two years, 185 over one years, 1073 over six months and 8304 less than 6 months. Targets were fixed that no case would remain pending investigation over three months within next hundred days. It was also ensured that the Investigating Officers together with their supervisory officer would personally discuss with the State Police Chief, the reasons for delay in finalizing investigation within the stipulated period. The most common irritant against the police in the public eyes was the discourtesy, indifferent attitude and rude behaviour. Reluctance to register cognizable crime was found to be a common malpractice. Urgent measures were called for to improve the image and effectiveness of the police. It was, therefore, ensured that the police personnel at all levels woul.. thoroughly understand and assimilate:

(i) That the police was a service dedicated to the protection of the citizens and to suppress the elements of lawlessness and disorder;

(ii) That the police was an important part of the democratic society and the citizens had every right to organize and express themselves in peaceful manner; dissent was not to be construed as a threat to law and order unless there was grave apprehension of breach of peace;

(iii) That policemen were in the business for extending help to the people in trouble and their attitude should be to render it to the best possible manner and

(iv) That the police was the helper, protector, a willing guide and the veritable friend of the people.

It was necessary to instill self-confidence in the public that police was entirely to render assistance to the aggrieved persons. Large size signboards of 8 X 4 square feet were displayed outside the gate of every police station and police post at conspicuous places, depicting various do's and don'ts, for the guidance of police personnel and the visiting public. The Supervisory Officers were advised that they would be held vicariously responsible for the lapses committed by their subordinates in the discharge of their duties in the law and order matters.

All the senior police officers in the state as well as their subordinates rose to the occasion and performed their respective role commendably. When the overall situation was reviewed after hundred day's period, the results were found to be very encouraging. Print media, generally critical of police working was found often coming up with stories of commendable police performance, particularly the marked change in their behaviour and improved police-public relations. The Chief Minister was often heard saying good words for the over all performance of the police. Appreciation of the CM for tackling the challenging law and order situation became apparent when he recommended my name for the coveted Award of President's Police Medal for Distinguished Service on Independence Day 1986, as mentioned earlier.

By the time, I had left Madhuban in early July 1986, there were 39 residential quarters for the gazetted officers, 777 for the other ranks beside 14 barracks, which could accommodate 1400 other ranks. The Model School as mentioned earlier had progressed upto sixth class and plans were on hand, to raise the level of the School upto 10+2 by adding a class every year. The concerned authorities were approached to get the school affiliated with the CBSE. To make it a residential School, hostel accommodation was being constructed. As State Police Chief, I submitted quite a few proposals to the government mostly aiming at the general welfare of the force. These proposals included (i) an additional grant of Rs. 2,00,000/- for the completion of Haryana Police Martyrs Memorial already under construction with initial grant of Rs.1,23,000/- (ii) a grant of Rs.1,60,000/- for the purchase of X-ray machine for the police hospital at Madhuban and

(iii) Purchase of 50 new vehicles as replacement of the old vehicles. These proposals got the nod of the government. The completion of construction of Haryana Police Martyrs Memorial was expedited. Other proposals still pending under consideration with the government were: (i) Sanction of matching grant towards the Police Welfare Fund. (ii) Special pay to the trainers posted in the Police Training College. (iii) Mid-day meal for those police personnel who had to remain on duty continuously for more than eight hours. (iv) Provision for two sets of warm uniform every three years period, instead of four years period already in vogue. (v) Ration allowance for the non-gazetted police personnel of the HAP. (vi) Sanction of city compensatory allowance to the police personnel stationed at Madhuban at par with the police personnel stationed at Karnal (all those residing in Police Complex Madhuban depended on Karnal City for all types of shopping). (vii) Monthly motorcycle allowance to all the non-gazetted police personnel posted in the various districts. (viii) Grant for the construction of additional residential quarters for the police personnel of districts Faridabad, Hisar and Ambala. (ix) Sanction for raising a commando company. M. L. Jain, the State Home Secretary hotly pursued all these proposals in the finance department where these were stuck up on the plea of financial constraints. It was entirely because of the helping hand extended by Sh Jain that some proposals particularly for the construction of residential and barrack accommodation at Madhuban were expeditiously sanctioned by the government.

Chief Minister's Visit to Madhuban

Various proposals enumerated above were still pending sanction with the government in the finance department. I thought that government sanction for these proposals might be expedited if the Chief Minister visited Madhuban on some occasion and these proposals reiterated and brought to his attention on that occasion. The construction of the Haryana Police Martyrs Memorial was completed by the middle of October 1986. I planned to invite the Chief Minister to Madhuban for the inauguration of the Haryana Police Martyrs Memorial on Police Martyrs Day falling on 21st October 1986. It was on 21st October 1959 that all members of a police party from the Central Reserve Police Force (CRPF), while on routine patrol duty on Indo-China Border, were killed by the Chinese troops in an ambush. This day is observed by holding a serene police parade all over the country with a view to pay tributes to the police personnel, who had laid down their lives at the altar of duty. The Chief Minister readily agreed to visit Police Complex Madhuban on 21st October 1986. He went around the entire Complex on foot. The idea to have such a sprawling Police Complex at Madhuban was conceived during the year 1968 when Bansi Lal had become the Chief Minister of Haryana for the first time. It was then, considered as an invaluable gift by the Chief Minister to the Haryana Police. In 1986, this Police Complex had come up as the best of its kind in the country, to be a pride place of Haryana Police. A Model School, built up out of the Police Welfare Fund and started for the children of the police personnel, had come up very well with 273 children including 226 children of the constabulary. Building for the hostel was the need of the time. The Chief Minister was visibly very happy on going around the Complex. After inaugurating the Haryana

Police Martyrs Memorial and the hostel for the schoolchildren, he was to address the police personnel assembled at the Parade Ground. Before inviting the Chief Minister to address the gathering, I availed the opportunity to briefly mention about the various proposals pending sanction with the government in the finance department and requested him for their early sanction. The Chief Minister, during his address, not only applauded the police role in excellently handling the law and order situation after his assuming the rein of the state, he also observed that the proposals made by the State Police Chief seemed to be genuine and he would ensure early sanction there of. Thus, the visit of the Chief Minister to Madhuban was a great morale booster for the Haryana Police.

Adverse Effect of CM's Rigid Style of Functioning

Considerable improvement in the state administration was conspicuously visible during the first three months of the Bansi Lal government. The evils of red tape and other mal-practices had almost disappeared. The "Nyay Yudh" agitators remained subdued. Bansi Lal was a strict disciplinarian. But the rigidity of the style of functioning of the CM soon started pinching both the government servants, political worker and even the senior politicians in the Congress Party. The grassroot Congress workers started losing enthusiasm. General Elections for the State Assembly were due in June 1987. In the meanwhile, Bansi Lal was yet to be elected as MLA within six months of his taking over as the Chief Minister of the state. For this purpose, 23rd November 1986 was fixed for holding by-election to Tosham Assembly constituency wherefrom Bansi Lal proposed to contest. Sometime in the middle of October 1986, Bansi Lal had called me to discuss general law and order situation in the state. To a general query about the stance of the opposition parties I mentioned that Congress Party could have won big majority of seats if the General Elections were advanced and held within six months of the change of guards at the top, as the opposition parties were then in disarray. I could easily discern from Bansi Lal's facial expression that he felt uneasy on hearing my assessment. He ended the meeting abruptly.

PC Wadhwa IPS, Director General of Prisons, the senior most IPS officer in the state Cadre, was due for superannuation at the age of 58 years on 31st October 1986. I thought it to be an appropriate gesture and befitting in the best tradition of the force, to organize a farewell dinner party in the manner befitting to his rank and seniority, on the eve of his superannuation. I decided that all IPS officers of and above the rank of Superintendent of Police should participate in the said farewell dinner, at Police Complex Madhuban on 31st October 1986. Therefore, all concerned were informed accordingly well in advance. On 30th October 1986, the Home Secretary talked to me on the telephone and conveyed indirectly that the Chief Minister would not like this. I explained to the Home Secretary that I was only upholding the tradition of the service and it would not be possible to cancel the already fixed programme and if necessary, I would explain the matter to the Chief Minister. The farewell dinner was held as scheduled; because I firmly believed that the personal disliking of the Chief Minister for a particular officer should not have come in the way of service traditions. Later I learnt that the Chief Minister expressed his utter unhappiness over this matter.

K K Zutshi IPS (1959-RR) was then on deputation with the Government of India. During the days of Emergency of 1975-76, Shri Zutshi was posted as Superintendent of Police, district Hisar. Shah Commission appointed by the Janata Party government at the centre, held inquiries into the alleged excesses committed by the police during the days of Emergency. It had been alleged that the excesses were committed at the behest of Bansi Lal, the then Union Cabinet Minister. When Shri Zutshi was examined by the Commission, he had taken the stand that the police action, allegedly dubbed as excesses, was taken in the interest of maintenance of law and order under his own directions and supervision and Bansi Lal had no role in that regard. Bansi Lal was naturally very appreciative of Shri Zutshi's taking the onus of police actions on himself. As the human psychology works, every IPS officer aspires to hold the top position as State Police Chief. Shri Zutshi was naturally keen to grab such an opportunity at the earliest. Bansi Lal, in his best wisdom, decided to appoint Shri Zutshi as the State Police Chief. The state government issued orders on 29th October 1986, appointing Shri Zutshi as State Police Chief. I was shifted and posted as Director General of Prisons, Haryana. S S Brar, who was senior to Shri Zutshi, was posted as Director General State Vigilance Bureau, Haryana. Shri Zutshi joined his new assignment on 4th November relieving me from the post of State Police Chief.

Chapter – 18

As Director General Prisons, Haryana

I joined as Director General Prisons on 4th November 1986. Since I was due to superannuate at the age of 58 on 31st July 1988, I thought that it was my last assignment in the Indian Police Service and that I was perhaps, destined to superannuate from the Prisons Department itself. I therefore, decided to settle down in the right earnest to grapple with the problems in the Prisons Department. After taking over the charge, I called on the Jail Minister and found him lukewarm giving me the impression that he perhaps had the view that I was in the category of rejected officers by the Chief Minister. This did not bother me much. I started visiting every jail with a view to understand in-depth, the problems of the inmates. Posting to Jail Department was viewed by me as a God sent opportunity for serving the human beings, who having gone off the track, were placed generally by the people at large in the category of wretched and fallen persons.

I was still in the process of closely studying the problems being faced by the inmates in various jails when by-election to Tosham Assembly constituency was held on 23rd November 1986. Bansi Lal as Chief Minister was the Congress candidate facing a common candidate sponsored jointly by all the opposition parties. Pre-poll electioneering by the supporters of both the Congress and opposition candidates had generated much heat. Many of the supporters of the opposition candidate had landed in various jails for the alleged violation of law and indulgence in breach of peace. I advised all the Jail Superintendents not to display any sense of discrimination against such 'guests' in the jails as dissent was a fundamental right of the people and it was not to be construed as an anti-social activity unless the allegations disturbing peace and harmony in the society are serious in nature. The by-election was held under very tight police arrangements. The results were startling both for the Congress and the opposition parties as well as for the public at large. 92.45% of the electorate came out to vote and Bansi Lal; the successful candidate secured an unbelievable 98.15% of the valid votes. D R Chaudhary a noted academic and keen observer of Haryana Socio-Political Affairs wrote in the *Indian Express* "A mafia gang was assembled in the area of influence of an important political figure of Haryana to browbeat his political opponents. Terror was so all pervasive that fair and free election became unthinkable. This was reflected most poignantly in the Tosham Assembly election." The spectacular results instead of demoralizing the opposition parties, acted as catalyst for them to spring up with much vigour and determination to turn their defeat into victory. Political atmosphere warmed up with frequent confrontations like 'wrestling bouts' forcing the state police to remain on toes all the times. I was watching the developments with great interest while continuing with my job in the Jail Department, in the right earnest.

General Administration of Prisons Department

It took me about two months to visit all the jails for in-depth study of the problems of the inmates, as obtaining on the grounds. There were 11 jails in the state. The building for the 12th jail at Kurukshetra was still under construction. The sanctioned general administration of the department included DG/1, Addl IG/1, Superintendents/14, Dy Supdts/17, District Probation Officers/12, Sr. Assistant Superintendents/1, Asst. Supdts/43, Sub-Asst. Supdts/7, Headwarders/57, Female Warders/3, Matrons/12 and Warders/527. There was shortage of staff in every rank in varied degrees. This shortage had to be made up on priority by taking up the matter with the Jail Department.

Problem of Overcrowding Jails

In all, there were about 7000 inmates in all the 11 jails of the state. These included 2300 convicts and 4700 undertrials. The authorized accommodation available was only for 5000 inmates. The overcrowding to the extent of 2000 inmates was beyond the seams of the available accommodation in every jail of the state.

Central Jail Hisar located in the heart of the city, over an area of 42 acres of land had too inadequate accommodation for the inmates lodged there. It involved huge expenditure to make the jail buildings worthy of reasonable living. To ease the problem of overcrowding, quite a few new barracks were required to be built. The best alternative was to shift the Jail from its present location to new premises outside the city. The land of its present location being in the heart of the city was worth several crores. Only a portion of the sale proceeds of the present sprawling land would meet the expenses of shifting of the jail outside the city, including the cost of the land and construction of the building at the new site.

District Jail Karnal built over an area of four and half acres of land was located in the heart of the city. An additional piece of land measuring over 5 acres was also attached with the jail for kitchen garden etc. Available accommodation was meant for only 200 inmates and against that over 350 inmates always remained lodged there. Here again the jail buildings required huge expenses for repairs and provision for additional new barracks. The Jail Department also owned about 23 acres of land at village Naval on Kunjpura Road, 6 km away from the existing jail location. Further, Jail Department also owned roughly 200 acres of land on Kaithal Road, about 8 km away from Karnal Municipal limits. Out of this, 75 acres of land were under forest and the remaining about 125 acres were under cultivation, under the direct supervision of local jail authorities. This huge area of about 200 acres of land could be utilized for locating new district jail buildings including an Open Air Jail, in tune with the modern concept. The sale proceeds of roughly 10 acres of land under the jail buildings etc and 22 acres of land situated on Kunjpura Road, also belonging to the Jail Department, could yield funds much more than required for building the new jail together with an Open Air Jail over the roughly 200 acres of land, lying on Kaithal Road.

Districts Jail Sirsa was housed in an old dilapidated fort, which was absolutely unfit and dangerous for human habitation. It could accommodate a maximum of 70 inmates. Against this 250 to 300 inmates remained lodged there. This heavy overcrowding was adding woefully to the miseries of the inmates, particularly with regard to hygiene sanitation and general environment. A new jail building was under construction over an area of about 20 acres of land with accommodation provision for a little over 200 inmates. The pace with which the construction of the new jail buildings was going on, it appeared to me that not less than one decade would be taken for its completion. As I could visualize, the new jail buildings would be inadequate by the time these were completed.

Either new buildings for District Jails at Kurukshetra, Jind and Sonepat were under construction or the government had approved their construction plans. As per the sanctioned plans, the barrack accommodation for these three district Jails seemed to me inadequate to meet the requirements in the coming years.

Central Jail Ambala had authorized the available accommodation only for 1000 inmates whereas 1500 inmates, on an average were always lodged there. There was an urgent need to provide additional barracks to ease the problem of overcrowding. A farmland available with this Jail had been taken over by Haryana Urban Development Authority (HUDA). It must have yielded huge revenue to the State Exchequer. Still additional barracks to cope with the overcrowding problem squarely, were not provided.

District Jail Gurgaon had accommodation only for 120 inmates against which roughly 400 to 450 inmates remained lodged there. To meet the increasing requirements of Southern Districts of Haryana, there was an urgent need to have new buildings for locating Central Jail at Gurgaon, at an appropriate place away from the centre of this fast developing city. In Gurgaon also, a big chunk of land belonging to the Jail Department had been handed over to HUDA, yielding huge revenue to the State Exchequer.

The general maintenance and cleanliness of the jail buildings all over the state was rather poor. The most pathetic sights in these jails were the toilet blocks, which were woefully lacking in, even an average standard of sanitation. Hygiene and sanitation were the casualties mainly for lack of adequate supply of water.

Medical Facilities in Jails

There was no regular cadre of medical staff in the Jail Department. Medical staff used to come on posting from Health Department on deputation basis, which was a satisfactory system. It was generally seen that the provision of medical staff in every jail was inadequate. On various occasions, even the sanctioned staff was not provided in full strength. A good number of inmates were daily referred to Medical College Rohtak and Civil Hospital at District Hqrs. Police escorts were not readily available; the delay adversely affected the patient's health. Regarding the provision of medicine the indents placed by the local jail authorities would generally mature very late and often with heavy cuts. The aged and sick convicts, particularly those suffering from terminal diseases like cancer, aids etc needed to be treated with humane touch, for prematurely releasing them, in tune with the concept of a welfare state.

Provision of Food and related Problems

Total ration provided per head to the jail inmates was quite adequate. However, the timings of serving food, system of cooking and provision of certain items in the menu needed changes. Improvement in this regard was ensured by me by making internal arrangements in consultation with the Jail Superintendents. However, I found that cooks were drawn from amongst the inmates. The entire cooking was being done in every jail centrally, in one cooking house. This was very unsatisfactory arrangement. There was need for having more than one cooking house, depending upon the number of inmates. Further, there seemed the necessity of providing for every cooking unit, a trained cook, employed on regular basis at government expenses, to organize the cooking operations with the help of cooks drawn from amongst the inmates. Cooking was done on fuel wood, an unhygienic and anti-environment practice. There was an urgent need to switch over from the fuel wood to the cooking gas.

Necessity for Imparting Vocational Training and Provision for Handsome Wages

An innovative programme for improving the living conditions of the jail inmates needed to be devised. A huge army of inmates remained generally idle. It was sheer wastage of work force. No developing state can afford to allow holiday to any citizen much less to a convicted criminal. By properly exploiting and developing human resources, available as inmates in the jails, spectacular results could be achieved. The educated convicts, who had studied upto and beyond matriculation could be given vocational training by setting branches of Government Industrial Training Institutes (ITIs) within the Central Jails at Ambala and Hisar, for training in the vocations like repair of radios, TVs, air conditioners, refrigerators, two-wheelers, electrical gadgets, electrical fitting works, tailoring and carpentry etc. Those completing successfully the laid down training programme could be awarded certificates at par with that of ITIs. Depending upon their good conduct, such trained convicts could be allowed to pursue their vocations on call from the public on normal wages, during the day. Idleness rusts both body and mind, apart from making it a den of evil thoughts, true to the saying, " An empty mind is a devil's workshop".

Provision for Entertainment Facilities

The factors like idleness, overcrowding, unhygienic conditions and total isolation from the families, cumulatively breed irritation, frustration and cynicism, leading to volatile temper, I thought it to be an urgent requirement to provide plenty of opportunities to the jail inmates with opportunities to smile, to laugh, to giggle and mentally relax. Therefore, various measures to kill idleness had to be thought out. Adequate facilities for recreation and entertainment in the nature of colored TV in every barrack, public address system with cassette player, centrally operated to play both 'devotional and film' songs at different timings, indoor games like carom boards, chess, snake ladder and sports like volleyball, badminton, basketball etc. Even provision for screening periodically entertaining, informative and educative movies, under arrangements of state's Public Relations Department was considered the need of the time. The inmates needed to be encouraged to hold cultural programme devised by the inmates themselves, with sprinkling of professional male artist here and there, provided by the Public Relations Department.

Proposals submitted to the State Government

I personally tried my best to meet many of the above requirements from within the resources available to me, with the assistance of Jail Superintendents. Inter Jail Competitions in the sports as kabaddi, basketball and volleyball were organized in the Central Jail Ambala. To break the invisible glass ceiling that civilian women should not be taken inside the jail, I took my wife and daughter and invited some senior female government functionaries at the District Hqr to witness the sports competitions amongst the jail inmates. Things did improve considerably but only to a limited extent. I prepared a detailed note highlighting the above problems and the measures required to be taken at the government level. It was specifically pointing out that there could not be any legitimate plea of financial constraints at the state government level as the Jail Department land already handed over to HUDA and various pieces of land could still be auctioned in the market to generate huge funds to the state exchequer. I handed over a copy each of my note to the Chief Minister and the Minister holding the portfolio of Jail Department and discussed with them the details. They appreciated my ideas and the efforts to improve the system. However, the Minister holding the jails portfolio was somewhat evasive for pursuing my proposals involving huge funds on the constructions of new jails. His argument was that the General Elections to the State Assembly were due in June 1987 and the opposition parties would exploit to their advantage that the Jail Minister was wasting funds for constructing new jails instead of pursuing developmental programmes for the common person.

Award of President Police Medal for Distinguished Service

In early January 1987, the Bansi Lal government once again recommended my name to the Government of India for the Award of President's Police Medal for Distinguished Service on Republic Day 1987. I had earlier been awarded Police Medal for meritorious service on Independence Day 1977. The excerpts from the recommendation then made for the award of the said Medal are mentioned earlier. In addition to briefly repeating the crux of those recommendations, the excerpts from the additional recommendation of the Haryana government for the award of President's Police Medal for Distinguished Service are mentioned below.

- On his repatriation from Central deputation to Haryana state in October 1978, Shri Swan was posted at DIG Hisar Range. Under his able guidance and effective supervision, the Police was successful to maintain admirably law and order affairs in the Range. He was conveyed special appreciation of the Chief Minister Haryana vide DO letter dated 4th May 1979 for the outstanding work done by him ensuring foolproof police arrangements made for *Sammelans* held simultaneously by the Akalis and Nirankaris at Hisar on 14th April 1979.
- He was posted as DIG/HAP Madhuban in which capacity, he was found to be highly intelligent and willing to accept any responsibility, not only for the task entrusted to him but also for consequences of his actions.
- In August 1980 while posted as DIG Administration and Training, the State IGP found him to be highly intelligent, very methodical in his work, prompt in taking decisions and that too intelligently and proved to be an officer with lot of initiative accepting responsibility willingly and bravely; he was adjudged as an outstanding officer.
- In December 1982, his services were once again placed at the disposal of the Government of India for appointment as DIG/CISF of the newly created Western Zone at Bombay. He harnessed his vast experience with admirable dedication for organizing Zonal Headquarter.
- After his repatriation to Haryana state in early May 1985, he was posted as DIG Welfare and Rules. He appreciably organized the welfare machinery to make it more effective. His qualities of being highly conscientious, completely professional and thoroughly conversant with the Police working amply reflected from his being fully devoted to duty by producing, in a short spell, thoughtfully revised four important chapters of the police rules.
- In May 1985, he was posted as Inspector General of Police, Madhuban Police Complex, with assignments including command and control of HAP, State Police Training College and State Forensic Science Laboratory. With his valuable experience of men and matters and thoroughly objective and humane approach, he provided very good leadership, made significant contribution to control law and order situation arising out of extremists' threat. He amply displayed his flair for writing papers on subjects of professional interest and participating in various police seminars.

- Shri Swan was posted as State Police Chief on 5th July 1986 and later as DG Prisons. Throughout he exhibited qualities of leadership, razor sharp intellect, sincerity of purpose and devotion to duty of a very high order.

The President of India was pleased to award President's Police Medal for Distinguished Service to the Author on Republic Day 1987.

Criminal Activities by the Convicts

It was widely known that some incorrigible criminals serving different terms of sentence, lodged in the jails, would conspire to commit various type of crime with the overt or covert support of corrupt persons among the jail staff. A very close watch was required to be kept to thwart such evil plans. I told the Jail Superintendents and their Deputies in clear terms that they would be held squarely accountable and responsible if any instance came to my notice that any member of the jail staff was found aiding or abetting any convict in pursuing any such evil plan. In fact, I was thinking of setting up a wing of intelligence staff to keep close watch on the activities of notorious convicts in Central/District Jails. However, my tenure in the Jail Department was too short to plan and introduce such a surveillance system.

Chapter – 19

Second Tenure as State Police Chief

General Situation in the State

As the General Elections to the State Assembly were due to be held in June 1987, the state politics warmed up and all the political parties started their preparations as early as March 1987. At the time of Tosham Assembly by-election rigging had taken place openly. To counter effectively the rigging of coming General Elections of June 1987, Lok Dal led by Devi Lal raised his own *Sena* called 'Green Brigade' from amongst the hefty built young persons of his followers. During the various political meetings and rallies held by Lok Dal-BJP pre-poll alliance, the "Green Brigade" created lot of nuisance, disturbing the law and order situation in the state. With every new day, the stance of the said Alliance was getting more and more aggressive. As and when the state police resorted to strong-armed measures to tame the aggressive posture of the opposition parties particularly the "Green Brigade" boys, the later gained more and more strength. It appeared that for holding the General Elections peacefully, the state police would need to formulate their plans very meticulously. The Election Commission of India was monitoring day-to-day developments. Well before the polling day, adequate re-enforcement of the local police was made by deploying a few companies of CRPF.

As scheduled, the elections were held in third week of June 1987. The political rivals of the ruling group organized a parallel "force" to fight the mafia. The earlier beneficiary of this game played on 23rd November 1986, was administered a dose of their own medicine, at most of the constituencies. Out of 90 Assembly seats, the opposition parties together won 85 seats; merely 5 seats went into the kitty of the Congress Party. Chief Minister Bansi Lal had contested again from Tosham Assembly constituency. In the by-election of the November 1986, he got 98.17% of the valid polled votes from this constituency whereas in the General Elections of June 1987, he got only 30,361 votes out of the 65779 valid polled votes, which were merely 46.15%. He was badly trounced by Dharamvir, a Lok Dal winning candidate who got 32,547 valid votes. General Elections of June 1987 proved to be a serious setback to the Congress party in Haryana and it was a humiliating political waterloo for Bansi Lal. Devi Lal was the undisputed leader of opposition parties getting unparalleled mandate of the electorate to rule the state for next five years. He took oath of the office of the state Chief Minister in Haryana Bhawan, New Delhi on 20th June 1987.

Normally senior officers of all the departments attend the Chief Minister's oath taking ceremony. However, I could not attend the oath taking ceremony of Devi Lal as I reached Delhi half an hour late after the oath taking ceremony was over. The Governor was still in Haryana Bhawan. I called on him. He inquired why I was not seen during oath taking ceremony of the Chief Minister. I explained the reasons. K K Zutshi IPS, the DGP was also still there in the adjoining room. I met him and he told me that there was a strong rumour of my being posted as the State DGP. Devi Lal had felt exhausted because of intense touring undertaken by him during the electioneering. After the oath taking ceremony, he had gone to the Ram Manohar Lohia Hospital, New Delhi for general check up. I went to the said hospital to convey my congratulations to him for winning the General Elections with thumping majority and assuming the office of the Chief Minister. Sharad Pawar, a Janata Party leader and M L Jain IAS, Haryana State Home Secretary were waiting outside the room where Devi Lal was admitted. I apprised the aide of Devi Lal standing outside the room that I wanted to pay respects to the Chief Minister. I was immediately called in, while the other two bigwigs were still waiting for their turn to meet the CM. I paid my respectful compliments to him and inquired about his health. He bid me to sit down on the chair laid by his bed side and inquired, to my utter surprise, whether I had taken over the charge as State Director General of Police. I told him that I had not yet received any such orders. He told me to go back to Chandigarh and take charge. He then casually told me that the administration of Ramakrishan Hegde, Chief Minister of Karnataka was very popular with the masses and advised me to bring about improvements in the working of the Haryana state police like that of Hegde's government in Karnataka. After about five minutes stay with him, I took his leave saying that Sharad Pawar and Haryana State Home Secretary were waiting outside the room for meeting him.

From the hospital, I went again to the Haryana Bhawan. I met there Ranjit Singh son of Devi Lal. He had also been elected as MLA during the General Elections of June 1987. He told me "the Chief Minister is very fond of you and is thinking of posting you as State DGP but one thing is against you that you have the reputation of being pro-scheduled caste". His remarks startled me. I told him that my policy, throughout my police career, had been, to uphold the rule of law. If in the process, I have ever found injustice being done to any scheduled caste person I did intervene to ensure justice within the framework of law and I would continue doing this irrespective of the post held by me in future. He then backtracked from his earlier statement and told me "you are known as an efficient and bold officer and I do not mean to cast any aspersion on your capability". Thereafter we interacted for about 15 minutes in a very cordial and friendly atmosphere. On return to my residence at Chandigarh, my wife told me that there was a telephonic message that the Home Secretary wanted to talk to me. The Home Secretary was still at Delhi when I talked to him. He told me that the Chief Minister had approved my posting as State DGP and the necessary orders had since been issued and I should take charge of the new assignment at the earliest. I received the written orders on 22nd June 1987 and I assumed the charge of State DGP on the same evening. Thus, with my appointment as State DGP the invisible glass ceiling was broken for the first time in India after Independence, by an IPS officer from a scheduled caste with two coveted awards of Police Medal for Meritorious Service in August 1977 and President's Police Medal for Distinguished Service in January 1987.

In making appointments to the key posts of the administration, Devi Lal was seen trying to dispel the notion that he was a jat leader only. A S Bhatotia IPS, an *ahir* was posted as DIG/CID. Dr K V Singh, collateral of Devi Lal was appointed as his OSD a key assignment by all standards. L C Gupta IAS and MC Gupta IAS were appointed as State Chief Secretary and Home Secretary respectively. Naseem Ahmed, IAS was appointed as Principal Secretary to the CM– a prized post. Both M C Gupta and Naseem Ahmed were known as affable officer of roven efficiency and integrity. R D Rao, an ahir was appointed as Deputy Principal Secretary to the Chief Minister. S S Brar, IPS and K K Zutshi, IPS had been promoted to the rank of DGP along with my promotion vide order dated 29th October 1986 by the Bansi Lal government. Both Shri Brar and Shri Zutshi were reverted to the rank of IGP. Shri Brar continued as Chief of State Vigilance Bureau and Shri Zutshi was posted as OSD Police Rules, in the office of the State DGP. However, better sense soon prevailed and they both were restored to the rank of DGP by cancelling their reversion orders. M S Bawa IPS, who had been holding the post as OSD Police Rules, was posted as DG Prisons. In the Police Department, quite a few other changes were made at the district and range levels.

At the political level also, Devi Lal made very cautious move to dispel the jat leader notion, right from the distribution of party tickets in the just concluded General Elections. He had given only 24 tickets to jats and remaining to other castes including eight to Brahmins, five each to Sainis, Sikhs and Muslims and so on. While constituting his Cabinet, besides himself Devi Lal took only two jats, Virendar Singh as Irrigation and Power Minister and Prof. Sampat Singh as Home and Industries Minister. Banarasi Das Gupta was given the portfolio of Finance; he was later elevated as Deputy Chief Minister. Suraj Bhan from the BJP and K R Punia from the Lok Dal, both belonging to scheduled caste were given the portfolios of Revenue and Development & Panchayats respectively. The Chief Minister unofficially assigned the task of assisting him in the political affairs to his elder son Om Prakash Chautala and in administrative affairs to his younger son Ch Ranjit Singh.

Massacre of Innocent Humans by wayward Humans

The state government had hardly settled down to grapple with the administrative problems when a gruesome tragedy took place on 6th July 1987 at Lalru, a small town of district Patiala, Punjab, about 25 km away from

Chandigarh, on the highway to Ambala. In this ghastly tragedy, a Haryana Roadways bus was way-laid and 40 of the passengers travelling in this bus were killed by the terrorists in a flash attack. On 7th July, I spent the whole day in issuing instructions telephonically and through Tele Printer Message (TPM) on the wireless network, to the Range Deputy Inspectors General and District Superintendents of Police to take all precautionary measures to forestall any likely backlash by the Hindus against the Sikh minority community in the state. The senior police officers posted in the Haryana districts bordering Punjab, were also alerted and directed to remain on the guard by taking action on the ground to forestall a similar assault by the terrorists in their areas.

Late in the evening on that day, a similar alarming tragedy took place near village Daryapur, Police Station Fatehabad, district Hisar. A Haryana Roadways bus No HYN-6301 was on its way from Delhi to Sirsa. At about 8.00 pm it left bus stand Fatehabad for its onward journey toward Sirsa. When the bus was near village Daryapur, it was overtaken by an Ambassador car and stopped. Certain armed persons alleged to be terrorists, came out from the Ambassador car and fired at the passengers of the bus. As a result, some passengers were killed and some others sustained injuries. The driver of this bus, finding a chance, jumped out and thus escaped from suffering any gun shot injury. After the assailants left the scene, the bus driver returned and drove away the bus to Civil Hospital Fatehabad. In the meanwhile, another Haryana Roadways bus No HRT-5366, starting from Sirsa at 7.10 pm for Hisar, reached a spot known as *Ding Mod* where it was stopped by a jeep after overtaking it. Four armed persons from the said Jeep boarded the bus while two remained sitting in the jeep. Those four persons first looted the bus passengers of their jewellery and other valuable items and thereafter opened indiscriminate fire on them. As a result certain bus passengers were got killed while some others were injured.

During the firing resorted to by the assailants, one of their companions also received gun shot injuries. Thereafter they escaped from the spot, in another vehicle deserting the jeep there. The bus driver had suffered fatal gun shot injuries and the conductor too was amongst the injured. Zile Singh, one of the passengers who knew driving, brought the bus to Civil Hospital Fatehabad and from there he went to the Police Station Fatehabad and lodged the FIR. From amongst the passengers of both the buses, 34 passengers had died and 23 had suffered gun shot injuries.

The local police immediately came into action. District SP Hisar and DIG Hisar Range rushed to Fatehabad to take up the process of investigation. The panic-stricken senior officers overlooked inadvertently to inform me or anybody else at the State Hqr about this ghastly tragedy. Bhajan Lal the then Union Cabinet Minister at Delhi was informed telephonically about this ghastly tragedy at about 9.30 pm by somebody from Fatehabad. Bhajan Lal comes from that area and naturally has close network of his supporters to keep him informed about all incidents of significance. He talked to me on telephone from Delhi at about 10.00 pm. First, he congratulated me for my appointment as State DGP by the Devi Lal government and then quickly inquired about the details of Daryapur tragedy. I got stunned after listening from Bhajan Lal that 'dozens' of people travelling in two Haryana Roadways buses were killed by the terrorists near Fatehabad, a short while back. I immediately requested the district telephone manager to connect me to DIG Hisar Range, District SP Hisar and Police Station Fatehabad, on top priority. STD facility on the telephone was not available during those days. It was only the clerk of the Fatehabad Police Station, whom I could get on the telephone and got some sketchy details from him. All senior officers were stated to be busy in organizing treatment to the injured and for nabbing the culprits. I informed both DGP Punjab and Rajasthan states about this ghastly crime and requested them to alert the senior officers of their respective state districts, bordering Hisar district. Similar alert was sounded to the Superintendents of Police in all the Northern districts of Haryana. In the meanwhile, I had given information to the Chief Minister, the Chief Secretary and the Home Secretary, whatever was available to me by then, about this tragedy and the action, till then taken by me. I had also mentioned to the Chief Minister that information of this tragedy had been given to me, first in time, by Bhajan Lal only and it was later that with the assistance of district telephone manager that I could make contact with the police officials at Fatehabad. Bhajan Lal had rushed from Delhi to Hisar and had visited Fatehabad during the small hours of 8th July 1987.

Aftermath of Daryapur Tragedy

The news about this ghastly crime spread like wildfire. The Governor accompanied by the Chief Minister and Banarasi Das the Finance Minister, visited the scene of crime at Daryapur village and also interacted with the people at Fatehabad, Sirsa and Hisar cities. I had also accompanied them. The people in these cities were naturally very agitated, anguished and pained over these two ghastly incidents. Fatehabad, Hisar and Sirsa witnessed incidents of arson and looting. In Sirsa, 6 shops were set ablaze and 22 were ransacked. In Fatehabad 4 shops were burnt and 6 were looted. The enraged crowd killed one person of the Sikh community who had used his 0.12 bore gun to scare away the infuriated mob at Fatehabad. A number of incidents of arson and looting took place in Hisar. The places targeted by the mob included Shops/20, Residential Houses/09, Hotel/01, Cinema Hall/01, Trucks/07. A person from the Sikh community used his 0.12 bore gun to scare away the enraged mob. A young boy by the name Daya Ram from the scheduled caste was accidently killed by his gunshot. This infuriated the mob and the Sikh gunman was killed. Elsewhere in the city, another Sikh person was killed by the mob. In other districts of the state only stray incidents of stone pelting took place. In Yumunangar town of district Ambala, one Sikh person was killed. In Kalka town of district Ambala windowpanes of three Punjab Roadways buses were smashed. In Jhajjar town of district Rohtak three trucks driven by Sikh drivers, were set ablaze.

All the dignitaries visiting Sirsa, Fatehabad and Hisar made fervent appeal to the people at large in the state to maintain utmost communal harmony. They also had face-to-face talk with various respectable persons from both the Hindu and the Sikh communities. The Chief Minister announced ex-gratia grant of Rs. 20,000/- each to the next of the kins of the deceased persons, Rs. 10,000/- each to the seriously injured persons and Rs. 5,000/- each to other injured persons from amongst the victims of both Lalru (Punjab) and Daryapur (Haryana) tragedies. We had noticed that there was some laxity on the part of quite a few police personnel at Sirsa, Fatehabad and Hisar in taking timely action to avert the incidents of communal disharmony between the Hindus and the Sikhs, resulting in numerous incidents of arson and looting. Those police officials, who were prima facie, found guilty of not rising to the occasion to prevent the communal disharmony and incidents of arson and looting, were placed under suspension. Inspector Satbir Singh, SHO Police Station City Hisar had left the Police Station at 5 am on 8th July 1987 purportedly for making arrangements with regard to law and order situation in City Hisar and had returned to the Police Station on 11th July 1987 after spending about 80 hours continuously away from the Police Station. There were serious allegations against him that incidents of rioting, looting and arson happened right under his nose and in many cases he and the police party with him remained mute spectators. He was shifted from the post of SHO, PS City Hisar and posted to another district. Disciplinary action against him and the others placed under suspension was ordered.

The Chief Minister who was visibly very annoyed because of the laxity on the part of many officials, told me to take very stern action against the guilty ones. He was also very particular that the people who indulged in blatant arson and looting should be booked forthwith and looted property recovered. Red alert was sounded in the state and all available police resources were harnessed for the maintenance of communal harmony and adequate measures taken to forestall the recurrence of such incidents. Anti-social elements all over the state were either brought under close surveillance or rounded up. Buses plying as night service were provided armed escorts. All barriers on the highways, interior roads, particularly in the area bordering Punjab were activated. Village Defence Committees in the area bordering Punjab were strengthened by issuing weapons to them under the Village Defence Scheme. Mobile patrols were started all over the state dividing highways and the interior roads, into beats of 15 to 30 km. Anti-Riot Schemes were vigorously enforced in all the towns of Haryana. Night trains passing through Haryana were provided armed escorts and Railway Security Scheme was enforced providing adequate protection to the Railway tracks. Senior police officers from comparatively lesser important duties, were diverted to the law and order duties, which became our top most priority. Army Flag Marches were got staged in all the towns/cities considered to be communally sensitive. All the Ministers and senior political leaders of the ruling alliance and the senior officers of the civil/police administration visited the affected towns/cities to enforce and supervise arrangements to restore the confidence in the minority communities and to ensure that anti-social elements were strongly suppressed.

With regard to Daryapur episode, case FIR No.225 dated 07.07.1987 u/s 302, 307, 394, 341, 506, 120B, 148, 149 IPC and u/s 3/4/5/6 of the Terrorists and Disruptive Activities (Prevention) Act, 1985 and u/s 27/54/59 of the Arms Act, was registered. Regarding the various incidents of arson and looting, 7 criminal cases under various sections of the IPC were registered.

In addition, 3 cases of murder had also been registered. The local police at Hisar was heavily reinforced and all resources available in the Police Department were harnessed to effectively control the law and order situation and to restore the communal harmony. Roughly, 150 persons who were accused or suspected of indulging in rioting, arson and looting were booked. Some 131 victims were identified. They had reported the total loss of property worth Rs.1,21,20,000/- in arson and worth Rs. 90,56,000/- in looting. On police verifications, the property lost in arson was estimated worth Rs.1,13,03,000/- and looted property was estimated worth Rs.77,17,500/. The police was able to recover and restore to the rightful victims, property worth Rs. 22,26,800/-. Some of the persons booked by the police included some close relations and committed supporters of Bhajan Lal. Special measures were devised to haul up the culprits involved in this tragedy.

Politicization of Daryapur Tragedy

The Congress Party had ruled the state continuously from 29th June 1979 to 4th June 1986 with Bhajan Lal as the Chief Minister. Sensing that the popularity graph of the party was slipping down, the Congress High Command had replaced him by inducting Bansi Lal as the Chief Minister on 5th June 1986, hoping that he, with all his experience and dynamism, would salvage the party from the "morass". However, Bansi Lal failed to retrieve the situation and was very badly mauled in the General Elections held in June 1987, losing himself from his own Tosham constituency to a young Lok Dal candidate who was a new entrant in politics. The Congress Party as a whole could win only 5 seats and was thus badly humiliated by the Lok Dal-BJP alliance under the over all leadership of Devi Lal, which won 77 seats out of the total of 90. The information about the Daryapur Massacre trickled down to the state Headquarter, when Bhajan Lal talked to me at about 10.00 pm on the day of gruesome tragedy. Thereafter, he paid a flying visit to Hisar and Fatehabad. Within a few hours after the tragedy, the incidents of rioting, arson and looting took place. All these factors were construed by the politicians in the ruling group as if Bhajan Lal had prior knowledge about the blitzkrieg attack by the terrorists, resulting in massacre of 34 bus passengers. Conspiracy by the Congress Party spearheaded by Bhajan Lal to destabilize the Devi Lal government, became a political plank. Alarming stories of serious allegations against the Congress Party, in general and Bhajan Lal in particular, started appearing as headlines in the newspapers. Similarly, Press statements by Bhajan Lal refuting all such allegations and on the contrary blaming the Devi Lal government for utter failure, appeared in various newspapers. In this political game of allegations and counter allegations, I felt highly embarrassed when some persons very close to Devi Lal the Chief Minister, started suggesting to me that I should come out with a Press statement that the needle of suspicion was pointing at Bhajan Lal. However, I refused to toe their line. When I found undue pressure was being mounted on me, I explained to Devi Lal that the Police had not found any substantive evidence in support of any conspiracy or the hand of

Bhajan Lal. I felt relaxed when Devi Lal in his magnanimity told me that I should not bother about the political game being played and instead devotedly continue making efforts to ensure proper law and order situation in the state.

Restoration of Communal Harmony and Law and Order Situation

The entire police machinery in the state rose to the occasion and succeeded in restoring the law and order situation to complete normalcy within three days. The Range DIGs and all District Superintendents of Police in the state displayed commendable leadership qualities, particularly A S Bhatotia IPS, DIG/ CID worked very hard and made immensely commendable contribution in making anti-terrorist measures effective and result oriented. The burden on Shri Bhatotia was indeed very heavy. To give him some relief, M S Malik IPS, Director PTC was shifted from Madhuban to Chandigarh and was entrusted with the job concerning the entire terrorists' related problems, which was hitherto being supervised by Shri Bhatotia. There were a couple of instances of laxity on the part of some senior officers; these were odd aberrations. In due course, they were replaced with those known for dynamic leadership qualities. Lt General J S Arora, the "Hero" of Indo-Pak War of 1971, who had earned the distinction of forcing General Niazi of Pakistan Army to surrender before him at Dhaka (Bangladesh) with 90,000 troops had become a Member of Parliament and President of the Sikh Forum. He visited Hisar and Fatehabad on 16th July 1987 and talked to the victims who had suffered in the incidents of arson and looting in the wake of Daryapur tragedy. In his Press statement, he appreciated the speedy action taken by the Haryana Police in arresting the suspects, recovering of looted property and initiating disciplinary proceedings against police officials found guilty of inaction against the rioters. He was also very appreciative of the expeditious relief provided to the affected families by the state government. During his meeting with the Chief Minister, he expressed his gratitude to Devi Lal for his initiative in controlling the situation firmly and his personal commitment to preserve communal harmony in the State. On 12th July, five Akali Members of Parliament in a joint statement hailed the Haryana Chief Minister Devi Lal for taking prompt action against those responsible for attacking the Sikhs, following the massacre of bus passengers.

The Tribune Chandigarh dated 10th July 1987, a premier English Daily of the region, stated in the Editorial column, "A cautious sigh of relief is in order at the stoic way Haryana has conducted itself in the wake of gruesome bus killings. It has refused to be provoked into violence on the scale that the terrorists dearly hoped for and the few stray incidents of murder and arson – regrettable though they are – do not threaten to start or sustain a cycle of massacre leading to massacre. In this sense, the terrorist had failed in his most diabolical game of setting people against people, with himself providing the initial burst of deaths. Everyone in this region has reason to be doubly thankful that Haryana until now more or less a stranger to the ways of the men with the stenguns, has quickly pulled itself together and not succumbed to searing emotions as other regions did on other occasions. After the common person, the next to claim credit are the law and order machinery........"

The macabre tragedy of Daryapur massacre became almost a forgotten story at the Justice Delivery stage during early nineties. The police had pursued the investigation with admirable commitment but at prosecution stage that sense of commitment had completely disappeared and sheer callousness and negligence had taken over the earlier zeal. Seven accused persons were sent up for trial on 4th January 1991 in the court of MK Bansal, Sessions Judge acting as judge Designated Court Bhiwani. During the peak trial days, Bhajan Lal was the Chief Minister and his favourite IPS officer Kalyan Rudra was the State DGP. In all, 144 prosecution witnesses, including police personnel connected with the investigation, were examined in the Court. Civilian PWs, 38 in number, were very material to nail the accused persons. However, none of these 38 PWs supported the prosecution story and they totally resiled from their statements given before the investigating officers u/s 161 CrPC. Even those witnesses who had recorded their statements u/s 164 Cr PC before the Magistrate resiled while deposing before the trial court. The result had to be disastrous for the prosecution and the police. In the last para of the judgment delivered on 4th December 1992 the trial court remarked "In the present case though the crime is heinous and the accused are going unpunished but the court has to go by the evidence on the file. As in the present case there is no evidence on the file to connect the accused with the crime, so they are acquitted of the charges."

With the changed complex of the state administration, perhaps nobody bothered to follow the case during the trial. Sad development indeed!

State Police Priorities

There were many impending challenges before the state police. During the earlier Congress regime, majority of the non-gazetted officers (NGOs) and the constabulary were availing the patronage of Congress politicians and thus, compromising their sense of neutrality, which is a very basic and necessary quality for the government servants. Instances of malpractices and irregularities were galore. In the wake of Lalru and Daryapur tragedies the force was required to be toned up by arranging special training for the existing force, its reinforcement in number, making adequate provision for requisite weaponry, Gypsy jeeps, Motorbikes and updating communication system. Reshuffling of gazetted officers at all levels was also very necessary for the placement of the right person at the right place. I discussed all my plans, for effectively containing the monster of terrorism in the state, with the Chief Minister. He assured me that all my proposals would be considered with concern on priority. M C Gupta, IAS the new State Home Secretary was down to earth a practical man, very sober, cool headed and pragmatic in approach. He proved to be extremely helpful and keenly cooperative and anxious for bringing about improvements in the police machinery to enable it to face the emerging challenges effectively and successfully. For pursuing vigorously the investigation of the Daryapur massacre case, Special Investigation Cell was created under the overall command and supervision of M S Mallik IPS. His substantive posting was DIG Railways and Crime as well as Director of the Police Training College Madhuban. The Special Cell included SP Hisar, Raj Roop Singh Dy SP

Faridabad, Ram Kumar Dy SP from HAP, Rajpal Singh and Sumer Singh Inspectors CID, Inspector SHO Police Station Fatehabad and Inspector CIA Hisar. A few more specially selected non-gazetted officers and constabulary, as well as one trained commando platoon were provided to the Special Cell. Necessary arms and equipments including Gypsy jeeps, Motorbikes, Walkie-Talkie Wireless sets etc were placed at the disposal of the Special Cell. I personally oversaw the day-to-day progress made in the investigation of the case with a view to ensure that it was progressing on the right track.

In the small hours of 12th November 1987, a party from the Special Cell raided a terrorists' hide-out in district Faridkot, Punjab and nabbed a dreaded terrorist, believed to be involved in Daryapur tragedy. Based on his disclosure statement, another hideout of terrorists in Punjab was raided wherefrom two terrorists were nabbed. The interrogation of these three terrorists led to the recovery of a stolen jeep, one 9 mm sten machine carbine with two magazines and 110 rounds of ammunition and three 0.38 revolvers/pistols with 60 rounds of ammunition. During their interrogation these three terrorists not only narrated the details as to how Daryapur massacre was planned and executed, the arrest of their co-accused of Daryapur tragedy was also facilitated. The persons who harboured the dreaded terrorists and provided shelter to them were also booked. With the arrest of all the accused persons connected with Daryapur killings, not only the mystery of Daryapur tragedy was solved but many other barbarous acts of terrorism committed by them at different places in Punjab and Haryana states were solved. They also confessed their complicity in the commission of various robberies and dacoities in the states of Assam, Rajasthan, Maharashtra, Delhi and Haryana. Another hair rising revelation made by the terrorists was their harbouring unfathomable malice and grudge against Shiv Sena and the terrorists' elaborate plans to eliminate Hindus in large number, at different places of Punjab, Haryana and Delhi to foment communal disharmony.

Thanks to the excellent efforts put in by everyone drafted to the Special Investigation Cell, particularly the role played by MS Mallik, with dash and drive that the assailants in this dastardly tragedy were hauled up without much delay. Some police personnel on the Special Investigation Cell displayed commendable spirit of devotion and dedication to the duties assigned to them. They were richly rewarded. The role of Inspector Rajpal Singh was found to be extraordinarily commendable. He was recommended for appointment as a Probationary Dy SP. This recommendation was readily approved by the state government.

High Level Meeting at Delhi

The Union Home Secretary convened a high level meeting about two weeks after the Daryapur tragedy to review the law and order situation prevailing in Haryana state and the progress made towards nabbing the culprits. This meeting was attended by the Union Cabinet Secretary, Principal Secretary to the Prime Minister, Union Home Secretary, Director Intelligence Bureau, Haryana State Chief Secretary and myself as Haryana State DGP. Before leaving for Delhi, we had taken instructions in the matter from the Chief Minister. I had prepared a detailed note for the information of all the top officers participating in the said meeting, pertinently highlighting our requirements of additional work force from the Paramilitary Forces and also for the provision of sophisticated weaponry. During the discussion in the meeting, I strongly made a point that the response of the Union Home Ministry and the Chiefs of Paramilitary Forces had not been encouraging when SOS messages were made by both the State Chief Secretary and the State Home Secretary. Even my personal pleadings with the Special Home Secretary, an IPS officer overseeing the deployment of the Paramilitary Forces in the country, were all in vain. Intervening, the Union Cabinet Secretary said that the point made out by the State DGP was well taken but he should not get over excited. I strongly resented the remarks made by the Union Cabinet Secretary saying, "I am not excited much less overexcited. My deep concern is for meeting the emerging challenges resulting from the ghastly massacre of Haryana people, both at Lalru in Punjab and Daryapur in Haryana state on 6th and 7th July respectively. The general perception with the common man building up was that politics was coming in the way of the Union Government for quickly extending requisite helping hand to Haryana administration to squarely face the situation." The State Chief Secretary lending strong support to my viewpoint said that any recurrence of such horrible incidents would lead to acute communal disharmony and the safety of about 10 lakh Sikh community persons settled in Haryana State would be at stake. The discussion in the meeting generated some heat. However, the Principal Secretary to the Prime Minister intervened and assured that the Union Government would certainly meet the requirements of Haryana Police to the extent possible. In due course, work force from the Paramilitary Forces and supply of sophisticated weaponry started pouring in. There was no terrorist related incident for quite some time in the state.

Special Meeting of Senior Police Officers at Madhuban

Law and order situation in the state and the state of preparedness of the police force to meet the new challenges in the wake of spurt in the terrorist activities in and around the state, were required to be reviewed. For long-term measures to effectively meet the new challenges, I held a meeting of all Deputy Inspectors General, Superintendents of Police, including Commandants of HAP Bns at Police Complex Madhuban on 24th July 1987. On my request M C Gupta IAS, the State Home Secretary, not only remained present in the meeting throughout, he actively participated in the discussion and lucidly made very useful and encouraging suggestions. All the police officers present in the meeting spiritedly made out their viewpoints.

After thoroughly reviewing the law and order situation in the state, important decisions were taken to sort out various complex problems being faced by the police department.

I had associated the Home Secretary in this all-important meeting, so that he could appreciate, in the right perspective, the various difficulties and problems coming in the way of the police department in facing the challenging situations, emerging in the wake of terrorist activities, in the otherwise peaceful state of Haryana. The outcome of the meeting was, indeed, very encouraging. Not only all the police officers attending the meeting got admirably enthused to face the new challenges ahead, the state government was quick in according sanction to our various pending proposals, thanks to the personal interest taken by M C Gupta IAS, the State Home Secretary. The additional work force sanctioned by the government comprised four commando companies, Dy SPs/2, Inspectors/9, SIs/17, ASIs/17, HCs/56 and Consts/448.

Solar Eclipse Mela at Kurukshetra

The state police was still busy in devising, rehearsing and implementing all possible measures to check the reoccurrence of any ghastly crime like that of Lalru and Daryapur massacre when the Solar Eclipse Mela became due to be held on 23rd September 1987. Lakhs of devotees were expected to visit Kurukshetra to take a dip in the Holy Tanks there. In the wake of Daryapur tragedy, there was a strong apprehension that the terrorists might strike to achieve their evil motives of killing a large number of innocent devotees gathered at Kurukshetra. Even the use of an insignificant explosive like the firecrackers could result into a devastating tragedy by stampede out of sheer panic. Therefore, the need of the time was to make foolproof police arrangements to guard against all such eventualities. Much ahead of the scheduled day of Solar Eclipse, I thoroughly examined all the pros and cons of the problem with the assistance of G L Puri, Superintendent of Police, district Kurukshetra. This district had been created in January 1973 by bifurcating Karnal district. The new district then had three sub-divisions; Guhla, Kaithal and Pehowa, with Ladwa, Shahabad, Guhla, Kaithal and Kurukshetra as the main towns.

Kurukshetra is a place of great historical and religious importance, revered all over the country for its association with epic *Battle of Mahabharata* during which Lord Krishna preached his philosophy of *Karma* as enshrined in the *Bhagwad-Gita.* It has a large number of holy places, temples and tanks associated with the ancient Indian traditions and the "*Mahabharata War*". Apart from 27 religious places of Hindus in and around Kurukshetra, there are five religious places of the Sikhs also. Typical religious places of Hindus include *Brahma Sarovar* of the size of 1220 meter X 609 meter, *Sannhit* which is nearly 472 meter long and 137 meter wide, *Jyotisar* about 8 km from Kurukshetra, on Pehowa road with its length of 394 meter and 197 meter width. The religious places of the Sikhs include *Gurudwara 9th Patshahi, Rajghat Gurudwara, Manji Sahib Gurudwara* located at Kaithal and *Gurudwara 6th Patshahi.* Large number of devotees visits all these religious places on various festivals.

Geographically, district Kurukshetra has very long common border with Punjab state. Guhla sub-division, comprising Police Stations Guhla, Pehowa and Thaska Neeranji shared nearly 80 km long border with district Patiala of Punjab State with Ghaggar River in between, which was easily crossable throughout the year except the monsoon months. Small pockets of area of both district Patiala and district Kurukshetra fall across Ghaggar River, at some places. It was therefore, very easy for anybody to enter district Kurukshetra through any of these routes from Punjab. Most of the villages of Guhla sub-division and partly of Kaithal sub-division were inhabited by Sikhs settlers. Police Stations Guhla, Pehowa, Thaska Neeranji and Sadar Kaithal had about 270 villages with 1700 Sikh *Dhanis* (Cluster of a few farmhouses). The crime profile of district Kurukshetra, revealed that during the period from May 1985 to December 1986, 15 criminal cases had been registered, one each u/s 302 IPC and Explosive Act and the remaining 13 u/s 3/4 Terrorists and Disruptive Activities (Prevention) Act 1985, at various Police Stations of the district. Nine such cases were registered at Police Station Pehowa only.

In the context of the above stated background and in the wake of Daryapur massacre of 7th July by the terrorists, Kurukshetra's vulnerability to the terrorists' attack on the occasion of Solar Eclipse *Mela* appeared to be very imminent. This *Mela*, the first big fair being held at Kurukshetra, an internationally known religious place of Hindus, since terrorism raised its ugly head in a big way in this part of our country, was an acid test for the Haryana Police of their efficiency and competency to handle the situation ensuring trouble free state of affairs. To ensure that no person entering Kurukshetra on Solar Eclipse *Mela* day carried any thing, which could ignite any trouble was really an uphill task. The complexity of the problem was compounded as numerous *Sadhus* from different *Akhara*s were to take out their processions and various god-men of different standings were to come for holy dip and their followers to throng for their *Darshan*. Detailed arrangements were drawn up in collaboration with various civil departments and a large police work force was mobilized to ensure the smooth flow of the devotees from one to another religious place. The entire 80 km long border of Kurukshetra district with Punjab was sealed. Day and night surveillance in all the villages bordering Punjab, inhabited by the Sikh population, particularly various *Dhanis* was intensified. Accompanied by SP Kurukshetra, I visited various villages and *Dhanis* inhabited by the Sikh population and interacted with them, with a view to seek their cooperation. My knowledge of Sikh Guru's *Bani,*particularly *Japuji Sahib*, committed to my memory from the school days, stood me in good stead in establishing close rapport with elderly persons from Sikh community. Many of them voluntarily came forward to extend every possible help and assured me that they would discourage even their close relations residing on the other side of the border, to visit them during the *Mela* days. I must thankfully place on record my gratitude that numerous Sikhs of the area spiritedly extended their helping hand in the matter.

Devotees from different parts of the country, attired in their traditional colourful dresses started pouring in droves about a week ahead of the Solar Eclipse *Mela* day. The entire 50 sq km area of the *Mela* ground was roughly divided into 8 self-contained sectors with a strong police post in each sector. Ram Rachpal Singh IPS (1961-RR), an Inspector General of Police was put on police *Bandobast* duty as *Mela* incharge with Raj Kumar, DIG as second in command. Besides 70 officers of the rank of SP, ASP and DSP, 1200 non-gazetted Officers and 1000 head constables and constables, mostly in uniform and some according to duty requirements in plain clothes, were detailed for *Mela* duty. 1474 police recruits/trainees including 526 from Haryana and 848 from Himachal Pradesh, attending various courses at Police Training College Madhuban, were also detailed on *Mela* duty. Seven watchtowers manned by National Security Guards with snipers, equipped with high-powered binoculars, were set up. Close-circuit television sets were installed to monitor traffic and crime. Strong barricades were erected leaving no room for stampede. Mobile Armed Police contingents were put on duty for constantly patrolling the entire periphery of Kurukshetra city. Reinforcements from the Central Reserve Police Force, Border Security Force and Armed Police of Maharashtra and Madhya Pradesh had also been pressed into *Mela* duty. Police was fully equipped with wireless sets where necessary. Both AS Bhatotia DIG/CID and MS Mallik DIG Anti-extremists Cell were kept free of any specific *Mela* duty, so that they could closely follow their own respective areas of operations which required utmost caution and commitment in the context of keeping the *Mela* free from the devilish eyes of anti-social elements, the extremists in particular. They did exceedingly well in their respective area of responsibilities. Adequate arrangements were made to detect explosives by providing "hand detectors" for use extensively by the police parties. A helicopter was kept handy. I used this facility to oversee the over all arrangements and issue instructions where necessary. The Chief Minister also flew over the *Mela* area on about half a dozen occasions. It was ensured that the flow of the devotees from one religious place to the other was unhindered.

About 15 lakhs of devotees took a dip in the holy tanks on the Solar Eclipse on 23rd September 1987 morning. The devotees in large number covered over a 10 km distance on foot to reach *Sannhit Tanks* and *Brahma Sarovar*. Continuous singing of devotional songs and chanting hymns by the devotees till they had a dip, rented the sky. Jagadguru Swaroopanandji Shankaracharya of *Dwarkapeeth*, at the head of a procession of about one lakh *Sadhus* took the dip in the *Brahma Sarovar* at 9.00 am. *Sadhus* also performed a ceremony after the Eclipse to "wash away its evil effects". Although several prominent religious and political leaders attended the *Mela*, the star attraction was controversial god-man Chandra Swami, who along with Devi Lal the Chief Minister, washed his hands and face in the *Sarovar* and performed a special *Puja* for the well being of the Chief Minister. Among the colleagues of Devi Lal, who took the dip were, Banarasi Das Gupta, Suraj Bhan, Ram Bilas Sharma, OP Bhardwaj, Dr Kamla Verma, Dharamvir, Balbir Singh Saini and Nar Singh Dhanda.

A Central Broadcasting Centre (CBC) was set up by the Public Relations Department. About 10,000 devotees who lost link with their near and dear ones or fellow-devotees, were announced as missing. CBC helped to re-establish their mutual links. While 200 children, who were separated from their parents, were restored to their guardians without much delay, 25 remained missing for over 24 hours. Out of about 100 valuable items reported to be missing, 60 were restored to the owners. A rumour, which was in fact a hoax, that a bomb had been planted at the local Railway Station, created a lot of panic and the devotees tried to run helter-skelter. However, the presence of the Police in strength and repeated announcements from the CBC instilled a sense of confidence among the devotees and normalcy was quickly restored. Most of the devotees started melting away for return to their homes, on 24th morning, but a large number of *Sadhus* stayed back to take part in a nine-day *Mahachandi Yajna* being organized by Chandra Swami from the day following the Solar Eclipse.

All police officers and policemen connected with the *Mela Bandobast* performed their respective duties devotedly except a few aberrations here and there. The role of RR Singh, IGP as overall incharge and Raj Kumar DIG as second in command was exceptionally commendable. As the *Mela* passed off free from any major incident, the Chief Minister publicly applauded the police *Bandobast*. Appreciations in each deserving case were conveyed to the officers and rewards were liberally sanctioned to the deserving policemen. The Chief Minister personally conveyed his fulsome praise to me for peaceful passing of the Solar Eclipse fair. MC Gupta, Financial Commissioner and Secretary to Government, Haryana Home Department, conveyed to me vide his DO letter dated 20th November 1987, Haryana government's appreciation. "My dear Swan Sahib, government have appreciated the excellent law and order arrangements made by the Haryana police under your guidance and supervision on the occasion of the Solar Eclipse at Kurukshetra on the 23rd September 1987. I am desired to convey government's appreciation to you for the efforts made by you in this behalf".

Chandra Swami and launching of Second "Nyay-Yudh" by Devi Lal

High-flying, tall, portly, bearded, self-styled god-man, then 38 years old Chandra Swami was under the scanner of the officials of Directorate of Enforcement. Custom officials at Madras Airport searched the Swami and four of his disciples on 19th September 1987 evening, after they had arrived from Singapore on an Indian Airlines Flight. He had returned to India after spending six months abroad, during which he visited Nepal, Italy, Austria, Denmark, Sweden, Sierra, Brazil, France, Britain, Spain, Switzerland and Singapore. The Swami was asked to appear at the Enforcement Directorate office on 21st Scptember 1987, where he was interrogated for clues in connection with the *Bofors* scandal. In the meanwhile, he was granted anticipatory bail by the Delhi High Court on 21st September 1987. He had been directed by the Directorate of Enforcement to appear again on 6th October 1987. He reached Kurukshetra on 22nd September 1987 and was extended VIP treatment on his arrival at Karnal Airport, where he was received by the Chief Minister and some members of the State Cabinet. At Kurukshetra, before taking a holy dip in *Brahma Sarovar*, he took a full round of the Sarovar along with the Chief Minister. He also took an aerial view of Kurukshetra city with the Chief Minister. He was a star among quite a few other god-men gathered in the afternoon where he announced the start of a nine-day *Yajna* to exorcise the evil of corruption, during which period he would observe *maun vrat* (vow of silence) barring two hours in the evening and his diet would be only honey and water. Devi Lal, the Chief Minister of Haryana proclaimed, in the gathering of the *Sadhus* that he launched his earlier "Nyay-Yudh" from Kurukshetra and swept the polls. Now with the help of numerous saints in the country including Chandra Swami, he was launching his "Nyay-Yudh" against the Central Government from the same historic Battle Ground of Kurukshetra. In fact this proclamation made by Devi Lal was an interlude to a Non-Left opposition parties to launch stir against the Central Government for which a meeting at Surajkund (Haryana) was already fixed to be held on 23rd September 1987.

Ten political parties and Congress (I) rebels were represented by about thirty top leaders with the significant absence of Left parties. Political parties, which were represented included Lok Dal (B), Telugu Desam, Bharatiya Janata Party, Congress (S), Assam Gana Parishad, Akali Dal (Badal), DMK, National Samajwadi Congress and Nagaland National Party. The participating leaders included Devi Lal, NT Rama Rao, LK Advani, Atal Behari Vajpayee, Chandra Shekhar, RK Hegde, Madhu Dandavate, Biju Patnaik, VP Singh, Arun Nehru, Aarif Mohammad Khan, Mufti Mohd Sayeed, HN Bahuguna, Karpuri Thakur, Sharad Yadav, SS Mahapatra, K Manoharan and Shaminder Singh. However, Devi Lal and N T Rama Rao were the star speakers. The conclave concluded after all the leaders unanimously resolved that a national JP-type movement should be started for the ouster of the Rajiv Gandhi Government at the Centre. The issues which were taken up included national unity, communal harmony, corruption, electoral reforms, inflation, unemployment, Centre-State relations, decentralization of power and workers' participation in management.

On the eve of conclave day Rameshwar Singh, a former MP and Vice President of Lok Dal had given vent to his antagonism against Devi Lal, by holding a Press statement, which sent shock waves down to the grass root workers of Lok Dal in Haryana State. He levelled nepotism charge against Devi Lal for giving key positions in the Haryana government to his sons and near relations. Devi Lal's eldest son Om Prakash Chautala was the President of the Haryana Lok Dal as well as member of the Rajya Sabha. His second son Ranjit Singh was an MLA and his third son Pratap Singh was made Chairperson of the Haryana Social Welfare Board. His nephew Dr K V Singh was assigned all-important duty as OSD to CM. His son-in-law Atamjit Singh Nehra was made Advocate General and many more near relations were made to occupy high offices in the state. This criticism of Devi Lal by his own Party's National Vice President did not augur well in the context of his initiative to hold high level all-party-conclave, targeting the Congress government at the Centre for its deficient governance.

While the devotees at Kurukshetra had just started returning to their homes by and by and their peaceful dispersal had to be ensured, I had on my hands another important task to ensure proper security arrangements at the venue of the conclave of the leaders of opposition parties at Surajkund. Therefore, I had to make hurried trips between Kurukshetra and Surajkund. I heaved a sigh of relief on the peaceful conclusion of the said conclave.

Revamping Police Administration in the State

The state police had faced two serious challenges soon after my taking over as State DGP. Firstly, the terrorists killed mercilessly the passengers of Haryana Roadways buses at Lalru (Punjab) and Daryapur (Haryana) in early July 1987. These tragic incidents had sent shock waves in the entire country and had generated lot of public resentment. The state police however, faced the challenge with courage and fortitude. Secondly, the Solar Eclipse held at Kurukshetra within a little over two months of the Lalru/Daryapur tragedies, posed a challenge of its own kind. The Solar Eclipse *Mela* passed off peacefully without any major incident. After successfully grappling with these two challenges, there was opportune time for me to revamp the police administration in the state to curb the evil of corrupt practices and dishonest dealings in the police department. I had earlier issued instructions to the field officers on 14th September 1987 wherein emphasis was laid on identifying the police personnel who were either known corrupt or suspected to be corrupt, so that they could be removed from the posts where they had greater chances of indulging in dishonest practices. Lists of such officers were still in the process of being finalized, when I called a meeting of senior police officers at Mdhuban on 11th October 1987 to find out ways and means, to firmly suppress the evil of malpractices and dishonest dealings in the police department, in the context of various legal safeguards already available.

The general consensus was that the supervision by the gazetted officers over the working of Police Stations' staff in their capacity as supervisory officers, if effectively exercised by ensuring the strict compliance of the laid down procedure, the evil of corrupt practices and dishonest dealings could be considerably curbed. Accordingly, I issued the standing order no. 46/1987 (Annexure-3) pinpointing the common underhand methods resorted to by the corrupt police personnel, in throttling the legal provisions and the measures to be strictly adopted to tame such wayward policemen.

The District SPs had earlier been asked in mid September 1987 to prepare the lists of notoriously corrupt and suspected to be corrupt police personnel. Such lists were prepared and finalized at the level of the Range DIGs. Strict orders were conveyed to the District SPs not to deploy such persons in the Police Stations and on other duties, which facilitated easy opportunity for indulging in corruption and malpractices. The District SPs and the Range DIGs were instructed to tighten up their supervision by frequent surprise visits to the Police Stations and the traffic staff. The Dy SPs are the cutting edge of the supervisory level. They were told that if their subordinates continued to indulge in the malpractices of any nature, the presumption would be that they either were lazy, negligent, callous, incapable, and incompetent or down right in league with the corrupt subordinates. Neither of these positions would be tolerated and any of them falling under any of these categories would expose himself to the charge of failure in maintaining integrity, commitment and devotion to duty.

The said DGP's standing order, attracted wide attention of the media. It earned deep appreciation of the public at large. The media highlighted, very prominently all the measures mentioned in the standing order to check the corruption. For many days, during the month of October 1987, different newspapers like *The Tribune* Chandigarh, *Indian Express* Chandigarh, *Punjabi Tribune* Chandigarh, Hindi *Jan Satta* and Hindi *Nav Bharat Times* Delhi continued highlighting the contents of the said standing order. It helped a lot in improving the quality of police working at the police station level and bolstering the image of the state police at large, in the eyes of public.

Controversy in the Management of Gurudwara Sahib–Sinister Role of Anti-Social Elements

Gurudwara Nada Sahib, a historically famous Sikh shrine is situated on the bank of Ghaggar River at the foothills of Shivaliks, on the Panchkula-Barwala Road, about 3 km from City Centre Panchkula. This Gurudwara dates back to 17th century. Legend goes that Guru Gobind Singh together with his warrior followers halted here while travelling from Paonta Sahib to Anandpur Sahib. During their stay, a farmer and follower, by the name Bhai Nadu Shah extended admirable hospitality to Guru Gobind Singh and the accompanying warriors. In appreciation, the Guru named the shrine as Gurudawara Nada Sahib.

About 130 persons representing various panchayats of the area submitted a representation dated 19th December 1987 to the Chief Minister. They alleged that the management of the Gurudwara had been forcibly taken over by some persons having close links with Punjab terrorists and huge money collected in the Gurudwara as 'offerings' from the devotees, was being fraudulently siphoned off for their personal use. The Chief Minister asked me to hold in-depth inquiry in the matter and submit report to him early. We in the police department were also lately much concerned as the intelligence reports revealed that anti-social and undesirable elements had established their base at this Gurudwara. Detailed inquiry made startling revealation.

During the investigation of Lalru Tragedy in which 45 passengers travelling in Haryana Roadways bus were massacred on 6th July 1987, dubious role of Harkirat Singh and Kala Singh who were holding the management of Gurudwara Nada Sahib for quite some time past was discovered. Then it became known that Kala Singh had been killed by Punjab police in an encounter and Harkirat Singh went behind bars in Punjab. In the absence of Harkirat Singh and Kala Singh, the former's father Daya Singh had taken over the management of Gurudwara Nada Sahib. He went underground after his son Harkirat Singh was arrested by the Punjab police, in a terrorists' related case. Baba Santa Singh Nihang at this stage usurped the management of the Gurudwara and appointed Mohan Singh as the sole manager of Gurudwara. However, within a week Gurmeet Singh Nihang who once used to be an associate of Harkirat Singh forcibly entered into the Gurudwara in August 1987 and took over the management with the support of a few shady characters. The whole kitty of "offerings" made at the Gurudwara by the devotees, used to be distributed amongst themselves, leaving some money for passing on to the terrorists. They had the patronage of a top Akali Dal leader of Punjab who had been released from the detention a few days earlier. The said Akali Dal leader had talked to me on telephone on a few occasions recommending some favours to be done to those people. I had to tell him plainly that those persons had close links with the Punjab terrorists and posed a potential threat to law and order in Haryana State and he should not entertain them at all. I had brought this fact to the notice of Devi Lal with whom the said Akali Dal leader was believed to have friendly relations.

According to Intelligence Reports, they contacted some hardened terrorists at Gurudwara Harmandir Sahib Amritsar on 9th March 1988 and cooked up cock and bull stories that Haryana police had committed atrocities on the Sikhs during the investigation of Daryapur episode of 7th July 1987. The Intelligence Reports further revealed that Gurmeet Singh was able to enlist the support of many terrorists and planned to intensify terrorists' activities for targeting the Haryana police officers and their family members. In view of such alarming Intelligence Reports, we carefully devised our action plan and forcefully implemented it to neutralize such evil designs of the Punjab terrorists. Details as above were brought to the notice of DGP Punjab, IGP UT Chandigarh and Joint Director Intelligence Bureau based at Chandigarh, through the letter dated 19th April 1988.

The complex of this historic Gurudwara has completely changed after it was taken over by the Shiromani Gurudwara Prabandhak Committee Amritsar. New constructions have come up with a happy blend of tradition and modernism at this Gurudwara and recitation of hymns from "Guru Granth Sahib" goes on from 4 am to 9 pm. Grand chandeliers adorn this space where devotees come from far and wide. Lakhs of devotees visit Nada Sahib Gurudwara on the full moon day (Pooranmashi) of every month.

Democracy taken for a ride in the State

While we in the police department were mobilizing all our resources to the maximum to provide protection to the people against the evil designs of the terrorists, the street politicians in the state were indulging in cheap politicking, to promote their own stakes. The genesis of the problem traced to the two overambitious sons of Devi Lal who were engaged in the intense battle for succession, even before Devi Lal became the Chief Minister in June 1987. It was as if both of them were individually planning for their father's political demise, even during his lifetime. The battle had begun with ticket distribution for the Assembly Elections slated for June 1987. In the selection of candidates, Devi Lal depended largely on his elder son, who was not only a good political organizer but had also emerged as the most vocal opponent of Ajit Singh son of Charan Singh from Uttar Pradesh who happened to have a short stint as Prime Minister of India. Ajit Singh was keen to acquire strong foothold in Haryana. Devi Lal's sudden illness immediately after the June Assembly Elections also helped the emergence of his two sons as the most important mediators between him and the party. Until then everyone had prospered in the shadow of Devi Lal's patronage. However, suddenly his two sons became the "power brokers". They were seen as green horns or leaders-in-waiting, whose advice the ailing patriarch heeded. It also seemed that the political ambitions of elder son were fuelled by the fact that HN Bahuguna, the then National President of Lok Dal openly expressed that he would be the fittest person to head the State Unit of the party.

As stated earlier, Devi Lal had proclaimed the second "Nyay-Yudh" from Kurukshetra at the time of September 1987 Solar Eclipse *Mela* and had organized a conclave of prominent leaders of non-Left opposition parties at Surajkund. Barely, within a few months of his new government coming into power in the state, Devi Lal had set his eyes on National Politics while his two sons had a field day in the state. They emerged as leaders of two extremely powerful factions. A young educated jat leader holding the prized portfolios in the Cabinet was a close confidante of the Chief Minister. This Cabinet Minister emerged as chief advisor of the Chief Minister's elder son, who with the assistance of the said Minister gained the support of the Chairmen of 28 out of 34 state government Boards and Corporations besides consolidating his hold on the bureaucracy and the police in five crucial districts – Jind, Hisar, Bhiwani, Rohtak and Sonepat – by manipulating administrative appointments. On the other hand, younger son was believed to have won the support of 18 out of 23 Ministers as well as the allegiance of District Magistrates and senior police officers in the remaining several districts. On the top, he had the support of Virendra Singh Narnaud, the then Irrigation & Power Minister, who was at one time Devi Lal's right hand man and held the prestigious Home Portfolio in the previous Devi Lal government of 1977. The younger son also counted among his advisors, Ran Singh Mann, the one time office secretary of the Haryana Sangharsh Samiti and the Chief Parliamentary Secretary to the Chief Minister. He also had the support of Banarasi Das Gupta who had by then been elevated as Deputy Chief Minister and Kirpa Ram Punia, bureaucrat turned politician, holding the portfolios of Minister for Agriculture and Technical Education. Shri Punia had earlier also held the portfolio of Scheduled Caste Welfare Department. He was divested of this important portfolio at the behest of elder son of the Chief Minister.

In his interview given to *Daily Hindustan* New Delhi (Hindi Edition) dated 8th January 1988 Gulab Singh Jain, Co-ordinator of Haryana Chamber of Commerce, a wing of Lok Dal (B) had alleged that Banarasi Das Gupta, Virendra Singh Narnaud, KR Punia and Ran Singh Mann, were misleading the Chief Minister with sinister designs. Khurshid Ahmed, Subhash Katyal, Narbir Singh and Narsingh Dhanda were the other Cabinet Ministers backing younger son. In this game of one upmanship, both the brothers were quite often at loggerheads when it came to distribution of spoils of office. But the group of elder son became much more powerful than that of his brother. The intelligence reports reaching me revealed that in this "war of succession" some people holding prestigious positions in the government were playing dirty role. It may ruffle a few feathers by knowing that the game plan of Virendra Singh Narnaud was, indeed, very subtle; in that, younger son of Chief Minister was to succeed his father Devi Lal as Chief Minister of the state in the first instance and then in due course to be pulled down by installing himself as the Chief Minister. This was a stark reality being followed quite intriguingly.

The situation reminded of tragic historical episode of Emperor named Nero who fiddled while Rome was aflame. Bharat Bhushan, a Press Correspondent with *The Times of India*, very objectively analyzed the situation accordingly in his article dated 9th January 1988.

In early September 1987 the Devi Lal government issued an order cancelling the allotment of plots of the Chief Minister's discretionary quota considering that this measure would enhance its popularity. This order covered about 2500 plots allotted under the discretionary quota system between 1977 and

1986. Of this, as many as 1122 plots were doled out in just one year of the Bansi Lal government between June 1986 and May 1987. In fact, the first considered decision to allot plots at the discretion of the government was taken by the Devi Lal government in the year 1978, making it applicable to the plots at Faridabad and Panchkula only. The Bhajan Lal government extended this policy in 1981 to other Urban Estates as well. The legality of the Devi Lal government order cancelling the allotment of plots from the discretionary quota became an intense debating point amongst the legal luminaries and the majority of the top legal experts condemned the government decision as "obnoxious" and "flagrantly" violative of the principles of natural justice. Congress Party had been very badly mauled by the Devi Lal wave of "Nyay-Yudh" in the Assembly Election held in June 1987. Its top leaders had gone into hibernation. However, they sensed that Devi Lal was losing his grip on the state administration in the wake of "battle of succession" launched by his two sons and his self created controversy by issuing order for the cancellation of plots allotted out of discretionary quota. They found it an opportune time, towards the end of December 1987, to come out of their hibernation and launch campaign against the Devi Lal government. While announcing on September 10th the decision to cancel all discretionary allotments, the Cabinet Minister for Urban Estates and Town & Country Planning, had described the discretionary quota allotments as "an immoral act and a corrupt practice". The Congress Party alleged that this decision was to create a situation amenable to make money. Thus, the Congress Party had openly levelled charges against elder son and the Minister for Urban Estates. Together with such charges, the apparent nepotism of Devi Lal and the doings of his sons and their fratricidal fight became a major plank of the Congress campaign.

In an attempt to clip the wings of his two sons and at the same time take the wind out of the sails of the Congress; Devi Lal got both of them to resign. Although the elder son also volunteered to resign from the Rajya Sabha, yet he also made sure that his supporters launched an agitation urging that he continued both as the state Lok Dal President as well as Member of Rajya Sabha. Devi Lal secured voluntary resignation of his entire Cabinet as well as that of the Chairmen of various state government's Boards and Corporations in a bid to demonstrate that he still called the shot in Haryana. Elder son was divested of presidentship of the state unit of the Lok Dal but that did not help curtail his career as an extra-constitutional centre of power. As he had already built up a powerful network of henchmen, it was difficult to dislodge him without triggering a major political crisis. *The Times of India,* New Delhi dated 9th January 1988, in its editorial captioned "Like Father, Like Son" summed up the Haryana situation "The bizarre goings on in Devi Lal's "court" in Haryana are reminiscent of the tragicomedies of the twilight decades of the Mughals in Delhi; it has all the elements of that drama. There is an ageing patriarch; there are his rebellious and arrogant sons; and there are the conspiring courtiers." *The Tribune* Chandigarh dated 18th January 1988 in its editorial captioned "The Haryana Charade", analyzed the situation in the words: "After a fortnight of noise over a non crisis, Haryana has had a non-solution and Mr. Devi Lal heads a second ministry which looks almost the same as the first one. The rationally minded will ask the purpose of an exercise, involving the resignation of an entire Ministry, if at the end of it, but two of the Ministers are back in their official perches. Is it all a drama, an elaborate farce intended to confuse movement with action?......."

In the wake of turmoil in the ruling family, the senior administrators in the state had to face, at times, very embarrassing situations. Those days were very difficult for me. I had to tread very cautiously and tried my best to keep an image of neutrality and also to keep in check the wayward police personnel. Even then, the leaders of both the groups suspected my stance of neutrality and neither of them was happy with me. However, the Chief Minister reposed complete trust in my objectivity and commitment in dealing with the law and order affairs. Fortunately the political storm which had unnecessarily raised dust, passed off and the political situation returned to near normalcy. However, the cunning elements in the civil and police administration took full advantage of the state of political uncertainty, which prevailed in the state for quite some time and indulged in all sorts of malpractices.

Terrorists' attacks in Ambala City and Shahabad

With various anti-terrorists measures taken by the Haryana state police, the evil of terrorism remained very subdued for more than six months after the Daryapur tragedy of 7th July 1987. However, on 1st January 1988, two unidentified cycle-borne persons stopped at the sweet shop at Ambala City around 8.00 am and ordered for tea. Shiv Prashad, MLA from BJP, the owner of the shop was reading a newspaper. They inquired from him who was Shiv Prashad? When he told them that he was the man, they fired four pistol shots at him. A worker at a nearby shop tried to grapple with the assailants, but was fired upon by the fleeing assailants, killing him on the spot. Shiv Prashad was rushed to PGI Chandigarh after some initial treatment at Civil Hospital Ambala City. He had suffered bullet injuries in his chest, abdomen and the leg while the fourth bullet pierced through his arm. He struggled between life and death for a few days in the PGI Chandigarh and was fortunate enough to survive.

Since the incident had happened right in the midst of the main bazaar of the city, it created a lot of panic all around. Further, the terrorists had struck in the state after a long lull, therefore it had shaken the self-confidence of the public at large. The victim targeted by the terrorists being a sitting MLA from BJP, a National Political Party, it was bound to assume political overtones attracting various leaders to the city to express their sympathies with Shiv Prashad and his family. The city had quite a sizeable Sikh population. Therefore, backlash affecting adversely the communal harmony was strongly apprehended.

The task before the police was quite complex in the sense that security in the city was required to be beefed up immediately, the assailants had to be nabbed without delay, shaken confidence of the people of the city urgently restored and likely communal disharmony was to be kept under check. AS Bhatotia, DIG/CID and MS Mallik, DIG Anti-Extremists Special Cell came into quick action to identify the assailants. VIP security was quickly strengthened. I accompanied by DIG Ambala Range and District SP Ambala, led from the front, flag march of roughly four hundred armed police personnel through the main interior roads of Ambala City. Respectable persons, both from the Hindu and Sikh communities, were called upon to exercise their influence to ensure that the hooligans between both the communities were kept in check from igniting any communal tension. Anti-terrorists plans already in place since the Daryapur tragedy, which perhaps had somewhat slackened due to total silence of the terrorists in the state for over six months, were activated by issuing telephonic and wireless instructions to all concerned in the state. The prompt action by the police, spiritedly aided by the civil administration like the Divisional Commissioner and Deputy Commissioner of the district achieved fair degree of success in keeping cool the temper of the people.

While the police was busy in dealing with the situation emerging from the murderous assault on the BJP MLA at Ambala City, the terrorists struck again on 9th March 1988 when they attacked Dr Harnam Singh CPI MLA and his family members at his residence in Shahabad town. In this incident, one terrorist was killed on the spot in the crossfire. This incident sent shock waves in the entire state. Every MLA started clamouring for strengthening his/her security. It was risky to ignore the need for adequate security of VIPs including MLAs. This caused extra strain on the police department already insufficient in number to meet the abnormal law and order situation. However, the hard work, vigorous and untiring efforts put in by the Police Intelligence and Investigating Agencies, achieved remarkable success in identifying the assailants in both the terrorists' related incidents of Ambala City and Shahabad. One of the two accused in the Ambala City case was also found to be an accused in Shahabad case. He was being hotly chased by the Haryana police when he was confronted by Punjab police at a *Nakka* near Banur district Patiala and was shot dead in the encounter. Another known terrorist, an accused in Shahabad incident was an army jawan who had deserted the army in the wake of 'Blue Star Operation' of 1984 at Gurudwara Sri Harmandir Sahib (Golden Temple) at Amritsar (Punjab). He had surrendered before the Punjab police during an operation conducted at Golden Temple Complex. He was arrested in the Shahabad case and proceeded against as per law. The second accused in Ambala City case continued evading arrest for quite a long time. He had already been declared a proclaimed offender by Punjab police because of his complicity in quite a few heinous crimes committed in Punjab. A few persons who were either privy or harbourers of the accused of Shahabad incident were also booked.

Welfare aspect of the Police Force

The entire police machinery had been under stress for quite some time to tackle the law and order problems. Nonetheless, the welfare needs of the police force did not escape my attention. I had submitted to the government quite a few welfare proposals for sanction. However, in view of the pressing demands of the law and order situations, these proposals could not be given serious thought by the government. Therefore, I thought of requesting the Chief Minister to visit Madhuban on some important occasions. In the Police Training College (PTC) Madhuban, 488 Police recruits from Himachal Pradesh and Haryana were completing their initial training by the middle of

March 1988, apart from roughly 200 police personnel of different ranks completing their in-service training. Thinking this to be an opportune occasion, I requested the Chief Minister to bless these trainees at the time of their passing out parade at the PTC, Madhuban. As per Chief Minister's convenience, 25th March 1988 was fixed for the passing out parade. Sampat Singh, the Home Minister also agreed to accompany the Chief Minister. In my welcome address, I highlighted the various pending welfare proposals of the force before I requested the Chief Minister to bless the huge police gathering. Following were the pending proposals:

Construction of Residential and non-Residential Buildings for Police Personnel

As on 25th March 1987 the subordinate staff in the police department comprised Inspectors/206, Sub Inspectors/732, Assistant Sub Inspectors/1250, Head Constables/4492 and Constables/14707, in all the twelve districts of the state having 136 police stations and 102 police posts. As per the norm fixed by the Punjab Police Commission 1962, the police official of the rank of Inspr, SI, ASI and HCs were entitled to 100% rent free residential accommodation and Constables entitlement was up to 60% only; remaining 40% Constables were to be provided barrack accommodation. However, the availability of residential accommodation was glaringly short of their entitlement. For 206 Inspectors and 732 Sub Inspectors, only 21 residential quarters were available. For 1250 ASIs, only 813 quarters were available. For 13316 other ranks, that is 4492 Head Constables and 8824 Constables (60%), only 1272 quarters were available. Regarding barrack accommodation for the 40% Constables, that is 5883 in number; accommodation was available only for 4305 Constables. I pointedly mentioned that in the changing times, the traditional joint family system was cracking and the girls marrying police personnel not only prefer but also insist on staying with their husbands instead of staying with the husbands' parents and extending helping hand in agriculture operations. This new social phenomenon was creating tension in the families and in the process, the efficiency of the police personnel was being adversely affected.

My impassioned appeal to the Chief Minister to consider this issue very favourably and on high priority touched his heart.

The Issue relating to Initiation of ACRs of Superintendents of Police

As per the system of initiating ACR as in vogue earlier, the Range DIG used to be the initiating officer. As mentioned earlier elsewhere Bansi Lal after becoming the Chief Minister in 1968 had issued orders that ACR of the District SP would be initiated by the Deputy Commissioner. Later when Devi Lal became the Chief Minister in 1977, he reversed that order restoring status-quo-ante. However, Bhajan Lal after succeeding Devi Lal again brought back the system introduced by Bansi Lal, but subsequently ordered status quo ante. This issue had been a cause of great irritation for the District Superintendents of Police. I briefly stated the background of this issue and pointed out that this matter was very hotly discussed in the meeting of the senior police officers held at

Madhuban on 24th July 1987. The State Home Secretary was also present in the said meeting. I made a fervent appeal to the Chief Minister to consider restoring the same system which he had introduced in 1977, particularly in the context of the District SPs facing very complex and difficult law and order situation as created by the terrorists.

Better Pay Scales for Deputy Superintendent of Police

A Dy SP is the cutting edge of the gazetted police officers in the state. He is the person who in the real sense is a field officer cadre closely supervising the day to day function of the police stations under his charge. He has to perform all types of complex duties in the maintenance of law and order. However, with regard to his emoluments, he was placed below the Haryana Civil Service (HCS) officers. They had been demanding parity with the HCS officers with regard to the pay scales. I emphatically supported their demands.

Construction of an Auditorium at Madhuban

Police Training College at Madhuban was catering to the training requirements not only of Haryana state police department, but also to that of some other states like Himachal Pradesh and some Eastern states. The state level meeting of the senior police officers also used to be held at Madhuban. There was no proper place for holding seminars and lectures by the guest teachers to trainees in the PTC. The need for the construction of an auditorium, thus, could not be overemphasized.

Indoor Shooting Range

In the context of extremism and terrorism raising its ugly head, the police force was required and kept in fine trim in the use of small, modern and sophisticated weapons, by practicing very frequently at the firing range. Therefore, the urgent need of a proper indoor shooting range at Madhuban was vital.

Well-Equipped Gymnasium

Physical fitness of the police personnel was a basic requirement. The availability of a well-equipped gymnasium with the PTC, Madhuban was an essential requirement.

Swimming Pool

The requirement of a swimming pool in the Police Complex Madhuban was imperative not only for general fitness and training of the police personnel but also for grooming them for National Swimming Competitions. It is a soothing, morale boosting and entertaining sport as well.

Extension to the Police Public School Building

An English Medium Public School for the children of subordinate police personnel started at Madhuban was progressing very well. However, a few extra classrooms and hostel accommodation needed to be added urgently. The School building was initially constructed out of the Police Welfare Fund and built up out of the voluntary monthly contribution made by all ranks of the police department. The stateg has been providing matching grant. However, more funds from the government in addition to the matching grant were needed to meet the accommodation requirement.

Devi Lal, the Chief Minister, like a true patriarch as if he was the benign head of police family, highly applauded and appreciated the Haryana police for firmly dealing with the terrorists' related crime, particularly the arrest of those terrorists involved in Daryapur massacre and other terrorists' related cases. He announced that the pay scale of the Deputy Superintendent of Police would be brought at par with the Haryana Civil Service scale. The confidential reports of District Superintendent of Police would not be written by the Deputy Commissioner but would be initiated only by the concerned Deputy Inspector General. Regarding the remaining proposals submitted by me as above, he announced the constitution of a committee consisting of Chief Secretary, Finance Secretary, Home Secretary and State DGP, headed by the Home Minister, to closely examine the proposals and those endorsed by this Committee would be sanctioned on priority.

Escalation of Terrorist Activities in Punjab

Right from January 1988, the terrorists in Punjab had escalated their orgy of killing innocent people. On 1st April 1988 when 37 persons were gunned down, the total number had reached 600 killings during 92 days period since 1st January 1988. The situation had assumed alarming proportions. Almost the entire Nation was having anxious moments for fear of uncertain future move, which could be taken by the security forces and the terrorists indulging in such gruesome crimes. The law and order agencies in Punjab got extra vigilant to mount heavy pressure on the terrorists. Haryana police was neither taken into confidence nor posted with the nature of the action-plan pursued by Punjab law and order agencies. However, it was widely known that Punjab law and order agencies had completely sealed Indo-Pak Border to prevent any terrorist escaping to Pakistan. In the circumstances, it was strongly apprehended that the Punjab extremists might infiltrate into Haryana for taking shelter with their relations, sympathizers and even harbourers. Once in Haryana, they were likely to take to their usual criminal activities..

The investigation of Ambala City and Shahabad cases brought to surface the fact that terrorists had established their wide network of hideouts, harbourers and sympathizers in Haryana. I was thus, visualizing a very grim law and order situation in the coming days. At the same time, I was not quite optimistic of getting any required logistic and work force support from the Union Government. I accordingly apprised the state government through a detailed letter dated 4th April 1988 and also pointedly highlighted the police problems in this regard, in a meeting with the Chief Minister. He assured me of extending all possible help by quickly sanctioning all pending proposals already submitted by me. S M H Burney, Governor of Haryana was replaced by H A Barari in February 1988. The new Governor was an Ex-IPS officer and had retired from the country's top post of Director, Intelligence Bureau. I also apprised him about the police problems in the areas of work force and logistics. He was of great help. I accompanied by the Home Secretary called on the Union Home Minister and Union Home Secretary on 9th May 1988. We were promised that fifteen companies from the Paramilitary Forces would be provided to Haryana. Two companies of BSF and one company of the CRPF arrived within two days. The remaining twelve companies were to come on 19th May 1988 but these were diverted to Punjab in view of awfully deteriorating situation there. Thus, we were left high and dry, utterly short of requisite work force. However, our strong contingent of commandos sanctioned and raised in October last year was likely to be available for deployment soon. In the meanwhile, the Chief Minister endorsed my proposal to make up the work force shortage with the police, to some extent by calling out Home Guards in large number. Sanction was also accorded for recruitment of 500 Special Police Officers (SPOs) from amongst the ex-service men who were below the age of 45 years and had come on discharge from the Army within the last five years. They were to be paid fixed salary of Rs. 1000/- per month in addition to what they were getting as pension from the Army authorities. These SPOs were quickly recruited and detailed on routine police duties, relieving thus the trained police personnel for deployment on 'Anti-Terrorists' related duties. The other area of great concern was the utter shortage of sophisticated weapons. The Chief Minister made a fervent request at personal level to the Prime Minister to make up this shortage on priority. We were thus allotted 200 additional SLRs immediately followed by 250 stenguns subsequently. With all the extra work force and sophisticated weapons, we were able to execute our action-plan to an extent. State's Action-Plan against the terrorists' activities as already in place, was revised on the lines formulated by Punjab police and circulated to all concerned vide letter dated 2nd May 1988.

Letter of Threat by Punjab Terrorists

The Haryana police hotly pursued the investigations of terrorists' related cases of Ambala City and Shahabad. In the process, quite a few persons who were suspected to be providing shelter to the terrorists or having close links with them, had to be interrogated by the Special Anti-Terrorist Cell of the State. Soon the perpetrators of these two gruesome crimes were identified and booked. Firm and stern action taken by the police created some panic in the ranks of Punjab terrorists. One Amritsar based terrorists' organization sent a letter dated 4th May 1988 to Devi Lal, threatening that if Haryana DGP did not stop harassing the Sikhs on the pretext of investigation of some murder cases, he would be taught a befitting lesson for his misplaced sense of bravery. This was an utterly crude method on the part of some panic-stricken anti-social elements to try to demoralize the Haryana police. I had shifted my residence from government accommodation Chandigarh to my own house in Panchkula in late 1987. On receipt of this letter, the Chief Minster called me to his residence at Chandigarh in the evening and apprised me about the contents of the said letter. The way Devi Lal disclosed the contents of that letter to me and emphasized the importance of tightening up my own security, was reminiscent of my childhood days when my father and mother used to express their concern about my well-being. The wordings of Devi Lal's concern, richly blended with love and affection, while conveying the contents of the letter to me and showing his deep concern about my security, did touch my heart deeply and with so touched moist eyes, I saw in him a wonderful personality. When he bid good-bye to this mortal world on 6th April 2001, tears spontaneously rolled down my cheeks which perhaps remained treasured for this occasion, after the death of my father on 18th September 1985.

Assault by Terrorists in Panipat

After Shahabad terrorists' related crime of 9th March 1988, the terrorists struck again on 8th May 1988 at Panipat. This was the fourth terrorists' related crime in the state after the Devi Lal government had come into power and I assumed the charge as DGP on 23rd June 1987. A few families of a Nomadic Tribe from Rajasthan had come to Panipat on 30th April 1988 to sell their bullocks. They had set up their *dera* temporarily on the GT Road side, on the outskirts of Panipat town. They organized there, the marriage of their two girls on 8th May 1988. They hired a TV set and installed it in the open to entertain the marriage party. Possession of TV sets was the privilege of only few rich people during those days. A few Saini families in the profession of growing vegetables had their huts nearby. Some of them also came over to the marriage place to enjoy the TV entertainment. A group of terrorists from Amritsar was on a mission to avenge the alleged harassment and insult caused to the Sikhs, on the eve of Asiad' 82 Games. They could not spot the person on their hit list. They spent the evening watching a show in the local cinema hall. While retiring to their hideouts late in the evening, they saw the congregation celebrating marriage on the GT Road side. The said gathering was not on the hit list, marked by their "masters" at Amritsar, for assault by this group of terrorist. However, out of sheer fun and adventure, two of the terrorists opened fire from their AK-47 carbines from two sides on the marriage congregation. The bullets rained by them indiscriminately killed 14 and injured 25 persons from amongst the poor innocent people. This case was dealt with by the police as FIR No. 277 dated 8th May 1987 Police Station Panipat. I learnt about this tragedy at about 10.00 pm. The police immediately sealed all passages/ routes leading from Panipat to UP by laying strong *Nakkas* and started the combing up operations of various *Dhanis,* lying within a radius of 10 km from Panipat. By the daybreak, many suspects were rounded up. I reached Panipat early morning on 9th May and after inspecting the scene of crime, held discussions with the officers of district Karnal and Anti-Terrorist Cell. The Chief Minister was camping at Delhi on 8th May. While returning to Chandigarh he visited the scene of crime and met the relatives of victims. Our Special Anti-Terrorists Cell hotly pursued the investigation of this case and definite clues about the identity of the perpetrators of the crime were available soon.

After initiating necessary measures for arresting the perpetrators of Panipat tragedy, I met the Chief Minister in his office chamber to apprise him of the details. As I entered his office chamber Virendra Singh, Irrigation & Power Minister was discussing some matter with the Chief Minister. He was winding up his discussion with the Chief Minister and was about to leave when he, after looking at me said "*Chaudhary Sahib, police department ko jhanjhorhane kee aavsyakta hai" (*Police Department needs to be shaken). The Chief Minister did not make any comment. Virendra Singh went away. I discussed all the details of the Panipat tragedy with the CM and apprised him of the follow up action taken by the police all over the state. I also told him that the police had identified the perpetrators of the crime and they would be arrested soon.

After discussing the matter with the Chief Minister, I immediately met Virendra Singh in his office chamber. The language he had used in his curt comments about the working of the police department in the office of the Chief Minister was agitating my mind. Virendra Singh had held the Home portfolio in the seventies when Devi Lal had become the Chief Minister for the first time. He had taken it to his heart that he was a big expert in the matter of law and order and police affairs and was feeling somewhat disgruntled for not getting the Home Portfolio, again during the second term of Devi Lal as Chief Minister. I respectfully inquired from him as to what message he wanted to convey by his comments in the office of the CM, assuring him that his expert opinion on police affairs would certainly benefit me. I spent with him half an hour. He was advocating that I should follow *"bullet for bullet"* policy as advocated by Punjab State DGP and bluntly advised me to kill some Haryana domiciled persons suspected to be associated with the Punjab terrorists. I was shocked that a senior Cabinet Minister was prompting me to stage "fake encounters". I tried to explain to him the serious implications of following such a blatantly unlawful recourse in dealing with the situation. However, he was not convinced. I totally ignored what he had said, but a lurking suspicion started troubling my mind that the thinking like that of Virendra Singh, would not fit well with my scheme of things.

Terrorists' related Criminal Case FIR No. 176 Dated 19th June, 1988, Police Station Thaneshar (Kurukshetra)

The vulnerability of district Kurukshetra to the terrorists attacks has already been discussed in details. The long common border of Guhla sub-division of Kurukshetra district with Patiala district of Punjab with overwhelmingly Sikh population in that area provided easy access to Punjab terrorists for establishing their hideouts in various *Dhanis* of the border villages. The main thrust of our Anti-Terrorists Cell always focused on this area, ever since the Solar Eclipse fair held at Kurukshetra in September 1987. However, despite very close vigil by the local police, the Punjab terrorists taking advantage of the geographical situation of the area were able to establish their hideouts there. On the morning of 19th June 1988 Punjab terrorists struck at Thanesar. The scene of crime was Jagat Electrical Shop situated in "Chhota Bazaar" in the town where a Television was showing the serial "Ramayana" at about 9.50 am. The owner of the shop and the sales boys together with owners/workers from the adjoining shops were watching the serial at the Jagat Electrical Shop. Some passers-by and Riksha pullers had also assembled there to watch the serial. At about 10.00 am a big explosion took place emitting waves of dark smoke and fumes of fire. Many persons from amongst the onlookers suffered grievous injuries, which in a few cases proved fatal. The incident created a lot of panic in the entire City. The local police reached the spot within no time, arranged medical aid for the injured, and registered a criminal case, at the Police Station at 10.45 pm.

The Anti-Terrorists Cell took up the investigation and SP Kurukshetra intensified police patrolling in the city area, alerted and strengthened various *nakka* points on the Punjab border. DIG Anti-Terrorists Cell rushed to Kurukshetra to direct the course of investigation and activate plans to arrest the culprits.

The state Home Minister desired to visit the scene of crime and discuss the matter with the senior officers at Kurukshetra City. I had called a meeting of DIG/CID, DIG Anti-Terrorist Cell, DIG Ambala Range and SP Kurukshetra at PWD Rest House, Pipali. We all visited the scene of crime and thereafter the state Home Minister held detailed discussions with the senior police officers in the meeting at Pipali Rest House. During the discussion, the Home Minister made an oblique reference of *"bullet for bullet"* policy as once advocated by Shri Rebiero. DIG Ambala Range very enthusiastically offered that he was prepared to follow that policy but his boss would make a mince of him. I immediately snubbed him very severely. He started apologetically explaining that by using the word boss he did not mean the State DGP. This did not satisfy me and I really shouted at him for indulging in irresponsible talk during the meeting of the senior police officers. However, the state Home Minister intervened and apparently taking his side tried to defend him saying that the DIG did not mean any disrespect to the State DGP, but was only expressing his viewpoint that the *"bullet for bullet"* policy could be an effective way of deterring the terrorists from reckless killing of innocent persons. I made it very clear to everybody present in the meeting that I would applaud and highly appreciate if any terrorist, while resisting his arrest at gunpoint, was killed by the police in self-defence, but in no case any "fake encounter" would be condoned on the pretext of pursuing *"bullet for bullet"* policy. The DIG was a thorough gentleman by nature but his sudden turning to thoughtless behaviour puzzled me. It started dawning on me that somebody at the higher level had certainly tutored the DIG. The DIG did apologize for his act of indiscretion but it raised many questions in my mind for which I was anxious to find answer. DIG Anti-Terrorists Cell told me in confidence that he and his men would be prepared to take even the gravest risk in encountering the terrorists and would have no second thought in killing them in self-defence but in no case, he would be a party to any "fake encounter". Later in the evening, I learnt that DIG Ambala Range who had advocated the policy of *"bullet for bullet"* had accompanied the state Home Minister to Delhi to apprise the Chief Minister about the outcome of the discussions taking place in the meeting held at Pipli Rest House.

Terrorists' related Tragedy at Pehowa

In this gruesome tragedy, the terrorists indiscriminately rained bullets on the people when they were coming out of the Khushwant theatre located on the roadside, after watching the evening show at about 9.30 pm. As per the sequence of events gathered by the police from the persons who witnessed the crime, a few minutes before the tragedy, a Maruti car stopped on the roadside in front of the theatre and five persons in the age group of 20-30 came out of the car. Four of them were turbaned Sikhs and one was bareheaded clean-shaven person. Two of the Sikh persons were carrying an AK-47 carbine each. They took position at the two exit points outside the theatre and opened fire on the people coming out of the theatre, killing six persons including the two gatekeepers at the spot and seven persons suffered bullet injuries. The assailants immediately escaped in their Maruti car after committing the crime. This incident was a matter of great concern for everybody in the state administration because on the morning of the previous day the terrorists had struck at Thanesar City.

Soon after learning about this tragedy late at night, I apprised the Chief Minister camping at Delhi telephonically. He told me that accompanied by the Home Minister he would be reaching Pehowa in the morning. I accompanied by DIG/CID and DIG Anti-Terrorists Cell rushed to Pehowa and reaching there early morning, minutely studied the details of the incident. The Chief Minister accompanied by the Home Minister reached Pehowa at about 10.00 am. After staying for a few minutes at the Khushwant theatre – the scene of crime, he visited the families of the victims who were domiciled in Pehowa town. He announced ex-gratia grants to the families of the deceased and financial help for medical care of the injured persons. At the Pehowa Government Rest House, I apprised the Chief Minister, in the presence of the Home Minister, DIG/CID and DIG Anti-Terrorists Cell, the details of the incident and all the anti-terrorists measures which we had taken, on regular basis, prior to the incident as well as after this tragedy had taken place.

The Chief Minister, whom I had always found having composed and dignified posture, while interacting with the senior officers of the state administration, was very different in his attitude. I lost no time in making out that those who had raised and advocated the plea of *"bullet for bullet"* policy on the previous day at Government Rest House Pipali might have misled him. The Chief Minister had made some utterly unbecoming remarks, obviously at my cost. My inner conscience prompted me not to let the curt remarks of the CM lying down. I therefore, with all due regards to the Chief Minister submitted that as he had reposed trust in me I tried to redeem it to the best of my ability but within the framework of law of the land. This led to further discussion when he used some indecent words also. In the atmosphere surcharged with trust deficit, I respectfully requested the Chief Minister to allow me to proceed on leave until the date of my superannuation, which was 31st July 1988. The meeting with the CM, thus, ended abruptly. Saluting him respectfully, I came out of the Chief Minister's room while the Home Minister, DIG/CID and DIG Anti-Terrorists Cell remained sitting there. Outside, Om Prakash Chautala was present in the corridor of the Rest House. I tried to talk to him but he ignored me. It appeared to me that he was in hot temper. Soon the Chief Minister announced his departure from the Pehowa Rest House for Chandigarh. The Home Minister accompanied him in his staff car. DIG/CID and DIG Anti-Terrorists Cell travelled with me in my staff car from Pehowa to Chandigarh.

Reaching my office at Chandigarh, I sent an application for the grant of leave until 31st July 1988 –the date of my superannuation. After leaving the office, I went to the Haryana Raj Bhawan, met the Governor HA Barari, and explained to him the details of what happened at Pehowa. He applauded my stand of upholding the rule of law telling me, that acting in any manner violating the spirit of the rule of law was always fraught with dangerous consequences in the end. Next morning, I went to the office and found that orders posting SS Brar, IPS (1959-RR) as State DGP on my proceeding on leave had been issued on 21st June 1988 evening. I handed over the charge to him and with deep sense of relief for concluding my blotless albeit tumultuous IPS career, spanning over three decades, I left the Secretariat and hung up the police uniform.

As the curtain was drawn on the most important and adventurous saga of the challenging phase of my life journey, I gleefully recalled how I took the whole life as a wondrous play scripted by nature, moulding, adapting and playing my role to turn aspirations and sweet dreams nourished since adolescence, into reality. Taking life as challenge, I determinedly moved forward to meet it squarely turning hardships to pale before steely resolve. Taking life as a game, I played it in sportsman spirit and taking life as love, I enjoyed it in its intensity. An old testament says, "At night, when you retire to sleep, feel that you are entering the green room after the scene, but with the dress of your role on; for perhaps, the role is not yet over and you have not yet been permitted to take the dress off. Perhaps, you have to make another entrance the next morning. Do not worry about that. Place yourself fully at the disposal of nature. Nature has written the play and nature knows how it will end and how it will go on. Yours is but to act and retire." With the sparkling glow of the mysterious ray in the eyes gazing upwards in humility, though I stepped back to enjoy the bounties of the nature at home more leisurely and heartily with complete sense of fulfillment, yet still looking forward for the wondrous nature to unfold yet another vibrant phase of the voyage.

With the best wishes for my dear young and not so young colleagues, my parting message was "For carrying out the sacred duty of upholding the rule of law, assigned by the Indian Constitution, the police officers must not dither. It does not matter if there are no accolades. It also does not matter if there are brickbats. You will walk with your chin high enriched with complete sense of fulfillment in your mission of playing a fair game which no accolades can match."

Chapter – 20

Police, Politicians and Corruption

Police and Corruption

Who controls the police? What is the truth behind *khaki*? These two questions have been agitating the mind of every right thinking Indian. The answers to these questions are well explained by citing various episodes in different chapters of the book. However, I consider it to be appropriate to refer here those episodes in particular, in which I have to suffer the wrath of politicians for refusing to toe their lines, which I thought were unlawful. I never deviated from upholding the rule of law, taking in strides the consequences of my lawful stand. Some such episodes are described in detail in Chapters 9, 13, 14 and 19.

During the British period, the people had to suffer an inefficient, corrupt, oppressive and tyrannical police. With India becoming a Sovereign Democratic Republic in 1950, the people had entertained the high expectations and aspirations that the political leaders, who had endeared themselves to the Indian masses for their high integrity, as selfless freedom fighters, would bring about much needed improvements in the overall governance of the country. It is said that next to the blessings, which a nation derives from an excellent constitution and systems of general laws, are those which result from a well regulated and energetic plan of police, conducted and enforced with purity, activity, vigilance and discretion. Police has thus, come to occupy a very prominent position among the institutions that are recognized all over the world to be of importance in preserving democracy, freedom and liberty. Therefore, radical reforms in the character and functioning of policing system were expected to be a high priority agenda for the Government of India after Independence. Ironically, as the years rolled on all such high expectations and aspirations entertained by the people started sliding into the abyss of frustration and dismay. Earlier, the policing system was used by the British to promote the interest of "Empire" and to suppress any rebellious voice. After the Independence, every ruling party used the police to promote its own interest at the cost of all dissentient groups. Police personnel rarely conducted themselves in the manner, the connotation of the words "public servants" signify. Some of them unabashedly indulged in intrigues, revenge and sealing the ladder for others. Almost every police personnel would have some politician as his godfather and this rotten system suited both the politicians and the policemen, playing subservient of the former

Thanks to infamous Emergency of 1975, the brazen manner in which the police force were used by the authorities that were, to subvert lawful procedures and serve purely political ends, the real heat of the wretched and putrefied police systems, obtaining in the country, was experienced by one and all. Janata Party government at the centre constituted in 1977 National Police Commission (NPC) to make an in-depth study about the entire gamut of policing system and make appropriate recommendations for carrying out necessary reforms. Recommendations made by NPC in seven volumes, in early eighties, continued eating dust for years. Even the Supreme Court directive of 22nd September 2006 for enforcing some important reforms ended only in some cosmetic changes in the policing systems, because of the manoeuvring by those wily politicians who never wanted to lose complete control over the police.

If the politicians have continued keeping firm control over the police, the later in turn, have continued indulging in corruption and malpractices more or less in the same intensity, as it used to be during the British Rule. The various malpractices and dishonest dealings generally indulged into by the police with the evil intention of making money, were identified and pinpointed. Measures to stem this evil were available within the existing laws and police rules. But, these measures were not implemented by the senior officers because of they being either incompetent or down right in league with corrupt subordinates. I issued a standing order no. 46/1987 (Annexure-3) calling upon the senior officers to ensure that all the available measures to stem the evil of malpractices and dishonest dealings indulged into by the subordinate police personnel, are meticulously evoked. It did have some positive effect. However, I found that the said standing order notwithstanding, the evil of malpractices and dishonest dealings in varied degrees continued.

Corruption in Politics

During my long police career, I came across politicians of varied hues. I had occasions to discern their character, attitude and behaviour – relationship between bureaucracy, police and politicians. I also closely watched the approach, patterns, postulations, converses and unifications of various political forces. The instant conclusion was that barring a few honourable exceptions, the politicians at large were always on the look out to make money by every possible means. First time, I saw large-scale corruption in politics, playing sinister role, in the year 1967. Bhagwat Dayal Sharma of Congress Party formed his government after winning majority seats in the Haryana Assembly elections, held in March 1967. A group of dissident senior Congress Party MLAs dislodged his government. This group about a dozen MLAs had the support of many Congress MLAs, independent MLAs and all the Jan Sangh

Party MLAs. All those MLAs, who had joined this group, to form the government with Rao Birender Singh, a dissident Congress MLA, as Chief Minister, were prompted for pelf and power. This group of MLAs forming non– Congress government was christened as Samyukt Vidhayak Dal. Now came into play the sinister game of corruption. Almost every MLA in the state became saleable commodity. One MLA changed sides five times in a fortnight – thanks to the higher bid every time. The infamy of frequent defections of MLAs from one political party to the other one was contemptuously given the name to such vacillating characters as *Aaya Ram* and *Gaya Ram.* This sinister game of corruption in politics continued for eight months and the rot was stemmed, only when on the recommendation of Governor BN Chakraverty, Government of India clamped President Rule in the State. It was anybody's guess where from wads and wads of currency came for the appeasement of *Aaya Ram* and *Gaya Ram* frequently changing sides. In any case, the ugly dance of democracy stopped for the time being.

Mid-term polls were held for Haryana Assembly in May 1968. Congress Party won majority seats. Bhagwat Dayal Sharma though had not contested the polls, was yet the top aspirant to become the Chief Minister, but Congress High Command had some other plans. Bansi Lal then a junior Congress leader was made the Chief Minister, on the understanding that Bhagwat Dayal Sharma, after becoming an MLA, by winning in a by-election, might replace Bansi Lal. However, Bansi Lal soon started strengthening his position by developing good rapport with Congress High Command. An intense tug of war started between Bhagwat Dayal Sharma and Bansi Lal. Once again, sinister role of money power came into play. MLAs turned into saleable commodities. Consideration in cash or promise for pelf and power became the order of the day. This shameful game of money power continued for a few months and came to an end only when Congress High Command strongly intervened to tell Bhagwat Dayal Sharma that Bansi Lal would continue as Chief Minister for full five years term. In the meanwhile, Bansi Lal otherwise a man of integrity learnt that money power really mattered a lot in politics. An unfortunate development indeed!

In June 1977 Assembly polls, Janata Party won majority seats and formed government with Devi Lal as Chief Minister. But in 1979, serious fissures crept into the Janata Party MLAs that Party High Command had to think of replacing Devi Lal. Here came into play sinister game of money power. Balwant Rai Tayal and Dr Sarup Singh, both known for high integrity were top favourites and frontrunners for the top job of Chief Ministership. However, Bhajan Lal with the blessings of a son of the Prime Minister was installed as the Chief Minister, Haryana. As I have mentioned earlier, I had friendly relations with Balwant Rai Tayal. Soon after, Janata Party High Command made it known that Bhajan Lal would be the leader of the Janata Party legislative wing, Shri Tayal returned to his home town Hisar, where I was then posted as Range DIG. Shri Tayal met me in connection with some problem concerning law and order matters. On my casual inquiry as to how he lost the chance to get the top job of Chief Ministership, he sarcastically remarked that the Janata Party leaders, while languishing in jails during the Emergency days, were swearing to eradicate corruption in the country, once they came into power. Ironically, they were promoting corruption after getting power. Continuing in the same tone laced with sarcasm, he told me that only he who could shell out huge amount of Rupees fifty lacs could get the Chief Ministership. A stunning revealation indeed! Even though this ugly game was over, some of the Janata Party's MLAs continued projecting their own respective price and to appease them all sorts of bounties, were showered on them by the top beneficiary in the whole drama. Things did not stop here. Soon after Congress Party came into power with Indira Gandhi as the Prime Minister of India, after trouncing Janata Party in 1980 Parliamentary Elections. The Chief Minister of Haryana, together with entire flock of Janata Party MLAs jumped into the bandwagon of Congress Party. Some of the MLAs again got their price for following their leader. This whole drama, the most unethical in nature, was unprecedented in democratic India.

In early 1982, General Elections were held for Haryana Assembly. Congress Party led by Bhajan Lal, then Chief Minister won 33 seats, 12 less than the half way mark. Lok Dal led by Devi Lal had pre–poll alliance with BJP. This alliance had won only a couple of seats, short of half way mark; Lok Dal alone had a score of 32 seats. The Governor invited Devi Lal to form the government, he being leader of the Lok Dal–BJP alliance with majority seats. However, Governor soon changed his stance. Cancelling his earlier order asking Devi Lal to form the government, he invited Bhajan Lal to form the government in view of the later being leader of the Congress Party, which was the single largest party with 33 MLAs. Thus, Bhajan Lal became the Chief Minister and proved his majority on the floor of the House within the time stipulated by the Governor, by winning over to his side more than 12 MLAs required to cross half way mark of 45. In this game of numbers, sinister game of corruption came into play unabashedly. All sorts of bounties were showered on various MLAs by each side for keeping them immune from any attempted poaching by the other side. It was anybody guess in what manner and to what extent, both sides had to stoop low to appease their respective flock of MLAs.

In all the above cited instances many police officers and bureaucrats played nasty roles in their anxiety to help their respective political masters, whom they had been faithfully loyal throughout. This was certainly not because of their instinct of rendering selfless service, but certainly, with eyes on pelf and power, which readily flowed to them. Unfortunately, the governance in every instance was the casualty in the face of shameless manifestation of politicization of civil services – a sad phenomenon indeed, which has since acquired deep roots in the country. Thanks to the nexus between politicians and civil services, the evil of corruption has brought the whole gamut of administration under its tentacles. The unfortunate part of this ugly development is that this scourge is sapping the strength, vitality and energy of the nation. The former Vice Chairman of the National Knowledge Commission has aptly described the prevailing situation that the money and position have acquired the power to derail justice, which if delivered within a timeframe of honesty and integrity, can be a great equalizer. Governance and objectivity have become so anachronistic that politics and subterfuge have become synonymous.

Chapter – 21

Retreat in Public Life

Ever since my joining the College in 1949 till the last day of service career on 31st July 1988, my life journey has been a saga of struggle, aspiration, adventure, excitement, meaningful service to fellow human beings and complete fulfillment. The nature has been bounteous enough to bless me with needed skills, to negotiate cheerfully the undulating path strewn with thorns and flowers with a sense of contentment and pride. Some people have a dull, drab and routine retired life without any objective and productive purpose and take the abrupt change from the hectic life of power and glamour of the prestigious government service, as an occasion to move to the quiet general social mainstream. However, it has not been so with me. More than 2500 years ago, deeply grieved at the sight of disease, old age and death, Sidhartha, a young prince renounced his palace, a pretty princess and a sweet son to discover the cause and cure for these three inevitable states of life. He went from forest to forest and hill to hill, meeting the sages, saints and seers of repute and practicing severest of austerities and undergoing mortification to unravel the mysteries of life and the Universe. The enlightenment ultimately dawned on him and he became Gautam Buddha discovering the panacea of human sufferings and sorrows in the eight-fold middle path known as "Dhamma". Centre of his Dhamma is man and the relation of man-to-man in this life on this earth. He postulated that the men are living in sorrows, miseries and poverty. As the world is full of sufferings, the sole purpose of his Dhamma is how to remove the sufferings from the world and nothing else. Going by Buddha's postulates, I firmly believe that one can make substantial positive and meaningful contribution in mitigating the human sufferings to the extent possible by sincerely and actively playing his part in life at every stage. Therefore, I have been treading the path of my life journeying with the same spirit even after I hung up my police uniform some 23 year's back. I would highlight my retreat in public life as follows:

Emergence of Bharatiya Shoshit Samaj–A Social Apolitical NGO

India won Independence from centuries old foreign yoke in 1947. An ideal Constitution, based on the progressive principles of Democracy, Secularism, Social and Economic Justice, Adult Suffrage, Socialism, Equality of status and opportunity for all, Liberty, Fraternity and Human Rights et al, framed and adopted in the name of "We the people of India, provided a fresh starting point for us all Indians". Admirable safeguards exclusively for the depressed and downtrodden people were incorporated in the Constitution by way of providing Compensatory Justice to them for the social disabilities and indignities suffered by them for centuries.

During my long service of about 34 years, I got various opportunities to visit various places all over the country. Among other things, I closely studied the socio-economic and educational standards of the depressed people coming from the lowest strata of society and interacted with prominent social workers. I found enormous differences in outcome in Independent India, wherein people were faced with colossal economic and social contradictions. Dazzling prosperity of a minority lived with the dehumanizing poverty of teaming millions, the rich living in cities were totally callous and insensitive to the people in remote areas and slums close by. Bounded labour, child labour, trafficking in women and children, existed in varied degrees, all over the country. These children of lesser God were not getting justice neither at the hands of the police nor from civil administration. This position continues to exist more or less in the same intensity, even after 64 years of India's independence.

Untouchability was abolished under Article-17 of the Constitution. The Protection of Civil Rights Act No. 22 of 1955 and Protection of Civil Rights Rules, 1977 were brought on the Statute Book, thus providing a strong platform to tame wayward conduct of those professing, practicing, promoting, and privy thereto and abetting, in any manner, such pernicious acts and in the process to save this strata of society from savaged acts of barbarity and cruelty. However, instead of showing any sign of improvement, the situation continued further deteriorating, compounding the miseries of these unfortunate people, as the die-hard so called upper caste people would not accept the erstwhile downtrodden and untouchables as their equal in their social stream. Accordingly, Government of India decided to go in for stringent measures against the perpetrators of excesses on them. Thus, the scheduled caste and scheduled tribes (Prevention of Atrocities) Act No.33 of 1989 was brought on the Statute Book on 11th September 1989.

Dr BR Ambedkar father of the Constitution said, "Blessed are those who are awakened to their duty to those among whom they are born; glory to those who devote their time, talent and their all to the amelioration of slavery!" Inspired by such quotes of Baba Sahib, I floated an idea to organize a non-govt. organization (NGO), through a personal letter addressed to about 2000 elite intellectuals in the entire length and breadth of the country to elicit their considered views on the subject. The response was indeed very promising. In due course of time the top intelligentsia like the retired high ranking civil servants, social activists of eminence and men in trade industry from the oppressed classes, keenly and zealously debated and discussed for several months, the socio-politico-economic scenario vis-à-vis the problems of the downtrodden people by exchanging notes and holding seminars /meetings at Chandigarh and Delhi. The discussions, in sum, veered round the fact that there could be no other solution to all these ills except a complete "Social Revolution", which according to political thinkers, philosophers and analysts, could not be brought about by the protective laws alone. On the contrary, the moral and social conscience of the society, as a whole, was necessary for such a "Revolution". The "Upper Castes" constituting dominating part of the Indian society had deliberately not played their parts for fear of losing their centuries old hegemony and supremacy and to preserve their own selfish class interest. Obviously, the task was so stupendous and arduous that it placed a heavy responsibility on the intelligentsia of the victim community to come forward and rise as one rock unit to fight against the forces of repression and exploitation. Thus emerged in August 1989, Bharatiya Shoshit Samaj, an all India socio-economic non-political organization - a unique "Think Tank" wherein talents from diverse areas could be meaningfully pooled together. It was registered at Chandigarh under the Societies Registration Act (XXI) of 1960 as amended by Punjab Amendment Act, 1957. Justice A. Varadarajan, former Judge Supreme Court of India blessed the said NGO by taking on himself the duty to advise and direct its functioning as its founder patron. The writer was chosen unanimously as the National President with Sain Das, former Commissioner of Income Tax, as Secretary General and KC Sulekh an ex-Excise & Taxation Officer, a prolific writer and former editor of a famous magazine "Ujala", as the General Secretary. A National Council with eminent personalities was constituted and state councils in a few states were organized.

The NGO took off very well and functioned excellently for a couple of years. However, some overambitious people, actively associated with this NGO, started pressing for giving it a political colour. I continued resenting against this development rather strongly. Serious cracks developed in the organization. Some stooped as low as to sabotage the functioning of the organization. This was my greatest disappointment in life. Often the idea has been agitating my mind that those having harvested more benefits than were due to them, occurring mainly because of the life long struggle made by Dr BR Ambedkar, were the thieves of duties devolving upon them. Though the said NGO did not flourish as per the idea conceived by its founders, it did not discourage me and I continued rendering social service in diverse areas.

Empanelment as Advisor to UPSC and Academic Interest

I remained on the panel of the Union Public Service Commission (UPSC) as an advisor for the selection of candidates for All India/Central Civil Services from 1991 to 1995. This apart, I got many opportunities for participating in various group discussions, seminars, conferences and conventions where issues of vital national concern, like criminalization of politics, politicization of services, widespread corruption, caste based politics, social justice for the downtrodden segments of society, were broached upon.

Association with Anil IAS Study Circle as a Senior Faculty Member

This Institution was established by Prof Anil Kumar in 1995 with the object of imparting intensive training to make young boys and girls from North India who were aspiring to compete for Civil Services. I have been associated with this famous institution for the last fifteen years as a senior faculty member. This institution has rendered yeoman service to the youngsters of this area by churning out every year, dozens of its students to successfully compete for All India Services/Central Civil Services and State Civil Services of Punjab, Haryana and Himachal Pradesh.

My Foray into Active Politics

Devi Lal, the Chief Minister of Haryana had launched his second "Nyay-Yudh" against the Central Government on 23rd September 1987. He succeeded in his efforts and the opposition combine dislodged the Congress government headed by Rajiv Gandhi in the Election to the Lok Sabha held in 1989. V P Singh, a non-Congress leader became the Prime Minister of India with Devi Lal as the Deputy Prime Minister. Lok Dal Party, which Devi Lal had built up over the years and had completely swept the Assembly Polls in June 1987, went into doldrums after his shifting from Haryana state politics to the Centre. His elder son Om Prakash Chautala remained Chief Minister Haryana for five months and twenty days during 1989-90, for six days in July 1990 and for fourteen days in early 1991. In between BD Gupta was Chief Minister for 50 days and Hukum Singh was Chief Minister for a little over 8 months. Both of them were cronies of Devi Lal. BD Gupta had the infamous knack of playing the game of a rank sycophant at the opportune time. He was a rank crony of Bansi Lal in seventies, when winning his trust became Chief Minister for one year and five months on Bansi Lal shifting to Delhi to become Cabinet Minister in the Indira Gandhi Government. No wonder, Lok Dal Party of Devi Lal came to an inglorious end in June 1991 yielding meekly before the Congress Party lead by Bhajan Lal, a pass master in the art of playing political game.

Between the periods from June 1986 to June 1991 Bhajan Lal remained active in politics at National level holding high profile assignments. He bounced back as Haryana Chief Minister in June 1991 and continued until May 1996. This was his last inning as Haryana Chief Minister. He was elected to Lok Sabha in 1998 and continued as an important political figure of some reckoning in the state. After losing to opposition parties in June 1996, Congress Party bounced back to power after Assembly Polls of 2005. Bhajan Lal was a strong claimant of Chief Ministership, but this time Bhupinder Singh Hooda won the game to lead the state. A master political strategist Bhajan Lal, this time failed to compromise with his wanning acceptability to the Congress High Command. He miscalculated and left the Congress Party in a huff in 2007 to form Haryana Janhit Congress. Because of failing health of Bhajan Lal, his younger son Kuldeep Bishnoi, a stormy petrel in state politics took over the command of Janhit Congress and won six seats in 2009 Assembly polls. However, the political game of the Janhit Congress went into doldrums as five Janhit Congress

MLAs deserted the party. Bhajan Lal was the only non-Congress MP in Lok Sabha elected from Haryana during the Lok Sabha elections of 2009. He breathed his last on 3rd June 2011. A non-jat politician who had a meteoric rise and stayed at the commanding position for over two decades did not have glorious evening of his life. May his soul rest in peace!

Bansi Lal, after his humiliating defeat in the Assembly Election of June 1987 had lost his moorings in the Congress Party. By the time General Elections both for the Lok Sabha and the Haryana State Assembly, were due in April-May 1996, Bansi Lal had already floated a regional political outfit by the name Haryana Vikas Party (HVP). The BJP and HVP forged an alliance to contest the elections to Lok Sabha and Haryana State Assembly. I joined Bhartiya Janata Party on the persuasion of Prof. Rajinder Singh, the then Rashtriya Swayamsewak Sangh (RSS) Chief in March 1996 and was called upon to contest election as a BJP candidate to 11th Lok Sabha from Sirsa (Haryana) Parliamentary Constituency. The BJP-HVP alliance got majority in the State Assembly election. I secured over two lakhs votes in a multi-cornered contest to the Sirsa Lok Sabha constituency, but lost in the fray. In the Centre, BJP led by Atal Behari Vajpayee formed a brittle coalition government that lasted for thirteen days only and United Front government, a hotchpotch conglomeration of non-Congress and non-BJP parties, came into power. This government too failed and 11th Lok Sabha was dissolved in early 1998. The BJP-HVP alliance with Bansi Lal as the Chief Minister was then ruling the Haryana state since 11th May 1996. Election to the 12th Lok Sabha was held in February 1998 and I was again called upon to contest election from the same Sirsa Parliamentary constituency. Prahlad Singh Gillankhera, then a young dynamic and dashing leader of HVP and a staunch Bansi Lal's loyalist was leading the HVP workers team in support of BJP-HVP alliance. By his untiring efforts and firm commitment, he made commendable contribution in organizing campaign in my favour during the electioneering. Atal Behari Vajpayee the Prime Ministerial candidate from the BJP personally visited Sirsa constituency for electioneering in my favour. However, I again secured over two lacs votes but lost in the multi-cornered contest.

A socio-religious sect called "Sacha-Sauda" with headquarters at Sirsa, having a very large following had been taking active interest in the elections. For more than one month, the followers of this sect enthusiastically participated in canvassing in my favour during the Lok Sabha election of 1998. However, two days before the polling date, this sect was won over by Indian National Lok Dal (INLD) a political party, then headed by Om Prakash Chautala. This sudden u-turn of a big chunk of electorate proved a deciding factor in my losing at the hustings. This apart, I had rather a bitter experience about the indulgence of some senior state BJP leaders in making money and grinding their own axe on the pretext of mobilizing support in my favour. Om Prakash Chautala with his rock like determination and excellence in understanding, the dynamics of state politics succeeded in out-witting Bansi Lal. By winning over the BJP legislators, Om Prakash Chautala dethroned Bansi Lal and assumed the reins of the state administration as Chief Minister on 27th July 1999 for the fourth time. In alliance with BJP, he was a victorious 'general' to hold the reins of the state administration as Chief Minister for the fifth time for full term of five years since 2nd March 2000. Reduced to single digit in Assembly Elections of 2005, the INLD of Om Prakash Chautala made spectacular recovery by winning 32 seats in Assembly elections of 2010. The trio of Om Prakash Chautala and his two dynamic sons Abhey Singh and Ajay Singh, has kept the Congress on tenterhooks.

I remained member of the National Council of the BJP and as Vice-President of Haryana Unit of the BJP for three years term. Narendra Modi, presently the Chief Minister of Gujarat was incharge of Haryana BJP Unit during the days when elections were held in 1996 and 1998. Despite his being a strict disciplinarian and possessing commendable administrative qualities, he could not tame the senior BJP leaders in Haryana because of inherent deficiencies in the character of the so-called Haryana state BJP senior leaders. In fact, the BJP at no point of time could build up its strong base in Haryana. They had enjoyed political power in Haryana during 1977 and thereafter in 1987 riding piggyback of Devi Lal. Bansi Lal as Chief Minister who provided them (BJP) crutches from 11th May 1996 to June 1999.

The 21st century augured well for the BJP – thanks to Pakistan aggression in Kargil . This party with Atal Behari Vajpayee as Prime Minister of India led a coalition government at the centre until 2004. On the eve of General elections to the Lok Sabha slated for early 2004, the BJP leadership used to boast that their achievements during five years rule of the Vajpayee government excelled the achievements made by the Congress and other successive governments during the previous fifty years. I would not go into all such details.

But I was finding myself utterly misfit in the flock of the BJP. There was a glaring difference between percept and practice in the leadership of not only the Haryana unit of the BJP but also in the Party at the National level and the slogan of "A Party with Difference" was just a rhetoric exercise, I was feeling suffocated. Further, I had found the BJP rudderless, having no clear-cut agenda for the amelioration of socio-economic conditions of the downtrodden segments of the society and their policies smacked communal approach. I therefore, decided to say good-bye to active politics and resigned from the BJP on the eve of Parliamentary election for 13th Lok Sabha of 2004. In retrospection, I realize that it was a Himalayan blunder on my part to jump into active politics.

Enquiry Officer into the affairs of Haryana State Prisons as appointed by High Court

One Jagir Singh, a life convict, confined in District Jail Sirsa, submitted an application dated 10th July 1996, to National Human Rights Commission, with a copy to Hon'ble Chief Justice of Punjab and Haryana High Court. He prayed that a senior IPS officer might conduct an inquiry into the inhuman treatment meted out to the inmates of jail by the jail authorities. The Hon'ble Chief Justice of Punjab and Haryana High Court treated that application as Crl. Misc Petition registered as No. 15809/M-1996 and transferred to the Court of Justice ML Singhal. The said Court issued a notice to the state of Haryana to file reply. In reply filed on behalf of the Haryana state, it was stated that Jagir Singh denied having made any allegations. Hon'ble Justice ML Singhal of the Punjab and Haryana High Court passed the order dated 19th January 1997 that

"The matter appears to be serious in character. Without there being an enquiry into the truth or otherwise of the allegations made by Jagir Singh, a life convict lodged in District Jail Sirsa, nothing can be said about the truth or otherwise of these allegations. Shri HR Swan, Director General of Police, Haryana (Retd.) is appointed as Enquiry Officer to hold an enquiry into the allegations made by Jagir Singh....in his complaint. He is further directed to suggest ways and means to improve the living conditions of the under-trials/convicts lodged particularly in District Jail Sirsa and generally in all other jails in the state of Haryana....". The Hon'ble Court also laid down other terms and conditions. To start with the job assigned to me by the Hon'ble High Court I examined Jagir Singh. He totally denied that he ever submitted any complaint against the jail authorities and that he did not have any grievances at all. Despite that, I thoroughly looked into the various allegations mentioned in the said complaint and found no evidence, which could substantiate these allegations. However, as per direction of the Hon'ble High Court I conducted detailed study with a view to suggest ways and means to improve the living conditions of the under-trials/convicts in all the jails of Haryana. I completed the enquiry on 10th August 1998 and submitted my report in 36 sheets, to the Assistant Registrar (Crl.), High Court of Punjab and Haryana Chandigarh on 13th August 1998, suggesting comprehensive reforms in the jails. The Crl. Misc No. 15809/M-1996 was by then, transferred from the Justice ML Singhal to the Court of Justice KK Srivastava. This Court passed the order dated 5th February 1999 accepting the recommendations made by me in the inquiry report. The Hon'ble Court directed the state of Haryana to comply with the recommendations made in the enquiry report in right earnest and place on record within four months the report of compliance. After the compliance of complete report placed on record, the Registry would list this case for hearing before an appropriate bench.

Member Research Advisory Committee in the Ministry of Social Justice and Empowerment

Government of India, Ministry of Social Justice and Empowerment (Scheduled Castes Development Division) had a standing Research Advisory Committee with Secretary, Ministry of Social Justice and Empowerment, as Chairman and Deputy Secretary as Member Secretary, for sponsorship of research studies on the development of scheduled castes. I remained as non-official member of this committee for two terms in 2004 and 2005. Every year scores of scholars and NGOs used to submit their applications with synopsis of their proposed studies. Those applicants selected for sponsorship were sanctioned handsome grants for conducting the studies. The first meeting of the committee was held on 29th January for the year 2004. I learnt that the Research Advisory Committee had been functioning for years and different scholars and NGOs had conducted various research studies from time to time. On my inquiry, I found that the follow up action taken on the findings of such research studies remained limited only to the remarks "seen" finally at the Minister level. I therefore recorded a note that there was no point in wasting huge funds every year on sponsoring research studies if the follow up actions on the findings, made in such studies, were not to be taken to a logical conclusion. There was no answer to this except that the Secretary advised me to take up the matter, at my own level, with the concerned Minister. Sensing that the Secretary was in no mood to bring about any worthwhile change in the system of sponsorship of research studies, I decided to discuss the matter with the concerned Minister. He appreciated my viewpoint and assured me for taking appropriate action. However, during the year 2005, the already prevailing system continued. By then Vajpayee Government had gone and I could not take up the matter with the then concerned Minister, in the Manmohan Singh government.

Member Dr Ambedkar Foundation and Research Cell in the Ministry of Social Justice and Empowerment

I was a non-official member of the general body of Dr Ambedkar Foundation and was a member of Research Cell of Dr Ambedkar Foundation in the Ministry of Social Justice and Empowerment for the term 2002-05. I did not find any striking achievements made by these bodies. The members generally enjoyed the occasion of meetings as sorts of get together of people drawn from diverse sections of the society, with not much adequate knowledge about the philosophy propounded by Baba Sahib Dr B R Ambedkar.

Ch Devi Lal University, Sirsa

This University had come into existing soon after the death of Devi Lal. When this University was in the process of being set up, I remained member of Court of this University for three years and member of Executive Council of this University for the term 2003-05.

Founder Patron and Member of the North India Dr BR Ambedkar Social Forum

This social forum was established as a registered body in the year 2003 to provide a platform for the retiree officers, domiciled in the tri-city of Mohali, Chandigarh and Panchkula, to hold discussions on various burning problems concerning the downtrodden people and to devise ways and means to get redressed their grievances by approaching the concerned government authorities. Its constitution includes all such lofty objectives. The forum holds monthly meetings on every second Saturday of the month. From time to time detailed discussions and deliberations have been held by the members of the forum, on matters relating to welfare of the oppressed and marginalized sections of the society and implementation of different programmes/schemes initiated by the government and further measures requiring to improve the lot of poorer sections of society. TD Jogpal IAS, Former Financial Commissioner and Principal Secretary to Haryana Government and thereafter Haryana State Election Commissioner, a Constitutional appointment, has been working as Secretary General of the forum after his superannuation. He is a committed worker and plays pivotal role in the functioning of the forum. It goes to his credit that various deficiencies in the implementation of reservation of candidates from the scheduled caste in the Higher Technical Educational Institutions and disbursement of Post-Matriculation scholarship to the students from these classes, have been, not only pointedly highlighted on behalf of the forum, but most of these deficiencies have been got removed.

Apart from this Forum, I have been actively associated with half a dozen other non-political social organizations based in tri-city of Chandigarh, Panchkula and Mohali. I have induced the residents of my ancestral village to come forward for building a multipurpose Bhawan by contributing 30% of its cost extending 70% cost from my own sources. The Bhawan is almost at completion stage.

Member Haryana Saket Council

I have been the member of the Executive Committee, for the last many years of Haryana Saket Council of which Governor Haryana is the President and Chief Minister Haryana is the Chairman. Haryana Saket Council is a registered body under Societies Registration Act, 1860, a non-profit making organization running various activities for the welfare, treatment, rehabilitation and education of physically challenged persons including recently started Saket College of Physiotherapy offering Bachelor of Physiotherapy and Master of Physiotherapy courses recognized by Pt BD Sharma University of Health Sciences, Rohtak.

General Observations as a responsible Senior Citizen

Apart from the above mentioned specific post service activities I have been closely watching like any other responsible senior citizen, the socio-politico-economic developments taking place in the country. There cannot be any qualm with the fact that considerable modernization of the law enforcement agencies including the police has been speedily affected during the first decade of the present Millennium. However, the unfortunate part of it is that strength, vitality and energy of the Nation are being sapped by the scourge of corruption rampant all over in the central/state's administration– the politicians playing the major role. Talking about the police alone the state of affairs continues, more or less, the same as I found during the eighties. I had then as State DGP pinpointed certain common malpractices prevalent in the police and had issued directives in the form of standing order to tame the wayward policemen. The said standing order might be gathering dust in the record room or even might have been destroyed being part of old record. At the time of Independence in 1947, a deeply conservative and largely illiterate Indian society chose British model of Democracy with Universal adult suffrage guaranteeing equality to its entire citizen. Thus, Constitution empowered millions of our people, a majority of them deprived economically and educationally. Democracy came first, developments followed later. Over six decades after Independence, India is undergoing a transformation economically and socially. This is driving the people for assertively demanding the development to be inclusive, comprehensive and extensive and due share in the rapid growth of our country. Police in the country thus, need to be reoriented professionally to meet the demands of the changing times. The entire gamut of police reforms, endlessly debated and refined for over thirty years since the submission of comprehensive reports by Dharamvira Commission in 1980-81, have remained unimplemented. Even the Supreme Court directive of 22nd September 2006, for setting up of a regulatory mechanism – State Security Commission, Police Boards and Authorities which was to ensure political neutrality and autonomy of police, by reforming the institutional system of Indian police, has remained far from implementation in the right spirit. It is a crying shame that even after the Union Home Minister recent plaintive cry in Parliament that malafide transfers have reduced the police to football, nothing seems to have happened to end the charade.

Epilogue

Closing the narration of my tale so far, let me speak to the readers from my heart that human life is a wondrous momentary play that can be blissfully enjoyed by playing spontaneously as it comes. The panacea for perennial human sorrows, miseries and sufferings lies in being with loving and living, the moment that comes as everything happens in a moment in this momentary world. In fact, the essence of life is only a moment. Accepting the life as the bounty of the bounteous nature, I have loved, lived and relished the way it has come, moment by moment to me. Taking head on, when it came as challenge, realizing when it came as a dream and meaningfully playing it as a wondrous play of the wondrous nature, thanks to the pious souls of various sages, whose words of wisdom have always been the fountainhead of inspiration.

The elderly must feel that they are useful to society. They also need to remember the lives of people like Nirad Chaudhary, who lived for over a 100 years in UK. Bernard Shah, Annie Besant and many others who lived a full and busy life beyond the age of 100. There is no reason, why more people in our own country cannot live beyond a century.

With modest dietary habits routine of light physical exercise including 'Yogasna', frequent interaction with learned people, ever heartfelt gratitude to the wondrous nature and taking the age related events in strides, one can keep happening with the whiff of fresh and new life as it unfolds in the moment, where there is no room for tiring or retiring.

Gautama Buddha said, "The secret of health for both mind and body is not to mourn for the past, not to worry about the future, but to live the present moment wisely and earnestly".

In the last, I quote the following message of Rabindranath Tagore being worthy of emulation by us mortals of this Universe, young and old:

"Go not to the Temple to put flowers upon the feet of God,

First, fill your own house with Fragrance of love,

Go not to the Temple to light candles before the altar of God

First, remove the darkness of sin from your heart...

Go not to the Temple to bow your head in Prayer,

First, learn to bow in humility before YOUR FELLOWMEN...

Go not to the Temple to pray on bended knees,

First, bend down to lift someone who is DOWNTRODDEN...

Go not to the Temple to ask for forgiveness for your sins,

First forgive from your heart those who have sinned against you"

Annexure – 1

Statement U/s 161 CrPC of Sh. SP Sen Verma, Chief Election Commissioner of India

"14th May 1968, was fixed as the date of polling, in Bahadurgarh constituency. On the 12th May 1968, I sent one of my secretaries to the Election Commission, namely Shri K S Rajagopalan, to visit as many polling stations as possible, where poll was being taken, throughout the day. I did not go out on the 12th to see how polling was being conducted because I decided that I should visit some polling stations on 14th of May, the second day of poll. Accordingly, I left my house in Delhi at 7.00 am on 14th of May. Shri AN Sen, the second secretary to the Election Commission was also with me. I reached Bahadurgarh at about 7.35 am. The Deputy Commissioner of Rohtak, Shri Isa Dass, the Superintendent of Police Rohtak, Shri H R Swan and Shri P N Bhalla, the Chief Electoral Officer who was also the Home Secretary to the Government of Haryana received me, at the PWD Rest House. As far as I can recollect, there were two polling stations, in that building also. After I had witnessed the progress of the polling in those two polling stations for a few minutes, I started for village Mandothi, with the Chief Electoral Officer, the DC and the SP. The Secretary to the Commission had of course all along been with me."

"The principal reasons which impelled me to visit polling stations in Bahadurgarh constituency, on the date of the polling were as follows:-

I had already heard, even before I joined as Chief Election Commissioner of India (I was then the law Secretary to the Government of India) that at the time of the by-election in Bahadurgarh Assembly constituency, which was held in May, 1967, to fill in the casual vacancy caused by the resignation of Shri Hardwari Lal that a good deal of intimidation was practiced, specially, against Harijan voters. I was told that as a result of the intimidation of the Harijan voters, in a number of places in Bahadurgarh constituency, specially by the jats, many Harijan voters did not appear at the polling stations at all, to exercise their franchise or if they appeared, they marked their ballot papers, in the presence of the presiding officer, the polling officer and the polling agents of the candidates, instead of marking the same in the voting compartments."

In the second place when on 21st March, 1968, in pursuance of a letter from the Governor of Haryana, I visited Chandigarh, to make final announcement of the date of poll, before a meeting of the representatives of the political parties, whom I also met in December, 1967, practically the representatives of all the political parties present, represented to me that something should be done, to stop this intimidation of voters, specially Harijan voters, at the time of the poll. I asked them, if they were saying so especially with reference to what happened on the last occasion, in the Bahadurgarh constituency, most of them replied in the affirmative.

In the third place, when I addressed a meeting of all the Returning Officers of Haryana, on 8th of April, 1968, at Rohtak, in the hall of Zilla Parishad, I was again asked by some of the Returning Officers, if I remember aright, to do something to stop this intimidation of Harijan voters. The meeting went on for two hours. After the meeting the representatives of the Press met me. There, the representatives of *PTI* and of *The Tribune* asked me the same question and I told them that on my return to Delhi, I shall certainly do something in this regard."

"This is the background of my visit to Bahadurgarh constituency on the 14th of May, 1968."

"I had already heard that village Mandothi, which is a flourishing village, having a population of about 13,000, was likely to be a trouble spot. I, accordingly, with the Chief Electoral Officer, the DC and the SP and others reached Mandothi village, at about 8.00 am. If I remember aright, there were four polling stations in Mandothi village. After I had visited the polling stations and witnessed the voters standing in the queues at the different polling stations, which, by the way, were all contiguous, Shri Hardwari Lal, the Swatantra Party candidate, together with Prof Ranga, came to the polling stations, at Mandothi and met me in the open, in front of the two polling stations, on the right (as one moves in the direction of the polling stations). It was complained to me by Shri Hardwari Lal that the police was entering the houses of the villagers and intimidating them. Prof Ranga took exception to this. I told both of them that the police, of course, had no right, to enter the houses of the villagers except with warrant or unless any cognizable offence was committed therein, in the presence of the police, but the police could patrol the public roads for the purpose of maintaining law and order and preventing any breach of peace and also for ensuring that no voter was prevented from coming to the polling stations. The Chief Electoral Officer, Shri PN Bhalla was standing by my side and participating in these talks that were going on among us. I do not exactly remember whether the DC and the SP were near us, exactly at that point of time. Shri Hardwari Lal, in the presence of Prof Ranga, asked the DC that the police patrolling the village, should be withdrawn to which the DC did not agree at all on the ground that the presence of the police, on the day of the polling, was absolutely necessary, for maintaining law and order and for preventing breach of the peace and intimidation of the voters."

"At about 9.30 am or so I left the polling stations in Mandothi village with the Chief Electoral Officer, the District SP, the Secretary to the Election Commission, Shri A N Sen and the Supervising Officer Shri V S Allahavadi. While we were leaving the polling stations, along the narrow lane leading there too, the Sarpanch of the village along with a number of other persons was found talking, in my presence, to Shri Hardwari Lal and Prof Ranga, in a highly agitated mood, but I did not wait and left for Jakhauda and Asauda villages. At about that time Prof Ranga and Shri Hardwari Lal were also leaving that area. After visiting these two polling stations, I returned again to the polling station at Mandothi, when the DIG, Ambala Range, Kanwar Randip Singh, met me along the narrow lane leading to the polling stations. He was coming out of the polling stations and from a distance of about 25 feet, he told me "Sir, this is not going to be a free and fair election." I asked him "Why?" He told me "Sir, please come and see how my constables have been injured, by the villagers." The DIG took me to one of the rooms, in between the two polling stations, on the left hand side and the other two polling stations, on the right hand side and showed me the bodies of three police constables with injuries on their bodies. I was told by the DIG that these injuries had been caused by the brick-bats, thrown from the roof of the houses and also by *Lathies*. I waited there for a few minutes and left village Mandothi, at about 1.00 pm."

Annexure – 2

Notes dated 20th October, 1968, submitted by HR Swan IPS, SP Rohtak to Ch. Bansi Lal Hon'ble Chief Minister, regarding Official Relations Between DM and District SP

Respected Sir,

This note is apropos my submission to you during your recent visit to Rohtak. As per your advice, I am submitting a detailed note, tracing the historical background of the posts of District Magistrate and District Superintendent of Police, as follows:

(i) The system of police administration, as at present in force, was created by the Indian Police Act, 1861. There has been no serious re-thinking since then, although 108 years have elapsed and 21 years have gone after Independence of India.

(ii) When the East India Company of the British assumed governance of this country, the police administration followed the ancient pattern based on land tenure and collective responsibility of the villages. The system of Kotwals and Fauzdars, introduced by the Mughals had decayed. The authority of the village functionaries had also become ineffective. Extortion and oppression flourished unchecked. Life and property became insecure.

(iii) The first British attempt at reform of the police was the introduction of the Darogha system. Responsibility for the maintenance of law and order was transferred from zamidars to the Magistrates of the district who were provided with a staff of officers, known as Daroghas. The Daroghas had under them some men equipped with firearms and all the watchmen in the villages were under his control. Each Darogha had a jurisdiction of about 20 square miles under him. In cities, the office of Kotwal was retained and a Darogha, appointed for each ward of the city. The system was something similar to that prevailing in England at that time where Justice of the Peace combined the judicial and executive functions of administration and maintenance of law and order with the help of constables. The Darogha system was however, scrapped in 1808, as it proved unsatisfactory because of high handedness and corruption perpetrated by the Daroghas and his men on whom the Magistrates could not exercise adequate control. However, the authority of the Collector and his subordinate revenue official was retained and the system of village police was re-introduced.

(iv) In 1831, the police administration and lower criminal justice was transferred to the Collector and another officer called the civil judge was appointed to carry out the administration of civil and higher criminal justice. A further transformation took place between 1838 and 1845, when the Collector was left with the revenue administration and the District Magistrate was entrusted with the maintenance of law and order and administration of lower criminal justice.

(v) British administration in India had started with the limited objective of collection of land revenue. This was sought to be done as cheaply as possible. The functions of revenue collection were combined with lower judiciary and police, and placed in the hands of the same person. The real motive in this regard was to establish such a control in all parts of the country so that in the event of rebellion, the payment of revenue was not suspended and the contagion of rebellion stifled. Since revenue constituted the primary concern of the government, Sir John Shore wanted a union of the two functions. For collection of revenue, it was essential to create machinery for controlling the anarchical elements and maintaining law and order. The Police Administration sought to maintain law and order not primarily for the public good but to facilitate collection of revenue. Lord Cornwallis questioned the propriety of the system, which combined different functions in one hand. At his instance, functions of police and justice were taken away from the Collector and given to the Judge Magistrate. At that time, the combination of police duties with judicial responsibilities was not considered as incongruous even in England.

(vi) A re-union of the magisterial revenue functions in the hands of one and the same functionary took place in 1859, as a result of a powerful opposition to the scheme of Bird Committee from the ranks of civil servants. A new policy called the oriental theory of government was evolved. It postulated, "The true theory of Indian Government is the entire subjection of every civil officer, in a division to the Commissioner at the head of it and the entire subjection of every executive officer in a district to its executive chief." Separation of judicial power from executive responsibility was considered to be a scheme foreign and unintelligible to Asiatic notions as altogether founded on European ideals and habits. It was emphasized that separation of offices of Collector and Magistrate had been injurious to the character of Administration. This theory was strongly criticized. Sir T P Grant who very sarcastically wrote in his minutes in 1857 that the contention of all supporters of this union of Collector and District Magistrate must be narrowed down to the position "that the Mohamedan System, though abominable under the Mohamedans, yet became the best possible system for the country. However, they misgoverned when put in the hands of Englishmen. Confessedly, it is a system which is contrary to all English principles and practices and is disagreeable to the common place English mind." The common opinion was that police and revenue should be in different hand. This question had been examined in details by the Commissioner of Bengal. After full deliberation it was recorded that management of police of each district should be taken out of the hands of the Magistrates and be committed to a European Officer with no other duties and be responsible to a General Superintendent of Police for the whole Presidency. However, the hope of the sponsors of this policy was belied.

(vii) A serious charge was made in Madras Presidency that government revenue was being raised by use of torture by revenue officials, taking advantage of the combination of the Magisterial and fiscal powers in the Collector. The Torture Commission appointed to go into these charges recommended the separation of police and revenue functions and the placing of police establishment under independent European Officers who would be able to give their undivided time and energies exclusively to the control of the force. Accordingly, a plan was approved for the whole Presidency to have a separate police force, as a distinct department, under a Commissioner of Police, divested of judicial functions, with exclusive control and management of their own officers, under the direct supervision of the government. However, in the meantime, Sir Charles Trevelyan, a member of the covenanted Civil Service became Governor of Madras. He decided that the District Superintendent of Police should be placed under the order of the District Magistrate. Accordingly, changes to this effect were introduced in the Draft Act which was passed as Act, XXIX of 1859 and this Act was presented as a model to the Police Commission of 1860.

(viii) Sir Charles Napier, in 1846, had organized the Sindh police on the model of the Irish Constabulary, whereby the police became a self contained organization under its own officers. This was finally accepted as a model for the police forces of the country under the Indian Police Act, 1861. However, the Police Act, 1861 formulated on the recommendation of the Police Commission of 1860 had a rather rough passage in the Legislature. It came under heavy fire from Mr. A. Sconce, the Member for Bengal. Sir HBE Frere, the Home Member made very significant observation when replying to Mr. Sconce. He observed, "It was one thing to lay down a principle and another to act upon it at once and entirely when it was opposed to the existing system, to all existing forms of procedure and to prejudices of long standing. Under such circumstances, it was often necessary to come to a compromise. ..... In England, it took a very long time to carry out the principle of a police force separate from and independent of the judicial magistracy in the Metropolis....he hoped that at no distant period the principle would be acted upon throughout India as completely as his honourable friend Mr. Sconce could desire." Sir JF Stephen, the Law Member of the Viceroy's Executive Council had remarked, "It seems to me that the maintenance of the position of District Officer is absolutely essential to the maintenance of the British Rule in India. Neither for the improvement of administration of justice nor for any other purpose, should this position be allowed to be weakened." These written remarks of Mr. Stephen henceforward became the last word in respect of the position of the District Magistrate. There was complete stagnation on the theoretical side of thinking on police thereafter.

(ix) The Indian Police Commission of 1902-03 had been inter-alia, directed only to report on the adequacy or otherwise of the general supervision exercised by the Magistracy over the police. It was not in the terms of reference of the

Commission to go into the merits of combination of police and judicial functions in the District Magistrate. Even though the Commission admitted that "cases of abuse amounting to scandal" had been brought to their notice, they observed, "It was essential to preserve the responsibility of the District Magistrate for the general success of the criminal administration of the district." The Commission, however, reviewed critically the developments in actual practice of the relationship between the District Magistrate and the Superintendent of Police. They observed, "The intervention of the District Magistrate is not intended to be constant or detailed. It is intended to be of the nature of general control and direction to assume detailed or particular character only occasionally when necessity arises. This intention of the Law has been overlooked in most provinces, in some much more than in others. The Superintendent of Police is not the assistant of the District Magistrate in the sense in which an Assistant Collector is. It would destroy police work to keep him in that position. Unnecessary interference with the Superintendent should be not allowed. The police force though bound to obey the Magistrate's orders concerning criminal administration, yet it should be kept as far as possible, departmentally distinct and subordinate to its own officers. The District Magistrate should avoid acting so as to weaken the influence and authority of the Superintendent, for discipline is one of the most essential features of the police work." Referring to the receding control of Magistrates in England, the Commission observed, "the interference of the District Magistrates would become less necessary and less common in India as police became more efficient." The Commission also made a most significant observation about the quality of Superintendents of Police. They said, "The class of Superintendents found in all provinces is not what it should be....It would appear that almost any person was believed to be qualified for the performance of the work of Superintendent of Police. A most important element of the reform of the police must be an improved system of selection and training of Superintendents of Police." Sir Lloyd George, the then Prime Minister of England was of the opinion that "The Collector of the district had been an institution which built up the British Raj– the British Civil Service in India." He was holding this opinion only to strengthen the British Raj in India.

Your honour would kindly appreciate that the main anxiety of the Colonial Rulers was to establish, with deeper roots, the British Raj in India by suppressing any sort of rebellion, even a little dissenting opinion, with iron hand, following the policy of "nipping the evil in the bud." They, therefore wanted concentration of all sorts of power in one hand, at the District level. The District Magistrate was a convenient tool available to them, to serve the British Raj, as their best and loyal hatchet man. Even the right thinking people among the British, at times, thought that Superintendent of Police should be independent of District Magistrate and accountable only to superior authorities of the department. However, after India's Independence the entire complexion of governance has changed. Keeping in view the aspirations of the people of free India as per the provisions of the Constitution, the law enforcement agencies like the police are required in a welfare state like ours to imbibe a spirit of service with more emphasis on the moral, social and welfare of the society rather than mere prevention, detection and execution of crime. Thus, the task of enforcement of general laws and maintenance of law and order has become a highly specialized job. It is for all these reasons that Indian Police Service was instituted in 1948 by Sardar Patel, the most distinguished visionary, the first Home Minister of India. Highly educated young men are recruited to the IPS through Competitive Examination, conducted every year by the Union Public Service Commission. Very intensive initial training is imparted to the selected candidates after their induction in the IPS and then subsequently, through refresher courses their knowledge is updated keeping in view the changing times. The government of the day, therefore, needs to look forward to improve the system whereby the IPS officers become more and more efficient and confident for the discharge of their complex duties, instead of demeaning stature of the IPS officer at the district level through the regressive measures. Any erosion in the stature of the District Superintendent of Police would weaken his position in firmly superintending and ensuring proper discipline and work culture in the police force. It is a stark fact that the present day Deputy Commissioner remains over busy in connection with the development work and hardly finds any time to devote to multi-dimensional police role, which has become too specialized job in the Criminal Justice System. His role as a District Magistrate has become negligible with the separation of lower judiciary from the Executive. Even there is already a serious thinking going on to make prosecution agency independent of executive/police."

In view of all the details narrated above, the Hon'ble Chief Minister may kindly consider, in his best wisdom, to cancel the latest order of his government, which has given new dimensions to the already existing very cordial relations, between the District Magistrate and the District Superintendent of Police.

Annexure – 3

DGP's Standing Order No. 46/1987, regarding Evil of Malpractices and Dishonest Dealings in Police Department–Legal Safeguards against such Malpractices and the Role of Gazetted Police Officers

Introduction

1. To suppress the evil of corrupt practices and dishonest dealings in the police department, circular instructions had been issued vide Police Hqrs Office Memo/Endst No. 9474-91 SA-3 dated 14-09-1987. The emphasis in the said memorandum was laid on identifying (a) Known corrupt and (b) Suspected to be corrupt Police personnel of all ranks and then to proceed, either to remove them from the posts where they have greater chances of indulging in dishonest dealing or to retire them compulsorily or to punish them by taking disciplinary action against them. With that end in view, the field officers were requested to furnish lists of police personnel falling in above two categories, together with supporting material.

2. This subject was discussed in depth, in the meeting of senior police officers held at Madhuban on 11th October 1987. It was generally agreed that action as proposed in Police Hqrs Memorandum under reference should be firmly taken. It was strongly mentioned by a few officers that the proposed action must not remain confined only to the non- gazetted officers and other ranks but should equally be all embracing and the gazetted officers who come in the red categories, also likewise be firmly dealt with. The discussion, which was indeed very lively, showed tremendous enthusiasm and promise. The consensus was that at the senior level various factors, which individually or collectively contribute in promoting corrupt practices and dishonest dealings in the police department, should be vigorously tackled. Director General of Police emphasized that the police rules and criminal procedure code provide a foolproof system for effective supervision by the gazetted officers over the working of police station staff. If the supervisory officers ensure that the police station discharge their role in the administration of criminal justice system strictly according to the laid down procedure, the evil of corrupt practices and dishonest dealings can very considerably be curbed. The Director General

of Police proposed that the gist of the provisions of the police rules and the criminal procedure code having relevancy on the subject shall be reiterated. It is in this context that the present Standing Order is being issued.

3. Before the relevant provisions of the police rules and the criminal procedure code are mentioned, it needs to be reminded that corrupt practices and dishonest dealings amongst the police personnel are prompted only if the gazetted police officers exercising supervision over the police station staff are either lazy or inefficient or down right corrupt. The District Superintendents of Police and the Range Deputy Inspectors General of Police are therefore required to closely watch the performance of the gazetted officers working under them with a view to identify whether any of them falls in any of the three categories and then recommend action against the defaulters accordingly.

Common Underhand Methods throttling Legal Provisions– Measures to curb the Evil:

The relevant provisions of police rules and the criminal procedure code, which are not strictly adhered to, with evil motive of corruption and the principal methods adopted by corrupt elements in this regard are mentioned below.

I. First Information Report (FIR): (i) Delay in recording it. (ii) Intentionally recording faulty or incorrect FIR. (iii) Inclusion of false witnesses or accused in it and (iv) Changing the correct story to suit the convenience of the person willing to offer bribe.

Vide para 24.5 of the police rules, one copy of the FIR is to be sent to the *Illaqa* Magistrate and this provides a check on delay. In murder case, a special check is provided – in that the copy of the FIR is required to be sent to the *Illaqa* Magistrate in the Court or at his residence, wherever he happens to be at that time. If the Magistrate is out of station, it is to be submitted to the Duty Magistrate. If the Magistrate is not available, the same has to be left at his house after noting the date and hours of delivery and the causes of delay on account of defective communication on the cover. The Magistrate is also supposed to acknowledge the receipt of the copy of the FIR received by him after noting the date and hour of receipt on it. In certain categories of cases as narrated in para 24.12 and 24.14 of the police rules, read with instructions issued from time to time, special reports are required to be sent to higher officers and this also provides a suitable check on delay.

According to the provisions of police rules 25.17, the gazetted/supervisory officers are required to check delays at different stages beginning from the recording of the FIR. If supervision is properly exercising all sorts of delays, malpractices, intentional omissions and irregularities on the part of the subordinates can be prevented. In the Special Report cases, the District Superintendents of Police and the Range Dy Inspectors General of Police should also be in a position to exercise similar control.

There are appropriate columns in the FIR register itself, which also help in keeping delays under check, the date and hour of report have to be given in column No.1. Full explanation in respect of delay in recording the report has to be noted down in column No.5. Further, in column No.6, the date and hour of its dispatch from the police station are to be given. A careful checking of these columns, to ensure that they are correctly filled, also helps in eliminating delays.

Under section 154 of criminal procedure code, information given by the informant has to be read over to him and has also to be signed by him in token of its correctness. In case, the information is not correctly recorded, the informant can point out the facts to the officer incharge of the police station and get the FIR corrected. A copy of the FIR has also to be given to the complainant as required under police rules 24.5. The complainant can examine the FIR himself, or through counsel to see that, the same was correctly, recorded. What is to be ensured here by the supervisory officer is the fact whether or not a copy of the FIR is immediately given to the complainant and its contents are recorded correctly according to the version given by the complainant and without any delay of any sort. Further, law requires reports to be recorded in the Daily Diary with regard to the registration of the FIRs and their dispatch to various officers. These should provide a further check on delays.

The departmental orders require the gazetted officers, more specially the District Superintendents of Police, to pay visits to the spots of occurrence in cases of heinous offences and stay there for adequate periods to sort out details of their investigations. If this part of the work is undertaken seriously, any delays or other irregularities could not escape their notice.

The above will show that the legal provisions are available for very healthy checks for preventing delays and other irregularities in recording FIR. If the evil persist, it is primarily because the gazetted/supervisory officers and other superior officers are inclined to be superficial and casual in their supervisory work.

II. Case Diaries: (i) Intentional delays in recording statements of material witnesses. (ii) Including such witnesses as are likely to retract and (iii) Falsely making mention of such situations which should suit the convenience of the person willing to offer bribe.

Instructions regarding recording and dispatching of case diaries are contained in paragraphs 25.53, 25.54 and 25.55 of the police rules. It has been provided therein that the investigating officers should write case diaries in prescribed Forms only but promptly and that the case diaries should contain all information about the various steps taken by them during the course of investigation. The number and date of each case diary is required to be recorded on the reverse of police station's copy of the FIR and the time of receipt and dispatch to the supervisory officer has to be recorded in the appropriate column.

Similarly, section 172 of CrPC enjoins that every police officer making investigation should enter his proceedings in the Daily Diary setting fourth the time at which the information reached him and the time at which he began and closed the investigation together with a statement of the circumstances ascertained through the investigation. Delay in recording and dispatch of case diaries can be easily checked by proper and close supervision. Similarly the supervisory officer can check up false and incorrect statements recorded as result of ulterior and dishonest motives while checking the details of investigations as required under police rule 25.17.

III. Glaring Instances of Corrupt Practices during Investigations:

(i) Fabrication of evidence. (ii) Foisting of property on the accused. (iii) Delay in inspection of the scene of crime, medical and postmortem examinations. (iv) Scaring away defence witnesses. (v) Giving facilities to the accused in lock-up and during transit. (vi) Use of third-degree methods on suspects and accused persons. (vii) Suppression of documents which can be utilized as evidence against accused. (viii) Accepting evidence of false witnesses for purpose of identification of articles and suspects. (ix) Introducing stories of alibi and (x) Detaining persons at the police stations illegally.

Police Rule 25.17 lays down detailed instructions regarding supervision of investigation by gazetted officers. In important cases, they are required to supervise the investigations personally and visit the scene of crime. If they perform their supervisory role honestly, they can check delay and other irregularities and impart necessary guidance to the investigating officers. A properly maintained crime register by the gazetted officers can provide a sure and effective check on the various malpractices of the investigating officers.

It will be equally relevant to mention here that submission of special reports by the gazetted officers in serious and important cases as required under police rules 24.14, 24.15 and 24.17 also provide a further effective check at the higher level.

In nutshell, it should be the quality of the supervision exercised by the gazetted officers and the vigilant eye of the superior officers at the District and Range levels, which can produce desired results in curbing the malpractices and dishonest dealings at the level of the subordinates during investigation of cases.

IV. Arrests, Searches and False Recoveries: Under section 57 of the CrPC no police officer can keep in custody, a person arrested without warrant, for a longer period than under all the circumstances of the case, is reasonably required and such period shall not be, in the absence of special order of a Magistrate u/s 167 CrPC, exceed 24 hours. Further, u/s 58 CrPC as incorporated in Police Rule 26.8, the SHO has to report to the specified officers, the cases of all persons arrested without warrant within the limits of his station, whether such persons have been admitted to bail or otherwise. When the arrested person is produced before the Magistrate for getting remand u/s 167 CrPC, case diaries and other relevant papers have also to be submitted to the Magistrate. The accused and their counsels are at liberty to bring irregularities committed to the notice of Magistrate, at this stage. Similarly, police rules 25.23, 25.53 and sections 100, 165 and 166 of the CrPC afford adequate safeguards in respect of searches and property seized by the investigating officers. Information along with grounds of searches etc has to be sent to the *Illaqa* Magistrate. The provision of presence of two respectable witnesses of the locality at the time of the search also provides a sound check. It is thus, manifest that both the police rules and CrPC provide comprehensive and sound check on the corrupt and unscrupulous police officers.

It is noteworthy that as enjoined by Article 22 of the Constitution, the grounds of the arrest have also to be made known to the arrested persons and copies of the recovery memos concerning incriminating articles have to be sent to the *Illaqa* Magistrate and to the owner of the house under sections 165 and 100 CrPC. In nutshell, if the gazetted officer exercises his supervision closely and sincerely with a view to ensure that no person is detained without authority and arrests/searches are conducted and further follow up action taken strictly according to the law, the investigating officers can dare not indulge in malpractices and dishonest dealings.

V. Making Incorrect Reports regarding the Accused having absconded and not taking Effective Action against the Accused actually Absconded: A vigilant supervisory officer shall not brook any under-hand tactic on the part of investigating officer in showing the accused to be absconding, whereas actually they may be easily available for arrest. It is laid down in police rule 25.17 that all delays in the course of investigation are to be carefully examined by the gazetted officers and are to be stopped forthwith. Effective supervision on the part of gazetted officer will not leave any scope for the investigating officers to make false reports in the case diaries in this regard. Besides, in the event the accused absconds, the procedure as laid down in police rule 21.5 read with police rule 26.5 has to be strictly observed. Warrants for the arrest of the absconding accused should be got issued and action under sections 82/83 of the CrPC expedited. Under section 82 of the CrPC, any court may, at any time, issue a proclamation when it is satisfied that the said person has absconded or is concealing himself and the warrants for his arrest cannot be executed. The court may, at any time, after proclamation, order the attachment of any property movable and immovable belonging to the proclaimed person. In the event of his becoming proclaimed offender, his name is entered in surveillance register as per police rule 23.4. If the progress of action against the absconder is carefully supervised and the lapses or delays on the part of investigating officers taken note of the chances of investigating officers indulging in malpractices, in this regard can be eliminated.

VI. Lapses connected with various stages of the Cases in the Courts:

(i) Suggesting a probable line of defence or helping the accused in engaging a particular counsel. (ii) Postponing arrest until bail is secured from the court. (iii) Willful absence of the investigating officers on the date of hearing in the court. (iv) Putting pressure on prosecution witnesses or harassing/threatening the complainant and witnesses during the trial and (v) Non-effective *pairavi* of cases in courts.

The scrutiny of challans by the prosecuting agency before presenting in courts and their examinations by the supervisory officers along with a detailed memorandum prepared in terms of Police Rule 27.1(3) would help the senior officers to detect some of the malpractices, lapses and factual/legal flaws. Similarly any strictures and adverse comments made by the courts are also brought to the notice of the supervisory officers for necessary action against the defaulters. It needs to be emphasis that as per police rule 25.17 the supervisory officers are required to follow up the challans of the cases after they are put in the court. In fact, the gazetted officers are enjoined to watch the progress of the cases in courts closely and to study the grounds of discharges and acquittals, in order to check malpractices.

VII. Improper use of Discretionary Powers conferred by Section 157, 169 and 436 of CrPC: In cases of optional investigations, a specific check is provided in police rule 25.9(4), wherein all such cases are required to be brought to the notice of the District Superintendent of Police. Section 157(1)(b) of the CrPC does provide that the SHO shall not investigate the case if it appears to him that there is no sufficient grounds for entering on an investigation. However, police rule 25.9 at the same time also suggests that in practice it is seldom advisable for the SHO to avail himself of the discretion to refuse investigation, as very many cases which appear trivial in nature may, if investigated furnish clue to the operation of professional criminals or afford valuable material, at a later date for preventive action. The discretion not to take up investigation of cases is in practice not permitted to be used by the SHOs. Similarly abuse of powers in the matter of release of accused u/s 169 CrPC for lack of sufficient evidence or release of accused on bail under section 436 CrPC by the investigating officers can be affectively checked, if the gazetted oficers keep close watch on the investigation, as it progresses and deal with the Case Dairies etc, from day to day.

VIII. Torturing of Suspects to extort Confession: Police Rule 25.2(2) lays down that no avoidable trouble should be given to any person from whom inquiries are made during investigation of cases. Voluntarily causing hurt or grievous hurt to a person for purpose of extorting confession is punishable u/s 330 and 331 IPC. Action against the defaulting officers can be taken under these sections. It is no secret that the corrupt police officials resort to dubious methods and untrue confessions are extorted. At times, innocent people are tortured labeling them as suspects with evil motive of creating awe and fear in their minds, thus, to force them to yield to their demands for illegal gratification. This would be possible only if the gazetted officers remain callous in their supervision.

IX. Police Touts in and around Police Stations: There are some self-styled helpers of the administration, who act as intermediary to collect bribe money for the unscrupulous police officials. The presence of touts in the society is most obnoxious and damaging for the growth of healthy police public relations. The touts prosper and their trade flourishes only when there are corrupt official around in the police stations. Often the cunning and corrupt Police subordinates introduce such touts to the senior officers as valuable helpers of administration. Rewards are also got sanctioned for the touts by presenting wrong facts. It is hereby, directed that no tout should be allowed to lurk around the police stations and at no cost, they shall be associated with the police investigations or other police activities. It is therefore, directed that lists of such undesirable persons should be prepared and kept upto date all the times. These lists should be displayed at the police stations as well as at the office of Superintendent of Police in order to keep everybody on the guard against them. Legal remedy is also available against this class of persons u/s 162 and 163 IPC. The gazetted officers shall keep vigil to rope in the notorious touts accordingly.

X. Police Interference in Private Disputes: By virtue of the provisions, contained in police rule 24.3 and section 155 of CrPC, a police officer is not competent to interfere in any private dispute and non-cognizable offences. As laid down in section 155 CrPC, investigations into non-cognizable offences can be made only under the orders of a competent Magistrate. A watchful gazetted officer will not allow any subordinate police officer to interfere in any private dispute, particularly when it would be clear that the motive for such interference would be dishonesty.

General

I have tried to identify the softest areas and the most notorious methods generally adopted by corrupt elements in the police force. At the same time brief mention has been made of the legal provisions, which if properly implemented and enforced by the supervisory officer, can keep corrupt practices in the working of the police under control. It is to be admitted regretfully that this is not being done by a majority of gazetted officers for the simple reasons that they lack proper caliber, application to work and are not made to exercise close and continuous supervision on their subordinates. If the District Superintendents of Police and the Range Dy Inspectors General of Police really care to make the gazetted officers under them to properly understand and assimilate the statutory legal provisions enumerated above, with the intention of their total implementation and enforcement, they shall in turn, surely tighten their supervision on the police station staff. Corruption and corrupt practices in police working would automatically be cut down largely. The gazetted police officers who do not rise to the occasion and tighten up the supervision by enforcing the legal provisions reiterated above should be either lazy or incompetent or downright in league with corrupt subordinates. Niether of these positions can be tolerated and therefore the defaulters will have to be proceeded against accordingly.

Sd/- Hans Raj Swan IPS, Director General of Police Haryana.

Appendix – 1

Imprints and Impressions by Shyam Chand, Ex-Minister; Haryana

It is very seldom that a bureaucrat, especially from Haryana writes his autobiography or pens his memoirs. Hans Raj Swan the author of this book is a pioneer in this respect and deserves appreciation.

The author has provided plethora of material for sociologists and historians of contemporary politics in Haryana. The book can serve as a textbook of reference for the cops.

The life story of the author shows that adversity brings about the best in a man and worst in the system. It compels the readers to explore the complex dynamics of relationship between dalits and so called twice born. Dalits are tired of explaining their origin and have to endure the mockery of these 'superiors' in social order but beneath them in intelligence.

Dalits complain that the State does not intervene when atrocities are committed on them. However, when a bureaucrat like the author is subjected to kind of treatment the privileged and the powerful regularly inflict on their victims, the reader comes to understand that there is something wrong with the system.

The author at every juncture, either by way of advice or by way of solace or consolation or by way of applying healing balm on the 'fractured soul' of Hinduism, quotes eminent writers, poets, saints and philosophers. For all that, one Mukta Bai is enough. That 14 years old girl studying in one

---

Shyam Chand after doing Post Graduation appeared in All India Services/Central Civil Services Examination conducted by the UPSC in 1960. He made to the merit list but did not join. Instead, he went to UK and joined British Civil Service. He did two years course in Journalism from London School of Journalism. He returned to India and contested successfully election for the Haryana Vidhan Sabha in 1968. In 1972 Assembly Polls, he was re-elected as MLA and remained Cabinet Minister in the Bansi Lal Government upto 1977 holding the portfolios of Excise and Taxation Department, Urban Development Department, Food and Supply Department and Departments of Social Welfare and Welfare of Scheduled Castes and Scheduled Tribes. He has written two books "**Seeds of Slavery**" and "**Saffron Fascism**".

of the schools run by Mahatma Phule started writing her essay. 'Let that religion where only one person's privileged and the rest deprived, perish from the earth and let it never enter our mind to be proud of such a religion.' Her essay ends abruptly: 'Oh God! What agony is this? I will burst in tears if I write more about this injustice.'

Because of his social origin and activism, the author had to suffer humiliation and loss of job at the hands of social Darwins and political McCarthys.

The author is lucky that he got inspiration from Dr Ambedkar whom he met in person and support from Sh BN Dattar when he was crying for help. But Alas! There are no Ambedkars and Dattars now! Moreover, adversity had given the author strength and courage, the most outstanding values to stand this world.

A man from the lower structure of the Indian Society, instead of being appreciated is, brutally bruised if he tries to break the ceiling for vertical mobility. If the officer of the rank of DIG when not manipulated to be an instrument of exploitation, is put under suspension by an up start guttersnipe who becomes powers, that be, without any coherent reason but for stellenbosch, to make way, height of injustice can be fairly gauged.

The book becomes more interesting when it deals with the relationship between bureaucracy and politicians-intrigues, revenge, rewards sealing the ladders etc.

As Director General of Police, the author had carried out many far-reaching reforms for which the Police department should be grateful to him. His sense of social service after superannuation is a source of joy and fulfillments for him and inspiration for others.

Appendix – 2

Imprints and Impressions by PC Wadhawa, IPS

I have known Hans Raj Swan for many decades. I must confess that I had known him only as a well meaning and competent IPS officer and an affable, well-mannered and loveable human being. But, his book, an autographic details of his life's journey from childhood till he hung up his Police uniform on superannuation in July 1988 and further still going strong even at the age of 81 in pursuit of his wonderfully productive retreat in public life for the last 23 years, has revealed to me some stunning facts about his life.

As a senior colleague, I watched that the author had acquired the reputation of performing the tasks assigned to him in the true spirit of the dictum "Work is Worship". As State Police Chief, I discerned that the author was a staunch believer of discipline in profession, sanctity of system and hierarchy and was always leading his subordinates from the front, inspiring them with innovative ideas and instilling amongst them a sense of comradeship. He would tackle the

---

P.C. Wadhawa, M.A., LLB, IPS (1952-RR) from Haryana Cadre retired as Director General of Police. He has been practicing as an advocate in Punjab and Haryana High Court and Supreme Court of India, ever since his superannuation in 1986. He is member, Punjab and Haryana High Court Bar Association, Supreme Court Bar Association, Bar Association of India and International Council of Jurists (2010-15). When he was reverted from SP to ASP in 1958, he challenged the reversion order contending that his reversion was in violation of AIS Rules. His contention was upheld by the Supreme Court (AIR 1964 SC -423). When posted as DIG Vigilance HSEB, he was given neither any Special Pay nor Deputation Allowance. On challenging the matter in the Supreme Court, he got Deputation Allowance (AIR 1981 SC-1540). His ACR as State Police Chief was initiated by the State Home Secretary. He challenged the competency of the State Home Secretary to initiate his ACR. His contention was upheld by the Supreme Court that the ARC of State Police Chief had to be written by the Home Minister not by the Home Secretary (AIR 1987 SC-1201). All the above mentioned cases were argued by P. C. Wadhawa personally. He has established his reputation as a renowned Legal Luminary in service related matters and has many success stories to his credit in addition to the above mentioned cases.

complex and baffling situations deftly and quickly. The code of ethic, he devised for others was what he also meticulously practiced.

Endowed with multiple qualities of head and heart, he would instantly endear himself with whom-so-ever he came into contact. I have always addressed him affectionately by his first name 'Hans'.

The life of the author from childhood until he got into the Indian Police Service is a fabulously enchanting and highly absorbing story. None could ever predict that the sixth child, born to parents with meager resources, starting schooling at the age of 7, in a totally non-descript surroundings, a school drop out from fifth primary class to turn into the family cattle grazer for two years, exposed to caste prejudices – a curse in Indian Society, could achieve such heights as to become a State DGP. In addition, he earned two coveted decorations of Police Medal for Meritorious Service and President's Police Medal for Distinguished Service, beside half a dozen special appreciation letters from the different highest state political executives. Hats off for the grit, rock – like determination and indomitable industry displayed by this erstwhile cattle grazer!

As a police officer, the author was loved, trusted and admired by his various superiors and was respected by his junior IPS colleagues. The police constabulary, at large always looked to him as their benign benefactor because the author gave due priority to their welfare aspect even when he was amidst the difficult law and order situations created by the terrorists.

The author has vividly described quite a few episodes in which calculated efforts were made by a mafia gang of rogue and unscrupulous police officers to concoct cock and bull stories to tarnish his reputation while he was Superintendent of Police District Rohtak. How boldly and dauntingly, the author exposed the evil designs of this mafia gang, speaks volumes of the quality of his fighting spirit and admirable ability to steer successfully through storms and straits.

The author has quoted instances when he strongly resisted unwarranted political interference and remained firmly committed to hold the rule of law, least bothering about the consequences of vendetta game of politicians. Unfortunately, sycophants, intriguers and manipulators amongst the politicians and bureaucrats have always had field day in our political system. To come clean out of this filth is no mean achievement by an upright police officer.

Police has always been on the receiving end because of malpractices and dishonest dealings indulged by some wayward police subordinates particularly at the police station level. The author, while State Police Chief made admirable efforts to identify such black sheep and various lapses and irregularities/ illegalities committed by dishonest police officers at different stages of the dealings with crime and criminals. He laid down well thought of code of conduct to be followed by the senior police officers for dealing with the errant subordinates.

The book contains details of various political developments, which took place in Haryana state during four decades after its formation, indicating the rhythm, the thesis, the anti-thesis and synthesis of political forces of varied hues, at different times. The quality of civil and police administration including Criminal Justice System has been described in graphic details.

It is very rare that a State Police Chief comes out with his autobiography with as graphic details as the author has done. I appreciate the author's bold adventure. It should serve an eye-opener to the readers of all ages, that firstly there is no short cut to success in upholding the rule of law and secondly how-so-ever a man might be handicapped by harsh environments and caste prejudices, the righteous, honest, sincere, determined and gritty approach can take him to the pinnacle of success, without bending down to his knees to seek 'blessings' of all demanding politicians.

The author has thrown up plethora of material for the readers of all ages, more particularly the present day youth at large, aspiring politicians and promising civil servants, particularly gazetted police officers of all ranks to do some introspection by shedding stake to promote their own interest and instead, by playing their role proactively, to check the deterioration of moral values, fast creeping into the system of governance and delivery of justice to everyone.

I strongly recommend gazetted police officers of all ranks, not once but many a time, to go through this book. I am sure they will find in the author a role model to follow. I also recommend copies of this book be placed in all the police libraries at District, Range, Zone and State levels and all public libraries in the country.

Appendix – 3

Imprints and Impressions by Baljit Rai, IPS, Director General of Police (Retd.)

The book in hand by Hans Raj Swan is autobiography of an officer of Indian Police Service, who has just clocked eighty summers and retired from service 23 years ago. The author describes every stage of his life from childhood onwards, in graphic details. He conceals nothing. Therefore, we must begin at the beginning with one very important fact, which lends additional value, and weight to the entire narrative. That important aspect is that the officer belongs to the scheduled caste category of Hindu society. Although handicapped by caste factor he had inherited enough sensitivity and grit, which took him to the pinnacle of his dreams. There is no doubt, he not only dreamt well but also converted his dreams into reality and multiple successes and retired happily with gratifying fulfillment.

It sounds like fiction to say that a cattle grazer in his childhood had risen to be State Police Chief but that is too true. While in school, a teacher made some disparaging remarks about his caste, which forced him to drop out of

---

Baljit Rai comes from district Sialkot (Pakistan). He was pursuing his studies at Lahore, but for the B.A. final year, he had to join Hindu College Delhi in 1947. A post graduate in history from Ramjas College Delhi, he taught history as College Lecturer in D. S. College Ambala City from 1951 to 1954. He joined the Indian Police Service in 1954. On allocation to Composite Punjab State Cadre, he served as ASP and SP at various places in the said State until 1966. He was on deputation to BSF from 1966 to 1971. On reorganization of Punjab state, he was allocated to Himachal Pradesh/UT Cadre. His Cadre was further changed from UT to joint Manipur -Tripura Cadre. He was State Police Chief at Agartala for four years. Further, from 1975 to 1981, he was on deputation to CRPF and CISF. Back to his Cadre, he remained posted as Resident Commissioner for the Government of Tripura in Delhi. He was promoted as Director General of Police in 1986. He visited various European countries including Italy, USA and Canada also. With intellectual bent of mind, he has flair and special interest in writing books. He has authored five books, which include (i) **Muslim Fundamentalism in the Indian Subcontinent,** (ii) **Demographic Aggression against India - Muslim Avalanche from Bangladesh** (iii) **Is India Going Islamic?** (iv) **Explosion of Muslim Population in India and** (v) **History of Jihadi Terrorism in India from 1920 to 2010.**

school for two years, which he spent in looking after family's cattle and grazing them in the fields. Although he was not going to school, the spark in him to get educated never lost its glow. He rejoined the school and fortunately came under the spell and tutelage of some very kindhearted teachers who not only encouraged him but also restored his *amour prope* to forge ahead in life. How much we owe, in our lives to the guidance received from a good teacher, we rarely acknowledge or appreciate. It was at this stage in school years that the author learnt the beauty of *Japuji Sahib*–morning prayer of Sikhs. I mention this fact because years later the author, who was now State DGP, when he had to face the challenge of Khalistani terrorists, he spoke to the Sikh population in a language, vernacular and lore that they best understood. The marvelous effect of this interaction was that true to their word, the Sikh population of Kurukshetra and neighboring area in Punjab did not allow a single terrorist to operate in the area of his high responsibility during Solar Eclipse Fair attended by about fifteen lacs devotees from different parts of India. The peace and law and order were, so well maintained that this earned him the special appreciation of the government.

School years were happily over and the grazer and tender of cattle of yesteryears went to college from where he graduated. He had early marriage and moved to Delhi in search of employment and simultaneously pursuing Post Graduation studies by attending evening classes. He managed to secure an employment in his own merit in the Intelligence Bureau and later in Civil Secretariat. He never stopped dreaming and his new goal and horizon was to join All India Services/Central Services. He took the UPSC Examination 1956 and qualified for the Indian Police Service. This was a milestone in the life of the author. He joined the Central Police Training College (CPTC) at Mount Abu as IPS Probationer for one year training to be, moulded into, an officer worthy of Indian Police Service.

One of the most distressing aspects of this autobiography is the author's encounter with the Commandant (GK Handoo) of the CPTC. In a routine interview, the Commandant asked a few awkward questions which were quite humiliating and questioned the ability of a member of the scheduled caste community to join the Indian Police Service. The author has rightly castigated the Commandant for displaying totally unwarranted prejudice. GK Handoo as a Kashmiri Pandit had been, handsomely endowed with good looks but he had a mind severely corroded by caste prejudices and as such unfit to be the head of a prestigious institution like the CPTC. Regrettably, the author continued to be a victim of such taunts and barbs throughout his stay at CPTC. A stinker from Handoo followed the author for not doing well in Infantry Training and delivered to him at PTC Phillaur where the author was undergoing State Police Training. It could be very demoralizing for an IPS Probationer. Here now steps in another benefactor HRK Talwar, Principal of the school, who advised the author not to look back and brood over the past but look ahead, far ahead. This sound advice had salutary affect.

The author's continuously excellent performance earned him two decorations, Police Medal for Meritorious Service and President's Police Medal for Distinguished Service. Having become a seasoned police officer, he earned every promotion when it was due. As State Police Chief he fully recognized, appreciated and documented the welfare aspect of the NGOs and Others Ranks and the good work of junior IPS officers who also rose to be the Chiefs in their own right in their turn.

The phenomenon of *'Aya Ram Gaya Ram'* (politics of defection) is a special contribution of Haryana State to the larger cauldron of Indian politics. It touched its lowest ebb of degradation when Devi Lal – a stalwart – delivered a tight slap on the face of Governor G D Tapase. The sound of the slap will continue to resound for generations to come, to the ever-lasting shame of the State. The author has discussed this and other shenanigans of politicians in graphic detail.

In his personal and family life, the author had to pass through an extremely agonizing time, particularly a 14 years long spell, when his elder son was bed ridden, who ultimately succumbed to an incurable disease. The author has often referred to the inevitable circle of agony and ecstasy, one following the other. The author has concealed nothing in his autobiography and laid bare everything before the readers and police fraternity.

All in all this autobiography is not only an assertion of an individual's rights but also, a powerful vindication of the same in no uncertain terms.

The author's life has been a life of challenges and fulfillments, which is, distinguished by the fact that he is *Ajat Shatru*. He has no enemies, only friends!

Who would not like to salute this cattle grazer par excellence of yesteryears!

Index